Minorities, Free Speech and the Internet

Minorities, Free Speech and the Internet explores the regulation of free speech online and offline.

Views are divided as to how much regulation of the Internet is appropriate. Some argue that it should be an unregulated space for free content. On the other hand, in many democracies, online hate speech, harassment and xenophobia are prohibited and punished. This book provides a forum for leading international scholars to address domestic and comparative dimensions of this complex legal conundrum. First, the authors analyse the free speech and Internet regulations in different legal cultures, including the United States, Europe, China and Russia. Second, they study fake news, extreme right speech and the implications of hate speech on pluralistic society. Third, they examine different case law addressing minority sensibilities, historical discriminations, offensive propaganda and other issues particularly concerning minorities and free speech.

This book will be of interest to students and scholars interested in the topics of hate speech and minorities, democracy, misinformation and debates about the Internet, as well as political science researchers.

Oscar Pérez de la Fuente is Associate Professor of Philosophy of Law and Political Philosophy in the Department of International and Ecclesiastical Law and Philosophy of Law and in the "Gregorio Peces-Barba" Human Rights Institute at Carlos III University of Madrid, Spain. He has written on cultural pluralism, free speech and legal interpretation. He is Coordinator of the "Cultural pluralism and rights of minorities" workshop and Chair of the Research Committee 26 on Human Rights of the International Political Science Association.

Alexander Tsesis is Raymond & Mary Simon Chair in Constitutional Law and Professor of Law at the Loyola University in Chicago, United States, and Visiting Professor at George Washington University Law School, United States. He has written on cyber speech, constitutional interpretation, civil rights law and human rights. His scholarship focuses on a breadth of subjects, including constitutional law, civil rights, constitutional reconstruction, interpretive methodology, free speech theory and legal history.

Jędrzej Skrzypczak is Head of the Department of Media Systems and Press Law in the Faculty of Political Science and Journalism at Adam Mickiewicz University in Poznan, Poland. In 2016 and 2022, he was nominated as an official candidate for the National Broadcasting Board by the coalition of opposition parties. He is Chair-elect of the Research Committee 26 on Human Rights of the International Political Science Association and Vice President of the Polish Press Law Association.

Routledge Studies in Human Rights
Series Editors:
Mark Gibney
UNC Asheville, USA
Thomas Gammeltoft-Hansen
The Danish Institute for Human Rights, Denmark, and
Bonny Ibhawoh
McMaster University, Canada.

The Routledge Studies in Human Rights series publishes high-quality and cross-disciplinary scholarship on topics of key importance in human rights today. In a world where human rights are both celebrated and contested, this series is committed to create stronger links between disciplines and explore new methodological and theoretical approaches in human rights research. Aimed towards both scholars and human rights professionals, the series strives to provide both critical analysis and policy-oriented research in an accessible form. The series welcomes work on specific human rights issues as well as on cross-cutting themes and institutional perspectives.

US Counterterrorism and the Human Rights of Foreigners Abroad
Putting the Gloves Back On?
Monika Heupel, Caiden Heaphy and Janina Heaphy

State-Building, Rule of Law, Good Governance and Human Rights in Post-Soviet Space
Thirty Years Looking Back
Edited by Lucia Leontiev and Punsara Amarasinghe

Border Deaths at Sea under the Right to Life in the European Convention on Human Rights
Lisa-Marie Komp

Understanding Domestic Violence as a Gender-based Human Rights Violation
National and International Contexts
Jurgita Bukauskaitė

Minorities, Free Speech and the Internet
Edited by Oscar Pérez de la Fuente, Alexander Tsesis and Jędrzej Skrzypczak

For more information about this series, please visit: www.routledge.com/Routledge-Studies-in-Human-Rights/book-series/RSIHR

Minorities, Free Speech and the Internet

Edited by
Oscar Pérez de la Fuente,
Alexander Tsesis and Jędrzej Skrzypczak

First published 2023
by Routledge
4 Park Square, Milton Park, Abingdon, Oxon OX14 4RN

and by Routledge
605 Third Avenue, New York, NY 10158

Routledge is an imprint of the Taylor & Francis Group, an informa business

© 2023 selection and editorial matter, Oscar Pérez de la Fuente, Alexander Tsesis and Jędrzej Skrzypczak; individual chapters, the contributors

The right of Oscar Pérez de la Fuente, Alexander Tsesis and Jędrzej Skrzypczak to be identified as the authors of the editorial material, and of the authors for their individual chapters, has been asserted in accordance with sections 77 and 78 of the Copyright, Designs and Patents Act 1988.

With the exception of Chapter 1, no part of this book may be reprinted or reproduced or utilised in any form or by any electronic, mechanical, or other means, now known or hereafter invented, including photocopying and recording, or in any information storage or retrieval system, without permission in writing from the publishers.

Chapter 1 of this book is available for free in PDF format as Open Access from the individual product page at www.routledge.com. It has been made available under a Creative Commons Attribution-Non Commercial-No Derivatives 4.0 license.

Project 'New challenges of Law'. This work has been supported by the Madrid Government (Comunidad de Madrid-Spain) under the Multiannual Agreement with UC3M in the line of Excellence of University Professors (EPUC3M06), and in the context of the V PRICIT (Regional Programme of Research and Technological Innovation).

Trademark notice: Product or corporate names may be trademarks or registered trademarks, and are used only for identification and explanation without intent to infringe.

British Library Cataloguing-in-Publication Data
A catalogue record for this book is available from the British Library

Library of Congress Cataloging-in-Publication Data
Names: Pérez de la Fuente, Oscar, editor. | Tsesis, Alexander, editor. | Skrzypczak, Jędrzej, editor.
Title: Minorities, free speech and the internet / edited by Oscar Pérez de la Fuente, Alexander Tsesis, and Jędrzej Skrzypczak.
Description: Abingdon, Oxon ; New York, NY : Routledge, 2023. | Series: Routledge studies in human rights | Includes bibliographical references and index.
Identifiers: LCCN 2022054872 (print) | LCCN 2022054873 (ebook) | ISBN 9781032228358 (hardback) | ISBN 9781032228488 (paperback) | ISBN 9781003274476 (ebook)
Subjects: LCSH: Freedom of speech. | Hate speech. | Information society—Political aspects. | Internet—Political aspects. | Internet—Censorship.
Classification: LCC JC591 .M56 2023 (print) | LCC JC591 (ebook) | DDC 323.44/3—dc23/eng/20230106
LC record available at https://lccn.loc.gov/2022054872
LC ebook record available at https://lccn.loc.gov/2022054873

ISBN: 978-1-032-22835-8 (hbk)
ISBN: 978-1-032-22848-8 (pbk)
ISBN: 978-1-003-27447-6 (ebk)

DOI: 10.4324/9781003274476

Typeset in Times New Roman
by Apex CoVantage, LLC

Contents

PART I
Introduction 1

1 Introduction: minorities, free speech and the Internet—
  an overview 3
  OSCAR PÉREZ DE LA FUENTE

PART II
Legal cultures on free speech and Internet 17

2 Democratic values and the regulation of hate speech 19
  ALEXANDER TSESIS

3 Freedom of speech, minorities and the Internet from
  the European perspective: words matter 44
  JĘDRZEJ SKRZYPCZAK

4 Free speech and Internet: is there a new interpretation
  for human rights? With particular reference to Chinese
  and Russian approaches to Internet regulations 69
  OSCAR PÉREZ DE LA FUENTE

PART III
Democracy, hate speech and (mis)information 91

5 Manipulation and the first amendment 93
  HELEN NORTON

6 **Fake news published during the pre-election period and free speech theory** FILIMON PEONIDIS	108
7 **Misinformation and hate speech: when bad becomes even worse** GUSTAVO FERREIRA SANTOS	123
8 **Sexist hate speech against women: towards a regulatory model** IRENE SPIGNO	137
9 **Artificial intelligence and hate speech** MIGLE LAUKYTE	153

PART IV
Free speech and minorities 165

10 **Disentangling "cancel culture"** DAVID S. HAN	167
11 **Government speech and minority rights: the American view** WILLIAM D. ARAIZA	181
12 **SLAPP: between the right to a fair trial and the chilling effect in favour of free speech** JĘDRZEJ SKRZYPCZAK	197
13 **The freedom of speech and the protection of religious feelings: the case of Dorota Rabczewska—comparative analysis** TOMASZ LITWIN	212

PART V
Conclusion 227

14 **Conclusion** ALEXANDER TSESIS AND JĘDRZEJ SKRZYPCZAK	229
Notes on contributors	237
Index	239

Part I
Introduction

1 Introduction

Minorities, free speech and the Internet—an overview

Oscar Pérez de la Fuente

1. Is everyone online? However, Internet is worldwide

The Internet has altered how people communicate with one another and how they access to information and technology has progressively changed our everyday lives. Previous interpretations of political notions or how they are understood now need to be revisited or revaluated.

On the Internet, free expression and minority concerns, a number of false assumptions are still commonplace and there is an initial assumption that everyone is online. Paradoxically, the first Internet minority consists of individuals who do not have Internet access. This might be due to age, visual or oral impairment or economic factors. What is key is that governmental regulations are increasingly requiring an online-only format. This results in the exclusion of some sectors of the population.

The second misconception is that the Internet is a local phenomenon with local answers; in fact, it is global in scope. A country's borders are important for national law, but less so on the Internet. This means that legal solutions for the Internet must derive from international treaties, actors' self-regulation, international soft law and so on. Global cases require global solutions. Obviously, this does not mean online impunity. Human rights should be enforced online, in a reasonable approach since some form of regulation is required.

What might a reasonable Internet policy to safeguard minorities entail? This is an excellent question and the general subject of this book. It is also related to the third fallacy, which asserts that the Internet should be an unregulated place. Political notions such as human rights may change slightly when applied online but should be enforced equally offline and online. Some perspectives oppose the total freedom of the Internet from countries that use it to control and censor political opponents. However, we must find a reasonable middle term according to human rights.

2. The Internet as a new forum

Due to its capacity to accept, store and transmit a variety of information kinds, the Internet has become a new and vital resource in politics, international relations

DOI: 10.4324/9781003274476-2

and education, among other fields. Minority members' lives have transformed as a result of Information and Communication Technologies, particularly the Net.

One of the most important challenges is how the Internet affects politics and whether Internet-based political notions evolve, one of the most important of which is freedom. Internet freedom, roughly defined, is "the idea that universal rights, such as the freedoms of expression, assembly, and association, apply to the digital world" (Fontaine and Rogers, 2011, 9). It is essential to differentiate *freedom of the Internet* and *freedom via Internet*.

Freedom of the Internet refers to the freedom to freely express oneself on the Internet. This concept signifies freedom from censorship, government monitoring, distributed denial of service assaults and so on (Fontaine and Rogers, 2011, 9–10). This is related to the *negative liberty* concept, which essentially advocates "the freedom of every individual to talk freely" (Ross, 2010, 6). In the famous words of Isaiah Berlin, "I am considered free to the extent that no individual or group of persons interferes with my action" (Berlin, 2002, 169).

Freedom via the Internet can lead to greater offline freedom; the free movement of ideas over the Internet encourages democratisation (Fontaine and Rogers, 2011, 9–10). The *positive liberty* approach consists of "the public's freedom to hear from all social voices" (Ross, 2010, 6). Berlin characterises it as "the desire of an individual to be his or her own master. I wish my life and decisions did not depend on any external influences whatsoever. I desire to be the agent of my own actions of will, not those of other men" (Berlin, 2002, 178). It could be argued that Berlin's idea of *positive liberty* is ambiguous, and clarification is required as the opinions of many authors disagree. Regarding free speech issues, *positive liberty* refers to the notion of self-regulation.

On the Internet, the *negative liberty* concept defines freedom as "no interference" and is linked to the *freedom of the Internet* approach. *Positive liberty* may be seen as a notion of self-governance and is frequently connected with a *human rights-based approach* on the Internet. Both views will be analysed in the following making the difference between (a) *freedom of the Internet*-based approach and (b) *human rights in the Internet*-based approach.

2.1. Freedom of the Internet-based approach

There is the opinion that the Internet should be unfettered. Particularly criticised, especially for political reasons, is censorship. It has become "one of the most significant worldwide disputes on international freedom of expression and foreign policy" (Wagner, 2011, 20).

According to Popper's classical categories, closed societies are characterised by a "magical, tribal, or collectivist society," and open societies are characterised by "individuals facing personal decisions" (Popper, 2013, 165). At its best, a closed society is comparable to an organism (Popper, 2013, 165). Closed societies are characterised by "authoritarian regimes, economic success limited to elites, and restricted, state-imposed cultural and religious values" (Ross, 2010, 8). China is a *networked authoritarian* society (MacKinnon, 2011, 33). This indicates that the Chinese government employs numerous methods to electronically monitor the populace, including Internet filtering and second- and third-generation controls. Other regimes utilise these control systems, such as Iran or Russia (Mackinnon, 2011, 44).

According to Popper, in an open society, there are many people who "strive for social advancement and to assume the roles of other members. This might result in significant societal phenomena such as class strife. There is nothing comparable to class conflict in living organisms" (Popper, 2013, 165). An open society is characterised by democratic institutions that allow anyone to freely engage in the political process, an economic structure that allows individuals from all social and economic backgrounds to compete and achieve, and cultural and religious diversity (Ross, 2010, 8). It is difficult to identify whether a culture is open or closed, according to Ross, because "all nation states operate along a continuum" (Ross, 2010, 8). Nonetheless, some regimes prioritise the defence of civil and political rights and opposition to censorship, especially for political purposes.

Regarding Internet restrictions, there is public opinion in favour of Internet freedom and against censorship. Such examples include information from the Association for Progressive Communications,[1] the United Nations Internet Governance Forum[2] and the Global Network Initiative.[3] The paper "Internet Freedom: A Foreign Approach Imperative in the Digital Age" by the Washington think group Centre for New American Security presented eight principles in favour of this policy (Wagner, 2011, 21). "Lead the Effort to Build International Norms" is the title of one of them. The United States government should promote a liberal definition of Internet freedom in all relevant forums and resist attempts by authoritarian states to promote norms that restrict online freedoms of information and speech. It should also adopt international transparency push to persuade countries to disclose their policies on the restriction of internet content (Fontaine and Rogers, 2011, 6–7).

Cyberactivism can be interpreted in two different ways. The first term is "political action," while the second is "security." In the first interpretation, cyberactivism is "a relatively contemporary kind of political mobilisation made possible by computer and smartphone technologies" (Sorell, 2015, 393). Post-2010 instances of cyberactivism include the so-called Tunisian and Egyptian revolutions, the *Indignados* movement in Spain, the kitchen tool protest in Iceland and the *Occupy* movement (Sorell, 2015, 394). Traditional human rights safeguards such as the right to protest, free expression, the freedom to assemble and demonstrate and other fundamental political rights apply to cyberactivism (Sorell, 2015, 395). Not all political systems respond in the same manner to the exercise of these fundamental political rights, particularly by political dissenters.

The second interpretation is "security." Cyberactivists are mentioned as potential "sources of cyberattacks," i.e. as potential sources of data-destroying viruses and as risks to the access and control systems of vital civic infrastructure and even military equipment (Sorell, 2015, 393). Hacktivism is a kind of political activity that targets powerful corporations and governments (Sorell, 2015, 391). Wikileaks' claims to engage in democratic accountability processes with the revelation of select restricted papers (Sorell, 2015, 401) and Anonymous' unorthodox methods and notions for their actions are notable examples (Karagiannopoulos, 2018, 25–28).

Protection of intellectual property rights on the Internet is a common restriction on the Internet freedom approach. "Hadopi is an abbreviation for 'High Authority for the Dissemination of Works and Protection of Copyright on the Internet'" (Koester, 2012, 328). In France, a portion of the original "Hadopi" statute was ruled unlawful. The courts alone, and not administrative authorities, have the power to suspend offenders' Internet connection and levy fines against them (Koester, 2012, 328).

When it comes to hacktivism and violations of intellectual property rights, the position defending an unrestricted Internet provides fewer persuasive arguments than when it comes to safeguarding fundamental democratic rights. On the one hand, the quality of democracy and, in autocracies, the nature of the political system are called into question. On the other, national security or the commercial exploitation of intellectual works may be put at risk.

This also applies to chances for political involvement on the Internet, as open and closed societies do not recognise and protect political rights in the same way. A closed society is reluctant to employ a *negative liberty* approach to free speech and favours intervention or electronic speech control for political reasons, especially against dissenters. A society with a strong commitment to openness will not outlaw political speech until it can be properly justified following "strict examination." In some cases, some of these grounds include national security. This *negative liberty* strategy that prioritises unrestricted freedom must confront infringement of intellectual property rights. Internet cannot be equated to a new state of nature or a wilderness. The protection of political rights is an extremely advantageous component of freedom of the Internet liberty. However, there are no absolute rights, and freedom may be limited or constrained if the freedom of another is infringed upon or challenged. To protect rights on the Internet, some guidelines must be followed. This is the starting point for a human rights-focused Internet strategy.

2.2. *Human rights-based approach to the Internet*

The Internet rules' "human rights-based approach" shows that there are valid reasons to prohibit communication in some Internet domains. According to a 2013 resolution of the United Nations General Assembly, "the same rights that individuals enjoy offline must be respected online" (United Nations, 2013; Mihr, 2017, 58). For example, the World Summit on the Information Society advocates for the prevention of "illegal or other activities motivated by racism, racial discrimination, xenophobia, and associated forms of intolerance, hatred, and violence" (World Information Society Summit, 2003). According to the Internet Charter of Human Rights and Principles, "human rights and social justice shall serve as the legal and normative basis for the operation and governance of the Internet. This will occur in a multilateral and transparent way, based on the values of openness, inclusive engagement, and accountability" (UN Internet Governance Forum, 2014). This indicates that human rights should also be enforced online, and that those responsible for human rights violations must be held accountable. According to the Internet Rights Charter, "the public must have unrestricted access to effective and responsible channels for resolving rights abuses" (Association for Progressive Communication, 2006). At the European level, several regulations require States to criminalise online and offline incitement to hate and Holocaust denial. The Framework Decision of the European Union (2008) and the Additional Protocol to the Council of Europe Convention on Cybercrime make this very obvious (2003). Under the self-regulation strategy, the European Commission and numerous platforms have created the Code of Conduct to counteract illegal online hate speech (2016). Approving "criminal legislation and an extradition treaty that limit the transnational spread of hate speech" is another method of combating hate speech (Tsesis, 2002, 41).

In an intriguing exercise, Weaver considers where consensus is most likely—child pornography (United Nations, 2019) and obscenity—and where there is no consensus—Holocaust denial, hate speech, reputation protection against defamation and privacy (United Nations, 2013)—for a new international treaty on the Internet (Weaver, 2011, 202–219).

This is because different legal cultures exist. For example, Holocaust denial is considered a crime in various nations (Pérez de la Fuente, 2010). Weaver asserts that when interpreting Article 10 of the European Convention on Human Rights, the United States would apply the standard established in *Brandenburg v. Ohio*, where subversive speech could only be punished if it was "intended to incite or produce imminent illegal action and is likely to incite such action" (Weaver, 2011, 211).

The *freedom of the Internet approach* is more concerned with political liberties, such as protests and revolutions, in comparison to freedom of expression. The distinction between democracies and autocracies has an explanatory force here. Online human rights initiatives, on the other hand, are primarily oriented on "expanding and integrating components of internet freedom into existing human rights frameworks" (Wagner, 2011, 22). In certain respects, it is challenging to standardise the methods of the various legal cultures. Nonetheless, it is evident that the Internet is worldwide.

Initiatives connected to freedom of expression in foreign policy are beginning to develop, including: "a) a relationship to existing human rights frameworks; b) the perceived role of the internet in allowing or fuelling revolutions; and c) the problematic position of the private sector" (Wagner, 2011, 22). Depending on the legal culture, the notion that human rights should be implemented on the Internet might be perceived differently. This ambition is limited by the fact that the Internet is platformed by private middlemen and platforms with their own objectives and standards. The basic problem is the redefinition of the public and private domain, such as the question of whether Twitter and Facebook are public or private forums. Depending on the choice selected, legal repercussions may vary.

3. Minorities

Turning to the paradigm of the mythical canon is one way to comprehend what minorities are. The mythical canon has established what the human being is, just as the standard of the metre distance is a metre of platinum and iridium kept in the Bureau of Weights and Measures in Paris. Therefore, here, the canon recognised the white, Christian, proprietary, heterosexual, right-handed, able-bodied male self. It may be added that he also belonged to the main ethnic group and spoke the prevailing language. In each instance, the concept of minority has been defined by excluding these traits.

This suggests that the experience of being a minority may be more widespread than it may initially seem. Being a woman, left-handed, worker, homosexual, atheist, black or disabled can be a daily experience for many people. These identities come with legitimate expectations that society must uphold, and a unique perspective—of discrimination and exclusion, in many cases—that shouldn't stand in the way of their ability to develop their life plans under conditions equal to those enjoyed by those who belong to the majority identities (Pérez de la Fuente, 2015, 56).

Continuing along this line of reasoning, the aspect of the mythical canon is that the majority of people in the world do not, under any circumstances, place any value judgements on any of the traits that define who they are. It is impossible to provide a definitive response as the contextual nature of this devaluation judgement depends on the situation. However, we can discuss the prejudices and stereotypes that serve as a social construct regarding the various components of identity. This hidden type of discrimination and even social stigma explains one of the most pronounced characteristics of the minority notion.

In 1979, the Special Rapporteur of the Sub-Commission on the Prevention of Discrimination and Protection of Minorities of the United Nations, Caportorti, analysed the concept of minority in a seminal report that provided a legal definition on an international level. His notion of minority is determined by three objective and one subjective criteria. The impact of the Internet on the concept of minority will be analysed using the following criteria.

The first objective criterion used by Capotorti is "the existence, within a State's population, of distinct groups possessing stable ethnic, religious or linguistic characteristics that differ sharply from those of the rest of the population" (Caportorti, 1979, 96).

To delve deeper into the characteristics of the concept of minority, we must remember that it is connected to people having a particular trait that defines them as a group. This trait may fall under either innate categories or socialisation-dependent categories. Some moral theories draw a special distinction between circumstances that are outside an individual's control and are viewed as morally arbitrary and circumstances that are the result of that person's own free will, to which individual responsibility would apply.

It is notable that Caportorti's definition is based on a state framework that prevents immigrants as a whole from being a minority, from the International Law approach. Specifically, this is one of the shifts brought about by the Internet's predominantly global, non-local perspective. This has been supported by several case laws, including the well-known *Yahoo* and *Toben* cases. In such circumstances, the Internet and its legal repercussions extend beyond a physical border.

In the *Yahoo* case, an anti-racist association in France sued the *Yahoo* company for hosting an auction of Nazi objects on its website. *Yahoo* responded to this lawsuit by stating that its servers were in the United States and that the applicable law and jurisdiction should be American (Ziaja, 2011, 1–14). In the *Toben* case, Frederick Toben was a German immigrant in Australia who maintained a website claiming among other things that "the Nazis never used gas chambers to murder Jews, or others during the Holocaust." His website appears to be hosted on a U.S. server. Frederick Toben was arrested in 1999 while visiting Germany and was charged with violating German law for his website's content (Van Blarcum, 2005, 803–804).

Those who share a characteristic at any linked online location can share information, data and so on as a result of the Internet. This implies that the connection between identity and territory is less important than it formerly was. Instead, identities may be shared and strengthened internationally.

The second objective condition is "they must in principle be numerically inferior to the rest of the population" (Caportorti, 1979, 96). The idea of a minority appears to be connected to a group's numerical disadvantage in comparison to the majority. This is generally accepted as true. It is also true that there are instances in which majorities minoritised themselves or behave as minorities. The black population in apartheid-era South Africa is a classic example.

The third of the objective criteria from Capotorti definition is "the non-dominant position of the groups in question in relation to the rest of the population: dominant minority groups do not need to be protected" (Caportorti, 1979, 96).

This indicates that discrimination and helplessness are additional minority traits. Minority rights therefore provide a type of empowerment for members of minority groups. The term "minority" would have two conflicting meanings: the minority as an element discriminated against and undervalued by society and the minority as an elite composed of the most socially and economically powerful groups. The finest illustration is the debate between federalists and anti-federalists over the American Constitution and their respective worries about the overwhelming influence of the *many* and the powers of the *few* (Pérez de la Fuente, 2005, 229–231).

The elderly, the visually impaired and the hard of hearing are examples of emerging digital minorities or minorities disproportionately affected by new technologies. There are segments of the population that cannot properly access the Internet owing to age, disability or financial hardship. A further characteristic of the Internet referring to minorities is the proliferation of hate speech websites that insult members of minorities in an anonymous atmosphere. Online misogyny against LGTBI or disabled persons' hateful content can be found easily online. These are fresh manifestations of an old discrimination.

According to Capotorti, the subjective criterion in the concept of minority consists of "a will on the part of the members of the groups in question to preserve their own characteristics. The existence of such a will had to be formally established" (Caportorti, 1979, 96).

Minorities *by force* and cultural minorities *by will* are typically separated. Comanducci defines minorities by force as groups of individuals who, despite being as numerous as other groups (such as women), are, for historical, economic, political or other reasons and based on their racial, sexual, ethical, linguistic and so on characteristics, at a disadvantage relative to other groups of individuals in the same society (Comanducci, 2001, 321–322). Minorities *by force* are also known as social minorities and are often safeguarded by rules promoting individual rights, equality and non-discrimination. Liberalism recognises these social minorities (Pérez de la Fuente, 2005, 256–279).

On the other hand, Comanducci defines cultural minorities *by will*, if their difference from the majority is determined by one or more characteristics to which they attribute value, if they demand respect for their difference and their uniqueness and do not limit themselves to requesting protection against discrimination. What cultural minorities will always reject are homologation, assimilation and forced inclusion in the majority's cultural paradigms (or of whoever holds power). Through the attribution of positive cultural rights, cultural minorities can be voluntarily protected (Comanducci, 2001, 321–322). Cultural minorities are another name for minorities *by will*. Typically, they are safeguarded by group rights and are not acknowledged by an egalitarian liberal approach, but by a liberal culturalist or multiculturalist one (Pérez de la Fuente, 2005, 279–345).

The subjective criteria in the definition of Capotorti are usually applied to cultural minorities or minorities *by will*. However, the different approach to minorities from liberal culturalism and multiculturalism is remarkable. According to the former view, only cultural minorities, such as national minorities, indigenous peoples and immigrants, have group rights and are significant in multiculturalism (Kymlicka, 1998a, 17–26). Alternatively, multiculturalists accept that new social movements such as women, racial minorities, LGTBI minorities, persons with disabilities and so on are part of subcultural, perspective or communal human diversity—(Parkeh, 2000, 3–4)—and can have collective rights; a politics of difference must be applied. Kymlicka, adhering to the liberal culturalist perspective, sought to compare gay culture and the deaf community to ethnic groups to assess if they are eligible for group rights (Kymlicka, 1998b, 90–103).

The classical definition of minority offered by Capotorti considers:

> a group numerically inferior to the rest of the population of a State, in a non-dominant position, whose members-being nationals of the State-possess ethnic, religious or linguistic characteristics differing from those of the rest of the population and show, if only implicitly, a sense of solidarity, directed towards preserving their culture, traditions, religion or language.
> (Caportorti, 1979, 96)

As previously stated, this definition might be revised if it applies to online minorities.

Synthetically, it could be said that the idea of a minority stems from a particular aspect of the identity that a group of people shares, which is typically numerically smaller than the rest of the population, is discriminated against and is powerless. This definition of "minority" would be appropriate for the Internet context.

4. Free speech

Several world-renowned experts participated in a July 2021 webinar on "free speech, democracy, and the rights of minorities" to examine the most cutting-edge topics regarding free speech, minorities and the Internet. The first webinar, "Legal Cultures on Free Speech and the Internet," discussed the many legal approaches to free expression, with a focus on political speech. The second webinar session was "Democracy, Hate Speech, and (Mis)Information" and focused on fake news and its effects on democracy, gender-based hate speech and the relationship between artificial intelligence (AI) and hate speech. The third webinar session, entitled "free speech and minorities," examined government speech and minority rights, the discussion about cancel culture and the representations of migrants' rights in official visual and verbal discourses during the COVID-19 period in Russia. Other articles in this volume were given during the panel "Freedom of Speech, Minorities, and the Internet" at the Virtual World Congress of the International Political Science Association, IPSA, on 12 July 2021.

Given the format of these webinar sessions, this book is organised into three main parts: Legal cultures on free speech and Internet; Democracy, hate speech and (Mis)information and free speech and minorities.

In the part entitled "Legal Cultures on Free Speech and the Internet," Alexander Tsesis first discusses "Democratic Values and the Regulation of Hate Speech." He defends that the majority of democratic governments and international organisations regulate hate speech to protect their liberal democratic values and norms. Despite an increase in hate crimes, the United States continues to be an anomaly in its inability to ban hate speech. Following the history of widely interpreting the freedom of expression, American law does not give credit to the argument that hate speech promotes violence.

Second, Jędrzej Skrzypczak studies in his work "Freedom of speech, minorities, and the internet from the European perspective. Words matter" how the digital era necessitates a new, distinct strategy to guaranteeing minority groups' access to and protection from the media. Education, self-regulation and limited international or European legislation are the best solutions. In the digital era, international rules for preserving the rights of national, ethnic and linguistic minorities should also apply to LGBT+ minority

This part is concluded with the work "Free speech and Internet: is there a New Interpretation for Human Rights? With a Special Reference to Chinese and Russian Approaches on Internet Regulations" by Oscar Pérez de la Fuente. The Internet has changed how we conceive about and conduct politics since it is a spectacular form of communication and information source. Many political regimes have responded differently to the Internet, for instance in the manner they face criticisms. A typology of political systems is useful for determining whether political speech prohibitions are enforced. Under democratic systems, individuals have the right to express their opposition privately or publicly to the government, to organise, form parties and compete in elections. The regimes that place the fewest restrictions on the speech, organisation and representation of political preferences—and the chances accessible to government opponents—are the least restrictive. China and Russia's approaches to online free expression will be analysed from the perspectives of *liberalisation* and *public contestation* and *participation* and *inclusiveness*.

This book's next part is named "Democracy, Hate Speech and (Mis)information," and it contains three pieces on manipulation, fake news and misinformation. This is a current subject on the significance of information in democracy in light of technological advancements. In her chapter "Manipulation and the First Amendment," Helen Norton argues that the prevailing presumption under the First Amendment is that listeners can defend themselves from unwanted or hurtful speech through the traditional remedies of exit and voice, avoidance and rebuttal. She contends that manipulation should be added to the list of damages to listeners' interests that deserve legal protection.

In "Fake News and Free Speech Theory," Filimon Peonidis cites Axel Gelfert's description of fake news as the deliberate dissemination of (generally) false or misleading statements as news. What does the notion of free speech have to say about this type of political discourse? In liberal democracies, a few competing major media nearly monopolised the provision of political news. In his chapter "Misinformation and Hate Speech: When Bad Becomes Worse," Gustavo Ferreira Santos discusses the significance of enacting public regulations to address democratic dangers on the Internet, in addition to the laws that existed before the Internet. Examining countermeasures to these threats is necessary to prevent omissions in our response that might compound the hazards to democracy. As a result of hate speech, misinformation and speech manipulation, the conditions for democratic dialogue are reduced.

This part also analyses the topic of hate speech from two uncommon perspectives: gender-biased language and the applications and consequences of AI. Irene Spigno asserts in the chapter "Gender-based Hate Speech against Women: A Comparative Perspective" that hate speech aimed towards women on the basis of their gender is a kind of gender-based violence. Typically, gender-based hate speech directed towards women is inaudible and unnoticed. In truth, it represents a profound scorn and loathing that manifests itself frequently in violence towards women. The purpose of this chapter is to examine, from a moral and legal standpoint, the comparative evolution of approaches to hate speech directed against women. Migle Laukyte notes in her chapter "Artificial Intelligence and Hate Speech" that every second, large amounts of hatred are voiced on social networks, published on websites, tweeted between friends and co-workers and searched for on search engines. This chapter covers the various AI techniques employed for this purpose and whether or not AI might be used to prevent the spread of hate speech. It also examines the key problems that might hamper the development of artificial intelligence, such as difficulties in natural language processing and contextualisation of speech.

The next part is entitled "Free Speech and Minorities" and covers a wide range of subjects, including cancel culture, government speech, blasphemy case law, SLAPP judicial actions and migrants' visual portrayal. These are controversial themes with open debates in many countries. David S. Han discusses in the chapter headed "Disentangling 'Cancel Culture'" that the issue over "cancel cultural" has become a flashpoint in the current culture wars. In its widest definition, "cancelling" refers to the social shame and loss of support from persons or organisations in reaction to previous offences. This also refers to a form of social media-specific humiliation and exclusion. This essay attempts to untangle the numerous threads of the cancel culture argument, which includes social and cultural standards around free speech.

William D. Araiza attempts to answer the following issues in his chapter on "Government Speech and Minority Rights": What obligations does a democratic government have when it targets or criticises minorities? How much is the government obligated or authorised to recognise, defend and promote their discriminatory rights? Is the government permitted to hold such opinions? Does the answer depend on the constitutionality of genuine, non-speech-based sexual orientation discrimination? Or, is the government permitted to take a stand on such topics, even if such a stance conflicts with constitutional mandates?

SLAPP is quite a new term and means strategic lawsuit against public participation. In his work "SLAPP—between the right to a fair trial and chilling impact for Freedom of Expression," Jędrzej Skrzypczak asserts that SLAPP refers to systemic, planned activities against journalists and other public life actors, whistle-blowers and so on. The primary objective of such activities is to deplete financial and mental resources and induce the chilling effect. No EU member state has enacted unique anti-SLAPP legislation. This chapter will examine instances of anti-SLAPP legislation from the United States and a proposal for EU anti-SLAPP legislation.

Tomasz Litwin explains in his chapter "The freedom of speech and the protection of religious feelings—the case of Dorota Rabczewska—comparative analysis" that the Polish female singer and star, Dorota Rabczewska, was fined in 2012 for claiming that the Bible was written by a drug- and alcohol-addled author. The judgement was based on a provision that authorised a maximum two-year jail sentence.

The final part of this book is a conclusion by Alexander Tsesis and Jędrzej Skrzypczak, co-editors of this book, which includes some observations on the presented themes and proposals for additional debates or legislative or judicial fresh perspectives.

It is time to show gratitude to the "Free speech, democracy and rights of minorities" webinar organisation entities—first, the Department of International and Ecclesiastical Law and Philosophy of Law at the Carlos III University of Madrid, Spain, in addition to the Gregorio Peces-Barba human rights Institute, Carlos III University of Madrid and lastly, to the Research Committee 26 on human rights of the International Political Science Association IPSA.

14 *Oscar Pérez de la Fuente*

The source of finance for this enterprise is the Project "New challenges of Law" of the Department of International and Ecclesiastical Law and Philosophy of Law UC3M. This work has been supported by the Madrid Government (Comunidad de Madrid-Spain) under the Multiannual Agreement with UC3M in the line of Excellence of University Professors (EPUC3M06) and in the context of the V PRICIT (Regional Programme of Research and Technological Innovation).

Notes

1 "2.2 The right to freedom from censorship." The Internet must be protected from all attempts to silence critical voices and to censor social and political content or debate (Association for Progressive Communications, 2016, 1).
2 Expression and Association: everyone has the right to seek, receive and impart information freely on the Internet without censorship or other interference. Everyone also has the right to associate freely through and on the Internet, for social, political, cultural or other purposes. NETWORK EQUALITY: Everyone shall have universal and open access to the Internet's content, free from discriminatory prioritisation, filtering or traffic control on commercial, political or other grounds (Internet Governance Forum UN, 2014, 7).
3 "The right to freedom of expression should not be restricted by governments, except in narrowly defined circumstances based on internationally recognized laws or standards. [vii] These restrictions should be consistent with international human rights laws or standards, the rule of law and be necessary and proportionate for the relevant purpose" (Global Network Initiative, 2008, 1).

References

Berlin, I. 2002. *Liberty, Incorporating Four Essays on Liberty*. Hardy, H. (ed.). Oxford: Oxford University Press.

Caportorti, F. 1979. *Study on the Rights of Persons Belonging to Ethnic, Religious and Linguistic Minorities*. New York: United Nations.

Comanducci, P. 2001. "Derechos humanos y minorías: Un acercamiento analítico neoilustrado." En M. Carbonell (ed.). *Derechos sociales y derechos de las minorías*. México: Porrua: 321–322.

Fontaine, R. and Rogers, W. 2011. *Internet Freedom: A Foreign Policy Imperative in the Digital Age*. Washington, DC: Center for a New America Security.

Karagiannopoulos, V. 2018. *Living Con Hacktivism: From Conflict to Symbiosis*. Cham: Palgrave Macmillan.

Koester, A. 2012. "Fighting Internet Piracy: The French Experience With the Hadopi Law." *International Journal of Management & Information Systems* 16, no. 4: 327–330.

Kymlicka, W. 1998a. *Multicultural Citizenship*. Oxford: Claredon Press.

Kymlicka, W. 1998b. "Can Multiculturalism Be Extended to Non-ethnic Groups?" In W. Kymlicka (ed.). *Finding Our Way. Rethinking Ethnocultural Relations in Canada*. Toronto, Oxford, New York: Oxford University Press: 90–103.

MacKinnon, R. 2011. "Liberation Technology: China's 'Networked Authoritarianism'." *Journal of Democracy* 22, no. 2: 32–46.

Mihr, A. 2017. *Cyber Justice: Human Rights and Good Governance for the Internet*. Cham, Switzerland: Springer.

Parkeh, B. 2000. *Rethinking Multicultarism. Cultural Diversity and Political Theory*. Cambridge, MA: Harvard University Press.

Pérez de la Fuente, O. 2005. *Pluralismo cultural y derechos de las minorías*. Madrid: Dykinson.
Pérez de la Fuente, O. 2010. "Sobre el Holocausto: el imperativo de la memoria en el ámbito del derecho y de la Historia." *Anuario de la Facultad de Derecho de la Universidad de la Coruña* 14: 91–120.
Pérez de la Fuente, O. 2015. "Sobre el discurso de las minorías." en M. Abad Castelos, M. C. Barranco Avilés, M. C. Llamazares Calzadilla (eds.). *Derecho y minorías*. Colección Gregorio Peces-Barba. Madrid: Dykinson: 55–78.
Popper, K. 2013. *Open Society and Its Enemies*. Princeton: Princeton University Press.
Ross, A. 2010. "Internet Freedom: Historic Roots nd Rod Forward." *SAIS Review* 30, no. 2: 3–15.
Sorell, T. 2015. "Human Rights and Hacktivism: The Cases of Wikileaks and Anonymous." *Journal of Human Rights Practice* 7, no. 3: 391–410.
Tsesis, A. 2002. "Prohibiting Incitement on the Internet." *Virginia Journal of Law and Technology* 7, no. 5: 1–41.
Van Blarcum, Ch. D. 2005. "Internet Hate Speech: The European Framework and the Emerging American Haven." *Washington and Lee Law Review*: 781–830.
Wagner, B. 2011. "Freedom of Expression on the Internet: Implications for Foreign Policy." *Global Information Society Watch*. Thematic reports.
Weaver, R. L. 2011. "The Internet, Free Speech, and Criminal Law: Is It Time for a New International Treaty on the Internet." *Texas Tech Law Review* 44, no. 1: 197–220.
Ziaja, A. J. 2011. "Free Speech in the Balance: An Examination of Yahoo! Case." *Global Jurist* 11, no. 2: 1–14.

Regulations

Association for Progressive Communication. 2006. APC Internet Rights Charter, March 14.
Council of Europe. 2003. Additional Protocol to the Convention on Cybercrime of the Council of Europe, January 28.
European Commission. 2016. Code of Conduct to Combat Illegal Online Hate Speech of the European Commission with Several Platforms.
European Union. 2008. Framework Decision 2008/913/JHA of November 28, 2008 on Combating Certain Forms and Expressions of Racism and Xenophobia by Means of Criminal Law, 2008/913/JAI, November 28.
United Nations. 2013. Resolution of the General Assembly on the Right to Privacy on the Digital Age, December 18, A/RES/68/167.
United Nations. Committee of the Convention of the Rights of the Child. 2019. Guidelines Regarding the Implementation of the Optional Protocol to the Convention on the Rights of the Child on the Sale of Children, Child Prostitution and Child Pornography, 10 September 2019 CRC/C/156.
United Nations Internet Governance Forum. 2014. The Charter of Human Right and Principles of the Internet.
World Summit on the Information Society. 2003. Geneva, Porrúa, 311–348, December 10–12.

Part II
Legal cultures on free speech and Internet

2 Democratic values and the regulation of hate speech

Alexander Tsesis

1. Introduction

Democracies around the world rely on variously formulated hate speech regulations designed to safeguard pluralistic equality. International organisations, such as the United Nations, also find such laws necessary for maintaining a tolerant society. Hate speech does not advance philosophical, historical, artistic, sociological or inclusive thought. Laws that regulate hate propaganda are meant to secure equality by restricting modes of discourse that have historically been used to arouse animosity and inflame stereotypes. The United States continues to be an outlier in the international community, adopting a libertarian philosophy of free speech.

Dialogue is essential to the development of democratic institutions. Freedom to express political views is critical to representative governance. Free political exchange allows for communications between elected government officials and constituents, holds officials accountable and gives voice to concerns about unequal treatment. Countries whose constitutions respect expressive rights nevertheless find necessary the regulation of incitement and hateful messages. These forms of communications are outside the realm of protection. They are, rather, analogous to other unprotected forms of speech, such as defamation, copyright, trademark infringement and monopolistic collusion.

The spread of denigrating ideas has historically been essential for groups to amass followers willing to commit various injustices. Among the many examples of hate speech turning into violent conduct are the Rwanda genocide, Jewish Holocaust, black slavery and aboriginal removal. On these and many other occasions around the world, rhetoric can influence mass violence. Supremacist groups whip up collective harm by steadily appealing to easily identifiable prejudices and adopting them to win support for violent or discriminatory conduct.

2. Pressing and substantial concern

There is ample reason to be substantially concerned that hate propaganda, which denigrates identifiable groups, can promote discriminatory behaviour. Slurs often rely on readily identifiable stereotypes that motivate behaviour. Walter Lippmann,

DOI: 10.4324/9781003274476-4

who coined the term "stereotype," explained that stereotypes "determine what group of facts we shall see, and in what light we shall see them" (Lippman, 1992, xviii). Racial and anti-semitic slurs target individuals based on historical degradations; they aim to harm the reputations of entire groups of people. Denial of an identifiable group's dignity and humanity is common in racial, nationalistic or ethnocentric behaviours.

Stereotypes provide culturally identifiable expressions that can affect individual attitudes. The long-term effects of hate propaganda are best illustrated by historical and contemporary examples, some of which are briefly described in the following.

2.1. German anti-semitism

Nazi Germany relied on numerous historically anti-semitic stereotypes that commonly appeared in popular literature from the late nineteenth century, in the works of Otto von Glogau, author of *Die Gartenlaube* (*The Bower*) (Bracher, 1972; Volkov, 1989, 321–322); Wilhelm Marr, the creator of the term *Antisemitismus* (Pulzer, 1964; Volkov, 1989, 320–321); Alfred Ploetz, a eugenicist who founded the Society of Racial Hygiene (Weindling, 1993, 72, 150) and Paul de Lagarde, an acclaimed biblical scholar who called for *lebenstraum* (living space) for Germany, while characterising Jews as "trichinae and bacilli" (Bein, 1959, 7, 14 n. 19).

They all would feed into what became Nazi ideology.

The Nazi Party came to power on the heels of decades of anti-semitic propaganda (Niewyk, 1980, 82). Adolf Stoecker, a court preacher from Berlin, became the first German politician in Germany to realise the power of anti-semitic slogans to drum up votes (Gutteridge, 1976, 4, 8). An even more powerful example of how these popular works affected German propaganda is Julius Streicher's weekly *Der Stürmer*. Streicher published numerous perverse caricatures of Jews and characterised the Jews as Germany's misfortune on his newspaper's headnote (ibid., pp. 161–62) (by the 1930s, Streicher's newspaper was used as a teaching tool by elementary school teachers). His thought was but an embellishment of a long-held German tradition. In this cesspool of company, Streicher had copied the great German historian Heinrich von Treitschke's article. Published in the prestigious newspaper, *Prueussische Jahrbücher*, Treitschke had sad asserting that "*Die Juden sind unser Unglück!*" meaning "The Jews are our misfortune!" Another example is the popularity of a forgery purporting Jews were fomenting revolutions, called *The Protocols of the Elders of Zion* (Dawidowicz, 1975, 47) (the year *The Protocols* was published in German it sold 120,000 copies). Besides going through many editions in pre-Nazi Germany, both Adolf Hitler and his head of the SS, Heinrich Himmler, commented on how deeply the book influenced their sense of anti-semitism (ibid., 71–72).

2.2. American slavery

In the pre-Civil War American South, proslavery claims dehumanising persons of African dissent appeared plentifully in works like *Personal Slavery Established*

(1773) and Edward Long's *History of Jamaica*. They influence beliefs and practices throughout the United States, especially in the South. Racialism was endemic in a culture whose very Constitution, while not overtly proslavery, was widely understood to be protective of that peculiar institution.

Abolitionists made powerful normative declamations against it, but their message took long to become part of the American psyche and even longer to make its way into the Thirteenth Amendment, abolishing the institution that led to Civil War. Dehumanisation here played out in pseudoscience, for instance, as it was used to rationalise unequal treatment in all walks of life. Many writings justified slavery as a natural condition for blacks and claimed that slavery was for black religious and intellectual betterment (Jenkins, 1935, 7; Greene, 1942, 61–62; McCaine, 1842; Brookes, 1969). These arguments were made repeatedly in popular pamphlets, sermons and congressional speeches (Jordan, 1968, 494). The most effective apologetics for slavery were heard in the years leading up to the Civil War from the voice of John C. Calhoun, who at various times served as United States Secretary of State, Secretary of War, Vice President and Senator (Katz, 1974, 95) (Calhoun believed that slave owners improved the lives of Blacks who otherwise would be low, degraded and savage).

2.3. American Indian removal

From early settlement in the United States, Native Americans were spoken of and written about as savages who had minimal to no property rights, were heathens and lacked civilisation (Berkhofer, 1979, 13–14, 26). This reduced Native Americans into a homogenous group about whom stereotypes were plentiful. For example, John Winthrop, the first governor of the Massachusetts Bay Colony in the seventeenth century, believed Indian deaths from smallpox were attributable to God who thereby was clearing the land for British settlement (Winthrop, 1629, 141; Simmons, 1981, 70). Colonists justified the misappropriation of aboriginal lands by characterising them in official publications and colloquial speech as nomads, thereby denying the legitimacy of complex tribal systems of riparian and agricultural rights that North Americans had developed on the Continent (Josephy, 1991; Driver, 1961, 244–264; Kroeber, 1939, 143–146, 218–221). As one frontier saying had it, "they ain't no game like Injuns. Nossir, no game like Injuns" (Jahoda, 1975, 135).

Indian Removal, which displaced thousands in the nineteenth century, was predicated on the spurious belief that Indians had no attachment to property, home, sovereignty or ancestral ties. As with the pervasive, antagonistic stereotypes of Jews and blacks, derogatory images of Native Americans worked hand in hand with claims of superiority.

2.4. Mauritanian slavery

In Mauritania, where black slavery has existed since at least the twelfth century, stereotype continues to play a role. In 2018, there was an estimated 20% of the population who are still enslaved labourers or child brides (The Unspeakable

Truth about Slavery in Mauritania, 2018). Just as in the antebellum United States, blacks in Mauritania are taught that slavery is a religious institution and that obedience to their Berber masters is a virtue. Ancient Islamic stereotypes of blacks purport that slavery is a religious institution. Professor Bernard Lewis surveyed Arab literature and folklore and found that many "early Islamic poets . . . suggest very strongly a feeling of hatred and contempt directed against persons of African birth or origin" (Lewis, 1990, 22, 56–57, 92, 95). An elderly former slave explained why the parchment abolition of 1981 signifies so little to slaves:

> It is hard to ignore what they have been told all their lives, that without their master they cannot survive, that only he can ennoble them, give meaning to their life, and lead them to heaven. They believe this; so how can they also believe that they must escape the situation that promises to give them so much?
>
> (Human Rights Watch, 1994, 90)

Dark skin Africans, mostly the Haratine, continue to be enslaved to the lighter-skinned Arab Berbers. A Mauritanian common expression among slaves that keeps many from rebellion against the common order is that "Paradise is under your master's feet" (Esseissah, 2016, 3). The term Arabic term "abed" refers both to black persons and to slaves, effectively equating the two. The effect of slave rhetoric is so strong that many of the Haratine regard the system as fair because the Berbers are saints. Proverbs degrading black slaves as cowardly, criminal and even abominable are part of a culture of contempt for blacks more generally (Lewis, 1990, 25).

2.5. Rwandan genocide

In Rwanda, ethnic stereotyping and repeated media calls for the extermination of Tutsis led to a massive genocide perpetrated against them in 1994. The racist ideology took root in the 1950s through ethnocentric uses of slogans in Hutu politics, which eventually permeated the views of ordinary citizens. In the years prior to the event, radio broadcasters called for the destruction of the Tutsi population. Encouragement to destroy the population came from the Hutu-power *Kangura* newspaper, whose reporters casually and regularly dehumanised Tutsis.

Tomes of history are replete with examples of widespread group defamations, calls to violence, stereotypes and dehumanising stereotypes that rely on dogma, religion and pseudoscience to incite audiences to engage in acts of animus against discriminated objects of ire. The spread of ethnic and racial hatred continues in our time to elicit violence throughout the modern world.

The dissemination of ethnically charged messages has precipitated tribal clashes in Kenya (Inskeep and Thompkins, Kenya's Post-Election Violence, 2008; Nowrojee, 1997, 61–63; Oucho, 2002, 90; Oyaro, 2008; Quist-Arcton, 2008). Arab racial hate propaganda in Sudan has catalysed a government-sponsored attempt to "cleanse" black Africans in Darfur, Sudan (Bureau of Democracy,

2004; Steidle and Steidle, 2007; El-Tigani Mahmoud, 2004, 3). Likewise, in the Democratic Republic of the Congo, the government has relied on the incitement of ethnic hatred, creating a culture where ethnic murder is a routine militia practice (Scherrer, 2002, 283; HRW, 1998; Summers, 2017). Throughout the Arab world, Jew-hatred is spread without any interference from governments in Egypt, Syria, Lebanon and Yemen. Indeed, school texts that are "written and produced by Saudi government" teach children to kill Jews and to hate Christians and Jews (Applebaum, 2008).

***

One of the world's foremost authorities on the psychology of prejudice, Gordon Allport, discussed how hate rhetoric is intrinsic to organising hate movements: "Although most barking (antilocution) does not lead to biting, yet there is never a bite without previous barking. Fully seventy years of political anti-Semitism of the verbal order antedated the discriminatory Nürnberg [sic] Laws passed by the Hitler regime." In another part of the world, the Bahutu-influenced media, especially radio, denounced Tutsis as "devils" seeking to commit the most heinous harms against Hutus, one of the greatest inhumanities of mankind, a brutal countywide campaign at genocide that left about 800,000 Tutsis dead, many of them by machete wounds. Cultural hatreds against identifiable groups betimes portend extreme, cultural depravity.

Pogroms against Jews often began with the spread of a medieval myth that they kidnap Christian children, crucify them and use their blood as an ingredient in Passover matzah. Ethnocentric hatred emboldens acts of sadism and bloodthirst. Many lynch mobs in the United States were energised by rumours of a black man raping a white woman. In all these speech-act events, widespread prejudice translated into animosity and animosity energised bloodthirst, rape and larceny. Thus, there is a pressing and substantial concern about hate propaganda that provides a legitimate reason for legislative intervention.

Not all intolerant utterances are so blatant. Jokes more subtly relate harmful stereotypes about ethnic, racial, gender and sexual orientation groups. Through repetition, a group's negative attributes become clichés: "He jewed me down," "he gypped me" and "she's on the rag" are putdowns that refer to widely shared attitudes about Jews, gypsies and women. The stereotypes that are used are typically historically or culturally identifiable tropes. In the hands of charismatic leaders, bigotry based on historical stereotypes can energise movements to discriminate and sometimes commit violence against identifiable groups.

3. International consensus and nuance

There is an overwhelming consensus among democracies that some antilocution leads to discrimination, persecution and, in the worst-case scenarios, genocide. Moreover, many countries express a policy to improve civic and pluralist culture through narrowly tailored regulations of misethnic statements. The list of nations that restrict incitement of racism, xenophobia and infringement of rights are Austria, Belgium, Brazil, Canada, Cyprus, England, France, Germany, India, Israel, Italy and Switzerland (Jones, 1998, 189–224, 259–313; Lasson, 1997, 72 n. 286; Mahoney, 1996, 803; Tsesis, 2004, 396; Southerland, 2007, 192). All these nations have policies to promote inter-group tolerance through laws that penalise hate speakers.

Most recently, in December 2021, the European Commission on Human Rights extended and sought to create a uniform standard for future promulgation of a uniform European Union standard against crimes of hate speech and hate crimes. The document connects EU countries' efforts to combat intolerance with the commitment to safeguard "human dignity, freedom, democracy, equality, rule of law and respect for human rights." Consistent with Article 19 of the Treaty on the Functioning of the European Union, the document identifies prohibitions against hate crimes and hate speech to be consistent with freedom of expression in democratic and pluralist societies. Social media has increased the use of xenophobia, sexism, racism and anti-semitism for political gains (European Commission, 2021).

International human rights instruments, such as the Universal Declaration of Human Rights, the International Covenant on Civil and Political Rights and the European Convention on Human Rights, place barriers against the exploitation of democratic norms of free speech and free assembly to subvert the institutions of liberal democracy. For instance, the International Covenant on Civil and Political Rights provides:

> Nothing in the present Covenant may be interpreted as implying for any State, group or person any right to engage in any activity or perform any act aimed at the destruction of any of the rights and freedoms recognized herein or at their limitation to a greater extent than is provided for in the present Covenant.
> (United Nations, 1966)

That formulation is almost identical to that found in the Universal Declaration of Rights and the European Convention on Human Rights (United Nations, 1948).

Without such a uniform standard, European nations enforce closely related but unique statutory frameworks. The German Constitution, the Basic Law, to take an example, fleshes out detailed guarantees for securing "the right freely to express and disseminat[e]" ideas (Tomuschat et al., 2012, Article 5). It further guarantees the freedom "to express and disseminate his opinions in speech, writing and pictures" and "to gain information from others" (ibid.). Nevertheless, the Basic Law recognises that freedom of expression can be abused to "undermine the free democratic basic order, shall forfeit these basic rights" (ibid., Article 18). Section 131 of the country's criminal code prohibits distribution, display and supply of any:

> writings . . . which describe cruel or otherwise inhuman acts of violence against human beings in a manner which expresses a glorification or rendering harmless of such acts of violence or which represents the cruel or inhuman aspects of the event in a manner which injures human dignity.
> (Bohlander, 2008, §131(a))

Balance is required, favouring speech but also not being so absolutist as to allow authoritarian organisations and individuals to capture the reins of power and turn state power against minorities (*Klass and Others v. Germany*, 1979).

The problem in Germany has grown increasingly acute in recent years with most hate speech targeting Jews, migrants, asylum seekers and refugees (Article 19, 2018b, Germany). For instance, on New Year's 2019, a German man, identified as Andreas N., rammed into a group among whom were Syrians and Afghans, telling the police that he meant to kill foreigners (Basay, 2019). Despite German history with hate propaganda, which was at its cruellest apex in the years leading up to and including the Holocaust, the present government has not responded strongly in the face of new dilemmas, especially with the ease with which hate speech is disseminated across borders over the Internet, the German high court has been inconsistent in its interpretations. However, just recently,

> there have been considerably more convictions for incitement to hatred. The latest official crime statistics document 6,514 cases of "incitement to hatred" in 2016, compared with just 2,670 cases two years earlier, before the start of the 2015 refugee crisis. In June 2017, police departments in all but two German states conducted raids against 36 social media users for alleged hate speech.
>
> (Germany, Freedom on the Net, 2018; Steger, 2016; Leisegang, 2017; Suzuki, 2017)

Ambiguities have raised questions about the applicability of the most recent rule against hate speech, *Netzwerkdurchsetzungsgesetz*, or Network Enforcement Law (NetzDG), which requires social media companies to remove alleged hate speech within 24 hours of notification (Bundesministerium der Justiz, Act to Improve Enforcement of the Law, 2017). The new law has set off some confusion with everything from a Twitter parody of an anti-Muslim comment to a Twitter attack on Muslims as "rapist hordes of men" being pulled down (Eddy, 2018). Despite the current ambiguity, at least this much is clear, says German Justice Minister, Heiko Maas, spreading criminal content is unprotected (Faiola and Kirchner, 2017).

While platforms like Facebook, Google and Twitter have taken down thousands of flagged items within 24 hours, they rejected most of the complaints. Caution is most noticeable at Twitter, which "only identified a need to take action in roughly 11 percent of reported pieces of content" as being prohibited as of 2018 by NetzDG (Gollatz et al., 2018). Concerns include the worry that social media companies will censor too much materials to avoid lawsuits and that the law privatises law enforcement (Claussen, 2018, 10–16).

German courts have found hate speech legislation to be consistent with the nation's commitment to free speech. The German Federal Constitutional Court (Bundesverfassungsgeric) has upheld a criminal conviction for expressing support for the Nazis. In *BverG v. Rieger* (2009), the Constitutional Court "upheld legislation against incitement to hatred that bans public support and justification of the country's former Nazi regime" (Zeldin, 2009). However, the law must be one of general applicability since targeting individuals' opinion is in tune with autocratic states, such as Russia and Turkey, rather than liberal democracies, such as Germany, Australia and the United States. In a separate case, the Australian Federal Court of Justice in 2002 ruled that the county's law against Holocaust denial applied to Austrian-based, German Fredrick Toben (*Jones v. Toben*, 2002). However, the Constitutional Court has likewise set outward limits for actionable expressions. Hence, it found in 2016 *The Case of Mr. D.* that Article 5 of the German Basic Law protects exaggerations, such as those involving name calling such as "maniac" and "insane," against charges of insult and defamation (Des Herrn, 2016; Global Freedom of Expression, Case of Mr. D, 2016).

Other Western democracies have acted consistently with the principles articulated in German and Australia. The Spanish Supreme Court upheld the criminal conviction of a Spanish rapper, Jose Miguel Arenas (also known as Valtonyc), for spreading hate speech and inciting terrorism. He subsequently fled to Belgium. The Spanish court found his music lyrics glorified terrorist groups that called for violence against politicians because they supported the Basque pro-independence group. As a reporter explained, "The Court held that the lyrics constituted criminal offences because they created an atmosphere of fear and anxiety" (Global Freedom of Expression, Case of Jose Miguel Arenas, 2018a). The harm came from the lyrics themselves, even though the singer did not intend to attack anyone. The result is a mixed bag. While conviction for violating Criminal Code Articles 578 and 579 prohibition of "exalting terrorism and humiliating its victims" reflects efforts to preserve public safety, his conviction of Article 169.2 of the Code for "slandering and insulting the Crown" seems more like political repression. The standard of review used by the Spanish court—identifying hate speech to create "fear and anxiety"—would not be sufficient in the United States to exclude the speech from First Amendment protection (ibid.).

A Belgian court then refused to comply with a European Arrest Warrant requesting his extradition to Spain because the judge found the reason for concern that Beltran was being prosecuted for his political beliefs. The case was then appealed to the European Court of Justice in Luxembourg. The ECJ then ruled that extradition is not a given; rather, a Belgium court must first determine whether his lyrics violated Belgium law, leaving it to the Court of Ghent to determine whether to comply with the extradition warrant (Quell, 2020). Later still, in demonstrating its independence, the Belgium court of appeals later found that Valtonyc could not be extradited because his three-year punishment for political hyperbole against the Spanish monarchy did not exist when he first made the comments; as of the time of publication, Belgium planned to appeal this latest ruling (AFP, 2022).

The muddled differences of opinion among Europe Union countries demonstrate the difficulties prosecutors face in proving up that punishment for hyperbolic antigovernment speech that does not amount to any advocacy or conspiracy to engage in violence. Moreover, they raise concerns that an unclear balancing analysis can result in unpredictability and political prosecution for the use of politically violent rhetoric that fuelled destructive protests (Hasel, 2022). Hence, Belgium's concern is to prevent the stifling of political expression that goes against the orthodox government views of the King in Spain.

Presumably, the newest appeal of Valtonyc's case will and should address the European Court of Human Rights' holding in *Féret v. Belgium*. In that case, the ECtHR found Belgium had not violated Article 10 (freedom of expression) by taking measures to combat "racism, xenophobia, anti-Semitism, and intolerance." Such actionable conversation was an irresponsible use of speech "detrimental to dignity and safety" of the objects of hatred (*Féret v. Belgium*, 2009, paras. 72–73). That holding is consistent with the more general European Union courts' use of proportionality analysis that balances of right to expression with principles of dignity and equality (Douglas-Scott, 1999, 343). While such a balance seems only logical when state interests conflict with privacy rights, the Valtonyc case raises serious concerns about state overreach and judicial acquiescence.

The European proportionality approach requires courts to weigh speakers' rights, policy concerns, means/ends analysis and tailoring consideration. This is quite different from the categorical method used in the United States. European nations often limit political expression in ways that in the United States are too abstract to withstand First Amendment review. The Austrian criminal code bans the National Socialist German Workers' Party (Nazi Party). Hate speech infringes on personal autonomy and dignity. Austria criminalises the incitement of hostilities against religious, racial, ethnic, national groups and other groups because of it "jeopardize[s] the public order." Slandering these groups attacks "their human dignity" (United Nations, 2012).

Stirring up hatred against or verbally harassing statutorily identified groups is subject to up to two years in prison. Aggravated offenses can be brought for printing and broadcasting such content. Intent to cause incite another to carry out the proscribed act is criminally actionable. The crime can be committed by film, cartoons or pantomime; words are not the sole means to commit the offense (Article 19, 2018a, Austria). Countries like Austria that have anti-hate speech laws "wish to deter the violence and fighting they believe it encourages" (Delgado and Stefancic, 2004, 196).

Great Britain has long recognised a connection between destructive propaganda that makes "reference to colour, race, nationality (including citizenship) or ethnic or national origins" and the spread of racism and ethnocentrism that undermine representative democracy. Its earliest law against the breach of the peace, the *Public Order Act* of 1936, was enacted in response to fascist rallies that became increasingly volatile and anti-Semitic. Then in 1965, the *British Race Relations Act* prohibited persons from intentionally publishing written materials or giving public speeches that were threatening, abusive or insulting and likely to stir up racial hatred. That Act was amended in 1976 to eliminate the earlier requirement that litigants prove a speaker's intent, which is the key mental component in countries such as the United States and Austria. With Great Britain, as with Germany, intent is a factor for the court to evaluate in determining whether speech incites violence and other illegal activity against identifiable groups (Roth, 1992, 201; Lasson, 1987, 170–71; Barendt, 1985, 163–64; Article 19, 2018b, Germany).

The current law against stirring up hatred against any racial group in Great Britain (Part III, § 18 of the *Public Order Act* of 1986) uses a test of whether "racial hatred is likely to be stirred up" rather than the "intends to stir up racial hatred" language. The language used in the *Public Order Act* of 1986 likewise criminalises the use of threatening, abusive or insulting language or behaviour to stir up hatred based on colour, race, nationality (including citizenship) or ethnic or national origins. Likewise, § 19 prohibits distributing written material that stirs racial hatred, having regard for the circumstances, and § 21 prohibits the distribution of visual or audio material that intends to stir racial hatred. In *R v. Umran Javed and Others,* speakers were convicted of threats, abusive and insulting words intent on stirring up hatred in violation of § 18 during a public gathering convened to condemn cartoons that insulted depicting Mohamad (BBC News, Cartoon Protester, 2012a). The event took place shortly after the London bombings of July 2005, when tensions were high about terrorism (Pallister, 2007). Statements at the event urged murder. The appellate court's reasoning considered the circumstances under which the statements were made and the likelihood they would stir others to commit further offences. Javed and others were also later convicted of having data on his computer that could be used to recruit others to commit acts of terror (Public Order Act, 1986; Halstead, 2009, 334; BBC News, Umran Javed, 2012b; Law Soceity Gazette, 2007). The Racial and Religious Hatred Act 2006 amends Public Order Act 1986 to create a criminal cause of action for stirring hated against persons on religious grounds (Racial and Religious Hatred Act, 2006). The Public Order Act further prohibits intentionally stirring hated against persons based on sexual orientation (Public Order Act, 1086, Section 39B-29F; First Criminal Conviction, 2019). In the United Kingdom, even possession of inflammatory material is a punishable offense when it involves "threatening, abusive or insulting" language.

Curiously, the United Kingdom includes an exception for religion, presumably indicating how difficult, if not impossible, it would be to administer prosecutions of religious institutions: "Nothing in this Part shall be read or given effect in a way which prohibits or restricts discussion, criticism or expressions of antipathy, dislike, ridicule, insult or abuse of particular religions or the beliefs or practices of their adherents" (Racial and Religious Hatred Act, 2006, (c.1)). Yet, the provision often has minimal value as the case of Dr. David Mackereth demonstrates. He was forced out of his job with the Department for Work and Pensions when in 2018 he said that he would not use transgender pronouns because he believed "gender is defined by biology and genetics" and that the Bible also taught the male/female sex dichotomy (Cimmino, 2019).

Scandinavian countries likewise link hateful propaganda to extremist conduct. They find a constitutional guarantee of free speech to be consistent with the enforcement of hate speech regulations. Article 266b of the Danish Penal Code criminalises racist statements, making it illegal to publicly utter "with the intention of wider dissemination" of a statement or to impart to others "information by which a group of people are threatened, insulted or degraded on account of their race, colour, national or ethnic origin, religion, or sexual inclination." Violators of 266b can be fined or imprisoned (Denmark Criminal Code, 2005). The enforcement of 266b has been severely criticised by the right in Denmark claiming that the law is not narrowly tailored enough to prevent excessive prosecution of those criticising Islam (Gutiérrez, 2017). It would go too far to say Danish prosecution is limitless. Director of Public Prosecutions in 2006 determined not to file charges under 266b against *Jyllands Posten* newspaper for publishing the article "The Face of Muhammad," which contained 12 critical cartoons of Islam and Muhammad (Jakobsen, 2016).

Finland is another country that honours free expression as a fundamental right (Constitution of Finland, 1999, Ch. 2 §12), but its law nevertheless criminalises the use of racial, ethnic and religious threats, slanders and insults (Finland Penal Code, 1963, Ch. 11 §8; Klo and Ellil, 2007). An author and two newspaper editors were fined in 2007 under Finland's hate speech law for anti-semitic remarks made in a published letter (Freedom House, 2008; United States Department of State, 2008). Finland has recently increased social media responsibilities for hosting hostile and extremist hate speech, adopting new legislation in 2017 (Cohen-Almagor, 2017). Finland relies on agitating and inciting hatred against an identifiable ethnic group (Abeng, 2017). The Finish government launched a campaign against hate speech in February 2019 to better inform people of what constitutes hate speech and to encourage reporting to the police of hate speech (Finish Government, 2019).

A recent decision in Finland, however, was rather draconian. In 2019, a Finnish Congresswoman criticised the state church for participating in the LGBT gay pride parade. Moreover, she was later investigated for a book she wrote, *Male and Female He Created Them*. The Prosecutor General brought charges under the Criminal Code of Finland, Section 10. This is prosecutorial overreach. The judiciary did not fall for the prosecutor's office's effort to require state orthodoxy. The Helsinki court dismissed all charges, writing that "it is not for the not for the district court to interpret biblical concepts" (CNA Staff, Christian MP, 2022; Helsinki, Finnish MP, 2022).

The Swedish Constitution explicitly guarantees all citizens the rights "publicly to express [their] thoughts, opinions and sentiments, and in general to communicate information on any subject whatsoever on sound radio, television and certain like transmissions, films, video recordings, sound recordings and other technical recordings." A provision of the Swedish Penal Code, nevertheless, punishes anyone for spreading "statements or communication[s]" that "threaten[] or express[] contempt for a national, ethnic or other such group of persons with allusion to race, colour, national or ethnic origin or religious belief." A 2003 amendment to the law also criminalises incitement against homosexuals (Swedish Penal Code, 16:8; *Prosecutor General v. Green, Nytt Juridiskt Arkiv*, 2005). Chapter 16, Section 8 of the Penal Code (*Brottsbalken*, SFS, 1962, 700) provides that

> A person who, in a disseminated statement or communication, threatens or expresses contempt for a national, ethnic or other such group of persons with allusion to race, colour, national or ethnic origin or religious belief shall, be sentenced for agitation against a national or ethnic group to imprisonment for at most two years or, if the crime is petty, to a fine.
>
> (Swedish Penal Code)

The Swedish Supreme Court, in a 2005 decision, upheld this law. The opinion distinguished between "objective criticism of certain groups," which the country's constitution protects, and statements triggering criminal liability: "Naturally, the principles of freedom of speech and the right to criticize may not be used to protect statements expressing contempt for a group of people, for example, because they are of a certain nationality and hence are inferior" (ibid.). In a separate decision, the country's supreme court upheld the conviction against individuals for agitating in a case upheld by the European Court of Human Rights agreed, finding that the conviction for disseminating antigay pamphlets at schools did not violate the freedom of expression guarantee of Article 10 of the European Convention for the Protection of Human Rights and Fundamental Freedoms. The ECHR held that "[t]he interference with the applicants' exercise of their right to freedom of expression could therefore reasonably be regarded by the national authorities as necessary in a democratic society for the protection of the reputation and rights of others" (*Vejdeland v. Sweden*, 2012, para. 3; *Tammer v. Estonia*, 2003, para. 69; *Skaÿka v. Poland*, 2003, paras. 41–42).

The government of Sweden considers the problem not simply the symbols of hate, which are prohibited, but the ideologies of groups that use them to spread violence, intimidation, harassment and threats (Government of Sweden, 2019b, Summary). Sweden in 2016 adopted a national plan to combat racism. As part of Sweden's plan to combat anti-semitism, it hosted a conference in 2020 in memory of the Holocaust (Government of Sweden, 2019a).

Norway's penal code contains a provision, Article 135a, which criminalises discriminatory or hateful expressions uttered to the public "willfully or through gross negligence" (Norwegian Penal Code, n.d.). Article 135a covers racial, xenophobic, ethnocentric and homophobic propaganda which is directed at individuals. The offence carries a penalty of fines or a term of imprisonment not exceeding three years. Norway added the negligence provision to its criminal law in order to adhere to the decision in *Jewish Community of Oslo v. Norway*. In that case, the U.N. Committee on the Elimination of Racial Discrimination held in that case that the Supreme Court of Norway had erroneously found that only wilful threats could lead to conviction (*Oslo v. Norway*, 2005, paras. 2.1, 2.5, 2.7). The Committee held, instead, that the speaker violated the U.N. Convention on the Elimination of All Forms of Racial Discrimination by publicly asserting that "people and country are being plundered and destroyed by Jews, who suck our country empty of wealth and replace it with immoral and un-Norwegian thoughts" and calling on members of the Bootboy organisation to follow in the footsteps of the National Socialists "and fight for what (we) believe in." These statements, the Committee stated, were an "incitement at least to racial discrimination, if not to violence" (ibid., para. 10.1–10.6).

In a 2018 case, the Norwegian Supreme Court found that a defendant had violated 135a by calling his Somali neighbour, "'*expletive* darky [*jaevla svarting*]' and '*expletive* negro" (*jaevla neger*).'" That decision is consistent with a 2012 case, which found a party guilty of violating 135a by using racial slurs against a bar tender, who had denied the defendant entrance (Global Freedom Expression, 2012).

Other Western democracies where political speech is staunchly protected have enacted similar legislation. The Swiss Criminal Code (Article 261bis) punishes public incitement to racial hatred or discrimination, spreading racist ideology, denying crimes against humanity and refusing on grounds of race, ethnic origin or religion to supply a service intended for the public (Swiss Criminal Code).

Israel has also found that racist speech is incompatible with democratic politics, enacting legislation in 1985 that prohibits anyone to be a member of the Knesset, Israel's Parliament, who uses racist incitement (Basic Law: The Knesset (Amendment No. 9) Law, 1985). An Israeli Penal Law permits courts to sentence persons who publish material "with the purpose of inciting to racism" for up to five years in prison (Cohen-Almagor, 2012). Under Section 144B of the Israeli penal code, "If a person publishes anything in order to incite to racism" (Israeli Penal Code, n.d.). As recently as 2018, a Jewish Israeli was indicted for racist incitement on social media targeting Arabs and "leftists" (Staff, 2018). In an earlier case, an Israeli court found a defendant guilty of advocating the expulsion of Arabs (Cohen-Almagor, 2012, 50–51).

Likewise, in 1992, the Hungarian Constitutional Court noted that freedom of expression is essential to "social justice and human creativity" (Decision No. 30/1992 (V.18) AB, Constitutional Court of the Republic of Hungary, 1995). Section 332 of the Hungarian Criminal Code prohibits incitement against a community (Hungarian Penal Code, 2012). Nevertheless, Article 269(1) of the Hungarian Penal Code prohibits persons from communicating incitements to large gatherings and thereby adjuring them to hate persons based on nationality, creed or race. The Hungarian Constitutional Court upheld the constitutionality of that statute. The Court explained its decision by drawing attention to:

> The potential harms resulting from incitement to hate, the subjecting of certain groups in a population to denigrating and humiliating treatment is amply documented in the annals of human experience . . . the whipped-up emotions against the group threaten the honour, dignity (and life, in the more extreme cases) of the individuals comprising the group, and by intimidation, restrict them in the exercise of their other rights as well (including the right of freedom of expression).
>
> (Hungarian Constitutional Court, 1995)

Hungarian Constitutional Court has, however, taken a position on a matter such as group defamation that, just as in the United States, criminalises incitement against a person, rather than solely abstract apprehension of danger, to a targeted community (Molnar, 2012; Rosenfeld, 2003). The Court uses the clear and present danger test that includes a harm component and does not allow for criminalisation of abstract communications (Kolta, 2013). The question is whether a harm is likely to occur from the communication, which the criminal code requires prosecutors to prove is a form of incitement rather than simple agitation (Hungarian Penal Code, 2012, Art. 332). Likelihood, of course, is as ambiguous in Hungary as it is in the U.S. clear and present danger test.

Hungarian penal law, however, should not be mistaken as entirely influenced by U.S. First Amendment jurisprudence. In fact, the Hungarian law of incitement differs significantly from the U.S. approach. It is a crime in Hungary to deny the genocidal acts and crimes of humanity perpetrated by such historical nemeses as the Nazis and communists (ibid., Article 333). One may point out that those groups have not been particularly influential in the United States, but that would not gainsay the U.S. experience with racism in the form of proslavery thought embodied in the Confederate States, which sought to secede by civil war and its St. Andrews Cross Battle Flag in the 1860s.

A broad consensus of democratic states holds that exposing others to hatred is detrimental to society. European laws prohibit a range of free expression regarded to be dangerous to democratic order, individual autonomy and equality. Many of those laws regulate expression that the U.S. free speech doctrine treats as protected speech.

The greatest danger of these use is autocratic regimes that manipulate these laws to abusively rely on modern surveillance technologies to suppress communication essential to deliberative democracies for the debate about political ideas, personal convictions and the enjoyment of the arts (Morozom, 2011). Google returned to profit from the Chinese market, working with that country's government to censor searches as it had prior to 2010, after leaving because of the degree of governmental censorship (World this Week, 2018; Isaac, 2016). Russia was particularly successful in manipulating the U.S. Presidential elections in 2016 and 2020 (Kim, 2020; Abrams, 2019). In its own country, Russian repression runs deep with the continued tyranny of Vladimir Putin. Among his victims was the punk rock group Pussy Riot, whose members were jailed for political protest (*Alekhina v. Russia*, 2019). Elsewhere, false political advertisements have been used to subvert the democratic process by saturating the marketplace of ideas with false propaganda that instigates violence, as it has in countries from Sri Lanka to Indonesia, Libya, India, Myanmar and Mexico (Hogan and Safi, 2018; Taub and Fisher, 2018; Walsh and Zway, 2018). The problem becomes increasingly acute as Facebook displaces local media, with news stories imputing the reputations of identifiable groups like Jews, African Americans, Muslims and homosexuals going viral on social media and being taken up by violent organisations seeking to harm the spectres of their animus.

Around the world, officials have abused hate speech laws to repress legitimate political criticism. For instance, the European Court of Human Rights ("ECHR") overturned the conviction of Savva Terentyev under Russian Criminal Code Article 282, which prohibits incitement to hatred or enmity against a social group, for criticising police misconduct, including characterisation of them as pigs. That conviction, the ECHR found, was a violation of Terentyev's rights under Article 10 of the EU Convention on Human Rights, which protects the freedom of expression.

Terentyev's words, as ECHR determined, did not promote violence hated, or intolerance when examined against the background context for the statement (*Savva Terentyev v. Russia*, 2018; Russian Federation Criminal Code, 1996, Art.

282; Global Freedom of Expression, Savva). The same court overturned the decision of the Moscow City Court against a journalist who had criticised Russian Army's conduct in the Chechen Republic (*Stomakhin v. Russia*, 2018; Global Freedom of Expression, Stomakhim, 2018c).

In the hands of repressive governments, laws against incitement turn into another vehicle for political and religious repression. Vietnam's cybersecurity law is indicative of other autocracies, such as Turkey, which prohibit criticisms of government (Vu, 2019; Human Rights Watch, 2018). These countries interpret peaceful criticism of government and abstract calls to arms to be forms of hate speech, defamation and terrorism. The Pakistan government has arrested Facebook users for benign comments about religion blasphemous by the Pakistan government (Kohari, 2019). A Pakistani man, Taimoor Raza, received a death sentence for allegedly insulting Mohamed on the Internet for engaging in an online debate about the finer points of Islam (AFP, 2017).

4. American free speech law and hate incitement

U.S. Law and doctrine should be understood in the context of the increasing hate crimes perpetrated in the United State. The number has been increasing, in the last three years, with blacks and Jews continuing to be the most reviled and physically attacked groups. The Federal Bureau of Investigations is mandated by statute, 28 U.S.C. § 534 to collect data on crimes motivated by race, religion and sexual orientation. The FBI also gathers data on attacks based on disability, gender and gender identity. Currently, available statistics, available for 1995–2017, indicate an increase in occurrences (FBI Statistics, 1995–2017; Rushin and Edwards, 2018). The level of hatred spread through the Internet and other channels conducive for white supremacists to spread their hatred against groups, especially blacks and Jews, has contributed to synagogue and black church attacks (Lopez, 2017; Gormly et al., 2018; Paul and Mettler, 2019). And perpetrators, such as Dylan Roof, John Earnest and Brenton Tarrant, have found it necessary to promote their hateful and dehumanising views by publishing manifestos of their supremacist beliefs (Lavin, 2019; The Great Replacement, 2019; Robles, 2015; Neuman, 2015).

Hate speech continues to play a significant role in catalysing violent conduct in the United States. Explicit, hostile and degrading anti-semitic statements were expressed by those who attack and killed worshipers at the Pittsburgh and San Diego synagogues in 2018 and 2019 and the Charleston black church in 2015. Other examples of racially and anti-semitically motivated violence include the murders committed by Benjamin Smith, a follower of the white supremacist organisation the World Church of the Creator; the killings at Columbine High School by Klebold and Harris, who planned the atrocity to coincide with Adolph Hitler's birth date; the Oklahoma bombing, which Timothy McVeigh said was influenced by a depiction of a bombing in William Peirce's novel The Turner Diaries and the murder of James Byrd Jr. by William King, who had been exposed to white supremacism in prison while serving sentences for other crimes.

Hatred is not always manifest in immediate calls for violence. Hate speech is often a slow-moving but lasting force, harnessed by those who regard their efforts to disseminate aversion, contempt and supremacy to be a mission. Their aim is not simply catharsis, but indoctrination. Those who breed racial aversion pose a long-lasting social menace that reaches to the past for stereotypes to justify oppression. Blacks are often depicted verbally and symbolically as hypersexual, Jews as controlling the highest echelons of power, aboriginal Americans as savages, the Roma are regarded as born and socialised thieves, Hispanics are pictured as drunks, Poles as imbeciles, Kikuyu are referred to as baboons, Darfurians are mocked as gorillas and Tutsi are dehumanised as cockroaches. Not all purveyors of destructive messages are right-wing fanatics. Some groups claim they work in furtherance of civil rights—especially the Black Lives Matter Movement and the leaders of the Women's March Movement in the United States—have no qualms supporting anti-semitic tropes that displace Jews from reviled pariahs. They segregate the world into a racial construct of light-skinned and dark-skinned people, without historical nuance, cultural awareness or ethnic differentiation. Of late, in the United States, the intersectionality movement has regarded Jews to be white and privileged, despite their being the victims of two millennial of discrimination, pogroms and attempted genocide at the hands of light-skinned Europeans (Pildis, 2018; Valdary, 2018).

U.S. law remains out of step with other democracies, consistent with a benighted notion of free expression libertarianism. The Supreme Court out of hand rejects regulations based on the identity of the speaker (*Reed v. Town of Gilbert, Arizona*, 2015; *Citizens United v. Federal Election Commission*, 2010, 340; *Tuner Broadcasting System, Inc., v. F.C.C.*, 1994), rendering almost impossible to use contextual analysis to show how destructive messages are more dangerous when uttered by a leader of a violent, supremacist group. That is not to say that there is no legal recourse in the United States, but the avenues for redress are quite narrowly defined by several doctrines.

The United States has few constitutionally viable courses of action in this area. One approach is for city and state governments to prohibit fighting words directed at an individual likely to create an immediate violent fight. It is rarely used in American courtrooms, much reviled by academics, but still good law. Despite the steady criticism and claims that the doctrine has long past its relevance (Strossen, 1990, 508–514), the Supreme Court of the United States has steadily cited to the case and disproved naysayers by characterising it as a low-value category (*U.S. v. Alvarez*, 2012, 717; *Brown v. Entertainment Merchants Association*, 2011, 791). In the landmark case on the issue, *Chaplinsky v. New Hampshire*, the Court found that the First Amendment of the Constitution does not prohibit the government from criminalising speech whose very utterance inflicts injury or tends to incite an immediate breach of the peace.

A different doctrine is more useful for restricting the use of incitements to violence that results from expressions that use various racist or xenophobic stereotypes. True threats analysis, which first appeared in *Watts v. United States* (1969, 707–708), requires courts to evaluate surrounding circumstances, whether the communication is made in a private or public forum, speaker's intent, whether conditional or actual threat and audience reaction. The Court refined the meaning of true threats in *Virginia v. Black*. To fall outside First Amendment protections, the person must mean to communicate the "intent to commit an act of unlawful violence to a particular individual or group of individuals" (*Virginia v. Black*, 2003, 359). *Elonis v. United States* (2015) focused on statutory interpretation but did not alter the constitutional standard in *Black*. The democratic process, with its emphasis on debate for resolving disputes, provides constitutional protections for the expression of vituperation and opprobrium, but not for actual threats made to specific persons.

For any conviction, the "wrongdoing must be conscious to be criminal" (ibid., 2009). The Supreme Court should give additional clarity on the definition of true threats. This should involve a reflect that they have "little if any social value" and "inflict great harm" (ibid., 2016). This statement conceives true threats to be low-value expressions that have traditionally and historically been unprotected by the First Amendment.

But these categories only get the American litigant so far; they are no substitute for the robust international community's effort to impede dehumanising words, writings and symbols from sparking mass violence against identifiable groups. The U.S. incitement doctrine is the main hurdle, unlikely to be cleared by the current members of the Supreme Court who tend to be absolutist in the protection of speech accept in a limited number of cases (Tsesis, 2015, 495). The U.S. incitement doctrine dates to World War I when a threesome of cases established the clear and present danger test for examining whether speech is actionable: *Schenck v. United States* (1919), *Frohwerk v. United States* (1919) and *Debs v. United States* (1919). The current standard comes from a seminal case, *Brandenburg v. Ohio* (1969), which aims to add contextual clarity about the likelihood that the intended harm will follow imminently after the suspect expression.

U.S. case law also holds to a more narrowly constructed rule than fighting words, true threats or incitement. In *Holder v. Humanitarian Law Project* (2010, 40), the Supreme Court upheld the constitutionality of a federal statute prohibiting anyone from providing "material support or resources" to organisations that the Secretary of State has designated to be foreign terrorists. The statute contained a mental component, applying only to anyone who lent support with the "knowledge of the foreign group's designation as a terrorist organisation or the group's commission of terrorist acts."

References

1773. *Personal Slavery Established*. Philadelphia: John Dunlap.
Abeng, Z. 2017. "Guest Blog: Is Finland in Need of a Hate Crime Prevention Law?" *Ihmisoikeusliitto*, May 2, 2017. https://ihmisoikeusliitto.fi/blog-hate-crime-law.
Abrams, A. 2019. "Here's What We Know so Far About Russia's 2016 Meddling." *Time, Inc.*, April 18. https://time.com/5565991/russia-influence-2016-election/.
AFP. 2017. "Pakistani Gets Death Sentence for Blasphemy on Facebook." *Times of Israel*, June 10. www.timesofisrael.com/pakistani-gets-death-sentence-for-blasphemy-on-facebook/.

AFP. 2022. "Valtònyc: Belgium to Appeal Against Court Refusal to Extradite Spanish Rapper." *AFP*, March 1. www.euronews.com/2021/12/29/valtonyc-belgium-to-appeal-against-court-refusal-to-extradite-spanish-rapper.

Alekhina v. Russia, 68 E.H.R.R. 14 (38004/12). 2019. https://hudoc.echr.coe.int/fre#{%22itemid%22:[%22001-184666%22]}.

Applebaum, A. 2008. "The Saudi Guide to Piety." *Washington Post*, July 22. www.washingtonpost.com/wp-dyn/content/article/2008/07/21/AR2008072102357.html.

Article 19. 2018a. "Country Report: Austria: Responding to Hate Speech." www.article19.org/wp-content/uploads/2018/09/Austria-Responding-to-Hate-Speech-.pdf.

Article 19. 2018b. "Country Report: Germany: Responding to Hate Speech." www.article19.org/wp-content/uploads/2018/07/Germany-Responding-toE2%80%98hate-speech%E2%80%99-v3-WEB.pdf.

Barendt, E. 1985. *Freedom of Speech*. Oxford: Claredon Press.

Basay, E. 2019. "Germany Charges Car Attacker With Attempted Murder." *World Bulletin*, January 2. https://worldbulletin.dunyabulteni.net/europe/germany-charges-car-attacker-with-attempted-murder-h208246.html.

Basic Law: The Knesset (Amendment No. 9 to Section 7A), S.H. 196 (Israel). 1985. https://main.knesset.gov.il/EN/activity/Documents/BasicLawsPDF/BasicLawTheKnesset.pdf.

BBC News. 2012a. "Cartoon Protester Umran Javed Admits Terrorist Material Charge." *BBC News*, August 31. www.bbc.com/news/uk-19437715.

BBC News. 2012b. "Umran Javed: Jailed for Terror Material Found on Computer." *BBC News*, September 19. www.bbc.com/news/uk-england-derbyshire-19645280.

Bein, A. 1959. "Modern Anti-Semitism and Its Effect on the Jewish Question." *Yad Washem Studies* 3.

Berkhofer, R. 1979. *The White Man's Indian: Images of the American Indian From Columbus to Present*. New York: Vintage Books.

Bohlander, M. 2008. *The German Criminal Code: A Modern English Translation*. Oxford: Hart Publishing.

Bracher, K. 1972. *The German Dictatorship*. Translated by Jane Steinberg. London: Holt Rinehart & Winston.

Brandenburg v. Ohio, 395 U.S. 444. 1969.

Brookes, I. 1969. *A Defense of Southern Slavery: And Other Pamphlets*. New York: Negro Universities Press.

Brottsbalken [BrB]. 1962. [Criminal Code] 16:8 (Swed.). https://www.regeringen.se/49bb67/contentassets/72026f30527d40189d74aca6690a35d0/the-swedish-penal-code.

Brown v. Entertainment Merchants Association, 564 U.S. 786. 2011.

Bundesministerium der Justiz. 2017. "Act to Improve Enforcement of the Law in Social Networks (Network Enforcement Act, NetzDR)—Basic Information (2017)." *Network Enforcement Act*. www.bmj.de/DE/Themen/FokusThemen/NetzDG/NetzDG_EN_node.html.

Bureau of Democracy, Human Rights and Labor. 2004. "Sudan: Ethnic Cleansing in Darfur." *United States Department of State*, April 27, 2004. https://2001–2009.state.gov/g/drl/rls/31822.htm.

Cimmino, J. 2019. "UK Tribunal Declares Christian Doctor's Beliefs About Gender Incompatible With Human Dignity." *Washington Examiner*, October 2. www.washingtonexaminer.com/news/uk-tribunal-declares-christian-doctors-beliefs-about-gender-incompatible-with-human-dignity.

Citizens United v. Federal Election Commission, 558 U.S. 310. 2010.

Claussen, V. 2018. "Fighting Hate Speech and Fake News: The Network Enforcement Act (NetzDG) in Germany in the Context of European Legislation." *Media Laws*: 1–10. www.medialaws.eu/rivista/fighting-hate-speech-and-fake-news-the-network-enforcement-act-netzdg-in-germany-in-the-context-of-european-legislation/.

CNA Staff. 2022. "Christian MP Acquired on All Charges After Finland's Bible Tweet Trial." *Catholic News Agency*, March 30. www.catholicnewsagency.com/news/250833/verdict-in-finland-s-bible-tweet-trial-announced.

Cohen-Almagor, R. 2012. "Is Law Appropriate to Regulate Hateful and Racist Speech? The Israeli Experience." *Israel Studies Review* 27: 41–64.

Cohen-Almagor, R. 2017. "The Role of Internet Intermediaries in Tackling Terrorism Online." *Fordham Law Review* 46: 425–453.

The Constitution of Finland. 1999. www.finlex.fi/en/laki/kaannokset/1999/en19990731.pdf.

Dawidowicz, L. 1975. *The War Against the Jews 1933–1945*. New York: Holt, Reinhart, and Winston.

Delgado, R. and Stefancic, J. 2004. *Understanding Words That Wound*. London: Routledge.

Denmark Criminal Code. Order No. 909. 2005.

Des Herrn, D. 2016. "Bundesverfassungsgericht." www.bundesverfassungsgericht.de/SharedDocs/Entscheidungen/DE/2016/06/rk20160629_1bvr264615.html.

Douglas-Scott, S. 1999. "The Hatefulness of Protected Speech: A Comparison of the American and European Approaches." *William and Mary Bill of Rights Journal* 7: 305, 343.

Driver, H. 1961. *Indians of North America*. Chicago: The University of Chicago Press.

The Economist. 2018. "World this Week." *The Economist*, August 4.

Eddy, M. 2018. "German Lawmaker Who Called Muslims 'Rapist Hordes' Faces Sanctions." *New York Times*, January 2. www.nytimes.com/2018/01/02/world/europe/germany-twitter-muslims-hordes.html.

Elonis v. United States, 575 U.S. 723. 2015.

El-Tigani Mahmoud, M. 2004. "Inside Darfur: Ethnic Genocide by a Governance Crisis." *Comparative Studies of Asia, Africa, and the Middle East* 24, no. 2: 3–17.

Equal Rights Trust. 2019. "First Criminal Conviction in Britain for the Offence of Stirring Up Hatred on the Grounds of Sexual Orientation." *Equal Rights Trust*. www.equalrightstrust.org/news/first-criminal-conviction-britain-offence-stirring-hatred-grounds-sexual-orientation.

Esseissah, K. 2016. "'Paradise Is Under the Feet of Your Master': The Construction of Religious Gasis of Racial Slaver in the Mauritanian Arab-Berber Community." *Journal of Black Studies* 47, no. 3.

European Commission. 2021. "A More Inclusive and Protective Europe: Extending the List of EU Crimes to Hate Speech and Hate Crime." https://ec.europa.eu/info/sites/default/files/1_1_178542_comm_eu_crimes_en.pdf.

European Freedom. 2019. "The Great Replacement: The Manifesto of Brenton Tarrant—The New Zealand Mosque Shooter." *European Freedom*, March 16. www.europeanfreedom.com/2019/03/16/the-great-replacement-the-manifesto-of-brenton-tarrant-the-new-zealand-mosque-shooter/.

Faiola, A. and Kirchner, S. 2017. "How Do You Stop Fake News in German With a Law." *Washington Post*, April 5. www.washingtonpost.com/world/europe/how-do-you-stop-fake-news-in-germany-with-a-law/2017/04/05/e6834ad6-1a08-11e7-bcc2-7d1a0973e7b2_story.html.

FBI. n.d. "FBI Statistics, 1995–2017." https://ucr.fbi.gov/hate-crime.

Féret v. Belgium, Application no. 15615/07 E.C.H.R. 2009.
Finish Government. 2019. *Ministry Launches Against Hate Campaign to Combat Hate Speech*. https://valtioneuvosto.fi/en/article/-/asset_publisher/1410853/vihapuheen-vastainen-against-hate-kampanja-kaynnistyy.
Finland Penal Code. 1963. Chapter 11, § 8. www.finlex.fi/en/laki/kaannokset/1889/en18890039_19951010.pdf.
Freedom House. 2008. *Freedom in the World 2008: The Annual Survey of Political Rights and Civil Liberties*. New York: Rowman & Littlefield Publishers, Inc.
Freedom House. 2018. "Germany, Freedom on the Net." *Freedom House*. https://freedomhouse.org/country/germany/freedom-net/2018.
Frohwerk v. United States, 249 U.S. 204. 1919.
Global Freedom of Expression: Columbia University. 2012. "Norwegian prosecution Authority v. X." *Columbia University*, 2012. https://globalfreedomofexpression.columbia.edu/cases/norwegian-prosecution-authority-v-x-2012/.
Global Freedom of Expression: Columbia University. 2016. "Case of Mr. D." *Columbia University*. https://globalfreedomofexpression.columbia.edu/cases/case-mr-d/.
Global Freedom of Expression: Columbia University. 2018a. "Case of Jose Miguel Arenas." *Columbia University*. https://globalfreedomofexpression.columbia.edu/cases/case-jose-miguel-arenas-valtonyc/.
Global Freedom of Expression: Columbia University. 2018b. "*Savva Terentyev v. Russia*, Summary of Outcome." *Columbia University*. https://globalfreedomofexpression.columbia.edu/cases/savva-terentyev-v-russia/.
Global Freedom of Expression: Columbia University. 2018c. "Stomakhim v. Russia, Summary of Outcome." *Columbia University*. https://globalfreedomofexpression.columbia.edu/cases/stomakhin-v-russia/.
Gollatz, K., Riedl, M. and Pohlmann, J. 2018. "Germany: Removal of Online Hate Speech in Numbers." *Inform's Blog*, August 24. https://inforrm.org/2018/08/24/germany-removal-of-online-hate-speech-in-numbers-kirsten-gollatz-martin-j-riedl-and-jens-pohlmann/.
Gormly, K. et al. 2018. "Suspect in Pittsburgh Synagogue Shooting Charged With 29 Counts in Deaths of 11 People." *Washington Post*, October 27. www.washingtonpost.com/nation/2018/10/27/pittsburgh-police-responding-active-shooting-squirrel-hill-area/?utm_term=.92bd10fe31a7.
Government of Sweden. 2019a. "Measures to Combat Antisemitism and Increase Security." www.government.se/government-policy/democracy-and-human-rights/measures-to-combat-antisemitism-and-increase-security/.
Government of Sweden. 2019b. "Summary." www.government.se/49c405/contentassets/e077c68e03f2408a81b7b35d0e4ef004/racist-symbols.-review-of-practice-and-analysis-summary-in-english-sou-201927.
Greene, L. 1942. *The Negro in Colonia in New England 1620–1776*. New York: Columbia University Press.
The Guardian. 2018. "The Unspeakable Trust About Slavery in Mauritania." *The Guardian*, June 8. www.theguardian.com/global-development/2018/jun/08/the-unspeakable-truth-about-slavery-in-mauritania.
Gutiérrez, Ó. 2017. "The Price of Hate in Denmark." *El País*, January 31. https://elpais.com/elpais/2017/01/31/inenglish/1485868003_162080.html.
Gutteridge, R. 1976. *Open Thy Mouth for the Dumb!* Oxford: John Wiley & Sons.
Halstead, P. 2009. *Unlocking Human Rights*. London: Routledge.

Hasel, P. 2022. "Otro Detenido por la Quema de un Furgón Policial en las Protestas." *Crónica Global*, March 11. https://cronicaglobal.elespanol.com/vida/detenido-quema-furgon-urbana-protestas-pablo-hasel_617472_102.html.

Helsinki. 2022. "Finnish MP Wins on All Charges in Major Free Speech Trial." *ADF International*, March 30. https://adfinternational.org/free-speech-victory-finnish-mp-wins-trial-over-bible-tweet/.

Hogan, L. and Safi, M. 2018. "Revealed: Facebook Hate Speech Exploded in Myanmar During Rohingya Crisis." *The Guardian*, April 3. www.theguardian.com/world/2018/apr/03/revealed-facebook-hate-speech-exploded-in-myanmar-during-rohingya-crisis.

Holder v. Humanitarian Law Project, 561 U.S. 1. 2010.

Holt, Reinhart, and Winston. *Debs v. United States*, 249 U.S. 211. 1919.

Human Rights Watch. 1994. "Mauritania's Campaign of Terror." *Human Rights Watch*. www.hrw.org/sites/default/files/reports/MAURITAN944.PDF.

Human Rights Watch. 1998. "HRW Alarmed About Hate Radio Broadcast and the Incitement of Ethnic Violence in the DRC." *Human Rights Watch*, August 12. www.hrw.org/news/1998/08/12/hrw-alarmed-about-hate-radio-broadcasts-and-incitement-ethnic-violence-drc.

Human Rights Watch. 2018. "Turkey: Crackdown on Social Media Post." *Human Rights Watch*, March 27. www.hrw.org/news/2018/03/27/turkey-crackdown-social-media-posts#.

Hungarian Constitutional Court, Decision 30.1992 (V. 18) AB. 1995.

Hungarian Penal Code. 2012. Article 332.

Inskeep, S. and Thompkins, G. 2008. "Kenya's Post-Election Violence Kills Hundreds." *National Public Radio*, January 2. www.npr.org/templates/story/story.php?storyId=17774507.

Isaac, M. 2016. "Facebook Said to Create Censorship Tool To Get Back Into China." *New York Times*, November 22. www.nytimes.com/2016/11/22/technology/facebook-censorship-tool-china.html.

Israeli Penal Code. n.d. www.oecd.org/investment/anti-bribery/anti-briberyconvention/oecdantibriberyconvention.htm.

Jahoda, G. 1975. *Trail of Tears*. New York: Random House.

Jakobsen, S. S. 2016. "The Case Regarding the Danish Muhammad Drawings." *IRIS Merlin*, August. https://merlin.obs.coe.int/article/3951.

Jenkins, W. 1935. *Pro-Slavery Thought in the Old South*. Chapel Hill, NC: University of North Carolina Press.

Jewish Community of Oslo v. Norway. 2005. http://www.worldcourts.com/cerd/eng/decisions/2005.08.15_Jewish_community_of_Oslo_v_Norway.htm.

Jones v. Toben, FCA 1150. 2002.

Jones, T. D. 1998. *Human Rights: Group Defamation, Freedom of Expression, and the Law of Nations*. Springer.

Jordan, W. 1968. *White Over Black: American Attitudes Toward the Negro, 1550–1812*. Williamsburg, VA: Omohundro Institute and University of North Carolina Press.

Josephy, A. 1991. *Indian Heritage of America*. Boston: Houghton Mifflin.

Katz, W. 1974. *Eyewitness: The Negro in American History*. Dallas, TX: Globe Fearon Co.

Kim, Y. M. 2020. "New Evidence Shows How Russia's Election Interference Has Gotten More Brazen." *Brennan Center for Justice*. www.brennancenter.org/our-work/analysis-opinion/new-evidence-shows-how-russias-election-interference-has-gotten-more.

Klass and Others v. Germany. 2 E.H.R.R. 24. 1979.

Klo, L. and Ellil, M. 2007. "Ethnic Agitation, Preliminary Investigation." *Laiva On Taynna*, June 25. http://laivaontaynna.blogspot.com/search/label/english.

Kohari, A. 2019. "What It's Like to Be Thrown in Jail for Posting on Facebook." *Wired*, March 20. www.wired.com/story/what-its-like-to-be-thrown-in-jail-for-posting-on-facebook/.

Kolta, A. 2013. "Hate Speech and the Protection of Communities in the Hungarian Legal System." *Papers*, January 9. https://papers.ssrn.com/sol3/papers.cfm?abstract_id=2197914.

Kousmate, Seif. 2018. "The Unspeakable Truth about Slavery in Mauritania." *Guardian*, June 8. https://www.theguardian.com/global-development/2018/jun/08/the-unspeakable-truth-about-slavery-in-mauritania.

Kroeber, A. 1939. *Cultural & Natural Areas of Native North America*. Berkeley, CA: University of California Press.

Lasson, K. 1987. "Racism in Great Britain." *Boston College Third World Law Journal* 7: 161–181.

Lasson, K. 1997. "Holocaust Denial and the First Amendment: The Quest for Truth in a Free Society." *George Mason Law Review* 6: 35–86.

Lavin, T. 2019. "The San Diego Shooter's Manifesto Is a Modern Form of an Old Lie About Jews." *Washington Post*, April 29. www.washingtonpost.com/outlook/2019/04/29/san-diego-shooters-manifesto-is-modern-form-an-old-lie-about-jews/?utm_term=.402c3b5a37e2.

The Law Society Gazette. 2007. "Law Reports." *The Law Society Gazette*, November 15. www.lawgazette.co.uk/law/law-reports/4506.article.

Legislation Online. 1996. "Russian Federation Criminal Code." www.wto.org/english/thewto_e/acc_e/rus_e/wtaccrus58_leg_362.pdf.

Leisegang, Daniel. 2017. "Rechte Hetze im Netz und die Grenzen des Rechtsstaats [Right-wing Incitement Online and the Limits of the State Under the Rule of Law]." *Netzpolitik*, September 30. https://bit.ly/2HkY2E5.

Lewis, B. 1990. *Race & Slavery in the Middle East*. Oxford: Oxford University Press.

Lippman, W. 1992. *Public Opinion 126*. New Brunswick, NJ: Transactional Publisher.

Lopez, G. 2017. "The Trial of Dylann Roof for the Charleston Church Shooting Explained." *Vox*, December 7. www.vox.com/identities/2016/12/7/13868662/dylann-roof-trial-verdict-charleston-church-shooting.

Mahoney, K. 1996. *Hate Speech: Affirmation or Contradiction of Freedom of Expression*. Chicago: University of Illinois Law Review.

McCaine, A. 1842. *Slavery Defender From Scripture Against the Attacks on Abolitionists*. Cornell University Library.

Molnar, P. 2012. "Responding to 'Hate Speech' With Art, Education, and the Imminent Danger Test." In *The Content and Context of Hate Speech: Rethinking Regulation and Responses*. Cambridge: Cambridge University Press: 242, 272.

Morozom, E. 2011. *The New Delusion: The Dark Side of Internet Freedom*. New York: Public Affairs.

Neuman, S. 2015. "Photos of Dylann Roof, Racist Manifesto Surface on Website." *National Public Radio*, June 20. www.npr.org/sections/thetwoway/2015/06/20/416024920/photos-possible-manifesto-of-dylann-roof-surface-on-website.

Niewyk, D. 1980. *The Jews in Weimar Germany*. Manchester: Manchester University Press.

Norwegian Penal Code. n.d. www.un.org/Depts/los/LEGISLATIONANDTREATIES/PDFFILES/NORpenalcode.pdf.

Nowrojee, B. 1997. *Failing the Internally Displaced: The UNDP Displaced Persons Program in Kenya*. New York: Human Rights Watch.

Oucho, J. 2002. *Undercurrents of Ethnic Conflict in Kenya*. Leiden: Brill.

Oyaro, K. 2008. "Kenya: The Media Is Not Innocent." *International Press Service*, February, 2008. www.ipsnews.net/2008/02/kenya-the-media-is-not-innocent/.

Pallister, D. 2007. "Three Jailed for Urging Murder at Cartoon Protest." *The Guardian*, July 19, 2007. www.theguardian.com/media/2007/jul/19/pressandpublishing.cartoon protests.
Paul, D. and Mettler, K. 2019. "Authorities Identify Suspect in 'Hate Crime' Synagogue Shooting That Left 1 Dead, 3 Injured." *Washington Post*, April 27. www.washingtonpost.com/nation/2019/04/27/california-synagogue-shooting-multiple-injuries/?utm_term=.0eac702c0901.
Pildis, C. 2018. "Stop Erasing the Jewish Victims of Anti-Semitic Violence." *Tablet Magazine*, October 30. www.tabletmag.com/sections/news/articles/erasure-jewish-victims-anti-semitism.
Prosecutor General v. Green, Nytt Juridiskt Arkiv. 2005. [NJA] [Supreme Court]. https://opil.ouplaw.com/view/10.1093/law:ildc/200se05.case.1/law-ildc-200se05.
Pulzer, P. G. J. 1964. *The Rise of Political Anti-Semitism in Germany and Austria*. New York: John Wiley & Sons.
Quell, M. 2020. "Top EU Court Punts Extradition Case of Spanish Rapper." *Courthouse News Service*, March 3. www.courthousenews.com/top-eu-court-punts-extradition-case-of-spanish-rapper/.
Quist-Arcton, O. 2008. "Tracing the Roots of Ethnic Violence in Kenya." *National Public Radio*, January 31. www.npr.org/templates/story/story.php?storyId=18582319.
Racial and Religious Hatred Act. 2006. Chapter 1. www.legislation.gov.uk/ukpga/2006/1/pdfs/ukpga_20060001_en.pdf.
Reed v. Town of Gilbert, Arizona, 135 S. Ct. 2218. 2015.
Robles, F. 2015. "Dylann Roof Photos and a Manifesto Are Posted on Website." *New York Times*, June 21, 2015. www.nytimes.com/2015/06/21/us/dylann-storm-roof-photos-website-charleston-church-shooting.html.
Rosenfeld, M. 2003. "Hate Speech in Constitutional Jurisprudence." *Cardozo Law Journal* 24: 1523–1567.
Roth, S. 1992. "Curbing Racial Incitement in Britain by Law." *Israel Yearbook on Human Rights* 22: 193, 201.
Rushin, S. and Edwards, G. 2018. "The Effect of President Trump's Election on Hate Crimes." *Papers*, January 18. https://papers.ssrn.com/sol3/papers.cfm?abstract_id=3102652.
Savva Terentyev v. Russia, European Court H.R. 2018. https://hudoc.echr.coe.int/eng#{%22documentcollectionid2%22:[%22GRANDCHAMBER%22,%22CHAMBER%22],%22itemid%22:[%22001-185307%22]}.
Scheneck v. United States, 249 U.S. 47. 1919.
Scherrer, C. 2002. *Genocide and Crisis in Central Africa: Conflict Roots, Mass Violence, and Regional War*. Westport, CT: Greenwood Publishing Group.
Simmons, W. 1981. "Cultural Bias in the New England Puritans' Perception of Indians." *William and Mary Quarterly* 38: 56–72.
Skaÿka v. Poland, no. 43425/98 E.C.H.R. 2003.
Southerland, A. J. 2007. "The Tug of War Between First Amendment Freedoms of Antidiscrimination: A Look at the Rising Conflict of Homosexual Legislation." *Regent Journal of International Law* 5.
Staff, T. 2018. "Israeli Court Indicts Jewish man for Inciting Murder of Arabs, Leftists." *Times of Israel*, November 10. www.timesofisrael.com/israeli-court-indicts-jewish-man-for-inciting-murder-of-arabs-leftists/.
Steger, L. 2016. "Hennigsdorfer soll Geldstrafe wegen Volksverhetzung zahlen." *RBB Online*, April 26. http://bit.ly/2d3m8Uz.
Steidle, B. and Steidle, G. 2007. *The Devil Came on Horseback: Bearing Witness to the Genocide*. New York: Public Affairs.

Stomakhin v. Russia, E.C.H.R. 2018. http://hudoc.echr.coe.int/eng?i=001-182731.
Strossen, Nadine. 1990. "Regulation Racist Speech on Campus: A Modest Proposal?" *Duke Law Journal* 1990: 484–573.
Summers, H. 2017."Democratic Republic of Congo: 250 Killed in 'Ethnic' Massacres, Says UN." *The Guardian*, August 5. www.theguardian.com/global-development/2017/aug/05/democratic-republic-of-congo-250-killed-in-ethnic-massacres-says-un.
Suzuki, R. 2017. "Bundesweite Razzien gegen Hetze im Netz [Nationwide Raids Against Incitement Online]." 2019. *Süddeutsche Zeitung*, June 6. www.sueddeutsche.de/digital/hetze-online-razzien-bundeskriminalamt-1.4477107.
Swedish Penal Code. www.government.se/49cd60/contentassets/5315d27076c942019828d6c36521696e/swedis h-penal-code.pdf.
Swiss Criminal Code. www.admin.ch/opc/en/classified-complicaiton/1970083/201903010000/311.0.pdf.
Tammer v. Estonia, no. 41205/98 E.C.H.R. 2003.
Taub, A. and Fisher, M. 2018. "Where Countries are Tinderboxes and Facebook is a Match." *New York Times*, April 21, 2018. www.nytimes.com/2018/04/21/world/asia/facebook-srilanka-riots.html.
Tomuschat, C. et al. 2012. "Grundgesetz für die Bundesrepublik Deutschland [GG] [Basic Law] May 23, 1949, art. 5 (F.R.G.)." In *Basic Law for the Federal Republic of Germany*. Federal Ministry of Justice. www.gesetze-im-internet.de/englisch_gg/.
Tsesis, A. 2004. "Regulation Intimidating Speech." *Harvard Journal on Legislation* 41: 389–405.
Tsesis, A. 2015. "The Categorical Free Speech Doctrine and Contextualization." *Emory Law Journal* 65: 495–531.
Turner Broadcast System Inc., v. F.C.C., 512 U.S. 622. 1994.
United Kingdom. 1986. *Public Order Act of 1986*. Vol. Chapter 64: Arrangement of Sections Part I. www.legislation.gov.uk/ukpga/1986/64/pdfs/ukpga_19860064_en.pdf.
United Nations. 1948. "Universal Declaration of Human Rights." www.un.org/en/about-us/universal-declaration-of-human-rights.
United Nations. 1966. "International Covenant on Civil and Political Rights." www.ohchr.org/en/instruments-mechanisms/instruments/international-covenant-civil-and-political-rights.
United Nations. 2012. "International Convention on the Elimination of Racial Discrimination (Austria)." www.bayefsky.com/summary/austria_cerd_c_sr2190_2012.doc.
United States Department of State. 2008. "Finland." www.state.gov/g/drl/rls/hrrpt/2007/100558.htm.
United States v. Alvarez, 567 U.S. 709. 2012.
Valdary, C. 2018. "What Farrakhan Shares with the Intersectional Left." *Tablet Magazine*, March 26. www.tabletmag.com/sections/news/articles/what-farrakhan-shares-with-intersectional-left.
Vejdeland v. Sweden, App. No. 1813/07. E.C.H.R. 2012.
Virginia v. Black, 538 U.S. 343. 2003.
Volkov, S. 1989. "The Nazi Holocaust." In *Antisemitism as a Cultural Code: Reflections on the History and Historiography of Antisemitism in Imperial Germany*. New York: De Gruyter.
Vu, K. 2019. "Vietnam Says Facebook Violated Controversial Cybersecurity Law." *Reuters*, January 8. www.reuters.com/article/us-vietnam-facebook/vietnam-says-facebook-violated-controversial-cybersecurity-law-idUSKCN1P30AJ.

Walsh, D. and Zway, S. A. 2018. "A Facebook War: Libyans Battle of the Streets and on Screens." *New York Times*, September 4, 2018. www.nytimes.com/2018/09/04/world/middleeast/libya-facebook.html.

Watts v. United States, 394 U.S. 705. 1969.

Weindling, P. 1993. *Health, Race and German Politics Between National Unification and Nazism 1870–1945*. Cambridge: Cambridge University Press.

Winthrop, J. 1629. "Winthrop Family Papers." *Massachusetts Historical Society*. www.masshist.org/publications/winthrop/index.php.

Zeldin, Wendy. 2009. "Germany: Constitutional Court Upholds Free Speech Restriction in Banning Public Support of Former Nazi Regime." *Library of Congress*, 2009. www.loc.gov/item/global-legal-monitor/2009-11-20/germany-constitutional-court-upholds-free-speech-restriction-in-banning-public-support-of-former-nazi-regime/.

3 Freedom of speech, minorities and the Internet from the European perspective
Words matter

Jędrzej Skrzypczak

1. Introduction

Freedom of speech is one of the fundamental human rights constituting the basis for the functioning of democratic societies and, simultaneously, an indispensable condition for the development of the state and the individual. A digital age phenomenon is the dynamic development of Internet media, especially social media (Zafarani et al., 2014, 1). In this case, everyone can be the recipient of some content and the creator of the content. It functions by sharing specific subject matter among the users in the community. It could be a chance for minority groups (ethnic, racial, religious, sexual orientation and gender orientation minorities) to present and share their point of view. On the other hand, they are frequently the main target of hate speech or radical, unaccepted and harmful content. Furthermore, they can be blocked, and their accounts cancelled.

Undoubtedly, technological progress in broadcasting has dramatically impacted the functioning of the media and media systems (Psychogiopoulou, 2014, 10). The digital era is also characterised by diverse forms and shapes of rendered services. It can be said metaphorically that a new continent was discovered with the development of the Internet (Neuman, 2016, 1–3). "Colonisation" of this area resembles conquering new territories in times of great geographical discoveries. All types of analogue media can be found here (newspapers, radio stations and TV channels), but also new forms of communication activity (Ess, 2014, 10–13). A digital age phenomenon is especially the dynamic development of social media. These are examples of demassification of media and blurring of the boundaries between producers/broadcasters and users (Toffler, 1980).

In this case, everyone can be not only the recipient of some content but also the creator of the content. It functions by sharing specific subject matter among the users in the community. The message is usually personalised. Consequently, the communication could be based on patterns of one-to-many and one-to-one as well. This means that in the case of online media, especially social media, the issue of accessing the web should be understood differently than in traditional media. Not as the right to access the media for all minorities but rather

DOI: 10.4324/9781003274476-5

as the individual right not to block some content and persons representing such communities. Of course, it is possible to perform acts of general blocking of the Internet, like web blackout. However, these are usually shared and relatively short actions. We have many examples of such activities, especially in non-democratic States (Stockman, 2013, 23–27). When Russian citizens decided to take another protest to the Moscow streets in August 2019, the Internet in the capital of Russia was temporarily disabled by major Russian Internet operators. Officials also decided on the Wi-Fi shutdown order imposed on cafes and restaurants close to gatherings. The disconnection from the network prevented the protesters from communicating, organising, and what could harm the authorities most—reporting on the protests and broadcasting them live.

This focuses on two types of minorities, namely ethnic or national minorities and sexual minorities, and challenges to such groups in mainstream media and online media, especially social media. These two groups of minorities and two kinds of media are good examples of differences between the *modus operandi* of old and new media and challenges for protecting freedom of expression.

2. Freedom of speech in the digital era

As mentioned at the beginning, the freedom of speech (for the purposes of this chapter, the term "freedom of speech" is the same like "freedom of expression" and is used, inter alia, in relation to the right to express one's views, thoughts and impart information or ideas, without interference by public authorities and regardless of state borders, Benedek and Kettemen, 2013, 23–37) is one of the fundamental principles of liberty in democratic states, which is reflected in the Universal Declaration of Human Rights[1] (United Nations, 1948), the International Covenant on Civil and Political Rights (United Nations, 1966a),[2] the European Convention on Human Rights (Council of Europe, 1950),[3] the Charter of Fundamental Rights of the European Union (European Union, 2012)[4] and many other provisions of international or national law, binding and non-binding (Verpeaux, 2010, 13–15). Most of these regulations were adopted in the analogue era long before the advent of the Internet and social media. However, it seems that proper interpretation of these rules leads to the conclusion that they could still be relevant to the challenges of the digital age.

An example of such an attempt approach could be the Resolution adopted by the Human Rights Council in 2012 which affirms

> that the same rights that people have offline must also be protected online, in particular freedom of expression, which is applicable regardless of frontiers and through any media of one's choice, in accordance with articles 19 of the Universal Declaration of Human Rights and the International Covenant on Civil and Political Rights.
> (Human Rights Council, 2012; Benedek and Kettemen, 2013, 18–19)

The same opinion was worded in the European area by the European Court of Human Rights, in the case Editorial Board of Pravoye Delo and Shtekel v. Ukraine (*Editorial Board of Pravoye Delo and Shtekel v. Ukraine*, 2011). The Court stated:

> It is true that the internet is an information and communication tool particularly distinct from the printed media, especially as regards the capacity to store and transmit information. The electronic network, serving billions of users worldwide, is not and potentially will never be subject to the same regulations and control. The risk of harm posed by content and communications on the internet to the exercise and enjoyment of human rights and freedoms, particularly the right to respect for private life, is certainly higher than that posed by the press.

As can be seen in this decision, the European Court noticed and emphasised the potential of the so-called new media and at the same time their much greater "firepower" (Ibid.).

Those international acts state that everyone has the right to freedom of opinion and expression and specify that this right includes space to hold ideas without interference and to seek, receive and impart information and opinions through any media and regardless of frontiers. First, it guarantees freedom of thought and expression. Second, this right includes the freedom to hold opinions without any interference. Third, it should be the same understanding of this term for the functioning of traditional and electronic media, including social media (McGonagle, 2015, 9–30). The freedom of expression should include not only such statements that remain neutral but also derogatory statements (*Gąsior v. Poland*, 2012), However, it cannot be absolute—in particular situations, it may be subject to restrictions[5] (Skrzypczak, 2019, 83).

As it turns out, on the one hand, communication on the Internet is a new chance in terms of the possibility of sharing opinions, but on the other, there are new threats to the freedom of speech. In the digital era, not one but three actors bear particular responsibility for freedom of expression: states, international organisations and corporations. States are obviously of crucial importance here (*Roskomnadzor v. Twitter*, 2021). However, other mentioned entities play a more critical role. So, in the digital era, it is not only states that should be responsible for respecting freedom of speech. New entities keep appearing, including international organisations and particularly private corporations, which could be accountable for human rights violations in this sphere. This last group of entities includes Internet service providers (ISPs) and various content aggregators, e.g. social media platforms. The ISPs or social media platforms could play the role of a private censor. Online service providers, such as social networks, may restrict certain types of content and behaviour and block some persons or groups along with their content policies. We can observe the troublesome strategy of "privatisation of censorship" in some areas of the web. Such activity ensures actual control of sharing information and opinions exercised not by State agencies but by internet intermediaries or aggregators of content who could exert pressure to gag journalists or internet users seeking to publish critical opinions.

3. Majority and minority in the analogue and digital era

Various forms of discrimination against diverse minority groups are as old as the history of societies and states (UK Essays, 2018). The institutionalised actions of such non-dominant groups to preserve cultural, religious or ethnic differences were born when national states began to form on the world stage, that is, at the turn of the eighteenth and the beginning of the nineteenth century. Some historians point to a much earlier document, as the first treaty protecting religious minorities; in this case, it was the Augsburg Peace of 1555 (Ibid.).

At that time, however, this applied to minorities such as national, ethnic, linguistic or religious groups mentioned earlier. Under no circumstances would sexual minorities apply for such legal protection. It should be noted, however, that in numerous countries, also within Europe, homosexuality was not only not tolerated but outright punished by the criminal law binding at that time.

After 1918, the League of Nations took the first steps to protect minority rights under international law. The minority protection system adopted under the auspices of the League of Nations was established with the so-called Minority treaties (13 treaties). However, the League of Nations' attempt to establish a general strategy for the protection of minorities failed. Even then, the catalogue of minority groups was limited to national, linguistic and religious communities (Krasnowolski, 2011,5).

However, only the adoption by the United Nations of the International Covenant on Civil and Political Rights of 1966[6] (United Nations, 1966b; Views of the Human Rights Committee, 1992) and the Declaration of the Rights of Persons Belonging to National or Ethnic, Religious and Linguistic Minorities of 1992 (United Nations, 1992) ensured recognition and protection of the rights of persons belonging to certain minorities under international law (United Nations, 2010; Kędzia and Płowiec, 2010, 41–43).

However, these were essentially national, ethnic, linguistic or religious minorities. An interesting and unfortunate characteristic of the global legal system, there is no legal definition of a minority *per se* (Shaw, 1990, 13–14; Gardocka, 2010, 90–102; McKean, 1984, 908–913; Modeen, 1969).

Even the last-mentioned Declaration of the Rights of Persons Belonging to National or Ethnic, Religious and Linguistic Minorities does not also attempt to define ethnic or national minorities. Under Art. 2 of the Declaration,

> Persons belonging to national or ethnic, religious and linguistic minorities (hereinafter referred to as persons belonging to minorities) have the right to enjoy their own culture, to profess and practise their own religion, and to use their own language, in private and in public, freely and without interference or any form of discrimination. Persons belonging to minorities have the right to participate effectively in cultural, religious, social, economic and public life. Persons belonging to minorities have the right to participate effectively (United Nations, 1992) in decisions on the national and, where appropriate, regional level concerning the minority to which they belong or the regions in which they live, in a manner not incompatible with national legislation. Persons belonging to minorities have the right to establish and maintain their

own associations. Persons belonging to minorities have the right to establish and maintain, without any discrimination, free and peaceful contacts with other members of their group and with persons belonging to other minorities, as well as contacts across frontiers with citizens of other States to whom they are related by national or ethnic, religious, or linguistic ties.

(United Nations, 1992)

Francesco Capotorti, Special Rapporteur of the United Nations Sub-Commission on Prevention of Discrimination and Protection of Minorities, defined the minorities in 1977 as

A group numerically inferior to the rest of the population of a State, in a non-dominant position, whose members—being nationals of the State—possess ethnic, religious or linguistic characteristics differing from those of the rest of the population and show, if only implicitly, a sense of solidarity, directed towards preserving their culture, traditions, religion or language.

(Capotorti, 1979)

As can be seen, sexual minorities are not included in this definition.

Literature indicates that majority and minority groups usually could be defined in size (Leonardelli and Brewer, 2001, 468–485), participation in power or status in society (Blanz et al., 1998, 697–729; Sachdev and Bourhis, 1991). Those terms reflect positive or negative social conditions and treatment (Blanz et al., 1995, 231–247). A minority would usually denote negatively stigmatised, ostracised, oppressed and outcast individuals, whereas a majority denotes positively valued or high-status groups (Tajfel, 1981, 63–68).

One of the basic rules of the international human rights protection system is the principle of non-discrimination and equal treatment of all persons. It was expressed in Article 2[7] of the Universal Declaration of Human Rights of 1948, Article 2.1 and Article of 26[8] of the International Covenant on Civil and Political Rights and Article 2.2[9] of the International Covenant on Economic, Social and Cultural Rights (United Nations, 1966b).

As can be seen, categories such as race, colour, sex, language, religion, political or other views, national or social origin, property status, birth or other status are distinctly indicated here. None of the aforementioned documents directly refer to sexual minorities as a separate group protected by law, which does not mean that, based on these international standards, representatives of these groups cannot apply for legal protection, which will be discussed later.

On the European continent, identical rules have been guaranteed in the most important conventions that make up the legal system of the Council of Europe and the European Union (CEI, 1994). This catalogue should include, in particular, Article 14[10] of the European Convention on Human Rights and Fundamental Freedoms, Articles 20–26[11] of the Charter of Fundamental Rights of the European Union (European Union, 2012) and Article 10 of the Treaty on the Functioning of the European Union (European Union, 2007). Under Article 10, the Treaty on European Union and the Treaty on the Functioning of the European Union "In defining and implementing its policies and activities, the Union shall aim to combat discrimination based on sex, racial or ethnic origin, religion or belief, disability, age or sexual orientation" (underlined by JS).

As already mentioned, most of the aforementioned documents, both international and European, establish an open catalogue of legally protected features. However, nationality, language and religion are also mentioned additionally, but usually, sexual orientation is omitted. The exception is the quoted European Union documents, which clearly state that any discrimination based on sexual orientation is prohibited (Gerber et al., 2021, 5–12; Gerber, 2019).

However, it should be remembered that when the documents were adopted by the United Nations or the European Council, the social perception of LGBT+[12] representatives was fundamentally different than today. Still, the open formula of the aforementioned norms of international (UNHRC, 2004) and European law convinces without any doubt that the prohibitions of discrimination and the imperative of equal treatment also apply to persons belonging to the LGBT+ community (Bodnar et al., 2019, 21–26).

Certainly, however, the international and European legal bases for protecting the international, ethnic, linguistic and religious minorities are more expressly specified. As already mentioned, it stems from the fact that there is a long tradition of providing legal protection in this case.

The group of documents protecting the rights of national, ethnic, linguistic and religious minorities includes all the acts mentioned earlier of international law, making up the system of human rights protection, but the list does not end there.

After the collapse of the bloc of communist countries, European states signed the Document of the Copenhagen Meeting of the Conference on the human dimension of the CSCE. The Conference on Security and Cooperation in Europe (CSCE) was renamed after the fall of the Soviet Union as the Organisation for Security and Cooperation in Europe (OSCE) on 1 January 1995 (Barcz, 2010, 11–38).

The signatory states undertook to respect human rights, including the rights of national minorities, in line with the principles of parliamentary democracies. The Copenhagen document contained the basic assumption of the CSCE on human rights, including a guarantee that belonging to a national minority is a matter of the personal decision of every human being. Articles 32.1–32.6,[13] 33–36[14] detailed the warranties of rights that states-parties should grant to representatives of national minorities, respecting their ethnic, linguistic, cultural and religious diversity.

The Council of Europe adopted the European Charter for Regional or Minority Languages on 5 November 1992 (Council of Europe, 1992; Sobczak, 2010, 127–176). The Charter protects and promotes regional and minority languages in Europe. (The Charter applies only to the population traditionally residing in a given country, who is a minority in that country, whose language is not an official dialect of the country or the language of the migrants). The actual Act of European law is the Framework Convention for the Protection of National Minorities, which was drawn up in Strasbourg on 1 February 1995 (Council of Europe, 1995; Council of Europe, 2022).

As far as the legal basis for the legal protection of representatives of the LGBT+ community is concerned, all the aforementioned primary conventions and legal norms protecting human rights should naturally be listed in this catalogue. As already noticed, protection on the grounds of sexual orientation *expressis verbis* was granted only in legal acts of the European Union. Nevertheless, in recent decades, additional regulations have been adopted within the framework of the Council of Europe, which refers directly to representatives of the LGBT+ community. However, these documents are not as essential as the European Convention on Human Rights.

In this catalogue, recommendation on measures to combat discrimination on the grounds of sexual orientation or gender identity deserves special mention (Council of Europe, 2010). It is underlined here that

> Member states should take appropriate measures to combat all forms of expression, including in the media and on the internet, which may reasonably be understood as likely to produce the effect of inciting, spreading or promoting hatred or other forms of discrimination against lesbian, gay, bisexual and transgender persons. Such "hate speech" should be prohibited and publicly disavowed whenever it occurs. All measures should respect the fundamental right to freedom of expression in accordance with Art. 10 of the Convention and the case law of the Court. Member states should raise awareness among public authorities and public institutions at all levels of their responsibility to refrain from statements, in particular to the media, which may reasonably be understood as legitimising such hatred or discrimination. Public officials and other state representatives should be encouraged to promote tolerance and respect for the human rights of lesbian, gay, bisexual and transgender persons whenever they engage in a dialogue with key representatives of the civil society, including media and sports organisations, political organisations and religious communities. Member states should take appropriate measures to ensure, in accordance with Art. 10 of the Convention, that the right to freedom of expression can be effectively enjoyed, without discrimination on the grounds of sexual orientation or gender identity, including the freedom to receive and impart information on subjects dealing with sexual orientation or gender identity. Public authorities at all levels should be encouraged to condemn publicly, notably in the media, any unlawful interferences with the right of individuals and groups of individuals to exercise their freedom of expression and peaceful assembly, notably when related to the human rights of lesbian, gay, bisexual and transgender persons.
>
> (Ibid.)

Based on the experiences of minority communities worldwide and the contents of the international standards relating to minority rights—the following can be identified as major concerns: survival and existence, promotion and protection of the identity of minorities, equality and non-discrimination and practical and meaningful participation (United Nation, 2010, 7–19). It seems that the most significant challenges for minorities from the digital media perspective are, on the one hand, access to the media and, on the other hand, the protection of the dignity of persons from such groups.

When it comes to the first of the aforementioned issues, i.e. access to the media, it must be clearly emphasised that the digital age and the advent of the Internet have definitely changed this challenge. In the analogue era, access to the media, that is, newspapers, radio, and television, was dependent on the decisions of the editorial office of a given medium, which, in turn, was influenced by historical, social and primarily political and legal factors. In the era of the Internet and social media, as mentioned earlier, anyone can become a sender of media messages. Of course, it is possible to block access to social media, both holistically for a specific population, by public authorities. This happened, for example, after the Russian Federation attacked Ukraine in February 2022 (Tidy and Clayton, 2022). However, it is also possible to block specific users by the website administrator.

It should be noted, however, that unlike in the case of analogue media, where the access to the media itself was dependent on the prior decision of the media's editorial office, in the case of online media, access is generally guaranteed to everyone, although it is possible to block specific media users later. Regarding the second of the issues mentioned earlier, that is, the possibility of violating the dignity of representatives of minority groups, the Internet media have a much more significant "impact and 'firepower'" if only because of their global nature. In addition, the "life cycle" of an article in a newspaper, radio or television was limited to a few moments, hours, days or a maximum of several weeks in the case of monthly magazines, that is, until the next issue or episode of the programme was published. In Internet media, access is chiefly unlimited in time, and the media message "lives" indefinitely. Hence, it was postulated to introduce the so-called right to erasure or "right to be forgotten" on the Internet, which happened first in 2014 by the Court of Justice of the European Union (*Google Spain v. AEPD*, 2014) and then under Article 17 of the General Data Protection Regulation (European Union, 2016a).

One more issue should be mentioned here, related to the specificity of the digital age. The Internet space is actually a virtual space with a global reach, in which various types of hoaxes and manipulations are possible, as well as in terms of subjectivity and digital identification. This is due to the multiple types of trolls, Internet boots and algorithms that can create the illusion of belonging to a specific majority or minority. Finally, the global network blurs national borders, becoming a global space, and thus may disturb the weight of certain majorities and minorities. It must also be added metaphorically that just as the creation of the Internet can be compared to the discovery of a new continent, the emergence of social media platforms can be associated with the creation of separate virtual spaces, somewhat in the image and similarity of countries. If so, perhaps it should be considered that in the future, the freedom of speech in international law should be guaranteed not only by states and international organisations but also by corporations managing social media platforms.

4. The access of minorities to the media and the protection of the dignity

One of the most important issues from the minority's point of view is access to the media. It was imperative, in particular, in the case of mainstream media within analogue media. The issue of the entry of minorities into the media could be considered in terms of external pluralism, namely the presence of a different media of the representatives and organisations of national, ethnic and religious minorities on the one hand, and internal pluralism in the form of these topics being presented in the mainstream media. Appropriate legal guarantees in this area have been included in international and regional (European) conventions. This issue falls within the human rights protection framework, as clearly emphasised in the UNESCO Convention on the Protection and Promotion of the Diversity of Cultural Expressions of October 2005 (UNESCO Convention, 2005). In conformity with Article 6, item 2(h), the parties of the Convention[15] undertake to adopt measures aimed at protecting and promoting the variety of cultural expressions. Such actions may encompass activities aimed at enhancing the diversity of the media, including through public service broadcasting. Considering the topic of this study and the European perspective, particular attention needs to be given to the Framework Convention for the Protection of National Minorities. It should be remembered that Article 9 thereof recognises that the right to freedom of expression of every person belonging to a national minority includes the space to hold opinions and to receive and impart information and ideas in the minority language without interference by public authorities and regardless of frontiers. The parties to this international Convention also ensure that persons belonging to a national minority shall not be discriminated against in their access to the media and undertake not to hinder the creation and the use of printed media by persons belonging to national minorities. In the legal framework of radio and television broadcasting, the parties make certain, as far as possible, that persons belonging to national minorities are granted the possibility of creating and using their own media. The aforementioned guarantees do not prevent the parties from their right to require the licensing of radio and television broadcasting or cinema enterprises, which is clearly stipulated. In such cases, objective criteria are expected to be introduced, ruling out discrimination. In the framework of their legal systems, the Convention also requires that the parties adopt adequate measures to facilitate access to the media for persons belonging to national minorities, promote tolerance and permit cultural pluralism.

According to The European Charter for Regional or Minority Languages,[16] the parties undertake to facilitate the creation and regular broadcasting of at least one radio station and one television channel in the regional or minority languages. This provision applies to the territories where such languages are spoken according to the situation of each language in a given region. However, it is stipulated that the aforementioned principles should be implemented while respecting the independence and autonomy of the media. It is recommended that such tasks should primarily be conducted by public radio and television. It is also possible for national broadcasters to offer programmes in regional or minority languages.

Additionally, the Charter obliges the parties to facilitate the production and distribution of audio and audiovisual works in regional or minority languages. The European Charter also requires states to encourage and facilitate the creation of at least one newspaper in regional or minority languages or the publication of newspaper articles in regional or minority languages regularly to cover the additional costs incurred by the fulfilment of such tasks and support the training of journalists and other staff for media using regional or minority languages. The signatories of the Charter guarantee the freedom of direct reception of radio and television broadcasts from neighbouring countries in regional or minority languages. The European Charter forbids restrictions on freedom of expression and free circulation of information in the written press in a language that is identical or similar to a regional or minority language. The exercise of the freedoms mentioned earlier, however, may be subject to restrictions that are prescribed by law and are necessary for a democratic society, in the interests of national security, territorial integrity or public safety, for the prevention of disorder or crime, for the protection of health or morals, for the protection of the reputation or rights of others, for preventing disclosure of information received in confidence or for maintaining the authority and impartiality of the judiciary.

There is no doubt that the aforementioned guidelines remain formally valid also in the era of online media. However, the real importance of these guarantees in social media practice is now much smaller. Guarantees of access or creation of newspapers, radio and television stations in the digital space are of no great importance since anyone can create such a media message without obtaining a licence or state concessions. Though, of course, it must not be forgotten that mainstream media still plays a vital role in today's media systems. Thus, in this respect, the guarantees mentioned earlier of international law will continue to play a role.

As can be seen, the aforementioned regulations apply to national, ethnic or linguistic minorities. Indeed, a broader scope relating to various minorities, including the sexual ones, has provisions in Recommendation No. R (97) 21 of the Committee of Ministers to member states on the media and the promotion of a culture of tolerance (Council of Europe, 1997b). As emphasised here, the intolerance issue calls for reflection by both the public and the media. Experience in professional media circles has shown that media enterprises might usefully reflect on the following: reporting factually and accurately on acts of racism and intolerance; reporting sensitively on situations of tension between communities; avoiding derogatory stereotypical depiction of members of cultural, ethnic or religious communities in publications and programme services; treating individual behaviour without linking it to a person's membership of such societies where this is irrelevant and depicting cultural, ethnic and religious communities in a balanced and objective manner and in a way which also reflects these communities' own perspectives and outlook. Thus, satisfactory goals in ensuring equality in access to the media seem to be achieved not only through the creation of legal regulations, that is, hard law, but also through various types of soft law instruments, such as self-regulation and appropriate educational activities.

One of the symptoms of discrimination against various types of minorities may be hate speech, as defined in Recommendation No. R (97) 20 of the Committee of Ministers to member states on "hate speech" (Council of Europe, 1997a) as "all forms of expression which spread, incite, promote or justify racial hatred, xenophobia, anti-semitism or other forms of hatred based on intolerance, including intolerance expressed by aggressive nationalism and ethnocentrism, discrimination and hostility against minorities, migrants and persons of immigrant origin" (Ibid.). The aforementioned guidelines apply to both online and analogue media. An example of this is two cases concluded before the European Convention for Human Rights. The first relates to social media and the other to the cinema. It is worth mentioning the crucial decision of the European Court of Human Rights (ECHR) of 14 January 2020 in the case of Beizaras and Levickas v. Lithuania (*Beizaras and Levickas v. Lithuania*, 2020). The ECtHR

> found a violation of Art. 14 in connection with Art. 8 of the European Convention on Human Rights (Council of Europe, 1950). One of the applicants posted a photo of their kisses on his social network. Due to the hateful comments posted on the complainant's Facebook webpage inciting hatred and violence on the grounds of sexual orientation, the applicants contacted the domestic authorities. Still, the Lithuanian officials refused to initiate an investigation. The applicants complained that they had been treated differently by the domestic administration because of their sexual orientation. Treatment by public authorities solely based on sexual orientation and expression of affection should be protected by the Lithuanian officialdom in order to ensure the effective exercise of the rights and freedoms guaranteed by the European Convention (Council of Europe, 1950). The Court noted that such treatment by the domestic officials was not reasonably justified when the authorities were combating hate speech by applying criminal law. The Court found that the comments made on the applicant's Facebook post had breached the applicant's dignity, which fell within the sphere of private life. Stressing the importance of tolerance, democracy and pluralism, the Court ruled that the State of Lithuania had breached Art. 14 by failing to fulfil its positive obligation to observe the right to respect for private life under Art. 8.
>
> (Ibid.)

Another case related to the interruption of the projection of a film for LGBT rights by a group shouting out homophobic abuses (*Association Accept and Others v. Romania*, 2016). The Court held that

> there had been a violation of Art. 14 (prohibition of discrimination) of the Convention taken in conjunction with Art. 8 (right to respect for private and family life) as regards individual applicants, finding that the Romanian authorities had failed in their positive obligation to effectively investigate the verbal attacks against individual applicants constituted a homophobic offence. In doing so, the officials demonstrated their own prejudices against

members of the LGBT community. The Court also stated that there had been a violation of Art. 14 taken in conjunction with Art. 11 (freedom of assembly and association) of the Convention in the present case, finding that the officials had failed to ensure that the event in question (which was organised by the applicants' association and individual applicants) may continue peacefully, by sufficiently stopping homophobic counter-demonstrators.

(Ibid.)

5. Internet media—new challenges for minorities

The Internet, from the beginning, has been developing in the spirit of freedom from all control. It has been treated as a common good of all users. It is noticed that there are numerous differences in using freedom of speech in public space, traditional media and the Internet. However, we can observe the paradox of freedom of expression. Sometimes the sphere of liberty is abused here and falls prey to undemocratic entities. The spread of mis(dis)information through online media and social media, particularly, has raised serious concerns worldwide. Therefore, the Internet and social media can manipulate the media and seriously misinform the public. This makes them a powerful tool for influencing public opinion and could severely threaten freedom of expression.

The critical challenge in the contemporary world from the minorities' point of view is another issue: equal presence in these media and protecting the dignity of representatives of persons belonging to such communities. However, a critical challenge of the modern world from the point of view of minorities is another issue: equal presence in these media and protection of the dignity of representatives of individuals belonging to such communities. As the European Court of Human Rights stressed in the case Dink v. Turkey (*Dink v. Turkey*, 2010)

> States are required to create a favourable environment for participation in public debate by all the persons concerned, enabling them to express their opinions and ideas without fear. In a case like the present one, the State must not just refrain from interfering with the individual's freedom of expression but is also under a "positive obligation" to protect his or her right to freedom of expression against attack, including by private individuals.
>
> (Ibid.)

In view of its findings concerning the authorities' failure to protect Fırat Dink against the attack by members of an extreme nationalist group and relating to the guilty verdict handed down in the absence of a "pressing social need"—the Court concluded that Turkey's "positive obligations" concerning Fırat Dink's freedom of expression had not been complied with. There had therefore been a violation of Article 10 (Ibid.).

The necessity to undertake legal actions to counter the intensified appearance of harmful, dangerous and illegal contents was relatively quickly observed. It is correlative with the discussion of the possibility of qualifying the internet space as a public space. Thus, a thesis may be proposed that access to the Internet and open electronic communication could be considered a human right in the twenty-first century. However, on the other hand, we should underscore that such freedom should be under the protection of the law. The doctrine of space on the Internet, with its non-territoriality, presents a genuine challenge. It is rather obvious nowadays that the traditional idea of the limitation of the legal system to a given country in this sphere is anachronistic.

On the one hand, the following paradox of the web is the Internet as a global network; on the other hand, major players on the Internet market, such as Google and Facebook, are subject to national rules. UN Secretary-General António Manuel de Oliveira Guterres, in UN Strategy and Plan of Action on Hate Speech, stated,

> Around the world, we are seeing a disturbing groundswell of xenophobia, racism, and intolerance/. . ./Social media and other forms of communication are being exploited as platforms for bigotry./. . ./Public discourse is being weaponised for political gain with incendiary rhetoric that stigmatises and dehumanises minorities, migrants, refugees, women, and any so-called "other." Hate speech is in itself an attack on tolerance, inclusion, diversity, and the very essence of our human rights, norms and principles. More broadly, it undermines social cohesion, erodes shared values, and can lay the foundation for violence, setting back the cause of peace, stability, sustainable development, and the fulfilment of human rights for all.
>
> (Guterres, 2020)

Not only the States which were traditionally suspected of censorship but also private companies are ready to violate freedom of opinion and expression. There are allegations that media content aggregators sometimes block access to the Internet and social media for certain content with radical ideas. It is so essential to develop appropriate mechanisms, structures and legal instruments to evaluate such content. Otherwise, it may lead to preventive censorship prohibited by international standards (Benedek and Kettemen, 2013, 67).

Examples of attempts to regulate this sphere seem to be different approaches to addressing the fake news issue. It should be emphasised that fake news is often fuel for all kinds of propaganda and hate speech (McGonagle, 2017, 201).

In the absence of legislation that expressly addresses the objectivity of news posted on social media, some countries apply relevant provisions of existing civil, criminal, administrative and other laws regulating the media, elections and anti-defamation (Sweden and the United Kingdom), even though these laws, enacted in the pre-Internet era, do not always reflect current technology and telecommunications developments. Other countries are choosing to pass new and more focused legislation that imposes sanctions on social media networks that spread false news, usually imposing fines and ordering the removal of information identified as false (France and Germany). Another option is to engage election authorities and digital platforms to secure a well-informed electorate, either by identifying and blocking fake news, providing fact-checking resources for the general public or through the mass publication of "real" information during election season and beyond (the United Kingdom). Some countries are also addressing the issue more generally by educating citizens about the dangers of fake news (Sweden).

The Recommendations made by the Forum on Minority Issues at its 13th session on the theme "Hate speech, social media and minorities" (De Varennes, 2021, 3–11) deserve attention. According to these recommendations:

> States should encourage dialogue between stakeholders, States, international and regional organisations, and tech companies should support and facilitate the capacity-building of national human rights institutions, civil society and minorities in the necessary skills and technical expertise required to combat hate speech online; States should consider strengthening their support to national human rights institutions in order to provide them with the necessary capacity, skills and resources to effectively combat hate speech in online communications; social media platforms should engage with civil society organisations in order to monitor changes in online hate and to alert platforms to new manifestations of hate; independent statutory bodies, such as national human rights institutions and equality bodies, human rights organisations, civil society and other stakeholders should build and strengthen partnerships, both with each other and with minority communities; independent statutory bodies, such as national human rights institutions and equality bodies, should expand their work to collaborate with all major internet companies and social media platforms to tackle online hate speech against minorities with public education initiatives, in addition to the enforcement of anti-discrimination laws; independent statutory bodies, such as national human rights institutions and equality bodies, human rights organisations, civil society and other stakeholders should help to ensure safe spaces for minorities to discuss issues related to hate speech; civil society actors should undertake a broad range of activities to counter hate speech against minorities. Among others, those activities should include monitoring online hate; supporting victims of online hate; tracking the responsiveness of platforms to reports of online hate; monitoring the response of Governments to complaints about online hate; identifying new manifestations of online hatred; tracking threats and alerting relevant stakeholders, including the Government; supporting law enforcement by providing data for investigations; supporting other civil society organisations by providing specialist capacities when needed; developing platforms to promote greater coordination in monitoring hate speech; providing information and education to policymakers, platforms, educators, law enforcement, national human rights institutions and others; and supporting public education through programmes and media engagement; media institutions should promote correct, equitable representation of minorities and include information about human rights, diversity, non-discrimination and prejudice in their reporting; all stakeholders should involve young persons in their initiatives, including by creating targeted programmes in cooperation with schools and universities, in order to expose young individuals to the knowledge and skills needed to identify hate speech, which may enable them to counteract messages of

hatred; all stakeholders should support human rights defenders belonging to or advocating the protection of minorities, in particular those defenders who are victims of threats, intimidation and harassment and those who suffer burnout as a result of working under constant pressure and with minimal support.
(Ibid.; Sacchetti and El Hajaly, 2021, 19)

According to the European Commission Against Racism and Intolerance (ECRI) recommendation (Council of Europe, 2015, 5–10), hate speech poses grave dangers to the cohesion of a democratic society, the protection of human rights and the rule of law. Under this standpoint,

> effective action against the use of hate speech requires: a/recognition of the fundamental importance of freedom of expression, tolerance, and respect for equal dignity; b/identification of the conditions conducive to the use of hate speech and taking appropriate measures to remove them; c/the involvement and commitment of a wide range of private and non-governmental actors, in addition to public ones; d/raising public awareness of the importance of respecting pluralism and of the dangers posed by hate speech but also demonstrate both the falsity of the foundations on which it is based and its unacceptability; e/providing support for those targeted by hate speech both individually and collectively by, f/providing support for self-regulation by public and private institutions as a means of combating the use of hate speech; g/clarifying responsibility under civil and administrative law for the use of hate speech while respecting the right to freedom of expression and opinion.
(Ibid.)

We can observe different approaches to solve this issue in this field, self-regulation proposals as an example of soft law and hard law regulation (Mancini, 2005; Frost, 2000: 107–109).

In this first category, we should indicate the EU's Code of Conduct on countering illegal hate speech online (European Union, 2016b). In May 2016, European Commission and major IT companies (Facebook, Microsoft, Twitter and YouTube) tried to respond to the proliferation of racist and xenophobic hate speech online. The Code aims to ensure that requests to remove content are dealt with quickly. When companies receive a request to withdraw from their online platform content deemed illegal, they assess such a plea against their rules and community guidelines and, where necessary, national laws transposing EU law on combatting racism and xenophobia. The companies commit to reviewing most of these requests in less than 24 hours and removing the content if necessary while respecting the fundamental principle of freedom of speech. A few major companies have dived into the Code, notably Facebook, YouTube, Twitter, Microsoft, Instagram, Dailymotion, Snapchat, Jeuxvideo.com, TikTok (in 2020), Linked (in 2021), Rakuten Viber and Twitch in 2022. It is also worth noting that in December 2021, the European Commission announced an initiative to expand the list of "EU crimes" to include hate speech and hate crimes (European Union, 2021).

What is significant is that in December 2020, the European Commission also published a Digital Single Act (European Union, 2020) proposal combating included illegal content. The current liability framework for online intermediaries is governed by the e-commerce directive from 2000. In this legal framework, ISPs and intermediaries are not liable for illegal and/or harmful content, goods, or services that may be distributed via their channels if they fulfil certain conditions: intermediaries are not responsible if they remove illegal content or disable access to it as fast as possible once they are aware of its illicit nature or if they play a neutral, merely technical and passive role towards the hosted content. According to the DSA proposal for online platforms and hosting services, detailed notice and action mechanisms and more adequate appeal mechanisms are proposed. This combination would facilitate the fight against illegal online content while safeguarding user rights. Both online platforms and hosting providers would be required to place notice and action mechanisms enabling third parties to notify the presence of allegedly illegal content (Article 14) and provide a statement of reasoning when deciding to remove or disable access to specific information (Article 15). In addition, online platforms must comply with a new set of requirements to ensure trust in and safety of the products and services they provide. They will have to establish an easily accessible and user-friendly internal complaint-handling procedure for their users (Article 17). They will be obliged to engage with out-of-court dispute settlement bodies to resolve disputes with their users (Article 18).

Recently, several European Union countries adopted new legal regulations to prevent hate speech on the internet (Goodall and Walters, 2019). The German NetzDG Act (Germany, 2017), passed in 2017, was the first in Europe to propose a legal solution to combat hate speech. On 1 April 2021, KoPl-G, inspired by the German NetzDG, became binding in Austria (Austria, 2021). France currently issued an Act against hate and crime on social media platforms, but the Conseil Constitutionnel deemed it unconstitutional due to incompatibility with freedom of opinion. Legislative work on content moderation is also underway in the other Member States, including Poland. The Polish Ministry of Justice drafted provisions in December 2020—according to the will of the framers—that would help protect against fake news on the Internet (Poland, 2020). According to the proposal, social media would be prevented from deleting posts or blocking user accounts at their own discretion if their content does not violate Polish law. If the content is deleted or an account is blocked, the user would be able to file a complaint with the website. The project also provides for filing objections to block published content contrary to Polish law. In both cases, the website will have to handle the complaint within 48 hours. The user can turn to a court to issue a ruling within seven days if the complaint is rejected. The proceedings will be carried out entirely by electronic means before a specialised Freedom of Expression Protection Court, established at one of the regional courts. The project also provides for a new instrument, the so-called "John Doe lawsuit." Someone whose personal rights are infringed upon on the Internet by an unknown individual will be able to file a lawsuit to have these rights protected without naming the defendant. To file the lawsuit effectively, it is enough to cite an URL with offensive content, as well as the dates and times of publication and the user's profile name or login handle. As underscored in the justification of this proposal, likewise, the solutions recently presented by the European Commission in the Digital Service Act focus on removing prohibited content. For this reason, Poland wants to adopt its own regulations to successfully protect the constitutional right to freedom of expression so that when a dispute arises between a social media website and its user, it is the courts that would decide whether an infringement took place. As mentioned earlier, some domestic attempts to regulate these issues demonstrate how important it is to adopt the acquis communautaire in this sphere.

6. Conclusions

William Shakespeare wrote, "Conversation should be pleasant without scurrility, witty without affectation, free without indecency, learned without conceitedness, novel without falsehood." On the other hand, unfortunately, the thought contained in the epigram entitled "Their Strength" by nineteenth-century Polish poet C. K. Norwid is still valid (Norwid, 2010):

> Ogre'ous armies, belligerent commanders,
> Polices—secret, open and both-gendered
> –Against whom do they collude?
> —Against a few ideas . . . nothing new!

Freedom of speech can lead to intercultural or cross-cultural conflict. Since the Internet plays a vital role in connecting people worldwide, communication on it can increase such conflict where there are differing levels of free speech protection (Sangsuvan, 2014).

The digital age of the global internet network and social media naturally requires a new, differentiated approach to ensuring media access and protection for diverse minority groups.

It seems that the best solution to this issue is a multipronged approach. The best answers are education, self-regulation and limited international or European regulation. In a word—searching for the golden mean and balance between different values.

While in the analogue era, international standards for protecting the rights of national, ethnic and linguistic minorities have been developed; in the digital age, a similar precaution should be guaranteed for other minorities, particularly LGBT+.

In addition, it should be emphasised that the era of online media means that the existing international conventions containing specific guarantees for the protection of minority rights may turn out to be insufficient, given that private corporations managing social media increasingly appear to be "extra-territorial." It also seems that these entities should declare appropriate guarantees for representatives of all minorities. Thus, a critical question arises: if so, how to regulate their functioning?

In the end, it is worthy of drawing attention to an effort prepared by U.S. Embassy in Poland called #WordsMatter (U.S. Embassy Warsaw, 2021). It aims to read the comments under LGBTQI+ people's posts about equality. It is worth mentioning here that the situation of this group of persons in Poland has been difficult in recent years. There were words full of support but also comments that should have never been expressed (Amnesty International, 2022, 13–15). The main message from this video is "It is time to end the hate, we are all equal, and we should treat others as we would like to be treated ourselves" (U.S. Embassy Warsaw, 2021). It could be the best resume for this chapter.

Notes

1 Article 19 of the Universal Declaration of Human Rights declares that "Freedom of opinion and expression includes liberty to hold opinions without interference and to seek, receive and impart information and ideas through any media and regardless of frontiers."
2 In accordance with Article 19.1, of ICCPR. "Everyone shall have the right to hold opinions without interference. 2. Everyone shall have the right to freedom of expression; this right shall include freedom to seek, receive and impart information and ideas of all kinds, regardless of frontiers, either orally, in writing or in print, in the form of art, or through any other media of his choice."
3 According to Article 10.1, of ECHR, everyone has the right to freedom of expression. This right shall include freedom to hold opinions and to receive and impart information and ideas without interference by public authority and regardless of frontiers. This Article shall not prevent States from requiring the licensing of broadcasting, television or cinema enterprises. 2. The exercise of these freedoms, since it carries with it duties and responsibilities, may be subject to such formalities, conditions, restrictions or penalties as are prescribed by law and are necessary in a democratic society, in the interests of national security, territorial integrity or public safety, for the prevention of disorder or crime, for the protection of health or morals, for the protection of the reputation or rights of others, for preventing the disclosure of information received in confidence or for maintaining the authority and impartiality of the judiciary.
4 According to Article 11, the Charter of Fundamental Rights of the European Union, (1) everyone has the right to freedom of expression. This right shall include freedom to hold opinions and to receive and impart information and ideas without interference by public authority and regardless of frontiers. (2) The freedom and pluralism of the media shall be respected.
5 According to Article 19 par. 3 of the International Covenant on Civil and Political Rights, the exercise of the rights provided for this article carries with it special duties and responsibilities. It may therefore be subject to certain restrictions, but these shall only be such as are provided by law and are necessary: (a) for respect of the rights or reputations of others and (b) for the protection of national security or of public order (*ordre public*) or of public health or morals. Similarly, Article 10 par. 2 constitutes that "the exercise of these freedoms, since it carries with it duties and responsibilities, may be subject to such formalities, conditions, restrictions or penalties as are prescribed by law and are necessary in a democratic society, in the interests of national security, territorial integrity or public safety, for the prevention of disorder or crime, for the protection of health or morals, for the protection of the reputation or rights of others, for preventing the disclosure of information received in confidence, or for maintaining the authority and impartiality of the judiciary."

6 According to Article 27 ICCPR "In those States in which ethnic, religious or linguistic minorities exist, persons belonging to such minorities shall not be denied the right, in community with the other members of their group, to enjoy their own culture, to profess and practise their own religion, or to use their own language."
7 Everyone is entitled to all the rights and freedoms set forth in this Declaration, without distinction of any kind, such as race, colour, sex, language, religion, political or other opinion, national or social origin, property, birth or other status.
8 All persons are equal before the law and are entitled without any discrimination to the equal protection of the law. In this respect, the law shall prohibit any discrimination and guarantee to all persons equal and effective protection against discrimination on any ground such as race, colour, sex, language, religion, political or other opinion, national or social origin, property, birth or other status.
9 The States Parties to the present Covenant undertake to guarantee that the rights enunciated in the present Covenant will be exercised without discrimination of any kind as to race, colour, sex, language, religion, political or other opinion, national or social origin, property, birth or other status.
10 Under Article 14 of ECHR, "The enjoyment of the rights and freedoms set forth in this Convention shall be secured without discrimination on any ground such as sex, race, colour, language, religion, political or other opinion, national or social origin, association with a national minority, property, birth or other status."
11 According to Article 20 of the Charter of Fundamental Rights of the European Union Equality before the law Everyone is equal before the law. Article 21 Non-discrimination—(1) any discrimination based on any ground such as sex, race, colour, ethnic or social origin, genetic features, language, religion or belief, political or any other opinion, membership of a national minority, property, birth, disability, age or sexual orientation shall be prohibited. (2) Within the scope of application of the Treaties and without prejudice to any of their specific provisions, any discrimination on grounds of nationality shall be prohibited. Article 22 Cultural, religious and linguistic diversity—the Union shall respect cultural, religious and linguistic diversity. Article 23 Equality between women and men—equality between women and men must be ensured in all areas, including employment, work and pay. The principle of equality shall not prevent the maintenance or adoption of measures providing for specific advantages in favour of the under-represented sex. Article 24 The rights of the child—(1) children shall have the right to such protection and care as is necessary for their well-being. They may express their views freely. Such views shall be taken into consideration on matters which concern them in accordance with their age and maturity. (2) In all actions relating to children, whether taken by public authorities or private institutions, the child's best interests must be a primary consideration. (3) Every child shall have the right to maintain on a regular basis a personal relationship and direct contact with both his or her parents, unless that is contrary to his or her interests. Article 25 The rights of the elderly—the Union recognises and respects the rights of the elderly to lead a life of dignity and independence and to participate in social and cultural life. Article 26 Integration of persons with disabilities—the Union recognises and respects the right of persons with disabilities to benefit from measures designed to ensure their independence, social and occupational integration and participation in the life of the community.
12 LGBT+ or LGBTIQ acronyms stand for lesbian, gay, bisexual, transgender, intersex or questioning (queer).
13 See: (32 of CSCE) To belong to a national minority is a matter of a person's individual choice and no disadvantage may arise from the exercise of such choice. Persons belonging to national minorities have the right freely to express, preserve and develop their ethnic, cultural, linguistic or religious identity and to maintain and develop their culture in all its aspects, free of any attempts at assimilation against their will. In particular, they have the right (32.1) to use freely their mother tongue in private as well as in public; (32.2) to establish and maintain their own educational, cultural and religious

institutions, organisations or associations, which can seek voluntary financial and other contributions as well as public assistance, in conformity with national legislation; (32.3) to profess and practise their religion, including the acquisition, possession and use of religious materials, and to conduct religious educational activities in their mother tongue; (32.4) to establish and maintain unimpeded contacts among themselves within their country as well as contacts across frontiers with citizens of other states with whom they share a common ethnic or national origin, cultural heritage or religious beliefs; (32.5) to disseminate, have access to and exchange information in their mother tongue; (32.6) to establish and maintain organisations or associations within their country and to participate in international non-governmental organisations. Persons belonging to national minorities can exercise and enjoy their rights individually as well as in community with other members of their group. No disadvantage may arise for a person belonging to a national minority on account of the exercise or non-exercise of any such rights.

14 See: (33 of CSCE) The participating states will protect the ethnic, cultural, linguistic and religious identity of national minorities on their territory and create conditions for the promotion of that identity. They will take the necessary measures to that effect after due consultations, including contacts with organisations or associations of such minorities, in accordance with the decision-making procedures of each state. Any such measures will be in conformity with the principles of equality and non-discrimination with respect to the other citizens of the participating state concerned. (34) The participating states will endeavour to ensure that persons belonging to national minorities, notwithstanding the need to learn the official language or languages of the state concerned, have adequate opportunities for instruction of their mother tongue or in their mother tongue, as well as, wherever possible and necessary, for its use before public authorities, in conformity with applicable national legislation. In the context of the teaching of history and culture in educational establishments, they will also take account of the history and culture of national minorities. (35) The participating states will respect the right of persons belonging to national minorities to effective participation in public affairs, including participation in the affairs relating to the protection and promotion of the identity of such minorities. The participating states note the efforts undertaken to protect and create conditions for the promotion of the ethnic, cultural, linguistic and religious identity of certain national minorities by establishing, as one of the possible means to achieve these aims, appropriate local or autonomous administrations corresponding to the specific historical and territorial circumstances of such minorities and in accordance with the policies of the state concerned. (36) The participating states recognise the particular importance of increasing constructive cooperation among themselves on questions relating to national minorities. Such cooperation seeks to promote mutual understanding and confidence, friendly and good-neighbourly relations, international peace, security and justice. Every participating state will promote a climate of mutual respect, understanding, cooperation and solidarity among all persons living on its territory, without distinction as to ethnic or national origin or religion, and will encourage the solution of problems through dialogue based on the principles of the rule of law.

15 The UNESCO Convention defines cultural diversity as "the manifold ways in which the cultures of groups and societies find expression. These expressions are passed on within and among groups and societies. Cultural diversity is made manifest not only through the varied ways in which the cultural heritage of humanity is expressed, augmented and transmitted through the variety of cultural expressions, but also through diverse modes of artistic creation, production, dissemination, distribution and enjoyment, whatever the means and technologies used" (see Article 4 p. 1). According to Article 4, p. 2, "Cultural content" refers to the symbolic meaning, artistic dimension and cultural values that originate from or express cultural identities. According to Article 4, p. 3, "Cultural expressions" are those expressions that result from the creativity of individuals, groups and societies and that have cultural content.

16 The European Charter for Regional or Minority Languages defines regional and minority languages as languages that are traditionally used within a given territory of a state by nationals of that state who form a group numerically smaller than the rest of the state's population, and are different from the official language(s) of that state. This is accompanied by the reservation that it does not include either dialects of the official language(s) of the state or the languages of migrants.

References

Amnesty International Report. Poland. 2022. "They treated us like criminals". From shinking space to Harassment of LGBTI Activists, https://amnesty.org.pl/wp-content/uploads/2022/07/THEY-TREATED-US-LIKE-CIMINALS-report-on-LGBTI-activists-in-Poland-Amnesty-International-EUR3758822022english.pdf

Association Accept and Others v. Romania. 2016. App. No 19237, E.C.H.R. https://hudoc.echr.coe.int/eng#%7B%22itemid%22:%5B%22001-210362%22%5D%7D.

Austria. 2021. "Bundesrecht konsolidiert: Gesamte Rechtsvorschrift für Kommunikationsplattformen-Gesetz, Fassung vom." September 9. www.ris.bka.gv.at/GeltendeFassung.wxe?Abfrage=Bundesnormen&Gesetzesnummer=20011415.

Barcz, J. 2010. "Rola standardów KBWE w ustalaniu treści klauzul dotyczących ochrony mniejszości narodowych w traktatach bilateralnych Polski z pierwszej połowy lat dziewięćdziesiątych XXw." In: Prawa mniejszości narodowych, edited by Teresa Gardocka and Jacek Sobczak. Toruń: Wydawnictwo Adam Marszałek: 11–38.

Beizaras and Levickas v. Lithuania. 2020. App. No 41288/15, E.C.H.R. https://hudoc.echr.coe.int/fre#%7B%22itemid%22:%5B%22001-200344%22%5D%7D.

Benedek, W. and Kettemen, M. C. 2013. *Freedom of Expression and the Internet.* Strasbourg: Council of Europe Publishing.

Blanz, M., Mummendey, A., Mielke, R. and Klink, A. 1998. "Responding to Negative Social Identity: A Taxonomy of Identity Management Strategies." *European Journal of Social Psychology* 28, no. 5: 697–729. https://doi.org/10.1002/(SICI)1099-0992(199809/10)28:5<697::AID-EJSP889>3.0.CO;2-%23.

Blanz, M., Mummendey, A. and Otten, S. 1995. "Perceptions of Relative Group Size and Group Status: Effects on Intergroup Discrimination in Negative Evaluations." *European Journal of Social Psychology* 25, no. 2: 231–247.

Bodnar, A., Mazurczak, A., Mrowicki, M. and Adamczewska-Stachura, M. 2019. "Sytuacja prawna osób nieheteroseksualnych i transpłciowych w Polsce. Międzynarodowy standard ochrony praw człowieka osób LGBT i stan jego przestrzegania z perspektywy Rzecznika Praw Obywatelskich." *Biuletyn Rzecznika Praw Obywatelskich, nr 6, Zasada równego traktowania. Prawo i praktyka* 27: 1–26.

Capotorti, F. 1979. *Study on the Rights of Persons Belonging to Ethnic, Religious and Linguistic Minorities.* New York. https://documents-dds-ny.un.org/doc/UNDOC/GEN/NL7/903/66/PDF/NL790366.pdf?OpenElement.

CEI. 1994. "Central European Initiative Instrument for the Protection of Minority Rights, signed in Turin on November 19." https://www.cei.int/sites/default/files/publications/downloads/CEI_Publication_7_4_05.pdf

Council of Europe. 1950. "Convention for the Protection of Human Rights and Fundamental Freedoms." www.echr.coe.int/Documents/Convention_ENG.pdf.

Council of Europe. 1992. "European Charter for Regional or Minority Languages." www.coe.int/en/web/conventions/full-list/-/conventions/treaty/148.

Council of Europe. 1995. "The Framework Convention for the Protection of National Minorities." https://rm.coe.int/CoERMPublicCommonSearchServices/DisplayDCTMContent?documentId=09000016800c10cf.

Council of Europe. 1997a. "Recommendation No. R (97) 20 of the Committee of Ministers to Member States on 'Hate Speech' Adopted on October 30, 1997." https://rm.coe.int/CoERMPublicCommonSearchServices/DisplayDCTMContent?documentId=0900001680645b44.

Council of Europe. 1997b. "Recommendation No. R (97) 21 of the Committee of Ministers to Member States on the Media and the Promotion of a Culture of Tolerance (Adopted by the Committee of Ministers on October 30, 1997, at the 607th Meeting of the Ministers' Deputies." https://rm.coe.int/CoERMPublicCommonSearchServices/DisplayDCTMContent?documentId=090000168050513b.

Council of Europe. 2010. "Recommendation CM/Rec(2010)5 of the Committee of Ministers to Member States on Measures to Combat Discrimination on Grounds of Sexual Orientation or Gender Identity (Adopted by the Committee of Ministers on 31 March 2010 at the 1081st Meeting of the Ministers' Deputies)." https://search.coe.int/cm/Pages/result_details.aspx?ObjectID=09000016805cf40a.

Council of Europe. 2015. "European Commission Against Racism and Intolerance (ECRI) ECRI's General Policy Recommendation No. 15 on Combating Hate Speech." www.coe.int/en/web/european-commission-against-racism-and-intolerance/ecri-members.

Council of Europe. 2022. "About the Framework Convention for the Protection of National Minorities." https://www.coe.int/en/web/minorities/at-a-glance.

De Varennes, F. 2021. "Recommendations made by the Forum on Minority Issues at its 13th Session on the Theme "Hate Speech, Social Media and Minorities": Report of the Special Rapporteur on Minority Issues." https://digitallibrary.un.org/record/3901780.

Dink v. Turkey. 2010. App. No 2668/07, 6102/08, 30079/08, 7072/09, and 7124/09). https://webcache.googleusercontent.com/search?q=cache:ierUGL2uHg8J:https://hudoc.echr.coe.int/app/conversion/pdf/%3Flibrary%3DECHR%26id%3D003-3262169-3640194%26filename%3D003-3262169-3640194.pdf&cd=1&hl=pl&ct=clnk&gl=pl&client=safari.

Editorial Board of Pravoye Delo and Shtekel v. Ukraine [2011]. App. No. 33014/05, E.C.H.R.

Ess, C. 2014. *Digital Media Ethics*. Cambridge: Polity Press.

European Union. 2007. "Consolidated Versions of the Treaty on European Union and the Treaty on the Functioning of the European Union—Consolidated Version of the Treaty on the Functioning of the European Union—Protocols—Annexes—Declarations Annexed to the Final Act of the Intergovernmental Conference Which Adopted the Treaty of Lisbon, Signed on December 13, 2007 — Tables of Equivalences." *Official Journal C* 326: 0001–0390, October 26. https://eur-lex.europa.eu/legal-content/EN/TXT/HTML/?uri=CELEX:12012E/TXT&from=PL.

European Union. 2012. "The Charter of Fundamental Rights of the European Union." https://eur-lex.europa.eu/legal-content/EN/TXT/?uri=celex%3A12012P%2FTXT.

European Union. 2016a. "General Data Protection Regulation (GDPR)." https://gdpr-info.eu.

European Union. 2016b. "The Code of Conduct on Countering Illegal Hate Speech Online." https://ec.europa.eu/commission/presscorner/detail/en/qanda_20_1135.

European Union. 2020. "Digital Single Act. Proposal for a Regulation of the European Parliament and of the Council on a Single Market For Digital Services (Digital Services Act) and Amending Directive 2000/31/E." https://eur-lex.europa.eu/legal-content/en/TXT/?uri=COM%3A2020%3A825%3AFIN.

European Union. 2021. "The Commission Proposes to Extend the List of 'EU Crimes' to Hate Speech and Hate Crime." https://ec.europa.eu/commission/presscorner/detail/en/ip_21_6561.

Frost, C. 2000. *Media Ethics and Self-regulation*. Essex: Pearson Education Limited.

Gardocka, T. 2010. "Mniejszości narodowe i etniczne—zagadnienie definicyjne." In T. Gardocka and J. Sobczak (eds.). *Prawa mniejszości narodowych*. Toruń: Wydawnictwo Adam Marszałek: 90–102.

Gąsior v. Poland. 2012. App. No. 34472/07, E.C.H.R. www.google.com/search?client =safari&rls=en&q=ECHR+21 + 02 + 2012++G%C4%85sior+v.Poland&ie=UTF-8&oe=UTF-8.

Gerber, P. 2019. "LGBTIQ Rights Around the World: Marriage Equality and the Death Penalty Hide Wider Concerns." www.internationalaffairs.org.au/australianoutlook/lgbtiq-rights-around-the-world-marriage-equality-and-the-death-penalty-hide-wider-concerns/.

Gerber, P., Raj, S., Wilkinson, C. and Langlois, A. 2021. "Protecting the Rights of LGBTIQ People Around the World: Beyond Marriage Equality and the Decriminalisation of Homosexuality." *Alternative Law Journal* 46, no. 1: 5–12.

Germany. 2017. "Act to Improve Enforcement of the Law in Social Networks (Network Enforcement Act, NetzDG)." www.bmj.de/SharedDocs/Gesetzgebungsverfahren/Dokumente/BGBl_NetzDG.pdf;jsessionid=08326D5ADD0F7CABAB562FE5992F8 21E.2_cid297?__blob=publicationFile&v=2.

Goodall, K. and Walters, M. 2019. "Legislating to Address Hate Crimes Against the LGBT Community in the Commonwealth." www.humandignitytrust.org/wp-content/uploads/resources/Legislating-to-Address-Hate-Crimes-against-the-LGBT-Community-in-the-Commonwealth-Final.pdf.

Google v. AEPD. 2014. Google Spain SL and Google Inc. v. Agencia Española de Protección de Datos (AEPD) and Mario Costeja González. The Court of Justice of the European Union Judgement of the Court (Grand Chamber), May 13. https://eur-lex.europa.eu/legal-content/EN/TXT/?uri=CELEX%3A62012CJ0131.

Guterres, A. M. de O. 2020. "UN Strategy and Plan of Action on Hate Speech." www.un.org/en/genocideprevention/hate-speech-strategy.shtml.

Human Rights Council. 2012. "Resolution Adopted by the Human Rights Council A/HRC/RES/20/8, The Promotion, Protection and Enjoyment of Human Rights on the Internet: Resolution/Adopted by the Human Rights Council." https://digitallibrary.un.org/record/731540.

Kędzia, Z. and Płowiec, W. 2010. "Ochrona mniejszości narodowych w pracach Komitetu Praw Człowieka." In T. Gardocka and J. Sobczak (eds.). *Prawa mniejszości narodowych*. Toruń: Wydawnictwo Adam Marszałek: 39–53.

Krasnowolski, A. 2011. "Prawa mniejszości narodowych i mniejszości etnicznych w prawie międzynarodowym i polskim." OT-599, Kancelaria Senatu, March. www.senat.gov.pl/gfx/senat/pl/senatopracowania/17/plik/ot599.pdf.

Leonardelli, G. J. and Brewer, M. B. 2001. "Minority and Majority Discrimination: When and Why." *Journal of Experimental Social Psychology* 37, no. 6: 468–485.

Mancini, P. 2005. "Is there a European Model of Journalism?" In H. de Burgh (ed.). *Making Journalists*. Oxon: Routledge: 77–93.

McGonagle, T. 2015. "The International Human Rights Protection of Journalists." In O. Andreotti (ed.). *Journalism at Risk: Threats, Challenges and Perspectives*. Strasbourg: Strasbourg University Press.

McGonagle, T. 2017. "'Fake News': False Fears or Real Concerns?" *Netherlands Quarterly of Human Rights* 35, no. 4: 201–209.

McKean, W. 1984. "Equality and Discrimination Under International Law." *Michigan Law Review* 82, no. 4: 908–913. https://repository.law.umich.edu/mlr/vol82/iss4/35.

Modeen, T. 1969. "The International Protection of National Minorities in Europe." *Acta Academiae Aboensis. Ser. A, Humaniora* 37, no. 1: 1–159.

Neuman, R. W. 2016. *The Digital Difference. Media Technology and the Theory of Communication Effects*. Cambridge, MA and London: Harvard University Press.

Norwid, C. K. *Their Strength*. Transl. by Pacze Moj. http://paczemoj.blogspot.com/2010/11/their-strength.html.

Poland. 2020. "Projekt ustawy o ochronie wolności słowa w internetowych serwisach społecznościowych Draft of the Act on the Protection of Freedom of Speech on Social Media." www.gov.pl/web/sprawiedliwosc/zachecamy-do-zapoznania-sie-z-projektem-ustawy-o-ochronie-wolnosci-uzytkownikow-serwisow-spolecznosciowych.

Psychogiopoulou, E. 2014. "Media Freedom and Independence in Contemporary Democratic Societies." In *Media Policies Revisited. The Challenge for Media Freedom and Independence*. New York: Palgrave Macmillan: 22–40.

Roskomnadzor v. Twitter. 2021. No. 05-0779/422/2021, Russian Appellate Court. https://globalfreedomofexpression.columbia.edu/cases/roskomnadzor-v-twitter/.

Sacchetti, I. El Hajaly, J. Hate Speech. 2021. Social Media and Minorities, Report of the Interactive Dialogue with Special Rapporteur on Minorities Issues, https://www.gicj.org/images/2021/Final_Report_on_ID_with_SR_Minorities-A.pdf

Sachdev, I. and Bourhis, R. Y. 1991. "Power and Status Differentials in Minority and Majority Group Relations." *European Journal of Social Psychology*: 1–24, January–February. https://onlinelibrary.wiley.com/doi/abs/10.1002/ejsp.2420210102; https://doi.org/10.1002/ejsp.2420210102.

Sangsuvan, K. 2014. "Balancing Freedom of Speech on the Internet under International Law." *North Carolina Journal of International Law and Commercial Regulation* 39, no. 3: 702–755.

Shakespeare, W. www.goodreads.com/quotes/139335-conversation-should-be-pleasant-without-scurrility-witty-without-affectation-free.

Shaw, M. N. 1990. "The Definition of Minorities in International Law." *Israel Yearbook on Human Rights* 20: 13–43.

Skrzypczak, J. 2019. "The Right to Freedom of Opinion and Expression in the Universal Declaration of Human Rights—A Contemporary Perspective." In A. Sungurov et al. (eds.). *Current Issues on Human Rights*. Madrid: Dykinson: 81–92.

Sobczak, J. 2010. "Języki regionalne i etniczne a problem tożsamości narodowej." In T. Gardocka and J. Sobczak (eds.). *Prawa mniejszości narodowych*. Toruń: Wydawnictwo Adam Marszałek: 127–176.

Stockman, D. 2013. *Media Commercialization and Authoritarian Rule in China*. Cambridge: Cambridge University Press.

Tajfel, H. 1981. *Human Groups and Social Categories—Studies in Social Psychology*. Cambridge: Cambridge University Press: 63–68.

Tidy, J. and Clayton, J. 2022. "Ukraine Invasion: Russia Restricts Social Media Access." www.bbc.com/news/technology-60533083.

Toffler, A. 1980. *The Third Wave, The Classic Study of Tomorrow*. Morrow: Bantam.

UK Essays. 2018. "Types of Minorities and Their Societal Role." www.ukessays.com/essays/sociology/types-of-minorities-and-their-societal-role-sociology-essay.php?vref=1.

UN Human Rights Committee (HRC). 2004. "General Comment no. 31 [80], the Nature of the General Legal Obligation Imposed on States Parties to the Covenant." CCPR/C/21/

Rev.1/Add.13, May 26. www.refworld.org/docid/478b26ae2.html (accessed August 16, 2022).

UNESCO Convention. 2005. "On the Protection and Promotion of the Diversity of Cultural Expressions." https://legal.un.org/avl/ha/cppdce/cppdce.html.

United Nation. 1992. *Optional Protocol to the International Covenant on Civil and Political Rights-Fiftieth Session—Concerning, Communication No. 488*. New York: UN.

United Nation. 2010. *The Office of the High Commissioner for Human Rights, Minority Rights: International Standards and Guidance for Implementation*. New York and Geneva: UN. www.ohchr.org/documents/publications/minorityrights_en.pdf.

United Nations. 1948. "The Universal Declaration of Human Rights." www.un.org/en/universal-declaration-human-rights/.

United Nations. 1966a. "International Covenant on Civil and Political Rights Adopted and Opened for Signature, Ratification and Accession by General Assembly Resolution 2200A (XXI) of 16 December, 1966, Entry into Force, March 23." www.ohchr.org/en/professionalinterest/pages/ccpr.aspx.

United Nations. 1966b. "International Covenant on Economic, Social and Cultural Rights." www.ohchr.org/en/instruments-mechanisms/instruments/international-covenant-economic-social-and-cultural-rights.

United Nations. 1992. "The Declaration of the Rights of Persons Belonging to National or Ethnic, Religious and Linguistic Minorities of 1992." www.ohchr.org/en/instruments-mechanisms/instruments/declaration-rights-persons-belonging-national-or-ethnic.

U.S. Embassy Warsaw. 2021. "Polish LGBTQI+ People Read Comments from the U.S. Embassy Warsaw FB Page." www.youtube.com/watch?v=nbx7HFgSyno.

Verpeaux, M. 2010. *Freedom of Expression*. Strasbourg: Council of Europe Publishing.

Views of the Human Rights Committee. 1992. *Views of the Human Rights Committee Under Art. 5, Paragraph 4, of the Optional Protocol to the International Covenant on Civil and Political Rights-Fiftieth Session—Concerning, Communication No. 488*. New York: HRC.

Zafarani, R., Abbasi, M. A. and Liu, H. 2014. *Social Media Mining. An Introduction*. Cambridge: Cambridge University Press.

4 Free speech and Internet

Is there a new interpretation for human rights? With particular reference to Chinese and Russian approaches to Internet regulations

Oscar Pérez de la Fuente

1. Internet, polyarchies and hegemonies

The relationship between free expression and democracy is significant and has been customarily established in classic texts on constitutionalism and the majoritarian judicial approach in pertinent case law on the subject. The Internet is a new arena for political discourse and free expression. The various approaches to political speech on the Internet are a useful indicator of the strength—or weakness—of democracy and the implementation of human rights.

The Internet has altered how we conceive about and conduct politics as it is a spectacular form of communication and information source. Consequently, many political regimes have responded differently to the Internet, for instance, in the manner in which they face criticisms.

A typology of political systems is useful for determining if political speech prohibitions are enforced. Clearly, the limitations on political expression differ between democracies and autocracies. Dahl's books are a famous reference on democracy studies (1971, 1973). Regarding political systems, he distinguishes between democracies, hegemonies and polyarchies, stating that "while they never exist in pure form, they do imply a hypothetical continuum extending from one to the other" (Dahl, 1973, 2).

The primary distinction between democracies and pure hegemonies is that the latter takes into account the preferences of one person—or small and unified group—and "ignore or override all other preferences" (Dahl, 1973, 1–2). In contrast, in egalitarian democracies, everyone's political preferences "may be weighted equally, and the government would always respond to the preferences of the greatest number" (Dahl, 1973, 2).

Under Dahl's typology, hegemonies are political systems in which the political speech of dissenters or political opposition is clearly restricted. Therefore, the public expression of dissent to the current authorities, their policies and ideologies and the key social, economic and political systems is outlawed (Dahl, 1973, 3). These are regimes that put the strictest restrictions on the speech, organisation and representation of political views and on the chances accessible to government

DOI: 10.4324/9781003274476-6

opponents. Under these regimes, public dissent to the existing leaders, their policies and ideologies and the dominant social, economic and political institutions are outlawed. Any sort of organised protest or resistance is outlawed (Dahl, 1973, 3).

In contrast, polyarchies are political systems that safeguard political speech even from dissidents or political opponents. Under these democratic systems, the vast majority of individuals are effectively protected in their right to express their opposition privately or publicly to the government, to organise, form parties and compete in elections where voting is secret, unintimidated and honestly counted, and election results are binding according to the rules (Dahl, 1973, 3). The regimes that place the fewest restrictions on the speech, organisation and representation of political preferences, and the chances accessible to government opponents, are the least restrictive. Ordinarily, the use of violent measures is outlawed, and in certain circumstances, it is criminal to promote the use of violence for political goals (Dahl, 1973, 3).

To distinguish the different systems, Dahl alludes to the dimension of *liberalisation* or *public contestation*[1] and the dimension of *participation* or *inclusiveness*.[2] The extent and combination of these dimensions vary from country to country and the results form a sophisticated typology, which is redefined and analysed by Dahl in a specific work called *Regimes and oppositions* (Dahl, 1973). For instance, some mixed or intermediate regimes could be considered *near-hegemony or near-polyarchy* or *competitive oligarchy* (Dahl, 1973, 3–4). Although they never exist in their purest form, Dahl suggests a conceivable continuity between them (Dahl, 1973, 2).

One is the *liberalisation* or *public contestation* dimension, which refers to the amount to which institutions are freely accessible, publicly utilised and guaranteed to at least certain members of the political system who desire to contest the government's actions. The other is the *participation* or *inclusiveness* dimension: the proportion of the population (or of adults) that is entitled to participate on a more or less equal basis in controlling and contesting the conduct of the government—i.e. who are entitled to participate in the system of public contestation (Dahl, 1973, 2).

It is interesting because, in a 1973 work, Dahl defined hegemonies as the regimes that place the strictest restrictions on the options accessible to the government's opponents. They prohibit the formation of all political parties, as in Argentina's dictatorship, or they construct a uniquely favoured party organisation, as in the Soviet Union and Eastern Europe with the Communist Party (Dahl, 1973, 11).

In *Poliarchy. Participation and opposition*, Dahl explains "Some Requirements for a Democracy among a Large Number of People" where the following institutional guarantees are required:

> 1.- Freedom to form and join organisations; 2.- Freedom of expression; 3.- Right to vote; 4.- Eligibility for public office; 5.- Right of political leaders to compete for support, 5a.- Right of political leaders to compete for votes, 6.- Alternative sources of information; 7.- Free and fair elections, 8.- Institutions for making government policies depend on votes and other expressions of preference.
>
> (Dahl, 1971, 3)

The new media has effects on political action and campaigns and outdated categories need reformulation. The Internet is a spectacular source of communication and information and, depending on the kind of political system, political ramifications are possible. One of the new traits of the Net is that opinions can be communicated anonymously, which gives rise to problems of legal liability and guilt (Pérez de la Fuente, 2019, 95). This is important in the context of misinformation, fake news and political mobilisation, area in which the Internet has played a significant role, for instance, in the Arab Spring.

While the Internet is a global phenomenon, jurisdictions are local (Pérez de la Fuente, 2019, 95). As the Internet has no borders, legal solutions for the Internet cannot be entirely national in nature. Nevertheless, nations such as China have taken steps to guarantee their official versions and prevent dissenting perspectives. In other instances, these safeguards need specialised technology participation, such as the Chinese *great firewall*.

Although there is some diplomatic and academic disagreement as to whether the Internet is a free-for-all or if the law is also enforced online (Pérez de la Fuente, 2019): human rights are no longer argued as valid offline, but also online, according to Mihr's interpretation of United Nations resolution 68/167. However, the method by which governments follow these principles, or fail to execute them, differs from country to country (Mihr, 2017, 58). Restrictions on political Internet expression, particularly of dissidents, are common practises of hegemonies, which constitute violations of human rights.

A new interpretation is also needed for concepts such as public sphere and public opinion, which has been analysed by Habermas and Taylor. These notions are traditionally linked with liberalism and democracy. In 1974, Habermas defined the *public sphere* as "a realm of our social life in which something was approaching public opinion can be formed. Access is guaranteed to all citizens" (Habermas, 1974, 49). According to Taylor, the public sphere is a shared place in which people of a society gather via a range of media (print, electronic), and face-to-face interactions, to debate subjects of common interest, and, therefore, to be able to develop a consensus on such matters (Taylor, 1995, 259).

This new understanding of these notions may provide two hypotheses for further study: (a) is the Internet a new scenario for the public sphere or public opinion? Has anything changed in the meantime? (b) Is it conceivable for a hegemonic or hybrid regime to have a public sphere or public opinion?

To answer the first question, it can be confirmed that the public sphere now encompasses online discourse. The intricacies of this format shift, however, would need more research, which is one of the current focuses of deliberative democracy experts. The solution to the second question will be provided on the following pages. Public sphere and public opinion have always been intimately associated with democracy. In fact, they are a kind of precondition for a polyarchic government.

Under this traditional view, Taylor characterises modern society's self-justification as a free self-governing society, that is, as a society in which (a) people form their opinions freely, both as individuals and in coming to a common mind, and (b) these common opinions matter—they have some effect on or control government, is largely dependent on the public sphere (Taylor, 1995, 260).

The Internet's technology facilitates communication, encounter and information exchange and discussion, value and opinion exchange. Even in the case of hegemonies or hybrid regimes, some are interested in portraying online arguments as proof of the presence of a public sphere. Taylor could not be clearer in that the public sphere is a medium of democratic politics in and of itself (Taylor, 1995, 287).

China and Russia's approaches to online free expression will be analysed in the following from the perspectives of *liberalisation* and *public contestation*, and *participation* and *inclusiveness*. The specific hypothesis of the research is whether typology of what political regime these countries are and what is the concrete—or possible—role of public sphere and public opinion.

2. China's approach to free speech and the Internet

It is essential to discuss freedom of speech in China on the Internet based on human rights. As a result of free speech, the Chinese approach to politics is characterised by a number of peculiarities that make this topic particularly ideal for academic, political and journalistic study.

On the issue of *liberalisation* and *public contestation*, it is noteworthy that, according to inside sources, China's authoritarian State permits online debate to some extent. This is called *authoritarian deliberation*.

In the dimensions of *participation* and inclusiveness, China is a one-party system that persecutes dissenting opinions and people. For this aim, there are additional technical restrictions and Internet surveillance.

2.1. Liberalisation and public contestation: authoritarian online deliberation

The Internet has transformed politics. Political information and political mobilisation have changed since the advent of the Internet. The unique property of the Internet in China, which is well-known internationally, influences the strengthening of political control and political influence (Yang, 2003, 408). This is explained by the following factors.

First, there is a strong connection between ideological freedom and the right to free expression. The Chinese State's treatment of political differences and their manifestation can be comprehended by examining its conception of politics. One of the reasons why China cannot be labelled a polyarchy in Dahl's terminology is its treatment of pluralism and political differences. This issue has been regarded to be exacerbated by the Internet. According to Yang, "diffusion of the Internet will challenge undemocratic State behaviour and enhance pluralism" (Yang, 2003, 409).

A paradoxical phenomenon exists while Chinese dissidents want to spread their political influence via the Internet, the State appears to have "successfully limited this effect" (Zheng and Wu, 2005, 511). The Internet is a medium for the State and the official party, and dissidents, due to its worldwide reach; yet the State employs technological barriers to hinder opposition communication.

Free speech and Internet 73

Second, the Internet has had significant implications for China's public sphere, associational life and political activism (Yang, 2003, 409). Numerous terms may be used to describe the current discourse on the Chinese Internet, such as "digital opium," "echo chamber," "online vigilantism," "online lynch mobs," "the digital scarlet letter," "digital Maoism" and "cyber-ghettos" (Yang, 2011, 1047).

One may claim that the Internet affects political equality by increasing the public's access to political information (Zheng and Wu, 2005, 509). However, this must be interpreted in light of China's unique political characteristics. Other political names for the Chinese Internet approach include *networked authoritarianism* (MacKinnon, 2011, 33) and *authoritarian deliberation* (He, 2006, 135; Jiang, 2010, 4). This is a combination of technology with a certain political philosophy.

Authoritarian deliberation thereby represents the contradictory and complicated reality of Chinese local governance and displays a potential logic of democratisation (He, 2006, 135). Consideration of deliberation in an authoritarian State such as China acknowledges that contemporary authoritarianism depends on a mix of patriotism and legitimacy based on performance rather than ideology (Jiang, 2010, 4). The notion of authoritarian deliberation recognises "increased civic and political speech freedoms" in an authoritarian State that loosens its hold on political discourse in return for its legitimacy and survival (Jiang, 2010, 4). According to He, "China's extensive experience affords theorists such an opportunity to accomplish this potential" (He, 2006, 135).

Consequently, *authoritarian deliberation* reflects the "contradictory and complicated reality of Chinese local governance" and "demonstrates a possible logic of democratisation" (He, 2006, 135). Consideration of deliberation in an authoritarian State such as China acknowledges that contemporary authoritarianism depends on a mixture of patriotism and legitimacy based on performance rather than ideology (Jiang, 2010, 4). The notion of *authoritarian deliberation* recognises the higher civic and political speech freedoms that exist in an authoritarian State that loosens its grasp on political discourse in return for its legitimacy and survival (Jiang, 2010, 4). According to He, "China's extensive experience provides theorists such an opportunity to accomplish this potential" (He, 2006, 135).

Professor He cautions against the assimilationist approach of conceptualising deliberative democratic institutions in China via a Western lens and suggests incorporating "the Confucian moral code of deliberation and the formal institutionalisation of deliberative activities throughout the history of Chinese imperial governments" in the understanding of contemporary Chinese deliberation practises (He, 2014, 59). It is easy to contextualise the contemporary deliberative culture under authoritarian settings based on this deliberative legacy.

Using context or history for social analysis is intriguing; yet, political concepts have a meaning, although a wide one, but they obviously exclude particular understandings. It is interesting to identify (a) whether China is a hegemony, polyarchy or hybrid regime and (b) the (possible) role of the public sphere and public opinion in this country.

China's top leaders are not chosen under its single-party system, which precludes true competitive and pluralistic elections (MacKinnon, 2011, 33; He, 2006, 134–135). The Communist Party is the only authorised political party; all others are prohibited. Decisions are not decided through pluralistic elections with real alternatives. China has made the economic transition from communism to capitalism, but no political transition to democracy has occurred. Under these circumstances, it is evident that China is not a polyarchy; based on other criteria, China may be a hegemony or hybrid government.

However, *there is a forum for debate on the Internet*. There is a deliberative space online in China where various conversations about the country's challenges occur through websites and social media. The government monitors and/or regulates this online activity in which people may sometimes use the Internet to bring attention to social issues or injustices and even succeed to influence official decisions (MacKinnon, 2011, 33).

From a Western viewpoint, this structure is rather contradictory, since it entails deliberation yet happens under authoritarian circumstances (He, 2006, 134–135). As a collective discussion, politics may be a useful tool for addressing social challenges via the exchange of ideas and reasons among those concerned. Therefore, participants and local leaders exchange viewpoints, present explanations and counterarguments and adjust their preferences via public conversation (He, 2006, 134–135). However, this model lacks the citizen rights and safeguards required for a polyarchy-based society.

Respect for individual liberties, especially political rights, is insufficient. Individuals in China can feel free to speak and be heard in this online collective discussion "in ways that were not possible under classic authoritarianism" which is paradoxical (MacKinnon, 2011, 33). Even only a decade earlier, Chinese citizens "had more fun, felt more approachable, and had less dread of their government" (MacKinnon, 2011, 33).

Respect for individual liberties, particularly political rights, falls short. Individuals in China may feel free to talk and be heard in an online group debate in ways that were not conceivable under classic authoritarianism (MacKinnon, 2011, 33). Even as recently as a decade ago, Chinese residents had more fun, felt more accessible and feared their government less (MacKinnon, 2011, 33).

Even when there are violations of human rights by the government, the recognition and efficacy of fundamental rights is one of the distinguishing qualities of the Rule of Law in contrast to authoritarian regimes. Freedom of speech and political participation are fundamental rights that cannot be protected under a networked authoritarian State. For example, "those whom the rulers perceive as threats are imprisoned; truly competitive, free, and fair elections are not held; and the courts and the legal system are tools of the ruling party" (MacKinnon, 2011, 33), and the government is actively monitoring its people and censoring and manipulating online conversations" (MacKinnon, 2011, 33). Under these circumstances, it is difficult to organise an opposition movement.

Following He and Warren, it may be important to differentiate between deliberation and democracy. Deliberation is "a mode of communication in which participants in a political process offer and respond to the substance of claims, reasons, and perspectives in ways that generate persuasion-based influence," whereas democracy is the inclusion of individuals in matters that may affect them, realised through distributions of empowerments such as votes, voice and related rights (He and Warren, 2011, 271).

From this distinction, it is feasible to support deliberation without democracy. Therefore, Chinese deliberative institutions have formed, grown and will continue to grow even under one-party rule. The focus of deliberative institutions is not on competitive elections (He, 2006, 136). Formally, this may be accurate yet under an authoritarian regime, strengthening deliberative institutions is a sort of democratisation strategy in favour of a future stage of complete democracy.

Min Jiang applies the concept of *authoritarian deliberation* specifically to Chinese cyberspace, identifying four main deliberative spaces:

1. *Central propaganda spaces:* which refers to websites and forums built and operated directly by the government;
2. *Government-regulated commercial spaces:* which refers to websites and other digital platforms owned and operated by private companies but subject to government regulation, including stringent requirements for content censorship and user surveillance;
3. *Emergent civic spaces:* or websites run by non-governmental organisations and non-commercial individuals, which are censored less systematically than commercial spaces but are still subject to registration requirements and intimidation, shutdown or arrest when authors cross the line or administrators fail to control community conversations;
4. *International deliberative spaces*: or websites and services that are hosted outside of Chinese government control—some of which are restricted and need circumvention techniques to access—where information and discussions not authorised on local websites may be accessed, and where more internationally-minded Chinese Internet users want to engage in dialogues with a larger global audience (MacKinnon, 2011, 36).

According to the prevailing view, China has neither a public sphere nor a public opinion. It might be questioned if online deliberation could be politically significant to some extent.

2.2. Participation and inclusiveness: China's online censorship and electronic controls and surveillance

It has been stated that the *participation* or *inclusiveness* dimension in Dahl's theory refers to "the proportion of the population (or of adults) entitled to participate on a more or less equal basis in controlling and contesting the conduct of government"— i.e. who are entitled to participate in the public contestation system (Dahl, 1973, 2). In China, there is just one political party, and there is no public contestation system. There is officially restricted speech, and the government employs technology to block the views of opponents and dissenters.

The constitution of China establishes:

> Article 1. The socialist system is the basic system of the People's Republic of China. Disruption of the socialist system by any organization or individual is prohibited.
> Article 4. Discrimination against and oppression of any ethnic groups are prohibited; any act which undermines the unity of the ethnic groups or instigates division is prohibited.
> Article 36. No one may make use of religion to engage in activities that disrupt public order, impair the health of citizens or interfere with the educational system of the State (Zhang, 2015, 2).[2]

The State Security Act, another source of China's counterterrorism law, lists acts that are deemed to endanger state security in Article 4, stating as follows:

Act endangering State security:

(1) plotting to subvert the government, dismember the State or overthrow the socialist system;
(2) joining an espionage organization or accepting a mission assigned by an espionage organization or by its agent;
(3) stealing, secretly gathering, buying, or unlawfully providing state secrets;
(4) instigating, luring or bribing a State functionary to turn traitor; or
(5) committing any other act of sabotage endangering state security[3] (Zhang, 2015, 3).

China's Internet censorship is "pervasive and unobstructed." It is pervasive because anything published online may be entirely censored due to government control, which explains why domestic alternatives to prohibited services are so popular and most people are oblivious of or unconcerned about the limits of their digital environment (Griffins, 2019, 71).

There are opinions inside China that support the robust online public discussion of social, political and policy concerns, but mostly within the growing confines permitted by the State. A simple Western perspective on the Chinese populace as homogeneous and passive grossly misses the multiplicity and cacophony of public opinion in Chinese online today (Jiang, 2010, 2).

From alternative perspectives, it is evident that the State has monopolised cyberspace. This is particularly true for news websites (Zheng and Wu, 2005, 518). Since 2000, the Chinese government has detained or arrested Internet-based individual demonstrators or collective action organisers (Zheng and Wu, 2005, 518). This involves restricting the political liberties of individuals based on their Internet behaviour. It is intriguing that Chinese authorities have employed various legal, political and technical methods to monitor, regulate and restrict political dissidents or even imprison them. These distinct applications of technology, politics and the law distinguish the Chinese case internationally.

The following are the many technical applications used to regulate political opinions in Chinese cyberspace:

1. *First-generation controls:* they prohibit the public from obtaining restricted material by erecting access barriers or by restricting certain websites or pages. The *Great Firewall* of China is the prototypical illustration (Maréchal, 2017, 3; MacKinnon, 2011, 36–37).
   The stated justification for these monitoring techniques is anti-terrorism measures, but they are also generally utilised to find and harass or arrest nonviolent government adversaries (Mackinnon, 2011, 40–41). On the persecution of political dissidents, the most infamous instance of law enforcement cooperation gone awry occurred when Yahoo's local Beijing employees handed Chinese police account details of activist Wang Xiaoning in 2002 and journalist Shi Tao in 2004, resulting in their detention (Mackinnon, 2011, 40–41).
2. *Second-generation controls:* they entail the creation of legal and technical frameworks that allow public and private bodies to prohibit access to information on an individual basis. This strategy is exemplified by "just-in-time" blocking and intermittent Internet shutdowns tied to certain political events (Maréchal, 2017, 36).
   The government has formed the Internet policing agency. The government may now filter and prevent the flow of information thanks to advances in technology. The government has been successful in obstructing access to a number of websites maintained by political dissidents in exile and others, including Amnesty International, China Human Rights, exiled Tibetans and Falun Gong adherents. (Zheng and Wu, 2005, 518–519).
3. *Third-generation controls*: they combine legal and technological measures with a proactive public relations (or propaganda) campaign. Competing with possible threats through successful counter-information operations that discredit or demoralise the opponent is more important than restricting access (Maréchal, 2017, 36).
   "Astroturfing" and public outreach: the government mixes censorship and monitoring measures with proactive efforts to direct internet discourse. In 2008, Hong Kong-based researcher David Bandurski concluded that at least 280,000 individuals were employed as "online commenters" at various levels of government. In the Chinese blogosphere, these individuals are derisively referred to as the "fifty-cent party" because they are paid to write positive Articles about their employers in online chatrooms, social-networking services, blogs and comments sections of news websites (Mackinnon, 2011, 41).
4. *Cyberattacks:* the sophisticated, military-grade cyberattacks conducted against Google in late 2009 specifically targeted the Gmail accounts of Chinese or China-related human rights advocates. Websites operated by Chinese exiles, dissidents and human rights campaigners (the majority of whom lack the knowledge or means to defend themselves) have been the target of more aggressive cyberattacks in recent years, in some cases compromising computer networks and email accounts (Mackinnon, 2011, 39).

5. *Control of devices and networks*: in May 2009, China's Ministry of Industry and Information Technology (MIIT) decreed that by 1 July 2009, a particular software programme called Green Dam Youth Escort will be preloaded on all computers sold in China. While Green Dam was allegedly designed to safeguard children from unsuitable content, researchers in and outside of China immediately discovered that it filtered political and religious content, monitored user behaviour and sent this data back to the software developer's central computer server. The software's further flaws generated resistance among U.S. businesses. It included major programming weaknesses that made the user more susceptible to cyberattacks. It also breached the intellectual property rights of a filtration product manufactured by a U.S. corporation (MacKinnon, 2011, 39).

6. *Domain-name controls:* the government-affiliated China Internet Network Information Center (CNNIC) declared in December 2009 that it will no longer let people register Internet domain names ending in ".cn." Only businesses or organisations would be permitted to use the. cn domain extension. While officials indicated that this move was intended to eliminate pornography, fraud and spam, a group of Chinese webmasters objected that it infringed upon individual rights. Authorities claimed that more than 130,000 websites had been deactivated as a result of the operation. A Chinese publication said in January 2010 that the action had severely harmed self-employed people and freelancers operating Internet business. In February, CNNIC announced that people will once again be permitted to register. cn domains. Still, all candidates would be required to confirm their registration in person, present a government-issued picture ID and include a photo of themselves with their application (Mackinnon, 2011, 40).

7. *Localised disconnection and restriction:* in times of crisis, when the government wishes to guarantee that citizens cannot use the Internet or mobile phones to organise protests, connections are completely cut off or severely limited in certain areas. The most extreme situation is in Xinjiang, a predominantly Muslim area bordering Pakistan, Kazakhstan and Afghanistan in China's far northwest. After ethnic disturbances in July 2009, the whole province was without Internet, mobile text messaging and international phone connectivity for six months. No one in Xinjiang could access any website, local or international, or send an email. To speak with clients, businesspeople had to go to the neighbouring province of Gansu. Since then, Internet connection and phone service have been restored, but with severe restrictions on the quantity of text messages, people may send on their mobile phones each day, no access to foreign websites and little access even to domestic Chinese websites (Mackinnon, 2011, 40).

Some scholars focus on contextual aspects to comprehend how the Internet influences the political understanding of Chinese citizens. As Meng explains the question of whether the Internet will democratise China implies an essentially Western-centric view that treats China as the mysterious and inferior "other" waiting to be converted to "one of us." This is not to deny the universal appeal of democracy as a desirable goal for China to pursue, but to acknowledge the power relations embedded in setting the agenda for China's Internet research. Under the orientalist gaze of Western scholars and policymakers, the Internet is expected to be the newest tool for taming the "beast" in the East (Meng, 2010, 502). This approach does need to be necessarily successful in their goals because it lacks some kind of contextualisation.

Such online dynamics are indicative of several constraints on civic and political participation in Chinese society: (a) the dominance of a strong state over a weak civil sector; (b) a paternalistic political culture and (c) the absence of institutional and legal means to resolve social injustices, compelling citizens to appeal to higher authorities outside the justice system (Jiang, 2010, 14). An approach from the inside considers, according to Jiang, that many civic-minded Chinese users criticise the government via sarcasm, satire and humour. A precise balance must be struck between self-expression and self-censorship. Many intentionally choose to criticise local government leaders and isolated events instead of the central government or national policies that exceed the State's tolerance level (Jiang, 2010, 14).

According to Dahl's typology, there is general acceptance that China's current political system may be classed as a hegemony. Political opposition and dissenters are met with repression and jail. Political choices are made by a small number of individuals in a system with just one party and no plural elections.

3. Russia's approach to free speech and the Internet

In recent years, Russia has developed its own perspective on free speech and the Internet, additionally intriguing from the standpoint of human rights. Article 29 of the Russian Constitution recognises the freedom of expression in these terms:

> 1.- Everyone shall be guaranteed freedom of thought and speech. 2.- Propaganda or agitation, which arouses social, racial, national or religious hatred and hostility, shall be prohibited. Propaganda of social, racial, national, religious or linguistic supremacy shall also be prohibited. 3.- Nobody shall be forced to express his thoughts and convictions or to deny them. 4. -Everyone shall have the right freely to seek, receive, transmit, produce and disseminate information by any legal means. The list of types of information, which constitute State secrets, shall be determined by federal law. 5.- The freedom of the mass media shall be guaranteed. Censorship shall be prohibited.
> (Constitution of the Russian Federation, 12 December 1993, as amended on 1 July 2020, Article 29)

The Russian Federation ratified the European Convention on Human Rights (ECHR) on 5 May 1998. Article 10 of the Convention (ECHR, 4 November 1950, as revised 1 August 2021, Article 10) safeguards freedom of expression, which embraces both political speech and government criticism (ACCORD, 2022, 4).

However, the Council of Europe (CoE) suspended Russia's rights of representation in the Committee of Ministers on 25 February 2022, and on 15 March 2022, the government of the Russian Federation informed the CoE of its departure from the CoE and its decision to condemn the ECHR. On 16 September 2022, the Russian Federation will no longer be a member of the ECHR, and Russian nationals will no longer be eligible to bring cases before the European Court of Human Rights. Approximately 18,000 Russian lawsuits were pending in the European Court of Human Rights in April 2022 (ACCORD, 2022, 4).

3.1. Liberalisation and public contestation: broad concept of extremism as a Russian State target

Regarding public contestation, it is globally remarkable that Russia has a clear commitment to combating extremism, which is broadly defined in Law. This extremist term has been applied to many groups, including political opponents and dissenters.

There is an Extremism Act in Russia, which was enacted in 2012, and it has been amended several times to include additional definitions for extremism, the precise nature of which remains unclear. Instead, there is a "'very varied' list of violent and peaceful behaviours that are called extremist" (Roudik, 2015, 30). As an example, the initial wording of Federal Law No. 114 FZ on Countering Extremist Actions designated the following activities as extremist:

> the activity of public and religious associations or any other organisations, or of mass media, or natural persons to plan, organise, prepare and perform the acts aimed at:
>
> - the forcible change of the foundations of the constitutional system and the violation of the integrity of the Russian Federation;
> - the subversion of the security of the Russian Federation;
> - the seizure or acquisition of peremptory powers;
> - the creation of illegal military formations;
> - the exercise of terrorist activity;
> - the excitation of racial, national or religious strife, and also social hatred associated with violence or calls for violence;
> - the abasement of national dignity;
> - the making of mass disturbances, ruffian-like acts, and acts of vandalism for the reasons of ideological, political, racial, national or religious hatred or hostility toward any social group;
> - the propaganda of the exclusiveness, superiority or deficiency of individuals on the basis of their attitude to religion, social, racial, national, religious or linguistic identity;
>
> 2) the propaganda and public show of Nazi attributes or symbolics or the attributes or symbolism similar to Nazi attributes or symbolics to the extent of blending;

3) public calls for the said activity or for the performance of the said acts;

4) the financing of the said activity or any other encouragement of its exercise or the performance of the said acts, including by the extension of financial resources for the exercise of the said activity, the supply of real estate, educational facilities, printing and publishing facilities and the material and technical base, telephone, fax and other communications, information services and other material and technical facilities.[4]

After the 2006 amendments, the definition of extremism became even broader, and it became permissible to prosecute those who criticise federal and local governments and officials, official programmes, laws, conceptions, religious and political organisations and so on. In June 2011, the Supreme Court, ruling on the application of the Extremism Act in courts, added to this ambiguity by stating that criticising the professional activities of politicians and government officials must not always be considered an incitement of hatred and enmity and must be reviewed on a case-by-case basis, as the limits for criticising these individuals are broader than for criticising private individuals (Roudik, 2015, 31). According to Favret, this clause might be interpreted so broadly as to criminalise any forms of civic activism, critical speech and government protest, unless the action or speech is already prohibited by other new laws (Favret, 2013, 305). According to Dahl's methodology, this is a closed interpretation of the public contestation component.

The legislation on combatting extremist activity was amended in July 2020 to classify violations of the territorial integrity of the Russian Federation as extremist activity (Federal Law No. 114, 25 July 2002, as amended on 1 July 2021, Article 1). According to RFE/RL, "[t]hat provision appeared to be linked specifically to Russia's annexation of Ukraine's Crimean Peninsula in 2014" (RFE/RL, 29 April 2021) (ACCORD, 2022, 20). In the ongoing conflict between Russia and Ukraine, this legal provision has been utilised by the Russian government to try to suppress internal dissent. On 21 March 2022, there was "wide media coverage (DW, 21 March 2022; The Guardian, 21 March 2022; Al Jazeera, 21 March 2022) of the designation of Meta, the parent company to Facebook and Instagram, as extremist due to tolerating Russophobia and "hate speech towards Russian soldiers and Vladimir Putin in relation to the country's war in Ukraine" (The Guardian, 21 March 2022)" (ACCORD, 2022, 21).

When prosecuting under inciting violence, the Law does not need proof of a threat to use inciting violence for prosecution. As a consequence, Russia's antiextremism laws are increasingly being utilised against nonviolent religious organisations and individuals whose acts are judged to pose a security risk. Under Russia's Extremism Act, non-traditional religious groups such as Jehovah's Witnesses, Hare Krishnas and Scientologists have been persecuted on a regular basis. Stepanova observes that in Russia, terrorism and extremism are often defined as anything that may be called separatist (Cross, 2013, 13).

The Russian anti-extremism legislation has been criticised by the United Nations, the Council of Europe and academics for being excessively broad and ambiguous (Grigorieva; Richter; Verhovskij, Ledovskih and Sultanov). However, according to the Russian government, the anti-extremist legal concept is consistent with international human rights legislation and Article 29 of the Russian Constitution, which protects freedom of expression and prohibits all forms of censorship. Russia's invasion of Crimea exacerbated tensions between Russia and the Council of Europe. Russian authorities have often argued that the Council of Europe's criticism of the country's human rights status is solely politically motivated (Sherstoboeva and Pavlenko, 2018, 102).

Article 282 of the Russian Criminal Code, which criminalises certain activities, is the core of Russia's anti-extremist legal framework. However, Article 280 of the Criminal Code overlaps with Article 282 in that it criminalises "public appeals to extremism." Thus, the Russian government has developed a new legal category—*incitement to extremism*—that extends far beyond incitement to violence (Sherstoboeva and Pavlenko, 2018, 105). This notion is something that is too broad and unclear and goes against a criminal guarantees' approach, based on human rights.

Following the implementation of anti-terrorism legislation in 2006, Russia has outlawed not just terrorist activities but also the undefined "ideology of violence." The 2012 modifications to the anti-extremist statute enabled the classification of speech as extremist regardless of whether it incites violence. In Russia, the link between the legal categories of extremism and terrorism has become more ambiguous. Russia adopted the 2005 Council of Europe Convention on the Prevention of Terrorism on 20 April 2006. Although the Convention prohibited "public incitement" and provocation to terrorism, it established several criteria to distinguish between Article 10 of the ECHR-protected statements and terrorist speech, which the Russian legislation does not address (Sherstoboeva and Pavlenko, 2018, 108). The Council of Europe distinguishes between incitement to violence or armed resistance and strong criticism of government policies, administrations, or institutions. From the perspective of the Council of Europe, the former cannot be protected, but the latter may be protected under the ECHR since it encourages open conversations on subjects of public importance (Sherstoboeva and Pavlenko, 2018, 109). In the case of Russia, a different perspective exists.

There is no clear difference between incitement and violence from political criticism. For instance, recent investigations and accusations of extremist crimes include 21 instances in which local journalists were prosecuted for publishing Articles on neutral topics, such as the status of languages of diverse Russian ethnic minorities and the predominance of the Russian language in ethnic autonomous republics comprising the Russian Federation. Local authorities utilised these prosecutions to repress social activists and opposition members the majority of the time (Roudik, 2015, 29).

It is clear that the Russian government's fight against extremism extends online. Extremism is one of the most often cited reasons for restricting internet free expression and especially for regulating websites. Since 2005, the Russian Ministry of Justice has maintained a broadly defined blacklist of so-called "extremist content." As of 13 June 2018, the blacklist comprised 4,461 online and print magazines. Since harsh limits on free expression under the premise of fighting extremism may hamper the empowerment of citizens on the Internet, it is essential to analyse anti-extremist legislation in the context of Internet freedoms (Sherstoboeva and Pavlenko, 2018, 103).

The legislature enacted a new censorship bill targeting extremist online material in November 2012. The bill, called the Act for Information, authorises the government to block websites providing content considered harmful to children. Websites that promote child pornography, violence or drug misuse must be restricted. The declared goal of the law is to protect children from improper content; however, the rule can be broadly interpreted to ban much more. According to Russia's anti-extremism statute, a Moscow judge decided in November that all websites hosting *Pussy Riot* concert footage must be pulled down (Favret, 2013, 307–308).

Putin has extended his grip over the Internet through multiple legislative measures since December 2011. These laws were enacted in fast succession, and they all employed ambiguous wording to identify the parts of the Internet to which they apply and how they will be implemented. The quick adoption of legislation aimed at restricting the Internet and the freedom of its users has been described as an effort to establish a local version of China's "*Great Firewall*" around Russian web content. Putin has encountered no opposition in this endeavour; as reported by the Moscow Times, Russia's leadership and its loyalist legislature have a history of enacting so-called "blitzkrieg" measures that limit Internet access within weeks and without consulting the web community or IT business (Duffy, 2015, 3).

Additionally, the Kremlin of Russia targeted notable independent news websites. On 13 March 2014, the Russian prosecutor general sent a list to the country's ISPs. Several websites and social media accounts of opposition groups and their leaders were included on the list. In addition, it controlled Grani, a well-known opposition journal noted for publishing very critical pieces of the Kremlin. In an effort to prevent unauthorised demonstrations and ensure compliance with house arrest conditions, the authorities requested that ISPs block servers that transmitted offensive content (Duffy, 2015, 5). In 2017, Russian law prohibited anonymisers and virtual private networks and authorised the blocking of websites containing content from "undesirable" foreign or international organisations and "access information" to such content. According to the SOVA Centre, the new restrictions apply to connections to the websites of "undesirable" organisations and to websites displaying their material or urging participation in mass actions (Sherstoboeva and Pavlenko, 2018, 110).

On 4 July 2014, the Kremlin enacted a measure linked to data retention and data mining. The legislation forces Internet businesses, including American technology titans like Google, Twitter and Facebook, to locate servers processing Russian Internet traffic inside the nation and to keep user data on these servers for at least six months. Companies had until September 2016 to comply or face government obstruction (Duffy, 2015, 7). On 31 July 2014, a bill that further restricts Internet freedom and prohibits public Internet anonymity was signed into law. This law requires Russians to register with their phone number in order to enjoy public Wi-Fi. The businesses administering the networks are required to maintain the given personal information for at least six months. Russia has a variety of violent extremist threats, ranging from Islamist extremists to ultranationalist extremists (Cross, 2013, 8).

There are well-known examples of the Russian government's response to extremism and its democratic repercussions. During a church service in Moscow, members of the anonymous female punk rock band *Pussy Riot* staged a political protest. The performance was a protest against President Putin's increasingly autocratic authority and the rising influence of the Russian Orthodox Church in the political system. The duration was 41 seconds. Despite its brief duration, the uninvited concert became the focus of a criminal inquiry as a *YouTube* video of the song garnered over 600,000 views on the first day. Kirill I, the Patriarch of the Russian Orthodox Church, regarded the song's antagonism to President Putin ("Virgin Mary, Mother of God, put Putin away/Put Putin away, put Putin away!") to be an act of religious hate, and the ladies were prosecuted under the statute against extremism (Favret, 2013, 305). Russian authorities punished these actions with the anti-extremist law and the European Court of human rights found these punishments were against the European Convention of human rights.[5]

As seen in the cases of Terpmlin, Togliatti and Khimki, journalists are frequently harassed, harmed and even murdered. On occasion, though, strong and devoted journalists who are also human rights campaigners may make a difference and force local governments to account for their performance (Lipman, 2010, 158). Anna Politkovskaya was murdered in broad daylight in 2006, just prior to the release of her final book, *A Russian Diary: A Journalist's Last Account of a Country*. Moving backward, has been released, and *Putin's Russia: Life in a Failing Democracy* has recently been completed. The killer followed the popular journalist for five days but waited until Putin's birthday, 7 October, to kill her. Authorities concur that the goal of Politkovskaya's assassination was to intimidate Russian journalists who, like Politkovskaya, could be inclined to criticise President Putin (Favret, 2013, 313–314).

From the beginning of 2012, the Russian government's stance toward the Internet has moved from widespread apathy to a developing cyberphobia. According to Duffy, "We have observed a government push to achieve total control over the Internet access and activities of the Russian public" (Duffy, 2015, 2). Additionally, social network users are cognisant of the range of ideas. The dominating networks have fostered a variety of political identities. While *Twitter* and *Facebook* have traditionally been favoured by opposition elites, *VKontakte* and *Odnoklassniki* are more popular with pro-Putin Russians of the masses (Lipman et al., 2018, 177). According to Duffy, in terms of Internet freedom, Russia is among the most restrictive nations, on par with Kazakhstan and Egypt, which have a long history of repression. As Putin continues to strengthen his control over Internet filtering, Russia continues on its way to become one of the most repressive countries in the world (Duffy, 2015, 10).

As an example of this Russian government online restrictive free speech policy, it is the law enacted on 5 May 2014. It is known as the "Bloggers Law" and requires all web-based authors whose postings get more than 3,000 page views to register with the government since they are deemed media entities. At the time of the bill's adoption, some 30,000 Russian bloggers were required to fact-check and erase any mistakes from their writings, lest they risk having their websites deleted or banned. This rule is remarkable because it is more restrictive than a comparable Chinese regulation that restricts blogger freedom and puts the daily threshold at 5,000 page views (Duffy, 2015, 6).

Convincing the audience that online material is inaccurate, prejudiced, and hazardous is a further major mechanism that diminishes the democratic potential of the Internet. The digital divide in Russia allows for this. A significant segment of the population still lacks direct Web experience. Their awareness of its advantages and disadvantages is solely based on what they've learned via conventional media outlets (Ognyanova, 2010, 13–14).

Internet is a new means of expression for the *public sphere* (Habermas, 1974, 49), where individuals can exercise their civil and political rights. Some scholars, such as Jiang and He, have labelled China's current condition as *authoritarian deliberation* (He, 2006, 135; Jiang, 2010, 4). Ognyanoiva, on the other hand, believes that Habermas's notion of the *public sphere* cannot be applied to Russia. She recommends for Russia the word "*public scene*"—used by Zassoursky—and concludes by emphasising that "the Russian public sphere is artificial rather than genuine" (Ognyanova, 2010, 9).

3.2. Participation and inclusiveness: elections based on fake plurality and a ban on actual opposition

There are political elections in Russia, but pluralism is restricted and true opposition is legally repressed. According to the Freedom House report on human rights in Russia of 2022, the Kremlin carefully manages the multiparty system and tolerates only superficial competition against the dominant party. A 2012 reform loosened registration requirements for political parties, permitting the formation of hundreds of new parties. However, none of them constituted a substantial political danger to the government, and many of them appeared to be meant to sow discord and confusion among the opposition. The Justice Ministry has consistently denied Navalny's political party registration. In June 2021, the Anti-Corruption Foundation (FBK) of Navalny was deemed an extremist group, essentially barring its members from competing for the government (Freedom House, 2022, 5).

Between the irregularities in the Russian electoral system, new government limitations on the number of observers prevented the OSCE from sending an observation mission. Numerous breaches, such as vote buying, voter coercion, "clone" candidates and ballot stuffing, were documented by the Russian election monitoring group *Golos* and independent media (Freedom House, 2022, 4).

Access disparities and existing normative practises in Russia make it more challenging to view the Internet as a forum for free expression that facilitates evasion of censorship. Recent events have cast doubt on the utopian notion that communication technologies automatically empower and successfully promote democratic ideals (Ognyanova, 2010, 10). Even if the medium is open and accessible (to state authorities and everyone), its users have long regarded it as a semi-public, informal space. The viewpoint of the Russian Internet populace has evolved in recent years. The consequences of Internet posting are becoming ever more apparent. Several instances of editors being punished, website administrators being bullied and bloggers being imprisoned substantiate this assertion (Ognyanova, 2010, 9).

Putin's method relies on terror rather than physical force as a means of control. To terrify, the legislation was drafted as broadly as possible, the boundaries were continually expanded and the media rushed to the Kremlin to learn about what was now permissible (Soldatov and Borogan, 2015, 342). Although relatively well-known, Russia's system non-opposition parties and movements have failed to acquire the Internet audience's trust or participation in their operations despite being banned from television by the government. For this, novel ideas and procedures will be necessary. Even if new political leaders and groups arise, it is doubtful that they will be permitted to participate in elections very soon. Russia's political structure as it has evolved does not permit this (Volkov, 2012, 85).

According to Bobbio, one of the defining qualities of democracy is that no majority decision may infringe upon the rights of the minority, particularly their opportunity to become a majority on equal terms (Bobbio, 2005, 460). In its current situation, Russia is a far cry from being considered a democracy or, even, a polyarchy. Specifically, Dahl believes that the latter has defined, among others, the respect for these institutions: freedom of speech, alternative information and autonomy of associations.[6] These institutions are hard to locate in contemporary Russian's society and cyberspace. It is evident that Russia may be categorised as a hybrid regime, but the absence of these fundamental democratic institutions gives it more parallels to the near-hegemonies than to the near-polyarchies.

As is evident, methods to free expression on the Internet are more similar depending on the political regime type applied. Consequently, Russia, China, Tajikistan and Uzbekistan proposed a 12-point code of conduct at the United Nations General Assembly in September 2011, citing the "need to prevent the potential use of information and communication technologies for purposes inconsistent with the objectives of maintaining international stability and security and that adversely affect the inalienable rights of third parties." Additionally, the accord sought restrictions on the dissemination of material that incites terrorism, secessionism or extremism that affects the political, economic, social and spiritual environment of other states (Cross, 2013, 17).

As has been shown, this proposal for a code of conduct of the United Nations, especially referring to extremism, is a threat to online freedom of expression, democracy and the Rule of Law from hegemonies or near-hegemonies.

4. Some concluding remarks on the Internet and free speech policies of China and Russia

This work's study aim was to examine whether Dahl's political regime typologies are more applicable to China and Russia and the function of the public sphere and public opinion in these countries. The purpose is to comprehend how new technology developments, particularly the Internet, may alter the answers to these questions. The central question is whether human rights are likewise enforced online, or if a new interpretation of human rights is feasible owing to the peculiarities of the Internet.

China and Russia use technology to control political opposition and dissenters. They favour technical intervention rather than liberalism. They employ distinct control and monitoring mechanisms to restrict the opinions of their opponents. This is especially evident in China and Russia's employment of these control tactics to combat extremism.

A well-known argument contends that the proliferation of the Internet is beneficial to democracy and human rights. The experiences of Russia and China demonstrate that the Internet is politically neutral and may be utilised for many purposes depending on the context. A consideration of aims and means is required. This concept of *authoritarian deliberation* is a more formal than substantive adaptation.

This exercise of adaptation, such as the definition of democracy, requires a context. Another argument used in this regard is that political principles have various meanings in different geographic regions or political or legal cultures. Extremely, this argument asserts that the only way to tell whether a country is a democracy is to live there. Despite comparison being difficult without proper contextualisation, it is feasible to use Political Science terms such as polyarchy and hegemony based on empirical evidence.

It is especially evident that neither China nor Russia has a public sphere or public opinion. These concepts are well analysed by Habermas and Taylor as synonymous of democracy and liberalism. These two countries have developed online an *authoritarian deliberation*. For example, in the case of Russia, some extent of pluralism is permitted where real opposition is prohibited. One can argue that the Russian context demonstrates how to view the boundaries of plurality. Nonetheless, the expansive definition of "extremism" and the difficulty of any minority becoming the majority demonstrate that Russia is not now a polyarchy; rather, it is a near-hegemony. From within Russia, it is possible to live in the *public scene*, which is not the true public sphere.

It might be a debate of public affairs, but the accountability of public authorities is tied to the quality of democracy. This implies that persons in charge of public office should inform and justify their actions, and they are punished or rewarded accordingly. Typically, transparency is coupled with accountability. In democratic regimes, transparency is both a citizen right and an administration's duty. There is a lack of transparency in China and Russia, particularly regarding political discourse. Voices of the political opposition are censored, technologically constrained and prosecuted.

Referring to *liberalisation and public contestation*, it could be affirmed simultaneously that, in these countries, there is online deliberation, but under authoritarian premises. Political opposition is legally prosecuted in both countries and technology is actively used to restrict their speech. In the case of Russia, the terms "extremism" and "incitement to extremism" are applied in a manner that exceeds and confounds the European Court of Human Rights' difference between strong political criticisms and incitement to violence.

88 *Oscar Pérez de la Fuente*

On *participation and inclusiveness*, the case of Russia is something more subtle, based on fear and on a restricted view of pluralism, but with some weak legal options without the opportunity of becoming majority. In the case of China, there is only one political party, without pluralistic elections. However, the legitimacy of these countries requires that information and opinion be regulated. This involves establishing the boundaries and values of the *authoritarian deliberation*.

Is there any alternative online for the political regimes? The answer is the approach to free speech under polyarchies, which is to protect the political speech of everyone, including dissenters and political opponents. Citizens' political rights are properly safeguarded, and pluralistic elections with real alternatives are held.

There may be a gap between ideals and realities, but it is certain that polyarchies and hegemonies do not apply people's rights to the Internet equally. To keep these distinctions alive, democracy and human rights globally rely on this benchmark.

Notes

1 One is the *liberalisation* or *public contestation* dimension, which is the amount to which institutions are freely accessible, publicly utilised and guaranteed to at least certain political system participants who seek to contest the government's actions (Dahl, 1973, 2).
2 The other dimension is participation or inclusiveness: the proportion of the population (or of adults) that is entitled to participate on a more or less equal basis in controlling and contesting the conduct of the government, that is, who are entitled to participate in the system of public contestation (Dahl, 1973, 2).
3 Guojia Anquan Fa [State Security Law] (adopted by the NPC Standing Committee on 22 February 1993, effective on the same day), Article 10, 1993 Laws of China, 43, 47. (Zhang, 2015, 3).
4 "*The extremist organisation* is a public or a religious association, or any other organisation, in relation to which a court of law has adopted the decision that took legal effect on the grounds provided by the present Federal Law concerning the liquidation or the prohibition of its activity in connection with extremism in its functioning; *the extremist materials* are the documents intended for publication or information on other carriers which call for extremist activity or warranting or justifying the need for such activity, including the works by the leaders of the National-Socialist Worker's Party of Germany and the Fascist Party of Italy, publications substantiating or justifying national and/or racial superiority, or justifying the practice of committing military or other crimes aimed at the full or partial destruction of any ethnical, social, national or religious group" (Russian Federal Law No. 114 FZ on Counteraction of Extremist Activities 2002).
5 Case of *Mariya Alekhina and Others v. Russia*, 17 July 2018, Application no. 38004/12.
6 According to the definition of these terms by Dahl: *Freedom of expression*: Citizens have a right to express themselves without the danger of server punishment on political matters broadly defined, including criticism of officials, the government, the regime, the social economic order and the prevailing ideology,

Alternative information: Alternative information citizens have right to seek on alternative sources of information: Moreover, alternative sources of information exist and are protected by laws.

Associational autonomy: To achieve their values right, including those listed off. Citizens also have a right to form relatively independent associations or organisations, including independent political parties and interest groups (Dahl, 1989, 221).

References

ACCORD—Austrian Centre for Country of Origin & Asylum Research and Documentation. 2022. *Russian Federation: Political Protests and Dissidence in the Context of the Ukraine Invasion.* Vienna: Austrian Red Cross.

Bobbio, N. 2005. *Teoría general de la política.* Madrid: Trotta, translation by Antonio de Cabo and Gerardo Pisarello.

Cross, S. N. 2013. "Russia and Countering Violent Extremism in the Internet and Social Media: Exploring Prospects for U.S.-Russia Cooperation Beyond the Reset." *Journal of Strategic Security* 6, no. 4: 1–24.

Dahl, R. 1971. *Polyarchy. Participation and Opposition.* New Haven: Yale University Press.

Dahl, R. 1973. "Introduction." In R. Dahl (ed.). *Regimes and Oppositions.* New Haven, London: Yale University Press: 1–26.

Dahl, R. 1989. *Democracy and Its Critics.* New Haven and London: Yale University Press.

Duffy, N. 2015. "Internet freedom in Vladimir Putin's Russia: The Noose Tightens." *American Enterprise Institute.* www.aei.org/wp-content/uploads/2015/01/Internet-freedom-in-Putins-Russia.pdf (accessed August 23, 2022).

Favret, R. 2013. "Back to the Bad Old Days: President Putin's Hold on Free Speech in the Russian Federation." *Richmond Journal of Global Law and Business* 12, no. 2: 299–316.

Freedom House. 2022. *Russia: Freedom in the World.* New York: Country Report 2022.

Griffins, J. 2019. *The Great Firewall of China. How to Build and Control an Alternative Version of the Internet.* London: Zed Books.

Habermas, J., Lennox, S. and Lennox, F. 1974. "The Public Sphere: An Encyclopedia Article (1964)." *New German Critique* 3: 49–55.

He, B. 2006. "Western Theories of Deliberative Democracy and the Chinese Practice of Complex Deliberative Governance." In E. J. Leib and B. He (eds.). *The Search for Deliberative Democracy in China.* New York: Palgrave Macmillan: 133–148.

He, B. 2014. "Deliberative Culture and Politics: The Persistence of Authoritarian Deliberation in China." *Political Theory* 42, no. 1: 58–81.

He, B. and Warren, M. E. 2011. "Authoritarian Deliberation: The Deliberative Turn in Chinese Political Development." *Perspectives on Politics* 9, no. 2: 269–289.

Jiang, M. 2010. "Authoritarian Deliberation on Chinese Internet." *The Electronic Journal of Communication* 20, no. 3–4: 1–22.

Lipman, M. 2010. "Freedom of Expression Without Freedom of the Press." *Journal of International Affairs* 63, no. 2: 153–169.

Lipman, M., Kachkaeva, A., and Poyker, M. 2018. "Media in Russia. Between Modernisation and Monopoly." In D. Treisman (ed.). *The New Autocracy. Information, Politics and Policy in Putin's Russia.* Washington: Brookings Institution Press: 159–190.

MacKinnon, R. 2011. "Liberation Technology: China's 'Networked Authoritarianism'." *Journal of Democracy* 22, no. 2: 32–46.

Maréchal, N. 2017. "Media Networked Authoritarianism and the Geopolitics of Information: Understanding Russian Internet." *Policy and Communication* 5, no. 1: 29–41.

Meng, B. 2010. "Moving Beyond Democratisation: A Thought Piece on the China Internet Research Agenda." *International Journal of Communication* 4: 501–508.

Mihr, A. 2017. *Cyber Justice. Human Rights and Good Governance for the Internet.* Cham, Switzerland: Springer.

Ognyanova, K. 2010. "Careful What You Say: Media Control in Putin's Russia—Implications for Online Content." *International Journal of E-Politics* 1, no. 2: 1–15.

Pérez de la Fuente, O. 2019. "How Can the Internet Change Human Rights on Online Hate Speech Regulations?" En A. Sungurov, C. Fernández Liesa, M. C. Barranco Avilés, M. C. Llamazares Calzadilla, and O. Pérez de la Fuente (eds.). *Current Issues on Human Rights*. Colección Debates. Madrid: Dykinson: 93–104.

Roudik, P. 2015. "Russia." In *Legal Provisions on Fighting Extremism*. Houstan: The Law Library of Congress, Global Legal Research Directorate: 26–45.

Sherstoboeva, E. and Pavlenko, V. 2018. "Freedom of Expression and Regulation of Extremism in Russia in the Context of the Council of Europe Standards." In S. S. Bodrunova (ed.). *Internet Science. 5th International Conference, INSCI 2018, St. Petersburg, Russia, October 24–26, 2018, Proceedings*. Cham: Springer.

Soldatov, A. and Borogan, I. 2015. *The Kremlin's War on the Internet*. New York: Public Affairs.

Taylor, C. 1995. *Philosophical Arguments*. Cambridge, MA: Harvard University Press.

Volkov, D. 2012. "The Internet and Political Involvement in Russia." *Russian Education and Society* 54, no. 9: 49–87.

Yang, G. 2003. "The Co-Evolution of the Internet and Civil Society in China." *Asian Survey* 43, no. 3: 405–422.

Yang, G. 2011. "Technology and Its Contents: Issues in the Study of the Chinese Internet." *The Journal of Asian Studies* 704, no. 201: 1043–1050.

Zhang, L. 2015. "People's Republic of China." In *Legal Provisions on Fighting Extremism*. Houstan: The Law Library of Congress, Global Legal Research Directorate: 1–9.

Zheng, Y. and Wu, G. 2005. "Information Technology, Public Space, and Collective Action in China." *Comparative Political Studies* 38, no. 5: 507–536.

Legislation and case law

China

Legislation

—Constitution of China, adopted at the Fifth Session of the Fifth National People's Congress and promulgated by the Announcement of the National People's Congress on 4 December 1982; the last amendment adopted at the First Session of the Thirteenth National People's Congress on 11 March 2018.

—State Security Law, 22 February 1993.

Russia

Legislation

—Constitution of the Russian Federation, 12 December 1993, as amended on 1 July 2020, Article 29.

—Russian Federal Law No. 114 FZ on Counteraction of Extremist Activities (2002).

Case law

European Court of human rights

—Case of *Mariya Alekhina and Others v. Russia*, 17 July 2018, Application no. 38004/12.

Part III
Democracy, hate speech and (mis)information

5 Manipulation and the First Amendment[1]

Helen Norton[2]

1. Introduction

Nobody wants to be manipulated. Yet speakers have long sought to manipulate their listeners—in other words, to covertly influence their listeners' decision-making to the speakers' advantage without those listeners' conscious awareness (Susser et al., 2019, 26). As one of many examples, think of subliminal advertising, where sellers embed a visual message within an advertisement for a time too brief for the viewer's conscious mind to comprehend (Salpeter and Swirsky, 2012, 504).

Empowered by the ability to collect and aggregate information about users and then to tailor messages designed to shape those users' responses, today's digital technologies can facilitate manipulation unprecedented in its reach and success. As Susser et al. (2019, 41) observe:

> [T]he more information a would-be manipulator has about a person's specific vulnerabilities, the more capably they can exploit them. Rather than aiming only to exploit vulnerabilities almost all of us share, as television advertisements and static billboards often attempt to do, online manipulation targets individuals, exploiting vulnerabilities specific to them.

Contemporary technologies thus enable manipulation differently in both degree and kind from more traditional forms of manipulation.

As one of many illustrations of twenty-first-century manipulation, consider sellers' new ability to monitor changes in the speed and accuracy of your keyboarding to determine when you may be tired or even intoxicated (and thus potentially impaired in your decision-making) and then to craft specific advertisements targeted to exploit that vulnerability (Willis, 2020, 143). Examples abound in the political context as well: recall, for instance, Russian operatives' use of data collection and algorithms to target African-Americans with personalised messages intended to induce them not to vote in the 2016 U.S. elections (Overton, 2020, 1795–1796).

Here I examine new conceptual tools for understanding manipulation and its harms. More specifically, I draw from ethicists' insights to explain how

DOI: 10.4324/9781003274476-8

manipulation—and especially online manipulation—can inflict harms distinct from those imposed by coercion and deception, and to explain why addressing these distinct harms is a government interest sufficiently strong to justify appropriately-tailored interventions.

I then explore how these conceptual tools can also help us understand when, how and why government can regulate online manipulation consistent with the First Amendment. As a threshold matter, note that manipulative online interfaces and related design choices may be better understood as conduct, rather than speech protected by the First Amendment (Calo, 2014, 1036–1037; Cohen, 2020, 641; Langvardt, 2019, 133; Wu, 2013, 1518–1525). When we recall that the First Amendment fails to cover, much less protect, every use of language (Schauer, 2004, 1773–1774), we can plausibly understand the First Amendment's coverage to exclude data collection and the use of algorithms (i.e. instructions to machines) because they *do* things rather than *say* things (Greenawalt, 1995, 5). This important possibility deserves attention and consideration. For purposes of this essay, however, I assume arguendo that courts may characterise the sorts of manipulative practices discussed herein as speech covered by the First Amendment and I explore the constitutional implications of that assumption.

As we'll see, First Amendment law sometimes permits the government to protect comparatively vulnerable listeners from comparatively powerful speakers' false or misleading speech, nondisclosures or coercive speech. Think, for example, of the government's requirements that commercial actors provide accurate disclosures about their products—like laws requiring cigarette manufacturers to post warnings about the dangers of tobacco on cigarette packages and advertisements and laws requiring lenders to disclose the terms and costs of their services in standardised form to facilitate comparison-shopping.

In other words, differences in power and information sometimes matter to First Amendment law, permitting the government's interventions to protect comparatively vulnerable listeners. The same can and should be true of efforts to regulate the sorts of manipulative speech discussed here. In other words, I propose that we understand the First Amendment to permit the government to intervene to protect listeners from speakers' manipulative efforts in certain settings.

In commercial settings, more specifically, I propose that the Court should refine and extend commercial speech doctrine to add "manipulative" commercial speech (as defined herein) to the commercial speech it currently treats as entirely unprotected by the First Amendment because it frustrates listeners' interests. This move tracks the original theoretical justifications of the commercial speech doctrine as steeped in protecting listeners' First Amendment interests. When we recall that false and misleading commercial speech, as well as commercial speech related to illegal activity, loses its First Amendment protection precisely because it frustrates listeners' First Amendment interests, we can see that the same can be true of manipulative commercial speech: it frustrates listeners' interests by seeking to covertly influence those listeners' choices without their conscious awareness, targeting and exploiting their vulnerabilities.

Filling this doctrinal lacuna would also help fill enforcement lacunae within current law. Even though existing consumer protection statutes frequently prohibit "unfair" as well as "deceptive" trade practices, to date enforcement efforts have focused almost entirely on allegedly "deceptive" practices—largely because of the conceptual difficulty in defining and describing illegally "unfair" practices. Here too ethicists give us the conceptual tools to help us understand why manipulation can be regarded as "unfair" to listeners even when it is hard to characterise it as "deceptive" in traditional terms.

This then requires that we have a workable principle for identifying manipulative (and thus unprotected) commercial speech. To this end, I consider two possibilities: (a) identifying commercial speech that is sufficiently manipulative to lose First Amendment protection by requiring evidence of its manipulative success in changing consumers' choices and (b) identifying commercial speech that is sufficiently manipulative to lose First Amendment protection by targeting interfaces that display key manipulative features that increase the risk of manipulation as defined herein.

Finally, I briefly examine how online manipulation in the political setting poses harms of its own that may also justify appropriately-tailored regulatory intervention (even while recognising that the First Amendment barriers to such regulation are significantly greater in this context than in the commercial setting), and I close by highlighting some possible interventions that deserve consideration.

2. Part I: understanding manipulation and its harms

Thinkers have long struggled to define the concept of manipulation with precision (Spencer, 2020, 984–988). This part draws from thoughtful recent work co-authored by ethicists Daniel Susser et al. (2019, 26), who describe manipulation as "imposing a hidden or covert influence on another person's decision-making." More specifically, they focus on manipulation that covertly influences listeners' decision-making by targeting and exploiting their decision-making vulnerabilities: "That means influencing someone's beliefs, desires, emotions, habits, or behaviours without their conscious awareness, or in ways that would thwart their capacity to become consciously aware of it by undermining usually reliable assumptions" (Ibid.) The key features of manipulation—as they define it, and as I'll discuss it here—are thus a speaker's *hidden* efforts to shape listeners' decision-making that *target* and *exploit* those listeners' vulnerabilities in ways that the targets aren't consciously aware of and in ways that those targets couldn't easily become aware of if they were to try.

To further understand the concept of manipulation, let's consider how it differs from other efforts (some more ethical than others) to influence targets' decision-making.

First, manipulation differs from both persuasion and coercion in that the latter two efforts are apparent while manipulation is not. Susser et al. (2019, 3) define persuasion as "the forthright appeal to another person's decision-making power"

(Ibid. at 17). And since coercion "is blunt and forthright, one almost always *knows* one is being coerced" (Ibid.). In other words, both persuasion and coercion are transparent efforts to influence the target—although to be sure, persuasion is generally respectful of the target's autonomy while coercion is not. But neither persuasion nor coercion is sneaky.

Manipulation, in contrast, *is* sneaky: "[r]ather than simply depriving a person of options as the coercer does, the manipulator infiltrates their decision-making process, disposing it to the manipulator's ends, which may or may not match their own" (Ibid.). So, for purposes of this essay, the terms "manipulation," "persuasion" and "coercion" describe mutually exclusive concepts.

Turn next to the relationship between manipulation and "nudges," i.e. "interventions that steer people in particular directions but that also allow them to go their own way" (Sunstein, 2015b, 417). Nudges may be or may not be manipulative, depending on whether the nudger hides the intentions underlying, and the effects of, the nudge. As Sunstein explains, manipulative nudges are those that attempt "to influence people in a way that does not sufficiently engage or appeal to their capacities for reflective and deliberative choice" (Ibid. at 443). Subliminal advertising is a classic example of the non-transparent nudge (Ibid. at 446–47).

In contrast, nudges are *not* manipulative when they are transparent and when they "have the goal of increasing navigability—of making it easier for people to get to their preferred destination. Such nudges stem from an understanding that life can be simple or hard to navigate, and a goal of helpful choice architecture is to promote simpler navigation" (Ibid. at 476). Illustrations of non-manipulative nudges include nutrition labels with calorie information or utilities' notices to us about how our home energy use compares with that of our neighbours (Ibid. at 425).

Now consider the relationship between manipulation and deception. As Susser, Roessler and Nissenbaum explain (2019, 21–22), deception is a subset of the broader concept of manipulation: deception is a particular type of covert effort to influence listeners' decision-making through false or misleading representations about objectively verifiable facts. In the commercial context, for example, deception includes false representations about the quality or hazards of goods and services or about the actual terms and conditions of a transaction. But manipulation is not limited to deception: manipulation *also* includes a variety of hidden efforts to influence listeners' decision-making that don't involve factual misrepresentations but instead exploit listeners' emotional, cognitive or other vulnerabilities. In this essay, I set deception to the side and focus instead on these other forms of manipulation.

Twentieth-century exemplars of this sort of manipulation include subliminal advertising, and sellers' infusion of sweet scents throughout their stores that cause consumers to linger longer and more happily (Becher and Feldman, 2016, 475). Law professors Jon Hanson and Douglas Kysar have examined a wide range of additional twentieth-century examples of

> the possibility of market manipulation—that is, the possibility that market outcomes can be influenced, if not determined, by the ability of one actor to

control the format of information, the framing and presentation of choices, and, more generally, the setting within which market transactions occur.

(Hanson and Kysar, 1999, 630)

The many twenty-first-century examples of manipulation now include sellers' ability to target online advertisements to consumers when surveillance of social media posts shows those consumers to be sad or lonely and thus especially vulnerable to buying certain goods and services they wouldn't normally buy—or to paying higher prices than they'd normally be willing to pay (Langvardt, 2019, 149; Willis, 2020, 122–123). And using webcams and smartphone cameras "to analyse consumers' facial expressions as they looked at a sales website and instantaneously deliver offers personalised to those consumers' nonverbal responses to the websites" (Ibid. at 126). And controlling the content of individuals' newsfeeds to steer their emotions to anger or fear—emotional states associated with barriers to careful decision-making (Ibid. at 144–47).

Twenty-first-century technologies, including the use of predictive algorithms informed by the collection and analysis of huge amounts of data, thus create opportunities for manipulation different in both degree and kind from more traditional forms of manipulation. As legal scholars Jamie Luguri and Lior Strahilevitz (2021, 103) explain:

By running tens of thousands of consumers through interfaces that were identical in every respect but one, firms can determine which interface, which text, which juxtapositions, and which graphics maximize revenues. What was once an art is now a science. As a result, consumers' ability to defend themselves has degraded.

Law professor Julie Cohen (2020, 658) finds the same to be true in political settings:

Manipulation in platform-based information environments is neither occasional nor accidental; it is endemic and results from capabilities that platforms systematically design, continually reoptimize, and habitually offer up to third parties for their deliberate exploitation.

These technological changes inspired law professor Ryan Calo (2014, 999) to extend Hanson's and Kysar's work to "digital market manipulation" that "stands to generate dramatic asymmetries of information and control between firms and consumers." In other words, contemporary online manipulation not only exploits vulnerabilities but can even create them. As Calo (Ibid., 1018) observes:

[D]igital market manipulation combines, for the first time, a certain kind of personalization with the intense systemization made possible by mediated consumption. A firm with the resources and inclination will be in a position to surface and exploit how consumers tend to deviate from rational decision-making on a previously unimaginable scale. Thus, firms will increasingly be in the position to create suckers, rather than waiting for one to be born.

Online manipulation is far from harmless. Speakers' manipulation harms listeners' autonomy and welfare when it shapes those listeners' choices to their economic and other detriments. This is the case, Calo (Ibid., 1033–1034) explains:

> when a firm uses personal information to extract as much rent as possible from the consumer. The consumer is shedding information that, without her knowledge or against her wishes, will be used to charge her as much as possible, to sell her a product or service she does not need or needs less of, or to convince here in a way that she would find objectionable were she aware of the practice.

The case for regulation becomes even stronger when we recall that manipulation, by definition, covertly targets and exploits users' vulnerabilities, thus inflicting harm that its targets cannot avoid through the traditional self-help remedies of avoidance and counter-speech. As Cass Sunstein (2015a, 213) notes:

> For the legal system, a pervasive problem is that manipulation has so many shades, and in a social order that values free markets and is committed to freedom of expression, it is exceptionally difficult to regulate manipulation as such. But as the manipulator's motives become more self-interested or venal, and as efforts to bypass people's deliberative capacities becomes more successful, the ethical objections to manipulation become very forceful, and the argument for a legal response is fortified.

Of course, online manipulation is by no means inevitable. Instead, it is the product of conscious design choices, carefully studied and tested to maximise their effectiveness in shaping targets' choices without those targets' conscious awareness and deliberately unleashed to advantage some at the expense of others. Government and private actors alike have made legal, policy and design choices that have enabled increases in online manipulation and its attendant harms (Cohen, 2020, 161). So too can we choose instead to make legal, policy and design decisions that deter and prevent these practices and their harms.

As we've seen, ethicists like Susser, Roessler and Nissenbaum now provide us with powerful conceptual tools for thinking about these contemporary problems of manipulation—and how they relate, and differ from, the problems of coercion and deception (and the non-problem of persuasion). The next part explores how these conceptual tools can also help us understand when, how, and why the First Amendment permits the government to regulate manipulation.

3. Part II: the First Amendment implications of the government's interventions to protect listeners from manipulation

Challenging constitutional problems are often difficult because they force us to choose between important constitutional values—for example, between liberty and security, or among speech, religion and equality. More specifically, some First Amendment problems are especially difficult because they force us to choose between speakers' and listeners' First Amendment interests—interests that include autonomy, enlightenment and democratic self-governance (Massaro and Norton, 2021, 1658–1660). This is the case, for instance, when speakers wish to tell lies while their listeners hunger for the truth; when listeners pine for speakers to reveal information that speakers would prefer to conceal and when listeners hope for respite from speakers resolved to address them.

Bedrock First Amendment law frequently privileges speakers' interests over listeners' not only because speech is often so valuable but also because it presumes that listeners can usually protect themselves from unwelcome or harmful speech through avoidance and rebuttal. At the same time, however, First Amendment law sometimes permits the government's intervention where asymmetries of power and information between speakers and listeners not only increase the likelihood and severity of harm to listeners but also limit the effectiveness of listeners' traditional self-help remedies.

In these settings, courts sometimes interpret the First Amendment to permit the government to intervene on listeners' behalf by prohibiting false and misleading speech, requiring speakers to stay away from listeners who prefer to be left alone or requiring speakers to make accurate disclosures of material matters. In the commercial setting, think of governmental requirements that manufacturers and sellers affirmatively disclose the costs of, or dangers posed by, their products even when those speakers would prefer not to reveal that information. And in the context of public discourse, recall campaign disclosure and disclaimer requirements that serve listeners' informational interests in knowing the source of campaign advertisements and contributions—even though some of those campaign speakers and contributors would prefer not to disclose their identities.

In short, inequalities of information and power sometimes matter to the First Amendment doctrine. And online manipulative speech, as defined in Part I, inherently involves such inequalities: those who deploy manipulative interfaces enjoy informational advantages because their ability to collect, aggregate and analyse data about their listeners means that they often know more about listeners and their vulnerabilities than the listeners themselves know (Susser et al., 2019, 44). These informational advantages also often draw from, or exacerbate, power advantages (Balkin, 2018, 1156).

We can thus understand the First Amendment to permit the government to protect listeners from manipulation's harms in settings where listeners cannot protect themselves because they're unaware of their manipulation. The remainder of this part discusses more specifically what this means for manipulative speech in commercial and political settings.

3.1. Regulating manipulative speech in commercial settings

The Supreme Court's modern commercial speech doctrine took a transparently listener-centred approach by treating commercial speech as protected or unprotected depending on whether it provides value to consumers as listeners. As Felix Wu explains, "Commercial speech protection [] originated in and is justified by protecting consumers' rights to receive commercial information, not in protecting merchants' rights to frame that information" (Wu, 2019, 637). Under the Court's framework, the government's restriction of accurate commercial speech about legal activity (like accurate speech about prescription drug prices) triggers courts' suspicion in the form of intermediate scrutiny because such speech is generally valuable to listeners. At the same time, the Court treats commercial speech that is false, misleading or related to illegal activity as entirely unprotected by the First Amendment because such speech fails to further listeners' First Amendment interests and often frustrates them.

Ryan Calo (2014, 1048–1049) has proposed that we characterise online manipulation as commercial speech that is entirely unprotected under this precedent because it is misleading. Although I agree that some manipulation can be considered false or misleading (i.e. when it seeks to cause the listener to believe a false factual representation to be true), many manipulative practices instead target and exploit cognitive, emotional and other vulnerabilities rather than make false or misleading representations of fact (Luguri and Strahilevitz, 2021, 90).

For this reason, the Court's current commercial speech framework is incomplete in its failure to address a large volume of manipulative commercial speech—especially in today's online environment. To fill this doctrinal gap, I propose that the Court refine and extend current commercial speech doctrine to add "manipulative" commercial speech to the commercial speech that it already treats as unprotected by the First Amendment. This move tracks the theoretical justifications of the original commercial speech doctrine as steeped in protecting listeners' First Amendment interests. When we recall that false and misleading commercial speech, as well as commercial speech related to illegal activity, loses its First Amendment protection precisely because that speech frustrates listeners' First Amendment interests, we see that the same can be true of manipulative commercial speech in the online setting: it frustrates listeners' interests by seeking to covertly influence its targets' choices (to the speaker's advantage) without their conscious awareness and by targeting and exploiting their vulnerabilities.

Filling this doctrinal lacuna would also help fill enforcement lacunae within current law. Even though existing consumer protection statutes often prohibit "unfair" as well as "deceptive" trade practices, to date "[u]nfairness has been the basis for decision in only a handful of litigated cases" (Greenfield, 2000, 1877)—largely because of the conceptual difficulty in defining and describing illegally "unfair" practices (Willis, 2020, 120). Here too Susser et al. (2019, 1) give us the conceptual tools to help us understand why online manipulation—i.e. speaker's *hidden* efforts to shape listeners' decision-making that *target* and *exploit* those listeners' vulnerabilities in ways that the targets aren't consciously aware of—is "unfair" to consumers even when it is hard to characterise as "deceptive."

Treating manipulative commercial speech as unprotected by the First Amendment then requires that we have a workable principle for identifying such manipulative commercial speech. The remainder of this subpart explores two possibilities.

3.2. Focusing on manipulative effects

One approach to identifying manipulative (and thus unprotected) commercial speech is to require evidence of its manipulative success.

Recall that manipulative interfaces and other online practices are the products of conscious design choices, carefully studied and tested to maximise their effectiveness in shaping targets' choices without those targets' conscious awareness (Langvardt, 2019, 142). This means that academics and regulators can also measure their effects. Testing by legal scholars Luguri and Strahilevitz (2021, 46), for instance, found certain interfaces to double, triple, sometimes even quadruple consumers' willingness to accept sellers' offers and requests when compared to neutral choice architecture. These design choices include interfaces that make it harder for users to choose options that are popular to consumers but less lucrative for sellers, minimise material information with smaller print in less prominent locations or require users to jump through numerous hoops to reject or withdraw from a service or product (so-called "roach motels") (Ibid. at 47–52). Luguri and Strahilevitz thus recommend that regulators engage in testing of their own to identify illegally manipulative interfaces— i.e. design choices that should trigger regulatory interventions because of their measurably stark effects on consumers' decisions (Ibid.).

Indeed, algorithmic manipulation at times may be easier to identify and measure—and thus responsibly regulate—than that by manipulative humans. As Luguri and Strahilevetz (Ibid. at 48) note:

> [D]ark patterns are different from other forms of dodgy business practices because of the scale of e-commerce. There may be poetic justice in the fact that this very scale presents an opportunity for creative legal regulators. Now that scholars can test dark patterns, we can isolate causation in a way that's heretofore been impossible in the brick-and-mortar world. Unlike brick-and-mortar manipulation, dark patterns are hiding in plain sight, operate on a massive scale, and are relatively easy to detect.

Of course, we can imagine challenges in identifying baselines for neutral choice architecture. (But, as Luguri and Strahilevitz note (Ibid. at 98), that's not always the case: "It should not be hard to generate consensus around the idea that a single Yes/No, Accept/Decline prompt is neutral, provided that choices are presenting with identical fonts, colours, font sizes, and placement.") Effects-based approaches to identifying illegally manipulative practices may also invite objections that comparisons to so-called "neutral" baselines rely on a contested liberal understanding of the autonomous self that assumes that our preferences are stable: in other words, our preferences are not always consistent and in fact can be shaped by algorithms and other forces, both technological and otherwise (Kerr, 2017, 92). For these reasons, rather than (or in addition to) focusing on manipulative success, we might identify manipulative (and thus unprotected) commercial speech as that involving certain manipulative characteristics that signal the intent and tendency to interfere with our choices, an effort that we might objectively view as harmful in and of itself. The next section explores this possibility.

3.3. Focusing on manipulative features

A second approach to identifying commercial speech that is manipulative (and thus unprotected by the First Amendment) is to target design choices that display the three characteristics of manipulation as emphasised by Susser et al. (2019, 41)—*hidden* efforts that *target* and *exploit* users' vulnerabilities:

> [W]e should attempt to determine whether the influencer was trying to conceal their efforts, whether the influence was intended to exploit the manipulee's vulnerabilities and to what extent the influence was targeted. Manipulative practices—characterized as we have argued by concealment, exploitation of vulnerabilities, and targeting—are cause for concern, regardless of whether they succeed in every instance.

To be sure, much work remains to be done in defining each of these three characteristics more precisely. But to start, I'll suggest "hidden" to mean not apparent to the user; "target" to mean identifying specific users with certain vulnerabilities and "exploit" to mean deliberately deploying knowledge of those vulnerabilities in settings where there's reason to believe it will shape users' choices to the speaker's advantage. In other words, we can understand speakers' choice to deploy designs with features that display these manipulative characteristics as a proxy for those choices' intent and tendency to manipulate those listeners (Cohen, 2020, 655).

3.4. Regulating manipulative speech in political settings

While manipulation in commercial settings threatens harm to individual consumers, online manipulation in public discourse additionally threatens collective harm to our democratic self-governance. As Susser et al. (2019, 43–44) observe:

> When citizens are targets of online manipulation and voter decisions rather than purchase decisions are swayed by hidden influence, democracy itself is called into question. Add to this the fact that the tools of online manipulation are concentrated in only a few hands, and it is easy to see how the nexus of influence and information technology stands to make already problematic power dynamics far worse.

Recall, for instance, Cambridge Analytica's use of big data to microtarget messages to specific voters in efforts to influence those voters' choices in the 2016 U.S. elections (Kilovaty, 2019, 467–468). Authoritarians and others similarly seek to exploit the manipulative possibilities enabled by twenty-first-century platforms in ways that threaten democracy, as Julie Cohen (2020, 659) explains:

> Authoritarian information systems have developed sophisticated information strategies that leverage platform-based environments to undermine common knowledge about how democratic institutions function and, by extension, to destabilize the behavioral norms that lend such institutions continuing legitimacy. Such attacks, which are now well-documented, exploit platform capabilities for microtargeting, automaticity, and cascading, socially-networked information spread to stoke conspiracy theories and foster distrust—of government, of the "mainstream media," of scientific consensus around topics such as climate change and the efficacy of vaccines, and so on. Powerful domestic factions that should have mobilized to defend these assaults on our foundational institutions instead have adopted weaponization techniques to further their own ends. As such strategies become more powerful, they produce and amplify modes of public discourse about institutional actors that are incompatible with the knowledge structure of a stable democracy.

The existential democratic threats posed by today's manipulative online practices thus may now outweigh the traditional dangers of the government's regulation of speech in public discourse (Ibid. at 661–62).

Of course, speakers' efforts to manipulate listeners' decisions about voting and other core political activity occur in the realm not of commercial speech but instead in public discourse, an area where courts' suspicion of governments' regulatory interventions is considerably greater (and understandably so) than in the commercial context. Under the Court's long-standing First Amendment doctrine, the government's content-neutral regulation of speech (i.e. its regulation of expression's time, place or manner rather than its content) in public discourse triggers a form of intermediate scrutiny, while the government's content-based regulation triggers strict scrutiny. Either way (and here I focus on content-neutral possibilities), the challenge is to cabin the government's considerable potential for overreach through appropriately tailored regulation of manipulative speech. To this end, the government can tailor its intervention through its choice of regulatory target (i.e. *what* it targets for regulation), through its choice of regulatory tool (i.e. *how* it regulates its target) or both.

3.5. *Tailoring through targeting*

As explained in the preceding subpart, appropriately tailored interventions could target interfaces with certain manipulative effects, certain manipulative features or both. Here's a brief recap:

> First, interventions could target interfaces with particularly stark manipulative effects through A-B testing (where an "A/B test randomly distributes an 'A'

version of something to some people and a 'B' version to others and measures differences between the responses of the two groups") (Willis, 2020, 127). Indeed, those who design and deploy these features engage in this sort of testing themselves to identify effective means for influencing users' choices to click on, read or forward specific content in political as well as commercial settings: online actors deploy these manipulative interfaces precisely because they've tested them extensively and *know* they are effective in changing their target's choices (Cohen, 2020, 164–165). (In political settings, however, the causal relationship between design and outcome may be considerably more contested, as the decision whether or for whom to vote can be more causally complex than the decision to decide whether to buy a product or agree to a transactional condition.)

Second, interventions could instead target "[m]anipulative practices— characterized, as we have argued, by concealment, exploitation of vulnerabilities, and targeting—[as] cause for concern, regardless of whether they succeed in every instance" (Susser et al., 2020, 41). Along these lines, Cohen (2020, 655) emphasises that "[t]he First Amendment does not require legislators or judges to privilege design for automaticity and reflexive amplification"; she identifies particularly manipulative features in public discourse to include "predictive profiling and microtargeting based on behavioural and psychographic data; interface design to elicit automatic, precognitive responses; and algorithmic optimization to amplify patterns of cascading, socially-networked spread" (Ibid. at 660).

3.6. *Tailoring through tools*

Moving from the question of *what* to regulate (target) to the question of *how* to regulate (tool), this section highlights a few suggestions offered by thoughtful commentators; my objective here is to draw attention to a range of possibilities for further exploration rather than to detail (much less exhaust) them. In thinking through available options, recall that the choice of tool drives the level of suspicion under the Court's First Amendment doctrine: tools characterised as content-neutral receive "only" intermediate scrutiny, as compared to the strict scrutiny generally applied to the government's content-based regulation of protected speech. For this reason, I focus on content-neutral possibilities.

Kyle Langvardt, for instance, has described a variety of friction-creating restrictions of manipulative interfaces, like restrictions on infinite scrolls (that unceasingly feed users with new posts); restrictions on auto-play features that seek to manipulate users into remaining online for longer periods of time (during which time the users spend more money and shed more data) and restrictions that limit or delay users' ability to mass-forward (and thus amplify) content (Langvardt, 2020, 13–15).

Lauren Willis (2020, 119–120) urges that law "compel businesses to engage in fair marketing by design" by, for example, requiring that platforms or retailers refrain from directing materials to consumers "whose demographics or behaviours indicate persistent or transitory impairment." Ian Kerr (2017, 101–102) suggests that "technological defaults ought to be regulated in a manner similar to contractual defaults," urging that "the strictest privacy settings automatically apply once a customer acquires a new product or service," such that users need to make no manual change to their privacy settings to protect themselves to the fullest. And Woody Hartzog, who has written extensively on how law should "better reflect how design influences our perceptions and actions" (2018, 7), urges regulators to "discourage design that tricks us, lies to us, exploits us" and advises courts and regulators to ferret out an abusive design that seeks to exploit users' biases and vulnerabilities (Ibid. at 126).

Again, recognising the harm of online manipulation in political settings does not tell us *how* to prevent and address that harm. Much work remains to be done; here I've highlighted a few possibilities for further consideration and development.

4. Conclusion

Some may fear the government's restriction of manipulative interfaces as unacceptably paternalistic. But paternalism describes interference with autonomous choices that others think unwise, rather than interference with practices that themselves frustrate autonomous choice. Precisely because manipulation's targets are unaware of the ways in which online actors gather, aggregate and exploit their data to influence their decision-making, online manipulation occurs in a setting that defies the traditional First Amendment model of fully informed rational listeners freely choosing among available options. In other words, nobody consciously chooses to be manipulated because, by definition, targets are unaware of their manipulation, and thus can't take steps to protect themselves. As Langvardt observes, "If the regulatory goal is simply to make product design less manipulative, then regulation in principle exists to enhance rather than diminish tech users' freedom of choice" (Langvardt, 2019, 148).

Others may worry that any effort to regulate manipulation is folly because manipulation is endemic to the human condition. But so too are violence, discrimination and falsehoods—and yet the government at times restricts each of those choices precisely because of the harms they inflict. Rather than asking whether to regulate these all-too-human behaviours, the better question is when, why and how to regulate them.

To this end, in this essay, I've suggested that ethicists' understanding of manipulation and its harms gives us helpful tools for thinking more carefully about legal and policy responses. I then draw from these tools to propose that courts add manipulation to the list of harms to listeners' interests that sometimes justify the government's intervention in certain settings consistent with the First Amendment.

More specifically, we can understand manipulative commercial speech to be entirely unprotected by the First Amendment, with the government's regulation subject only to rational-basis scrutiny. Like commercial speech that is false, misleading or related to illegal activity—and thus treated as entirely unprotected by the First Amendment—manipulative commercial speech frustrates rather than furthers listeners' First Amendment interests. We can target commercial speech as manipulative (and thus unprotected by the First Amendment) by focusing on its effects (i.e. its manipulative success), its content (i.e. its deployment of certain manipulative features) or both. And although the First Amendment doctrine appropriately poses a considerably larger barrier to the regulation of manipulative speech in political settings, there too we can consider the possibility that the First Amendment permits certain interventions that are carefully tailored in terms of regulatory target, regulatory tool or both.

Many may understandably wonder whether the contemporary Court will be receptive to these ideas given the antiregulatory turn in its First Amendment doctrine, along with its inconsistent attention to the ways in which twenty-first-century technologies inflict harms that are different in degree and sometimes in kind from earlier counterparts. Even so, as constitutional law scholar Mark Graber reminded us in another context: "Advocating doctrines unlikely to be accepted immediately is still a worthwhile activity" (Graber, 1991, 223). Indeed, the challenges posed by twenty-first-century expressive technologies "may inspire more careful reflection about how to define and mitigate the harmful effects of covered speech, while preserving its manifold benefits" (Massaro et al., 2017, 2514).

Notes

1 This is an abridged version of *Manipulation and the First Amendment,* published in 30 Wm. & Mary Bill Rts. J. 221 (2021), https://scholarship.law.wm.edu/wmborj/vol30/iss2/2, used with permission.
2 Thanks to Ellen Miller for excellent research assistance. Thanks too for thoughtful questions and comments from Enrique Armijo, Elettra Bietti, Caroline Mala Corbin, Margot Kaminski, Kyle Langvardt, Migle Laukyte, Francesca Procaccini, Harry Surden, Alex Tsesis and the participants at the William & Mary Bill of Rights Journal Symposium on Algorithms and the Constitution, and at Yale Law School's Free Expression Scholars Conference.

References

Balkin, J. 2018. "Free Speech in the Algorithmic Society: Big Data, Private Governance, and New School Speech Regulation." *The U.C. Davis Law Review* 51: 1149–1210.
Becher, S. and Feldman, Y. 2016. "Manipulating, Fast and Slow: The Law of Non-verbal Market Manipulation." *The Cardozo Law Review* 38: 459–507.
Calo, R. 2014. "Digital Market Manipulation." *The George Washington Law Review* 82: 995–1051.
Cohen, J. 2020. "Tailoring Election Regulation: The Platform Is the Frame." *The Georgetown Law Technology Review* 4: 641–664.
Graber, M. 1991. *Transforming Free Speech.* Berkeley: University of California Press.
Greenawalt, K. 1995. *Fighting Words: Individuals, Communities, and Liberties of Speech.* Princeton: Princeton University Press.
Greenfield, M. 2000. "Unfairness Under Section 5 of the FTC Act and Its Impact on State Law." *The Wayne Law Review* 46: 1869.

Hanson, J. and Kysar, D. 1999. "Taking Behavioralism Seriously: The Problem of Market Manipulation." *The New York University Law Review* 74: 630–749.

Hartzog, W. 2018. *Privacy's Blueprint: The Battle to Control the Design of New Technologies*. Cambridge: Harvard University Press.

Kerr, I. 2017. "The Devil is in the Default." *Critical Analysis of Law* 4: 91–103.

Kilovaty, I. 2019. "Legally Cognizable Manipulation." *The Berkeley Technology Law Journal* 34: 449–502.

Langvardt, K. 2019. "Regulating Habit-Forming Technologies." *The Fordham Law Review* 88: 129–186.

Langvardt, K. 2020. "Platform Speech Governance and the First Amendment: A User-Centered Approach." *The Digital Social Contract: A Lawfare Paper Series*: 1–33.

Luguri, J. and Strahilevitz, L. 2021. "Shining a Light on Dark Patterns." *The Journal of Legal Analysis* 13: 43–109.

Massaro, T. and Norton, H. 2021. "Free Speech and Democracy: A Pragmatic Primer for 21st Century Reformers." *The U.C. Davis Law Review* 54: 1631.

Massaro, T., Norton, H. and Kaminski, M. 2017. "Siri-ously 2.0: What Artificial Intelligence Reveals About the First Amendment." *The Minnesota Law Review* 101: 2481–2526.

Overton, S. 2020. "State Power to Regulate Social Media Companies to Prevent Voter Suppression." *The U.C. Davis Law Review* 53: 1793–1830.

Salpeter, L. and Swirsky, J. 2012. "Historical and Legal Implications of Subliminal Messaging in the Multimedia: Unconscious Subjects." *The Nova Law Review* 36: 497–520.

Schauer, F. 2004. "The Boundaries of the First Amendment: A Preliminary Exploration of Constitutional Salience." *The Harvard Law Review* 117: 1765–1809.

Spencer, S. 2020. "The Problem of Online Manipulation." *The University of Illinois Law Review* 2020: 959–1006.

Sunstein, C. 2015a. "Fifty Shades of Manipulation." *The Journal of Marketing Behavior* 1: 213–244.

Sunstein, C. 2015b. "The Ethics of Nudging." *The Yale Journal on Regulation* 32: 413–450.

Susser, D., Roessler, B. and Nissenbuam, H. 2019. "Online Manipulation: Hidden Influences in a Digital World." *The Georgetown Law Technology Review* 4: 1–45.

Willis, L. 2020. "Deception By Design." *The Harvard Journal of Law and Technology* 34: 115–190.

Wu, T. 2013. "Machine Speech." *The University of Pennsylvania Law Review* 161: 1495–1533.

Wu, F. 2019. "Commercial Speech Protection as Consumer Protection." *The University of Colorado Law Review* 90: 631–652.

6 Fake news published during the pre-election period and free speech theory

Filimon Peonidis

1. Introduction

A recent study of Twitter made it clear that "falsehood diffused significantly farther, faster, deeper and more broadly than the truth in all categories of information and the effects were more pronounced for false political news" than any other categories of misinformation (Vosoughi et al., 2018, 1146). Since we do not live in Nazi Germany or in Stalinist Soviet Union—and I presume we do not want to—this is a cause of great concern. It involves not only governments and political leaders, including democratic ones, who are proved prone to mislead the public. Perhaps, what should worry us more are the rapid and unprecedented developments that are taking place in the news industry. In the past, a relatively small number of competing mainstream print, radio and TV outlets enjoyed an almost absolute monopoly on the dissemination of political news, and they had a strong interest in being responsible and trustworthy if they desired to stay in business. During the last two decades, the situation has rapidly changed, as the advent of the Internet and of various social media multiplied the sources of information and offered many people the opportunity to reach and communicate with huge audiences at minimal cost and (in many cases) without being accountable to anyone. Our tendency to turn anything to our advantage, often to the detriment of others if we are left unchecked, was given free rein here, and among the unhappy results it brought about is the aforementioned preponderance of falsehood over truth concerning political news.

In this essay, I will focus on a particular form of disinformation diffused through the Internet and other more conventional means, fake news. In the second section, I argue that fake news is lies with all the morally reprehensible connotations of the term. In the third, I offer a proposal for the legal regulation of political fake news published during the pre-election period. In the fourth, I explore whether this proposal can be defended in a manner that is consistent with certain tenets of mainstream free speech theory, and in the fifth, I critically discuss certain objections deriving from this tradition. The results of this inquiry are tentative, and they should be seen as generating further reflection, discussion and deliberation rather than signalling a battle cry for immediate legislative intervention.

DOI: 10.4324/9781003274476-9

2. Fake news is lies

The term "fake news" was not coined as part of a scientific discourse, and this fact gives rise to a significant semantic laxity regarding its use in various contexts (Katsirea, 2018, 160). The confusion is aggravated by certain politicians who do not hesitate to call fake news any sound criticism made by the opposition. However, one is entitled to assume that fake news is conceived as "news," and not as hoaxes, jokes, satire, rumours or works of fiction. Moreover, in contrast to "proper news," fake news is commonly understood as some kind of fraud pretending to be something that it is not, and on further scrutiny, it turns out to be intentionally deceptive. By taking into account these two rather obvious considerations, I will offer a conceptual analysis of fake news that conceives it as a particular category of lies.[1]

The producer of fake news lies to her target audience, meaning that:

a. She presents as news a statement or a set of statements she knows to be false. This means that she perfunctorily follows all the standard conventions concerning the presentation and circulation of news by mainstream media.[2] Moreover, she is epistemically justified in believing that her statement(s) is fabricated. Someone who writes a false report convinced that it is a genuine one may be accused of sloppy journalism, but she cannot be called a liar.[3]
b. She intends her statement(s) to be believed by a target audience. Her intention to deceive becomes manifest by the fact that she does not give any indication that her statement(s) might not be true. For instance, she does not state that it is based on unconfirmed reports or allegations, she does not make clear that she is being ironic, metaphorical or making a joke and she does not rush to retract it immediately after its publication to prevent confusion and misinformation.
c. She realises that her statement(s) is likely to be believed by at least a subset of her target audience. This belief is essential for distinguishing fake news from nonsense or bullshit[4] that is so obvious that no average person will believe them. Of course, the degree of probability for her statement to be believed depends on many factors such as the content of the message, the type of the audience, the prevailing circumstances and others that cannot be predicted, but I tend to agree with Gelfert (2018, 103) that

> for a claim to be considered fake news, it must *in fact* mislead a relevant audience—though precisely how large an audience may depend on the case at hand—and it must do so in virtue of the way it is designed to pass itself off as news.

The aforementioned account purports to capture the most correct uses of the term "fake news" in ordinary discourse, although one can expect the occurrence of borderline cases, where it is difficult to say whether a set of statements should belong to this type of misinformation or not. It makes room for fake news that appears in print or is broadcast on radio and television, but, as said before, here I am mostly interested in fake news diffused through the Internet. As far as the motives of its producers are concerned, we can assume that the pursuit of ideological, political and financial interests, pure malice, vanity, sheer fun or a combination of them are among the most common ones. Finally, following the recipe for successful propaganda, the false statements of fake news may be intermingled with true ones to make the basic message appear more convincing (Gelfert, 2018, 100).

One benefit of viewing fake news as a type of lying is that it makes its normative evaluation easier. There is a general moral presumption against lying and in favour of truthfulness. It is undergirded by the variety of individual and collective harms caused by lies among which stand out the multiple direct setbacks in the agents' interests (welfare, financial, professional, etc.), as well as the assault on individual autonomy[5] and the erosion of social trust that is necessary for constructive communication among people. There is also an old debate as to whether lying is always blameworthy. Immanuel Kant (1996, 613) notoriously argued that the duty to be truthful "in all declarations is a sacred command of reason prescribing unconditionally, one not to be restricted by any conveniences," even if a lie is necessary to thwart a prospective murderer. Nevertheless, this position is counterintuitive and most contemporary philosophers counter with the argument that certain limited and specified in advance exceptions have to be granted when the need to protect other values of paramount importance outweighs the duty to be truthful (Peonidis, 1994, chap. 3; Coady, 2008, chap. 5; Carson, 2010, chap. 3). Most people would find the publication of a fake news story morally justifiable if they were told that its author had to succumb to the demands of some shady characters who were credibly threatening to harm her family. To give another example, many would condone a misleading police announcement presented as genuine news if it is necessary for resolving a serious crime, such as a terrorist attack or a homicide (Norton, 2013, 165). Along similar lines, we are less harsh with someone who publishes fake news because she is a pathological liar.

However, it is my belief that those who are infuriated by the recent flood of fake news and its ramifications would not settle for a mere *moral* condemnation of most of it. They want something to be done to reduce its rate of appearance and its impact on Internet users. They also want prospective manipulators to be discouraged through sanctions from being engaged in its production and deliberate dissemination. In other words, they press for a *legal* regulation of fake news (Ball, 2021, 6–7). This move from moral reproach to legal regulation presents us with a serious issue. Suppression of fake news means suppression of speech, which is something in principle prohibited or disparaged within most liberal legal and constitutional traditions. Thus, a different type of quest becomes necessary, one that would inquire whether free speech considerations allow or disallow the regulation of fake news.[6]

3. A regulatory proposal

I will now defend the following assumption which paves the way for the legal regulation of a particular category of fake news.

> There are good prima facie reasons—which are supported by mainstream free speech theory considerations—to withhold constitutional protection from fake news with political content published during the pre-election period.[7]

The length of the pre-election period, which covers the last phase of public debate and campaigning of parties (or candidates) immediately preceding elections and referenda, depends on the customs of the land. Yet, the term should be generously construed to include the period between the Election Day and the inauguration of the new government or the president-elect, which signals the return to normality. As far as "political content" is concerned, there might be borderline cases we find puzzling, but I believe that, in most cases, the study of the context of the message will help us determine whether a particular communication is political or not. For instance, political factual assertions expressed in works of fiction, such as a TV sitcom, may be influential, but they do not count as political speech in the sense that interests us here. Finally, the term "mainstream free speech theory considerations" refers to specific positions taken from the huge bulk of theories, court rulings, arguments and assumptions developed during the last hundred years mostly by American judges, constitutional lawyers and philosophers in their effort to interpret and lay the foundations of the famous provision that "Congress shall make no law . . . abridging the freedom of speech, or the press" contained in the First Amendment of the U.S. Constitution.[8]

Why does this proposal opt for the regulation of only a small subset of fake news? The moral wickedness of fake news depends heavily on the messages communicated. It is one thing to present a misleading story about an actor's new girlfriend and a different thing to report falsely that the incumbent president had a secret meeting with a notorious mobster. It is better to start with a piecemeal and trial-and-error approach focusing on a particular category of fake news that has severe consequences for the body politic and the proper functioning of democracy and is not fully covered by existing legal provisions such as those concerning defamation. In addition, there are reasons pertaining to the "mechanics" of online political fake news which have recently started coming to the fore: "in times of uncertainty" fake news multiplies and is harder to be checked,[9] and, as said before, it seems to be disseminated faster than other false stories and to reach a wider audience.[10]

Before moving to the defence of the aforementioned assumption, I will give two fictional (but inspired by true events) examples of fake news to which I will refer throughout the rest of the essay.

> Example 1: "Last minute update! The bishop of Sin City asked the vicars in all the parishes under his jurisdiction to urge churchgoers to vote for the yellow party."

Example 2: "Last minute update! In Sin City two local officials responsible for the counting of votes were apprehended while trying to dispose of ten thousand valid ballots cast for the yellow party."

As it follows from these examples the category of fake news that interests me concerns news that is in principle verifiable.[11]

4. The main argument

One initial question that should be asked is whether the proposed regulation is content-based, in the sense of restricting a special category of speech, or viewpoint-based, in the sense of banning the expression of a particular point of view. What bothers us here is the use of lies in general in democratic elections and not particular lies that may or may not promote specific partisan interests. It would be unfair to regulate fake news that favours the yellow party, but not the remaining parties that are competing in the election. Thus, it is reasonable to assume that by proscribing mendacious political speech, we impose a content-based restriction on free speech.

However, Shiffrin (2014, chap. 4) has argued that the legal regulation of lies in general is more content-neutral than content-based. What we suppress is not the message but the act of asserting something one does not believe. We interfere with someone's intention to impose a false belief upon others. These considerations led her to the view that this regulation is closer to time, place and manner restrictions on speech, which are often regarded as plausible and necessary, and they do not raise significant First Amendment objections.[12] Is this the case? I do not think so. A widely accepted time restriction is the rule that no interruptions are allowed when a speaker has the floor in an official meeting. The idea is that you can say whatever you want to say, but you have to wait your turn. This rule does not have ceteris paribus any effect on the content of the message the interrupter would like to convey. It just postpones the time of its expression for reasons of fairness and equality. However, the regulation of fake news does not work this way. When an official authority characterises the Sin City electoral fraud story as fake news, it deprives it of any epistemic value it might have. It tells the public that this is bogus and that it should be withdrawn from circulation. Of course, some bigots may continue to take it at face value, but this does not alter the fact that there is sufficient evidence to reject it as false and misleading. When we criticise a mendacious message, we not only object to the liar's intention but also dismiss the whole message. This criticism cannot be content-neutral.

In First Amendment jurisprudence, content-based restrictions on speech are in principle treated with suspicion and disbelief, but they are not fully dismissed. They must meet strict scrutiny standards, which means that the government must have a "compelling interest" to impose them. There are indeed certain categories of mendacious communication that do not enjoy constitutional protection such as fraud, defamation, perjury and lying to government officials. The rationale underlying them is the following:

> False speech that causes certain *legally cognizable harms* can be punished or subjected to civil liability without raising significant First Amendment concerns. Government may punish or subject to liability the harm that defamation causes to reputation, that fraud causes to one's property rights, or that perjury causes to judicial truth-finding (Blitz, 2018, 70) [Emphasis mine].[13]

With the exception of defamation of public officials and figures, the mendacious political speech seems to be constitutionally tolerated, although the Supreme Court has sometimes acknowledged the overall potential unconstitutionality of deliberate falsehoods in politics.[14] Thus, it is of no surprise that the legislative efforts of States such as Minnesota and Massachusetts to proscribe false election and campaign speech were invalidated by State and Federal Courts (Sellers, 2018, 150–154). These rulings have recently attracted the criticism of commentators who find them "disheartening,"[15] "dishonest"[16] and "preposterous."[17]

Could it be argued that fake news with political content published during the election period constitutes a legally cognisable harm? In my view, this could be done as far as it can be shown that it undermines the integrity of the democratic electoral process and encourages attitudes that are harmful to the healthy political culture that supports democratic elections, campaigns and referenda and keeps them on the right track.

The damage caused is threefold. First, fake news can compel citizens to reach decisions that they would not have reached if they knew the falsehoods and the disinformation contained in them. "Many instances of misinformation disseminate false beliefs that impair individuals' ability to make sound normative judgments" (Brown, 2018, 207). The alleged support of the Bishop of Sin City for the yellow party might motivate certain voters to change their mind and vote for or against the yellow party, depending on their religious affiliations. The revelation of the truth later on is very likely to make them regret their vote, but the election cannot be repeated. Their decisions cannot be regarded as authentic, since they have fallen prey to manipulators who collude to make their target audience promote partisan goals without knowing it. Those who vote by believing in lies resemble those who are forced by threats or offers they cannot refuse to vote for a certain party or candidate. The only difference is that the deceived voters are not aware of their situation. In addition, political manipulators mock the principle of voting equality by creating a huge epistemic gap between themselves and the audience they deceive. They assume a morally unjustifiable position of epistemic superiority concerning a certain piece of politically relevant information which bestows them an unfair advantage over their fellow citizens in the voting procedure. It is hard to see how we can have free and fair elections—which are the main outlet for the legitimisation of the bearers of legislative and executive power—if citizens fall victims to lies and misinformation during campaigns and elections.

Second, political fake news not only misleads and disorientates citizens concerning their voting decisions but also motivates them, when tensions run high, to resort to violence and commit unlawful acts. For certain fanatics, the story about the alleged electoral fraud in Sin City is a good excuse for storming the building to "administer justice." There are examples of people from all over the world who have lost their lives because of actions triggered by fake news (Tandoc, 2021, 36–37). Note that fake news need not incite people to crime in a technical legal sense. The producers of the aforementioned story do not urge anyone to invade the City Hall, but they realise that under the circumstances some citizens are likely to do it. Of course, this does not absolve these fanatics of their responsibility for their actions, but all would be better off in the absence of such incendiary fake messages.

Third, the problem with political fake news is not only that people "will believe the wrong things" but that they "will fail to believe the right things" (Ball, 2021, 13). If it becomes common knowledge that lies, in the sense that interests us here, abound during the election period, citizens might not know whom to trust. Thus, they might decide that they have to rely only on what they already believe and refuse to seek any other source of information and alternative viewpoints in particular. The growing suspicion that other political actors are deceiving them may increase animosity and polarisation and stifle the desire to listen to the other side, let alone the desire to be engaged in a constructive dialogue with it. This epistemic isolation can cultivate self-righteousness and bigotry. Political fake news in huge quantities can lower the quality of a democracy, even if it is not taken at face value.

One might agree that mendacious political speech during the election period is harmful but may have doubts as to whether the compromising of the integrity of the electoral process is a legally cognisable harm requiring legislative intervention. There is, however, evidence that governments are regarded *legally* responsible "for the protection of the integrity and regularity of the election process." In 1934, the U.S. Supreme Court upheld the power of the Congress to protect the "purity" of election of the President and Vice-President with any means it considers appropriate:

> If this government is anything more than a mere aggregation of delegated agents of other States and governments, each of which is superior to the general government, it must have the power to protect the elections on which its existence depends from violence and corruption. If it has not this power it is helpless before the two great natural and historical enemies of all republics, open violence and insidious corruption.[18]

Things are clearer in Greece where Article 52 of the Constitution rules that:

> The free and unfalsified expression of the popular will as an expression of popular sovereignty shall be guaranteed by all State officers, who shall be

obliged to ensure such under all circumstances. Criminal sanctions for violations of this provision shall be specified by law.

The final question that should be asked in this section is whether the proposal discussed is consistent with contemporary theories that justify free speech as necessary for safeguarding and promoting democratic values that are of the outmost importance. I will focus first on Meiklejohn's theory, which, although it was developed in the forties and the fifties, continues to inspire current discussions with its simplicity and comprehensiveness. For Meiklejohn, freedom of speech "springs from the necessities of the program of self-government" (1960, 27). People are self-governed, not when they are subordinate to a ruling elite, but when they publicly deliberate on equal terms with the view of taking binding decisions for all concerning the common affairs of their community. However, their decisions run the danger of being mistaken and invalid if they are not allowed to listen to all the views and facts pertaining to the case under consideration. Thus, discussions should not be conducted for their own sake or for the self-gratification of those taking an active part in them. "The point of ultimate interest" in his theory "is not the words of the speakers, but the minds of the hearers. . . . The voters . . . must be made as wise as possible" (p. 26). In his view, the aim of the First Amendment is to secure that citizens should not be deprived of material that is essential for reaching informed political decisions, among which voting decisions stand out. In practical terms, this means that there are no ideas we should be afraid of and, thus, political speech in general should enjoy constitutional protection.

When it comes to exceptions, Meiklejohn withdraws protection from libel, slander and incitement to crime, but he remains silent about mendacious political speech. However, there are two reasons which make us surmise that he would not oppose its regulation. First, it is difficult to see how political fake news that is believed makes voters "as wise as possible." Rather, as previously stated, it leads them to decisions they would not have made if they knew the truth. It makes them feel foolish and confused and this is not something we can condone, since, in the final analysis, it undermines self-government. Second, he is wary of the increase in a person's powers of manipulation, which is "the destruction of self-government" (p. 13). Lying and deception are the par excellence acts of manipulation of human beings, and they ipso facto constitute threats to self-government.

In contrast to Meiklejohn, more recent theorists, such as Robert C. Post (2011, 2012), put forward the view that not self-government but "the free formation of public opinion . . . is the sine qua non of democracy" (2012, 15). This implies that "all persons within public discourse should be equally free to say or not say what they chose" (p. 22). By placing emphasis on the interests of the speakers and not of the listeners, Post insists that even citizens "who disagree with official versions of factual truth" should not be deprived of the opportunity to influence the formation of public opinion (p. 29). He makes it absolutely clear that no content-based restrictions of misleading speech are allowed. Instead "the rule of caveat emptor applies," meaning that the body politic should be responsible for what it believes or not (p. 23).

One can wonder what value public opinion that has been formed through lies and misinformation has for democracy. Alternatively, one could argue that democracy is not government by public opinion, which could be taken perfectly seriously in authoritarian regimes, but rule by the people. However, I will not pursue these lines of criticism. I think that Post's account encapsulates certain free speech theory concerns that militate against the regulation of mendacious political speech. I will turn to these concerns in the last section of this essay.

5. Possible objections

It could be argued that the constitutional protection of mendacious political speech as defined here is necessary "to prevent the chilling of truthful expression" (Norton, 2013, 169). Some authors insist that here we are caught in the horns of an unavoidable dilemma:

> Either we protect consciously false expression in the political arena—expression that will often mislead its recipients and threaten to seriously distort performance of the democratic process—or we invite widespread chilling of potentially valuable expression and place a dangerous weapon in the hands of those in power.
>
> (Redish, 2013, 170)

Is that so? It should be made clear that my account does not rule out cases of political fake news that *should* enjoy constitutional protection. I realise that it is not an easy task to enumerate the most significant ones in a statute, but the *morally* justifiable exceptions I mentioned in the second section may offer some guidance to the legislator. Having said that, I cannot imagine how the regulation proposed will have a chilling effect on the production and diffusion of proper political news during the election period. It is already known that news editors should vet their stories, double-check their sources, seek an independent confirmation and be ready to admit honest mistakes. They should not also present a piece of news whose epistemic status they are uncertain about as a fact. Moreover, those involved in political satire should inform their audience through the usual conventions that what they say should not be taken at face value. Staying on the side of caution is an asset in the news industry. It seems to me that the regulation proposed would encourage responsibility and professionalism and discourage liars, foreign and domestic conspirators and manipulators.[19]

Someone might claim that the public would be deprived of non-epistemically valuable speech. As great novels attest, speech can be valued for many more things apart from its correspondence with the external world as we know it. Thus, it may not come as a surprise that some people might express their admiration for (revealed) fake political news, praising its inventiveness and audacity. Yet should this admiration be given such priority to the extent of allowing the "noble" art of lying and deception to compromise the integrity of the electoral process?

Another argument against the regulation of mendacious political speech comes from the "counter-speech doctrine," namely the idea that it suffices to show through more speech what is wrong with particular tokens of speech without resorting to their suppression. As Justice Brandeis said in an often-quoted milestone opinion:

> *If there be time to expose through discussion* the falsehood and fallacies, to avert the evil by the processes of education, the remedy to be applied is more speech, not enforced silence. *Only an emergency can justify repression.* Such must be the rule if authority is to be reconciled with freedom [Emphasis mine].[20]

How does this apply to the case at hand? First, we should pay attention to the qualification Brandeis himself incorporated in his opinion. Severe time limitations may impede the exposure of lies through a prolonged discussion. If the fake news of the first example reaches the electorate just three hours before the opening of the polling stations, the remedy is immediate legal action not an exchange of views. An electoral result that is due to a certain extent to the spread of misinformation cannot change. Further, the term "more speech" seems misleading in the case of fake political news. To be accurate, what is often needed to disprove fake news is not "more speech" in general but a special kind of evidence citizens are unable to procure through their own means. In the second example, only the Sin City Police Department or the District Attorney's Office can declare after a thorough investigation that this incident never occurred. The Sin City electoral fraud can be contrasted with other cases where one does not need special evidence to challenge views she considers fallacious. For instance, if one disagrees with the view that God is perfectly good, she could argue that this seems inconsistent with the demise of so many young and innocent persons.

However, more needs to be said here. Up to now, I made the assumption that the citizens are "eternally vigilant" in exposing political fake news. Unfortunately, this is not the case. The electorate at large does not think like knowledgeable members of an academic philosophy seminar who are bombarding every speaker with scores of challenging questions. Many people tend to unquestionably believe fake political news at least for two reasons. First, because of a psychological phenomenon called *positive confirmation bias* which refers to our compelling and "natural tendency . . . to look for evidence that is directly supportive of hypotheses we favor" (Nickerson, 1998, 211). This means that some of us tend to blindly believe the fake news that is consistent with our political profile and that we choose to visit sites that "do not disturb our pre-existing view of the world" (Sunstein, 2001, 57). To put it in a more prosaic manner, the reaction expected from many political subjects concerning the two Sin City examples is more likely to be "Now do you believe me!?" rather than "This cannot be true." There is also empirical evidence that people with strong partisan commitments, who also claim that they are well versed in politics, are not moved by corrections of relevant false statements they consider to be true. In their case, these corrections might "fortify their original beliefs" (Sunstein, 2021, 78–81).

Second, a fake news story that is repeated without being exposed is easier to pass along as reliable news (Brown, 2018, 203). This might have serious implications. As a researcher put it,

> sufficiently prolonged or repeated exposure to fake news about a person might result in the formation of implicit bias against her, in the same way in which, plausibly, implicit biases against women or minorities arise, at least in part, from the negative portrayal in explicitly labelled fictions.
>
> (Levy, 2017, 31)

It is not my intention with this discussion to dismiss the general view that falsehoods can be remedied with more speech—sometimes they can—and to deny that the public should have some training in identifying fake news. My point is that all these interventions do not suffice when we have to deal with fake political news published during the election period. Applying the caveat emptor rule here betrays an indifference to the facts of the case.

The final concern draws on the old liberal fear that governments, even those democratically elected, could, if they are given the opportunity, abuse their powers to subject individuals under their rule. Regulation of mendacious political speech allows "the government's power to impose its own version of the truth upon the public" (Norton, 2012, 170–171, 2015). To this, it can be replied that the imposition of the government's truth, provided that this government is accountable to the people and willing to acknowledge its fallibility, is in many cases preferable to a stance of indifference towards the truth. For example, one cannot but praise democratic governments for vaccinating their citizens with a small number of independently approved vaccines instead of letting them buy any kind of medicine against COVID-19 they could find on the Internet. The problem lies elsewhere. A government may be a source of political fake news, and it cannot be the judge of its own case. A plausible solution to this problem, apart from the existence of an independent judiciary, is the establishment of a non-partisan authority, which will possess the know-how and the resources to detect fake news in a relatively short time and trace its source of origin. Its powers would include a warrant to investigate government-controlled services, although, of course, the enormous complexity of the existing technologies and the frequent involvement of foreign governments in the diffusion of fake news would make its job less easy.

6. Conclusions

Although there seems to be a prima facie case in favour of the legal regulation of political fake news during the election period, there is no doubt we are still at the beginning. Meticulous empirical research should be conducted to corroborate or dispel certain assumptions made here concerning the impact of political fake news on voting decisions. Further, the time-honoured hostility to content-based restrictions on political speech has produced additional objections that have to be discussed thoroughly. It has been suggested, for instance, that there should be only

Pre-election period and free speech theory 119

code-based interventions or that we should leave regulation to the market in the hope of making the production of fake news a less lucrative business (Verstraete et al., 2022). Other scholars put a very high premium on educating schoolchildren and on pushing big social media companies to come to a mutually binding agreement to protect users from deception and manipulation (Sorabji, 2021, chap. 3). Moreover, there are many legal issues such as those concerning the criminal and civil liability of the purveyors of fake news or the effectiveness of the proposed sanctions that lie beyond my expertise. Finally, yet importantly, one should deal with influential theoretical approaches that have more sympathy and tolerance for lying and deception in politics than mainstream moral philosophy (Jay, 2010). There is no royal road to the countering of political fake news, but I am convinced that the existing road, despite all its hurdles and the delays expected, is a road worth trying.[21]

Notes

1 In this section, I draw heavily on an earlier work of mine on the meaning and the value of lying and deception (Peonidis, 1994). For recent relevant general accounts, see Carson (2010), Saul (2012) and Stokke (2018).
2 Cf. Levy (2017, 20), Rini (2017, E45), Katsirea (2018, 186) and Fallis and Mathiesen (2019, 8). From this description, it follows that not any online fabricated story or report counts as fake news. For instance, a false report blaming the U.S. government for the 9/11 attacks that is published on a website conspicuously promoting conspiracy theories or hate speech against the government cannot be classified as fake news. Context is always relevant.
3 It should be noted that according to most general accounts of lying, it suffices for the liar to *believe* that her statement is false. Helen is lying to her teacher when she explains that she is late for class because of the sudden illness of her grandmother, on condition that she believes that this excuse is false, even if unbeknownst to her the grandmother has fallen sick. However, the publication of a news story which the author believes to be false while it is in fact true, although technically a lie, cannot be conceived as fake news. In addition, this account leaves out "negligent falsehood" that is "a falsehood propagated *without sufficient attention* to ascertaining the truth of the matter" (Saul, 2018, 247). This omission does not imply that news reports described as negligent falsehoods are harmless, but it is pertinent to start with the most paradigmatic and unquestionable cases of fake news.
4 For Frankfurt (2005, 61), the bullshitter, that is a person who takes great pains to make an impression, "does not reject the authority of the truth, as the liar does, and oppose himself to it. He pays no attention to it at all." See also Fallis and Mathiesen (2019, 6–7).
5 As Killmister (2013, 529) has argued "false beliefs affect autonomy by compromising the competency to comprehend a potential action, both in terms of what the action is, and what will follow from that action." However, even false beliefs not resulting in action are unwelcome by the autonomous agent, since, in contrast to a person who is credulous or never examines the nature of her beliefs, she wants to have true and justified beliefs to the extent that this is possible. This holds a fortiori for false beliefs that derive from the machinations of a third party who is tampering with her belief-formation procedures.
6 For a book-length proposal for regulating the Internet that aims at balancing between social responsibility and respect for freedom of speech, see Cohen–Almagor (2015).
7 A legal scholar, Joshua S. Sellers (2018, 145), without focusing on political fake news per se, argued that there are constitutional grounds for the proscription of lying in

campaigns and elections "(1) when foreign nationals engage in intentionally false speech that includes express advocacy, (2) when intentionally false speech is used to undermine election administration, and (3) when a campaign or outside political group intentionally falsifies a mandatory disclosure filing." The first two cases are covered by my own account, if false speech is presented as genuine news, but I am inclined to regulate many more cases of political lying in campaigns and elections than Sellers allows. For a summary account of the legal issues surrounding the publication of fake news in general in the United States, see Klein and Wueller (2017), and for a European perspective, see Katsirea (2018). Cf. also the French Law n° 2018–1202 against the manipulation of information, which among other things imposes an obligation on digital platforms to reveal many details about the sponsored content they host in election periods and allows courts to halt the circulation of fake news immediately.

8   Free speech theory as understood here is not only of American or legal interest. It offers valuable insights into theoretical discussions concerning almost any aspect of freedom of speech and expression.
9   "When people feel uncertain, they crave for information. This happens in situations such as disasters or elections. . . . Uncertain situations also get in the way of verifications, especially when alternative information sources are not immediately available" (Tandoc, 2021, 43).
10 According to Vosoughi et al. (2018, 1148), "False political news [on Twitter from 2006 to 2017] traveled deeper and more broadly, reached more people and was more viral than any other category of false information. False political news also diffused deeper, more quickly and reached more than 20,000 people nearly three times faster than all other types of false news reached 10,000 people."
11 On the methods journalists use to verify online information and the challenges they face, see Lecheler et al. (2019).
12 In her words "such regulations advance free speech values in ways analogous to time, place and manner restrictions that aim to ensure that speakers can be heard and are not drowned out by competitors or hostile audience members" (2014, 126).
13 On the contrary, the U.S. Supreme Court in *United States v. Alvarez* 567 U.S. (2012) struck down a 2005 Federal Act penalizing insincere claims that one has been "awarded a medal, decoration, or badge for service in the Armed Forces of the United States." The Justices in dissent (Alito, Thomas and Scalia) argued that the only reason for not suppressing false speech is the avoidance of the chilling effect it might have on true speech, something irrelevant in the case decided.
14 "That speech is used as a tool for political ends does not automatically bring it under the protective mantle of the Constitution. For the use of the known lie as a tool is at once at odds with the premises of democratic government and with the orderly manner in which economic, social, or political change is to be effected." *Garrison v. Louisiana*, 379 U.S. 64, 75 (1964).
15 "It is disheartening to think that the Constitution contains within it a right to lie in political campaigns" (Hasen, 2013, 76).
16 "There is an inherent and obvious contradiction in extending First Amendment protection to political deception in the name of freedom. It is a contradiction so glaring that it is almost offensive that it is not acknowledged in the legal arguments from the last three decades in particular" (Spicer, 2018, 48).
17 "[The Court's] ultimate ruling was wrong, even preposterous" (Sunstein, 2021, 42).
18 *Ex parte Yarbrough*, 110 U. S. 651, 657–58 (1884) quoted in *Burroughs and Cannon v. United States*, 290 U. S. 534, 546 (1934). I understand that there is a controversy in the United States as to whether the Congress or State governments are responsible for conducting elections, but this does not affect my argument. The regulatory proposal discussed here does not specify which government in a federal system will enact the relevant legislation.

19 I admit that my argument here is theoretical and it might be disproved by the way this regulation could work in practice.
20 *Whitney v. California* 274 U.S. 357, 376 (1927).
21 I would like to thank Migle Laukyte, Oscar Pérez de la Fuente and Alexander Tsesis for valuable comments and suggestions.

References

Ball, B. 2021. "Defeating Fake News: On Journalism, Knowledge and Democracy." *Moral Philosophy and Politics* 8: 5–26.

Blitz, M. J. 2018. "Lies, Line Drawing, and (Deep) Fake News." *Oklahoma Law Review* 71: 59–116.

Brown, É. 2018. "Propaganda, Misinformation, and the Epistemic Value of Democracy." *Critical Review* 30: 194–218.

Carson, T. L. 2010. *Lying and Deception: Theory and Practice*. Oxford: Oxford University Press.

Coady, C. A. J. 2008. *Messy Morality: The Challenges of Politics*. Oxford: Clarendon Press.

Cohen-Almagor, R. 2015. *Confronting the Internet's Dark Side: Moral and Social Responsibility on the Free Highway*. Cambridge: Cambridge University Press.

Fallis, D. and Mathiesen, K. 2019. "Fake News Is Counterfeit News." *Inquiry*. https://doi.org/10.1080/0020174X.2019.1688179.

Frankfurt, H. G. 2005. *On Bullshit*. Princeton: Princeton University Press.

Gelfert, A. 2018. "Fake News: A Definition." *Informal Logic* 38: 84–117.

Hasen, R. L. 2013. "A Constitutional Right to Lie in Campaigns and Elections." *Montana Law Review* 74: 53–77.

Jay, M. 2010. *The Virtues of Mendacity: Lying in Politics*. Charlottesville: University of Virginia Press.

Kant, I. 1996. "On the Supposed Right to Lie from Philanthropy (1797)." In M. J. Gregor (ed. and trans.). *Practical Philosophy*. Cambridge: Cambridge University Press.

Katsirea, I. 2018. "'Fake News': Reconsidering the Value of Untruthful Expression in the Face of Regulatory Uncertainty." *Journal of Media Law* 10: 159–188.

Killmister, S. 2013. "Autonomy and False Beliefs." *Philosophical Studies* 164: 513–531.

Klein, D. O. and Wueller, J. R. 2017. "Fake News: A Legal Perspective." *Journal of Internet Law* 20: 5–13.

Lecheler, S. et al. 2019. "The Use and Verification of Online Sources in the News Production Process." In J. E. Katz and K. K. Mays (eds.). *Journalism and Truth in an Age of Social Media*. New York: Oxford University Press.

Levy, N. 2017. "The Bad News About Fake News." *Social Epistemology Review and Reply Collective* 6: 20–36.

Meiklejohn, A. 1960. *Political Freedom: The Constitutional Powers of the People*. New York: Harper and Brothers.

Nickerson, R. S. 1998. "Confirmation Bias: A Ubiquitous Phenomenon in Many Guises." *Review of General Psychology* 2: 175–220.

Norton, H. 2012. "Lies and the Constitution." *The Supreme Court Law Review* 2012: 61–201.

Norton, H. 2015. "The Government's Lies and the Constitution." *Indiana Law Journal* 91: 173–120.

Peonidis, F. 1994. *Pseudologia kai Ethike [Lying and Morality]*. Thessaloniki: Vanias.
Post, R. C. 2011. "Participatory Democracy and Free Speech." *Virginia Law Review* 97: 477–489.
Post, R. C. 2012. *Democracy, Expertise, Academic Freedom: A First Amendment Jurisprudence for the Modern State*. New Haven and London: Yale University Press.
Redish, M. H. 2013. *The Adversary First Amendment: Free Expression and the Foundations of American Democracy*. Stanford: Stanford Law Books.
Rini, R. 2017. "Fake News and Partisan Epistemology." *Kennedy Institute of Ethics Journal* 27: E43–E64.
Saul, J. M. 2012. *Lying, Misleading, and What Is Said: An Exploration in Philosophy of Language and Ethics*. Oxford: Oxford University Press.
Saul, J. M. 2018. "Negligent Falsehood, White Ignorance, and False News." In E. Michaelson and A. Stokke (eds.). *Lying: Language, Knowledge, Ethics and Politics*. Oxford: Oxford University Press.
Sellers, J. S. 2018. "Legislating Against Lying in Campaigns and Elections." *Oklahoma Law Review* 71: 141–165.
Shiffrin, S. V. 2014. *Speech Matters: On Lying, Morality and the Law*. Princeton and Oxford: Princeton University Press.
Sorabji, R. 2021. *Freedom of Speech and Expression: Its History, Its Value, Its Good Use, and Its Misuse*. Oxford: Oxford University Press.
Spicer, R. N. 2018. *Free Speech and False Speech: Political Deception and Its Legal Limits (Or Lack Thereof)*. Cham: Palgrave Macmillan.
Stokke, A. 2018. *Lying and Insincerity*. Oxford: Oxford University Press.
Sunstein, C. 2001. *Republic.com*. Princeton: Princeton University Press.
Sunstein, C. 2021. *Liars: Falsehoods and Free Speech in an Age of Deception*. Oxford: Oxford University Press.
Tandoc Jr., E. C. 2021. "Tools of Disinformation: How Fake News Gets to Deceive." In S. Jayakumar et al. (eds.). *Disinformation and Fake News*. Singapore: Palgrave Macmillan.
Verstraete, M. et al. 2022. "Identifying and Countering Fake News." *Hastings Law Journal* 73: 821–859.
Vosoughi, S. et al. 2018. "The Spread of True and False News Online." *Science* 359: 1146–1151.

7 Misinformation and hate speech

When bad becomes even worse

Gustavo Ferreira Santos

1. Introduction

On 5 August 2012, 40-year-old Wade Michael Page stormed a Sikh temple in Oak Creek, Wisconsin, United States, killing seven people and then committing suicide. On 27 October 2018, 46-year-old Robert Gregory Bowersat broke into Tree of Life—or L'Simcha Congregation in Pittsburgh, Pennsylvania, United States, and shot those present, leaving 11 dead and six others wounded. On 15 March 2019, Brenton Tarrant, a 28-year-old Australian, entered the Al Noor Mosque and Linwood Islamic Center in the city of Christchurch, New Zealand, and killed at least 51 people, injuring 49 others.

What is common in these violent incidents? All were preceded by the radicalisation of their perpetrators in hate and intolerance forums on the Internet. These are spaces in which radical speeches against women, blacks, homosexuals, Jews, immigrants, Muslims and other social groups proliferate. The Unite the Right demonstrations were combined in these kinds of forums, which brought together more extremist sectors of the American Right in Charlottesville, Virginia, in 2017.

The Internet information flow, and especially social networks, is full of fake news, hate messages, conspiracy theories and junk science. There is a synergy between campaigns that spread falsehoods in politics and aggressive speeches against minorities. The agents are generally the same. There are countless cases in which political groups use speeches with false information or hate speech to attack their opponents.

However, these speeches are not the only instruments that extremist groups use to resist governments or that refute an imaginary "system." They have become auxiliary instruments in the daily political dispute. They have also become tools for governments themselves to garner support. Hungary under Viktor Orbán is an example of this. The government has already been accused of sponsoring campaigns with false content, saying that the European Commission supported illegal immigration (BBC, 2019), and campaigns promoting hatred against refugees, migrants, and more recently against non-governmental organisations (Article 19, 2018). Immigrants and refugees are the target of fake news, hate speech is used against them and they become victims of violence, including official violence, as

DOI: 10.4324/9781003274476-10

shown in the Human Rights Watch NGO's denunciation of Hungary's treatment of migrants at its borders (HRW, 2016).

The pandemic has deepened the problems of misinformation and hate speech worldwide with a set of falsehoods about death tolls or the vaccine, as well as aggressive speech against China and the Chinese people. And this hatred has overflowed from the Internet and materialised into attacks, making for a remarkable increase in the number of attacks on Asians in the United States (BBC, 2021).

Both combatting "hate speech" and countering "misinformation" face the challenge of defining these threats. Political posturing often tends to define hate speech or misinformation as the opponent's speech, unpleasant speech, inconvenient speech or undesired information. Regarding misinformation, it is vital to understand who spreads false information on the Internet, who consumes this information, and the reasons for this in order to plan public policies in response.

In fact, it is important to act against these threats. Although individuals enjoy the freedom of speech, they are accountable for any damage their words cause to others or to society. We are responsible for a set of personal expressions. The Constitution is complex and involves the protection of different rights and different interests. Freedom of expression coexists in the constitutional system with other norms. Considering it as unlimited would mean restricting other constitutional norms such as those which protect privacy.

If the coexistence between different rights and interests in the constitutional context was already a challenge before, the issues have become even more complex in the digital environment. We have yet to adapt our view of fundamental rights and democracy to this new forum with its strengths and weaknesses.

It is hard to precisely combat such threats because we must give freedom of expression as much protection as possible. The fight against threats to democracy contains additional risks in itself. Omission can turn the threat into something that cannot be stopped. A mistake can lead to imbalance and legitimise a super censorship entity. In both cases, the result may be the undermining of constitutional democracy.[1]

In this chapter, we highlight the problems of misinformation and hate speech, pointing out the necessity of specific public policies for their restraint, and discuss the particularities of combatting such harmful speeches on the Internet. The vision that is guiding this work involves a commitment to the idea of constitutional democracy. Therefore, we reflect on issues concerning the legitimacy of political power, the promotion of pluralism and the protection of basic rights.

2. What is "misinformation"?

The term "fake news" is the most commonly used in this debate about misinformation, especially in political discussions and media coverage. It was so extensively used in the aftermath of the 2016 U.S. presidential election that it was chosen as the word of the year by the Collins Dictionary in 2017. In the past few years, a significant part of the debate about the crisis of democracy has used the expression to refer to campaigns that spread false or inaccurate information as a political strategy. It has been used in the more general debate in society, as well as in academic texts that address the topic.

However, it does not have the scope or precision that the discussion requires or at least the theoretical discussion. First, it is not a term that captures the phenomenon as a whole. The news used to misinform is not necessarily false. Much information labelled as fake news is true information that is used in erroneous contexts, such as old news. However, populist political leaders misrepresent its use when they use the expression to target legitimate media outlets and opponents who criticise them. For example, it has been common to see Trump or Bolsonaro calling news that they dislike as "fake news" (Sullivan, 2020; Santana, 2020).

Another term that has populated the debates about manipulations in information in recent years is "post-truth." Although their uses are not intertwined, "fake news" and "post-truth" revolve around the same phenomena. "Post-truth" emphasises a loss of importance of facts, which come to be regarded as disputable, with "alternative facts" existing that would coincide with the beliefs of certain political groups (MacIntyre, 2018).

Claire Wandler and Hossein Derakhshan present a typology on the basis of the harm and falseness criteria that divides the phenomenon into three types of information disorder: (i) "Dis-information," which is false information deliberately created to target a person, a social group, an organisation or a country; (ii) "Misinformation," which is false information that was not created with the intent to cause harm and (iii) "Mal-information," which is reality-based information used to cause harm to a person, an organisation or a country. But this is not a distinction that is reflected in dictionaries.

Some people define "fake news" as an information disorder distinct from misinformation and disinformation, which is the case in Lazer et al. (2018). For them, "fake news overlaps with other information disorders, such as misinformation (false or misleading information) and disinformation (false information that is purposely spread to deceive people)." They have defined fake news as "fabricated information which mimics news media content in form, but not in organisational process or intent." As much as this appearance of legitimate news is adopted by many outlets that carry content used in disinformation campaigns, we prefer to abandon the use of the term due to the disadvantages and inaccuracies we have already reported.

If we want to use only a single term to define these information disorders, we think that the choice should be "misinformation." In consulting the Collins, Marian-Webster, and Cambridge dictionaries, we find that the expression "misinformation" has a broader meaning than "disinformation" because the latter refers to the intention to deceive. Therefore, we use the term misinformation in a wide sense herein, encompassing the aforementioned forms of information disorder. When specifically referring to false information intentionally used to deceive people, we will use "disinformation."

3. What is "hate speech"?

There is an initial difficulty in defining "hate speech." Primarily, because "hate" is a feeling, a subjective state. Those who deliver hate speech do not necessarily feel hatred. Many times the choice for this instrument is simply the choice for a political weapon. The concept of "hate speech" must detach itself from this feeling and confine itself to certain objective elements that are on the surface of the discourse.

"Hate speech" is obviously a kind of speech. Speech is a human manifestation that, first and foremost, should be protected in every constitutional democracy. Protecting freedom of speech is protecting freedom of thought itself. Freedom of speech is one of the foundations for the well-functioning of a democracy. However, it is precisely the need to protect democracy that gives us reasons—rooted in history—to consider expression that encourages hatred as dangerous.

A helpful starting point for the challenge of defining hate speech is international law. Article 20 of the International Covenant on Civil and Political Rights states that "any advocacy of national, racial or religious hatred that constitutes incitement to discrimination, hostility or violence shall be prohibited by law." It is a starting point because there are other reasons that justify protection against hate speech, such as gender and sexual orientation. In this definition of the Covenant, the characteristic of "incitement to discrimination, hostility or violence" is highlighted. It is a discourse that aims to drive an action.

German criminal law (1998) defines that a person commits a crime and is liable to punishment if they

> incite hatred against a national, racial, religious group or a group defined by their ethnic origin, against sections of the population or individuals on account of their belonging to one of the aforementioned groups or sections of the population, or calls for violent or arbitrary measures against them or violates the human dignity of others by insulting, maliciously maligning or defaming one of the aforementioned groups, sections of the population or individuals on account of their belonging to one of the aforementioned groups or sections of the population.

However, it is important to note that such acts are only punishable when they are done "in a manner which is suitable for causing a disturbance of the public peace."

In the case of hate speech, on the one side, there is tension between individual autonomy and the consequent freedom to express what the individual believes, and on the other side, human dignity. This kind of discourse stigmatises and discriminates specific social groups and tends to induce violence. Speech has an impact on each person who displays the characteristics that identify the group.

Jeremy Waldron (2012) accurately summarises the messages that hate speech passes on. To those against whom the speech is directed, it says:

> Don't be fooled into thinking you are welcome here. The society around you may seem hospitable and non-discriminatory, but the truth is that you are not wanted, and you and your families will be shunned, excluded, beaten, and driven out, whenever we can get away with it. We may have to keep a low profile right now. But don't get too comfortable. Remember what has happened to you and your kind in the past. Be afraid.

Misinformation and hate speech 127

For those whom the hate speech wants to convince, on the other hand, it says:

> We know some of you agree that these people are not wanted here. We know that some of you feel that they are dirty (or dangerous or criminal or terrorist). Know now that you are not alone. Whatever the government says, there are enough of us around to make sure these people are not welcome. There are enough of us around to draw attention to what these people are really like. Talk to your neighbors, talk to your customers. And above all, don't let any more of them in.

Taking all of these points into account, we can summarise by understanding that hate speech is a speech against a group of people which depreciates the dignity of that group, taking it as inferior to others and inciting other individuals to discriminate against them, with the group being identified as "different" because it has certain characteristics that distinguish it from the standard that constitutes the audience that the discourse is trying to incite.

4. Why are public policies against misinformation and hate speech essential?

We live in a period of democratic decline, which is explained by different reasons, including the increasing prevalence of misinformation and hate speech in recent years. Misinformation campaigns and hate speech lead to radicalisation of the political debate. They contribute to creating an ambience of distrust between groups, which undermines the capacity to dialogue and to consider different opinions. Moreover, these speeches can lead to more severe hostilities and, as a result, to actual acts of physical violence against members of the groups they target.

The world has a longer experience in identifying and countering hate speech. Nevertheless, there is a wide range of ways in which national legal systems address hate speech. Everyone knows the contrast between the United States' and Germany's approaches to the problem, real antagonists with greater or lesser restrictions on this type of discourse: "the American legal system prohibits hate speech as late as possible; only when an imminent danger of illegal acts exist. German jurisprudence cracks down on hate speech as early as possible" (Brugger, 2002).

Winfried Brugger builds a fictional protest poster in order "to dramatize the differences between the American and German approaches to hate speech." He considers decisions by the Supreme Court of the United States and the German Federal Constitutional Court that have examined speech restrictions and concluded in opposite directions. Carrying the same poster in Berlin or Washington would result in different consequences. In the first scenario, it would be a crime. In the second, the demonstrator would be exercising his freedom of speech. Let's take a look at the poster:

> Wake up, you tired masses, I have four messages that you better listen to, understand, and share! First, our President is a pig! I have painted two pictures

128 *Gustavo Ferreira Santos*

to demonstrate my point. Here is one showing our clearly recognizable President as a pig engaged in sexual conduct with another pig in a judge's robe, and here is another, showing our President having a sexual encounter with his mother in an outhouse. Second, all our soldiers are murderers. Third, the Holocaust never happened. Fourth, African Americans use the slavery lie to extort money from the American government in the same way Jews use the Holocaust lie to extort money from Germany. Something should be done about this!

The U.S. first amendment doctrine provides broad, almost absolute, protection for freedom of speech and sets the United States as a unique case in the world (Beausoleil, 2019). It is a safe way to protect speech since it shields it regardless of scrutiny over its contents. However, it is illusory, because we cannot consider freedom of speech insulated from other rights and interests that the constitution and international human rights treaties entrench. In order to safeguard individual speech, do we have to entrench the rights to insult, harass or discriminate against other people? Should the defence of the right to freely express opinions be guaranteed at the expense of people's dignity? We don't believe this is a reasonable choice. The bills of rights in constitutions are complex, full of diverse rights and aimed at protecting a wide range of interests. Interpretative practices that go beyond designing the protection of a specific right usually weaken other rights.

There are many voices in the U.S. constitutional debate calling for a change in understanding and an opening for the punishment of hate speech. For example, Lauren E. Beausoleil (2019) advocates a closer approximation of treating the first amendment doctrine in the United States to the treatment of hate speech question in other countries "so that it can properly combat, control, and contemplate the power of hate speech transmitted through social media communications." I also point out the critical essay by Jeremy Waldron (2012), who highlights the damage that hate speech causes not only to the dignity of the group but also to the dignity of each individual who is part of the group. He asserts that

> what hate speech legislation stands for is the dignity of equal citizenship (for all members of all groups), and it does what it can to put a stop to group defamation when group defamation (of the members of a particular group) threatens to undermine that status for a whole class of citizens.

As we have already mentioned, human rights treaties in international law embrace freedom of speech but emphasise that hate speech is not protected. The atmosphere in the post-World War II world included an awareness that speech could be dangerous. The first international human rights treaty after World War II, the 1965 International Convention on the Elimination of all Forms of Racial Discrimination, included a commitment by states parties to

> declare an offence punishable by law of all dissemination of ideas based on racial superiority or hatred, incitement to racial discrimination, as well as all acts of violence or incitement to such acts against any race or group of

persons of another colour or ethnic origin, and also the provision of any assistance to racist activities, including the financing thereof.

Moreover, it made commitments to "declare illegal and prohibit organizations, and also organized and all other propaganda activities, which promote and incite racial discrimination, and shall recognize participation in such organizations or activities as an offence punishable by law." In the same vein, the 1966 International Covenant on Civil and Political Rights prohibited "advocacy of national, racial or religious hatred that constitutes incitement to discrimination, hostility or violence shall be prohibited by law."

Maintaining public policies to combat hate speech is imperative because it provides a balance in the public space, giving groups targeted by such speech more suitable conditions to present themselves in the debate, and guarantees individuals from this group against physical and psychological violence. It is a way to seek to have a healthier democratic debate less burdensome for minority groups.

5. How the Internet has amplified misinformation and hate speech

Lying and hate speech already existed and played a role in politics before the emergence of the Internet. Rumour has always played an important role in political debate. These discourses have always been used as tools in political campaigns. In her famous essay on Truth and Politics, Hannah Arendt (2006) stated that "no one has ever doubted that truth and politics are on rather bad terms with each other, and no one, as far as I know, has ever countered."

The emergence of the Internet has added another dimension to such phenomena. In fact, it is important to point out that the most worrisome dimension of the problem came after almost two decades of Internet use. The Internet has obvious positive aspects. In particular, it provides faster communication and greater access to information. Unlike traditional broadcasting media, the Internet turns every person into a broadcaster. But it has also gradually become a place of radicalisation and polarisation. Some of these positive characteristics have also become a source of negatives. Individuals who had little audience for their speeches gathered a large following, and attacks began to be made instantaneously, with difficulty for contention and punishment. Another feature of the Internet that enables creation of hate and disinformation networks is the possibility of anonymity. Extremist militants hide their identities and feel free to express their hatred for specific social groups and spread lies.

Michał Bilewicz and Wiktor Soral have suggested that with the changes to the online digital environment the "default emotional responses to other people, such as empathy are replaced by intergroup contempt—an emotion fundamental to derogatory behaviors," and this contempt for the other "might be both a motivator, and a consequence of derogatory language."

There is overexposure to prejudiced speech in the online digital environment, which also leaves people more free to express their prejudices (Bilewicz and Soral, 2020). Conversely, social media have favoured polarisation and radicalisation of the debate. People were overexposed to political discourses with that they already agreed and the mutual feeding of convictions favoured the most radical forms of discourses against "the other," "the different."

The harm caused by these forms of discourse is evident. The instrumental use of lies and the radicalisation of the speech undermine democracy. The exposure to hate speech impacts the self-esteem of minority group members. There is an erosion of basic conditions for collective coexistence, which is fundamental for a well-functioning democracy (Bilewicz and Soral, 2020).

A number of studies have sought answers about what are the main motivations for sharing false content. This is still a question that requires extensive study. Inquiring about the reasons can lead to important insights for designing strategies to overcome the problem.

Many of these Internet attacks on minorities occur with the aid of bots. However, this sometimes leads to a loss of focus in the search for those responsible. Bots play an active role in starting disinformation campaigns. Research has shown that a strategy often used by bots is to mention influential users in tweets that use low-credibility content. Bots use this targeting strategy repetitively, and the message goes viral when shared by the influencer (Shao et al., 2018). But these campaigns would not have the impact they do if it were not for the widespread support of human users.

We cannot be under the illusion that the adherence to these disinformation and hate networks only derives from people's ignorance. Recent research has relativised the role of ignorance in adherence to misinformation campaigns. Osmundsen et al. (2021) mapped psychological profiles of over 2,300 American Twitter users linked to behavioural sharing data and sentiment analysis of over 500,000 news headlines and concluded that ignorance was not the main factor: "when examining direct measures of ignorance—cognitive reflection, political knowledge, and political digital media literacy—we did not find that fake news sharing reflected an inability to discern whether the information is true or false."

In the same direction in a focus group study with middle-class people in India, Shakuntala Banaji and Ram Bhat (2019) concluded that

> in a majority of instances, misinformation and disinformation which contributes to the formation of mobs that engage in lynching and other discriminatory violence appears to be largely spread for reasons of prejudice and ideology rather than out of ignorance or digital illiteracy.

The behaviour of the political leaderships counts a lot in the adoption or not by their followers of a harmful language. This seems quite evident on the Internet. Trump and Bolsonaro are two examples of congenital liar leaders who have fostered lies in their followers (Kellner, 2018; Biancovilli and Jurberg, 2020).

6. Social media as a locus of misinformation and hate

The Internet has changed a lot in its short history. To talk about "surfing the web" well-defined the user experience of the Internet in its first period, which was

Misinformation and hate speech 131

closer to surfing on the open sea. People accessed pages they had heard about by typing in the web address. We used to look for newspapers and magazines that we already knew, and we would get to know blogs of people and institutions that we would start to follow.

The early Internet landscape was filled with websites of institutions and companies, as well as blogs that were visited by users in different ways from different gateways. But, the advent of social media changed everything. They sucked in almost the entire Internet like a big black hole, and introduced a new and very attractive experience, and became the gateway to the internet. The numbers prove it: there are 4.6 billion Internet users in the world, while there are 4.2 billion social media users (Hootsuite, 2021). For some people, social media is synonymous with the Internet. It has allowed greater interaction, because it has reproduced relationships with people we already knew in the virtual world, and opened up a world of "friendships" to us. The Internet became more attractive with social media. However, we have become more limited by it.

In our current way of "surfing" the Internet, we are guided by algorithms and we only socialise with specific people, access specific information and receive specific advertising. An interesting account of the experience of an Iranian, Hossein Derakhshan, shows this process of Internet concentration on social media well (Kaye, 2019). He was one of the most widely read bloggers in Iran. He was subsequently arrested for criticising the government and spent from 2008 to 2014 in prison. When he got out, he found it strange that his blog no longer had an audience. The audience had migrated to social networks.

The users of social networks are the products. Along with search engines, social networks are among the most effective means of data collection. The social media "business model" leads to what Richard Deibert (2019) called "three painful truths": (1) social-media business model is based on surveillance of our personal data in order to target advertisements; (2) we allow this amazing level of surveillance voluntarily, if not fully consciously and (3) social media is far from incompatible with authoritarianism and indeed is proving to be among its most effective enablers. Social media is compatible with authoritarianism and is appearing as its enabler.

The role of algorithms in forming echo chambers, and hence radicalisation, is quite controversial. There are studies that attribute the creation of ideological bubbles to social network algorithms (Pariser, 2011), while others minimise this role, blaming it on human preferences (Cinelli et al., 2020). Of course, social media algorithms alone are not responsible for the ideological echo chambers that emerge on the networks. They exist because people have their own biased opinions and adhere to the groups they are identified with. However, algorithms make this meeting between equals easier.

In addition to open social media, messaging apps also play an important role in sharing lies and hate. WhatsApp was the main medium for spreading lies in the 2018 Brazilian elections and in spreading several rumours that resulted in mob violence in India. There is one peculiarity that differentiates it from social media: messages are encrypted. As a result, it is more difficult to identify the circulation of misinformation and furthermore to investigate and punish those responsible.

7. Hate speech and misinformation on the Internet demand an additional arsenal to combat it

There is already a worldwide perception that misinformation and hate speech on the Internet call for a response with specific tools. France and Germany are two large and well-established constitutional democracies that have chosen to enact new laws to contain the threats. In France's case, the new legislation has focused on disinformation campaigns, attempting to more thoroughly protect electoral processes and suppress foreign interference. The concern in Germany was more explicitly to target hate speech by creating a set of duties for social media companies to remove content that is considered unlawful.

The French law established that the big platforms have to be transparent in their policies, have representation in France and publish their algorithms. It created a legal injunction that will be used in cases where the information is manifestly false, is massively shared deliberately and is intended to create a disturbance of the peace or compromise the outcome of an election (France, n.d.).

The German law has established the following obligations for companies that own social networks:

> They must offer users an easily recognisable, directly accessible and permanently available procedure for reporting criminally punishable content.
>
> They must immediately take notice of content reported to them by users and examine whether that content might violate criminal law.
>
> They must take down or block access to manifestly unlawful content within 24 hours of receiving a complaint.
>
> Other criminal content must generally be taken down or blocked within 7 days of receiving a complaint. Alternatively, social networks may refer the concerning content to a "recognised institution of regulated self-governance" on the understanding that they will accept the decision of that institution. The institution must then also make its decision on whether the content is unlawful within 7 days.
>
> They must inform users of all decisions taken in response to their complaints and provide justification (Germany).

The law also created a set of duties for the social networks to report on their performance, established fines for failure to comply with their duties, required the appointment of responsible persons in Germany and imposed a duty to disclose details about the offenders to those affected by criminal offenses (Germany, 1998).

The French experience has the merit of highlighting the election period as one that deserves special attention. The time between the choice of candidates by political parties and the popular vote, in which the candidates present their proposals to society and discuss their positions with each other, is short and can have long-term consequences. Widespread misinformation in this period can misrepresent the popular manifestation of will. Disinformation must at least be addressed by the law and the authorities responsible for the integrity of the electoral process.

On the other hand, the German experience has the merit of working with definitions of illegal speech that the country has already adopted. Also praiseworthy are the duties that the law has created for the companies responsible for social networks.

Even when legislative changes are justifiable, it is preferable that no specific authorities are created for this purpose. The caution aims to avoid creating a censorship authority, or at least to avoid creating the impression in society that such an authority is being created. This does not mean that the option should be for omission. On the contrary, specific policies are needed, but they should be taken over by existing authorities that deal with areas affected by information disorder. One example is the authorities already responsible for the integrity of electoral processes, such as the electoral judicial branch that exists in some countries, like Brazil.

Government agencies committed to countering disinformation campaigns and hate speech on the Internet have to engage in close dialogue with the companies that operate social media. The mentioned laws of France and Germany have made companies more committed to action and transparency. However, we cannot justify excessive government intervention that replaces the problem of lack of action by social media with control of them by public authority. It is also not reasonable to turn social networks into savage forests, nor is it reasonable to turn them into powerful censors. The demand must be for clear policies and transparent practices to combat such problems.

Content moderation is already an activity that is in the DNA of social media companies. Offensive content has been able to be flagged or taken down since the emergence of these networks. This activity has expanded in recent years after pressure has grown on companies that were seen as lacking in the most serious cases of mass disinformation—as in several electoral processes—or of violence associated with hate speech—as in India.

Content moderation policies need to be effective, identifying organised groups and suspending accounts used for disinformation and hate campaigns, and they need to be transparent so that society knows that the interests being looked after are really collective. It is necessary to clarify that demanding an active moderation attitude against misinformation and hate speech from social networks does not correspond to authorising them to become new censors, arbitrarily choosing what can and cannot be published. Therefore, moderation policies adopted by social networks must be under the most extensive public scrutiny.

A change in the media ecosystem would be finding ways to put the traditional media back in a prominent position. They are institutions with history and the structure to take responsibility for the damage that the information they publish can inflict. They need to be islands of trust in this sea of uncertainty. Democracy requires interaction and dialogue. Public issues submitted for deliberation require to be understood as clearly as possible. The traditional media play a critical role, revealing aspects of the issues that are sometimes not very evident. But there are only advantages when citizens are informed by multiple sources. Our isolationist posture on social media excludes spaces for confronting ideas and interpretations. The result of isolation is radicalisation.

It is necessary to encourage the emergence of entities dedicated to fact-checking on social networks. This activity provides more information to social network users and serves to reduce the impact of misinformation and at least prevent people of good faith from joining disinformation campaigns. Developing habits of consulting fact-checking websites by users could even contribute to the legitimacy of more responsible and prudent media outlets, providing them with more audience.

Despite its limited reach, digital literacy is a strategy that has to be embraced to make users' relationship with the Internet healthier. Of course, it will not keep the ill-intentioned away from these disinformation and hate networks, but it will help those who share such content due to unfamiliarity with the medium. Since childhood, it is necessary to teach people to be more careful about the news they read. Therefore, digital literacy has to become part of the school curriculum among the subjects that are covered in school.

There is a surface on the Internet where a multitude interacts, and there are forums in the depths where smaller groups exchange even more hateful and resentful messages. While social networks take responsibility for moderating content, there is a tendency toward hate and intolerance networks migrating to such spaces with the emergence of new "limitless" networks and radicalised forums. It is not possible to imagine that there will be usage policies inspired by ethical standards and collaboration in these spaces. Thus, the only thing that can be done is police monitoring which allows us to anticipate the facts. This monitoring can break up criminal groups and reveal the plans of lone wolves.

8. Conclusions

The Internet has become an essential tool for the emergence of hate and intolerance networks that are responsible for the growth of hate speech and violence against minorities. In addition, the Internet has become the privileged space for the action of a neo-populist, nationalistic movement that is adaptable to the changing moods of its followers. They are not limited to the procedural consensuses of liberal democracy, and it attacks institutions when it favours them. Giuliano Da Empoli (2019) an Italian journalist who has studied the actions of those who act backstage in some of these movements, says that these new movements have adaptability comparable to the workings of algorithms.

It stands to reason that misinformation and hate speech need to be countered. However, since these are human communication phenomena that have always been documented, it would be an illusion to imagine instruments that could eradicate them. This does not eliminate the fact that it is urgent to restrict the most intentional and professionalised forms of the use of misinformation and hate speech in politics, leaving the arena in which political debate occurs a little healthier. To the extent that such threats are present, democracy itself is at stake.

There are some low- or non-intervention strategies that can be commonly adopted by non-state actors and public authorities, such as digital literacy and fact-checking. While demonstrating limited effectiveness, these strategies are auxiliary in overcoming the problems addressed herein and cannot be abandoned.

It is crucial that there is a crackdown on collectives that use these speeches as tools to mislead the public and attack minority groups. Nevertheless, the criminalisation of behaviour must be used with restraint. Broadening the scope of criminal law can lead to the very criminalisation of political activity with the use of instruments created in good faith to persecute critics and dissent. This concern recommends that criminal law enforcement measures be directed only at the most radicalised and violent groups.

It is important to take a closer look at France and Germany as countries that have changed their legislation to strengthen the tools to fight disinformation and fake news. We believe that both laws have virtues and were thought out with prudence. They can be starting points for debates in other constitutional democracies facing the same problems. In particular, it is important to monitor the execution of the two laws in order to learn from possible mistakes that practice will reveal.

Note

1 We use the term "constitutional democracy" as a formula that combines the elements of democracy, which emphasizes the popular legitimacy of power, and constitutionalism, which enshrines the power limited by a constitution. I recognize that this is a concept which encompasses very different national experiences given the variety of ways of understanding "constitutionalism" or "democracy" (Bellamy, 2015). However, it has the advantage of excluding some political forms, for example, states which do not recognize and respect fundamental rights or states in which there are no competitive elections and no alternation in power.

References

Arendt, H. 2006. *Between Past and Future*. New York: Penguin.
Article 19. 2018. "Hungary: Responding to 'Hate Speech'." *Country Report*. www.article19.org/wp-content/uploads/2018/03/Hungary_responding_to_HS.pdf.
Banaji, S. and Bhat, R. 2019. *WhatsApp Vigilantes: An Exploration of Citizen Reception and Circulation of WhatsApp Misinformation Linked to Mob Violence in India*. London School of Economics and Political Science. Research Report.
BBC. 2019. "EU Blasts Hungary 'Fake News' on Migrants." *BBC News*, February 19. www.bbc.com/news/world-europe-47294183.
BBC. 2021. "Covid 'Hate Crimes' Against Asian Americans on Rise." *BBC News*, May 21. www.bbc.com/news/world-us-canada-56218684.
Beausoleil, L. E. 2019. "Free, Hateful, and Posted: Rethinking First Amendment Protection of Hate Speech in a Social Media World." *Boston College Law Review* 60: 2101.
Bellamy, R. 2015. "Constitutional Democracy." In M. T. Gibbons (ed.). *The Encyclopedia of Political Thought*. New York: John Wiley & Sons.
Biancovilli, P. and Jurberg, C. 2020. "When Governments Spread Lies, the Fight is Against Two Viruses: A Study on the Novel Coronavirus Pandemic in Brazil." *medRxiv* [preprint]. www.medrxiv.org/content/10.1101/2020.10.20.20215962v1.full.
Bilewicz, M. and Soral, W. 2020. "Hate Speech Epidemic: The Dynamic Effects of Derogatory Language on Intergroup Relations and Political Radicalization." *Political Psychology* 41: 3–33.
Brugger, W. 2002. "Ban on or Protection of Hate Speech-Some Observations Based on German and American Law." *Tulane European and Civil Law Forum* 17: 1.

Cinelli, M., Brugnoli, E., Schmidt, A. L., Zollo, F., Quattrociocchi, W. and Scala, A. 2020. "Selective Exposure Shapes the Facebook News Diet." *PLOS One* 15, no. 3.

Da Empoli, G. 2019. *Les ingénieurs du chaos*. Paris: JC lattes.

Deibert, R. J. 2019. "The Road to Digital Unfreedom: Three Painful Truths About Social Media." *Journal of Democracy* 30, no. 1: 25–39.

France. n.d. "Against Information Manipulation." www.gouvernement.fr/en/against-information-manipulation.

Germany. 1998. "German Criminal Code (Strafgesetzbuch—StGB)." www.gesetze-im-internet.de/englisch_stgb/englisch_stgb.html#p1333.

Hootsuite. 2021. "Digital 2021, Report." https://wearesocial.com/digital-2021.

HRW. Human Rights Watch. 2016. "Hungary: Migrants Abused at the Border: Ensure Asylum Access; Investigate Cruel, Violent Pushbacks." www.hrw.org/news/2016/07/13/hungary-migrants-abused-border.

Kaye, D. 2019. *Speech Police the Global Struggle to Govern the Internet*. New York: Columbia Global Records.

Kellner, D. 2018. "Donald Trump and the Politics of Lying." In M. A. Peters, S. Rider, M. Hyvönen and T. Besley (eds.). *Post-Truth, Fake News*. Singapore: Springer.

Lazer, D. M. J., Matthew A. Baum, M. A., Benkler, Y, Berinsky, A. J.,Greenhill, K. M., Menczer, F., Metzger, M. J., Nyhan, B., Pennycook, G., Rothschild, D., Schudson, M., Sloman, S. A., Sunstein, C. R., Thorson, E. A., Watts, D. J., and Zittrain, J. L. 2018. "The Science of Fake News." *Science* 359, 6380.

MacIntyre, L. 2018. *Post-Truth*. Cambridge, MA: MIT Press.

Osmundsen, M., Bor, A., Vahlstrup, P., Bechmann, A. and Petersen, M. 2021. "Partisan Polarization Is the Primary Psychological Motivation Behind Political Fake News Sharing on Twitter." *American Political Science Review* 115, no. 3: 999–1015.

Pariser, E. 2011. *The Filter Bubble: How the New Personalized Web Is Changing What We Read and How We Think*. London: Penguin.

Santana, B. 2020. "Jair Bolsonaro Accused Me of Spreading 'Fake News': I Know Why He Targeted Me." *The Guardian,* June 22. www.theguardian.com/commentisfree/2020/jun/22/jair-bolsonaro-fake-news-accusation-marielle-franco.

Shao, C., Ciampaglia, G. L., Varol, O., Yang, K. C., Flammini, A. and Menczer, F. 2018. "The Spread of Low-Credibility Content by Social Bots." *Nature Communications* 9, no. 1: 1–9.

Sullivan, M. 2020. "What It Really Means when Trump Calls a Story 'Fake News'. April 13. https://www.washingtonpost.com/lifestyle/media/what-it-really-means-when-trump-calls-a-story-fake-news/2020/04/13/56fbe2c0-7d8c-11ea-9040-68981f488eed_story.html.

Waldron, J. 2012. *The Harm in Hate Speech*. Cambridge, MA: Harvard University Press.

8 Sexist hate speech against women

Towards a regulatory model*

Irene Spigno

1. Introduction. The problem of sexist hate speech

Words have weight.

Much of what we communicate in a simple conversation is a more or less voluntary expression of our sociocultural context and values. Often, our language is full of expressions and stereotypes based on sex or gender produced by a macho and patriarchal culture that has normalised such communication. Such expressions can generate countless instances of discrimination or verbal aggression. Many idioms, clichés and "funny" jokes about gender diversity contribute to creating a scenario that inevitably affects and conditions women's everyday life, amplifying a problem that is already cumbersome in our contemporary society.

It is an underestimated and belittled problem both on a social level and on a legal one, but it should be taken very seriously: the toxic narrative created by sexist language often acts as an antechamber to verbal and physical violence. It contributes significantly to a distorted perception of gender-based violence in all its forms and perpetuates gender inequality.

Threats, whether more or less veiled, for example, between a couple (with phrases such as "Try to speak to X again—which can be a friend, a colleague or an ex-boyfriend—and you will see what happens," or "I have already told you a thousand times, don't you dare contradict me") or degrading and manipulative expressions (also known as "gaslighting," with sentences such as "Shut up, you never understand anything" or "It is just your fault, do not complain if I get aggressive") are never justifiable and should be seen as alarm bells signifying possible situations of physical and verbal abuse. They are also the symptom of a relationship characterised by the dynamics of control and the imposition of strong limits on the freedom of choice and behaviour of the woman and which affirm an indisputable male authority within the relationship. Additionally, aggressive expressions in public debates (such as "a woman who speaks this way deserves a slap in the face" or, especially in the case of female human rights defenders "Given that she defends [migrants] so much, surely she wouldn't mind being raped by these people") are equally violent since they express the idea that women "who cannot stay in their place" deserve to be "corrected" and to face physical violence. Sentences like these cause damage on every front, leading to generalisations, accusations

DOI: 10.4324/9781003274476-11

and very serious insinuations, often belittled as exaggerations or even as light-hearted comments. All of these are forms of expression that affect women's daily lives and which, in addition to being unpleasant, must also be read in light of the data on gender-based violence against women that reveal a genuinely alarming reality. If we only consider the data relating to the most extreme violence, that constituting feminicide,[1] approximately 100,000 women die every year, around the world for reasons relating to their gender and therefore for the fact of being women[2] It is a silent Holocaust.

However, feminicide is only the most extreme form of violence against women. The number of women that are victims of many other types of gender-based violence is truly incalculable. Women (adults, children and adolescents) suffer domestic violence all around the world within their families or within their circle of acquaintances, through threats, physical and psychological abuse, persecution, stalking, beating, sexual abuse, honour killings and murder (whether a crime of passion or premeditated). Women also suffer from economic violence which consists of the control being taken over their money and properties by their partner, the prohibition of them to undertake work activities outside the home environment and the prohibition of any independent initiative with respect to the woman's assets. Women are also exposed in public places and workplaces to sexual harassment and sexual abuse, rape and sexual blackmail.

In many countries, young girls are victims of female genital mutilation and other types of mutilation, forced marriages and shotgun marriages, are forced into sexual slavery, prostitution and trafficking, war, ethnic rape and so on.

The list of the different types of gender-based violence is unfortunately very long and results from the unequal power relationship between men and women which is also continually fed by sexist and misogynistic discourses. Speeches that, in addition to reinforcing a suitable context for fuelling inequality between men and women, constitute in themselves severe forms of gender-based violence. Despite being a more subtle and less evident form of violence, sexist speech spreads, incites, promotes or justifies hate against women based on their sex.

Social networks and the media are full of this kind of message. Although sexist hate speech has taken on a new dimension through the Internet, its roots preceded technology and are fundamentally linked to the persistent unequal power relationship between women and men. Sexist hate speech is a form of violence against women and girls that perpetuates and exacerbates gender inequality.

Much work has been done in relation to racist hate speech, in terms of legislation, doctrine and jurisprudence, especially following the Holocaust and World War II, which provided the impetus for creating normative and jurisprudential standards to regulate hate speech and to generate a global consensus towards it. However, there is still no similar consensus regarding sexist hate speech.

This article argues that to overcome this lack of consensus and the consequent absence of regulatory standards, sexist hate speech must also be considered a form of hate speech and should be treated and punished as such (para. 2). In the third paragraph, this article will consider the elements of the debate, criticisms and some of the obstacles that stand in the way of extending the anti-hate speech racist regulations to sexist hate speech (para. 3). Paragraph 4 will analyse the regulatory models of racist hate speech obtained through the systematisation of comparative experiences, underlining which values each of them protects. Lastly, some reflections on which of the proposed models could be the most appropriate to regulate sexist hate speech will be offered in the concluding section (para. 5).

2. Hate speech and why sexist speech should be considered as such

The formula for "hate speech" includes expressive forms which are quite diverse from each other. Contemporary legal literature defines hate speech, almost unanimously, as those forms of incitement to hatred and/or discrimination directed against people by virtue of their racial, ethnic, national, religious, sexual or gender identity (Rosenfeld, 2003, 1523–1568). The consensus of the international community also converges on this position, claiming that states have a responsibility to adopt appropriate regulatory provisions to prohibit those forms of expression such as the spreading of theories about the superiority of a race or those that seek to justify or encourage any form of racial hatred and discrimination,[3] incitement to discrimination, hatred[4] and genocide[5] and the promotion of the crime of apartheid, as well as similar segregationist policies,[6] to punish any form of dissemination, incitement, promotion or justification of racial hatred, xenophobia, anti-semitism or other manifestations of hatred based on intolerance, expressed in the form of aggressive nationalism or ethnocentrism.[7]

Many national legislators are also on the same wavelength: regardless of the particularities of each one (e.g. some legal systems limit themselves to punishing incitement to racial or religious hatred, others incitement not only to hatred but also to discrimination, others even to violence).[8] The predominant tendency in most states with a pluralist democracy, most likely promoted by the same international law, is in the sense of repressing any form of public incitement to hatred, which is accompanied by an obvious discriminatory intention. Despite the consensus that has been achieved between doctrine, regulations and jurisprudence on the essential contents of a shared definition, it remains to be clarified precisely what "hatred" is transmitted through the use of the word or other communication strategies.

Cognitive psychology says that "hate" is the point of intersection between a "denied intimacy" (understood as "disgust" concerning what is different, although not repellent), "passion" (which is expressed in an explosion of "anger" and/or "fear" in the face of something that is perceived as harmful) and "determination" (as devaluation through "contempt" motivated by perceiving others as inferior[9]).

Almost in unison, the Canadian Supreme Court and the Italian Court of Cassation say that "hatred" is that feeling of an intense and extreme nature, different from a "generic antipathy, intolerance or rejection," capable of provoking "hostility," "resentment" and "contempt" for another person.[10]

Many scholars, concentrating on its potential consequences, consider that "hatred" is that strong feeling of "aversion" or "hostility" expressed towards other people by virtue of their ethnic, racial, religious, sexual, political identity and gender, due to issues related to age or to conditions of physical or mental disability, "which can generate" discrimination, prejudice, fanaticism, racism, misogyny, homophobia and xenophobia.[11]

If hate is all this, it seems clear that not all "extreme" speech is also hate speech[12] and it is only the latter which would reach the barrier of what is constitutionally admissible. To identify the expressive manifestations that would fall into the category of hate speech, it is necessary to consider two different perspectives, complementary to each other and not mutually exclusive. According to an initial content-based approach, hate speech—and therefore prohibited expressions—would be identified by its content regardless of its ability to cause an "imminent danger" to life or safety or other fundamental rights. On the alternative approach, the contextual/consequence-based approach would identify the prohibited expressions that are "capable" of endangering the security or the protection of the fundamental rights of others, since its dissemination would be capable of provoking violent actions.

Given that these are two perspectives that are not mutually exclusive and are complementary to each other, in the present work, the expression "hate speech" is considered inclusive of all expressive forms that result from the combination of both. Therefore, hate speech would include those expressions "capable," due to their "offensive, injurious or defamatory content," of "generating" hostility, resentment, contempt, discrimination, intolerance, prejudice, sense of rejection, fanaticism, racism, misogyny, homophobia or xenophobia, of destroying the identity of others and inciting people to commit acts of violence against other due to their belonging to a group identified for its unique differential characteristics.

The dissemination of such expressions, regardless of whether they lead to any violent act and judged only by the expression's ability to lead to or produce such acts, would justify the sanctioning intervention of the law and the consequent exclusion of such expressions from the public arena.[13]

Consequently, those expressions, which, although disagreeable, are not capable of causing harm and discrimination but instead only lead to an emotional conflict or a lack of respect or rejection of the points of view of others would not fit into the legal category of hate speech. These expressions, which are in no way linked to the presence of tendentially permanent characteristics,[14] would instead fit into the category of "extreme speech."

Sex and gender are also tendentially permanent characteristics, and sexist hate speech must be considered a form of hate speech against women for gender reasons. More specifically, hate against women is mainly related to sexism and misogyny. Sexism is to discriminate or judge someone (especially women) based on sex or gender,[15] while misogyny refers to hatred and identifies the rejection, aversion and contempt of men towards women and, in general, towards everything related to the feminine. This hatred (feeling) has frequently had continuity in negative opinions or beliefs about women and the feminine and in negative behaviours towards them.[16] This means that, although this is a very subtle line, a misogynistic utterance is always sexist,[17] but not all sexist expressions are also misogynistic.

Sexist hate speech is one of the expressions sexism may have, and it can be defined as any assumption, belief, statement, gesture or act that aims to express contempt towards a person, based on their sex or gender, or to consider that person as inferior or essentially reduced by their sex or gender. All women and girls are potential targets of sexist hate speech; however, younger ones and those with a public image (such as journalists, bloggers, influencers, politicians or human rights defenders) are a particular target of sexist hate speech, facing sexist hate speech in both the public arena and their work environment.

Even though the Recommendation No. R(97)20 on hate speech of the Committee of Ministers of the Council of Europe does not include sexist hate speech,[18] the Recommendation CM/Rec(2019)1 of the Committee of Ministers to member states on preventing and combating sexism, defines sexism as

> [a]ny act, gesture, visual representation, spoken or written words, practice or behaviour based upon the idea that a person or a group of persons is inferior because of their sex, which occurs in the public or private sphere, whether online or offline, with the purpose or effect of: i. violating the inherent dignity or rights of a person or a group of persons; or ii. resulting in physical, sexual, psychological, or socio-economic harm or suffering to a person or a group of persons; or iii. creating an intimidating, hostile, degrading, humiliating or offensive environment; or iv. constituting a barrier to the autonomy and full realization of human rights by a person or a group of persons; or v. maintaining and reinforcing gender stereotypes.[19]

The Convention on Preventing and Combating Violence against Women and Domestic Violence of the Council of Europe (better known as the Istanbul Convention) also recognises two forms of sexist hate speech identified in sexual harassment (Article 40) and stalking (Article 34). Moreover, the Istanbul Convention underlines that sexist hate speech is closely linked to violence against women. The approach proposed therein is that it is necessary to find solutions to gender violence by looking at all the different manifestations it may assume based on the idea of the inferiority of women or on stereotyped roles for women and men (Article 12), sexist hate speech being one of them.

So, according to the double-tier approach (content-based and context/consequence-based) to defining punishable hate speech, sexist speech should be considered as a form of hate speech in all those cases in which sexist and misogynistic expressions are "capable," by virtue of their "offensive, injurious or defamatory content," of "generating" hostility, resentment, contempt, discrimination, intolerance, prejudice, a sense of rejection and fanaticism, which are directed at destroying the identity of others and inciting others to commit acts of violence against people determined by their belonging to a group identified by special differential characteristics, regardless of the effective production of any violent act, but only under its ability to produce it.

3. How to regulate sexist hate speech?

The problem of sexist hate speech has not yet been deeply explored. Some states have included gender or sex in their anti-hate speech criminal laws (as in Belgium,[20] Canada,[21] France,[22] Lithuania,[23] the Netherlands[24] and Spain.[25] It was largely discussed in Italy[26]). Some include these two categories in their anti-discrimination laws (as in some Australian States, namely: the Australian Capital Territory,[27] New South Wales,[28] Queensland[29] and Tasmania,[30] as well as in South Africa[31]), in gender equality laws (as in Lithuania[32] and the United Kingdom[33]), and anti-harassment laws (Ireland[34] and Switzerland[35]), and in laws on the freedom of the press (Chile[36] and France[37]).

However, sexist hate speech is still less visible than racist hate speech as far as its legal treatment is concerned, and the low number of court cases confirms this perception. Recently, the Higher Regional Court of Cologne (*Oberlandesgericht Köln*) ruled[38] (decision issued on 15 June 2020) that even if the primary area of application of post-war German laws against hate speech is the protection of minorities, the wording, meaning and purpose of the law also cover attacks on the human dignity of women. The case at stake was about a man who managed a website that repeatedly addressed women as "second-class people," "closer to animals" and "inferior human beings." The Bonn Lower Administrative Court initially fined the homepage user, and the man was later acquitted in the second instance by Bonn High Court. Prosecutors were prompted to appeal in Cologne and requested a new trial. According to the appeal judge who acquitted the defendant, paragraph 130 of the German Penal Code prohibits hate speech [*Volksverhetzung*] and protects minorities, but not women, a word omitted in the paragraph.

Section 130 of the German Penal Code provides for the punishment to be a prison term between three months and five years. It considers two possible situations: the first refers to inciting hatred or even violence against "national, racial, religious group or a group defined by their ethnic origin," but the second is more general and applies to anyone who "violates the human dignity of others by insulting, maliciously defaming or defaming one of the groups mentioned earlier, sectors of the population or individuals."

According to the Higher Regional Court in Cologne, the paragraph's reference to "sectors of the population" may be applied to women since the *ratio legis* of this provision is to prevent discrimination. According to the Cologne judge's argumentation, the reference to the sector of the population provided by Section 130 of the German Penal Code cannot be interpreted as limited to the groups or characteristics expressly mentioned in the text (which explicitly refers to national, racial, religious groups or a group defined by their ethnic origin). Instead, the provision needs to be interpreted in an open way in order to include other vulnerable groups not explicitly mentioned, as in the specific case, women. Furthermore, according to the court, the defendant's description of the women as "inferior," the disregard for the principle of equality and his attacks on their human dignity amounted to incitement of the masses, punishable by Section 130 of the Penal Code.

We are, therefore, still in the early stages of a serious regulation of sexist hate speech. The need to regulate sexist hate speech has also emerged in Italy and was the subject of a heated debate that has overwhelmed Bill no. S-2005 (better known as the Zan Bill from the name of one of its proponents) and then blocked by the Senate in the session of 27 October 2021 according to Articles 96 and 133 of the Senate's Rules. These rules allow a senator to propose that an article of the examined bill not be examined through a vote that can be secret by at least 20 senators' request, and the Senate presidency accepts this proposal. In the case of the Zan Bill, after the general discussion of the bill, the individual articles and amendments presented were not examined. The practical consequence of this procedure involves the substantial rejection of the bill, the blocking of the entire parliamentary process and the need to restart with a new bill. This Bill proposed extending the Italian law on propaganda and incitement to crime for racial, ethnic and religious discrimination (Article 604 *bis* of the Italian Criminal Code) to also include reasons based on sex, gender, sexual orientation, gender identity or disability. This approach would have also applied to the specific aggravating circumstances provided for crimes punishable with a penalty other than that of life imprisonment, committed for the purposes of ethnic, national, racial or religious discrimination or hatred, or in order to facilitate the activity of organisations, associations, movements or groups that have among their purposes the same purposes (Article 604 *ter*).

Although the key point of the debate concerned, among other aspects, the introduction in a relatively conservative legal system of concepts such as "gender identity" and consequently the preference that would have been given to a perceived identity over biological sex, among the criticisms, the proposal also included those related to the fact that the Italian provisions are aimed at the protection of racial minorities and not of women, who cannot be considered a minority from a quantitative point of view (but nonetheless, who are a vulnerable group historically discriminated against).

The articles that this bill intended to modify were introduced in 1993 by the cd. Mancino Law[39] which is part of an overall regulatory framework aimed at sanctioning conduct attributable to fascism and racism.[40] The legislator was pushed to revise the previous provision as a reaction to the events that occurred in 1992–1993, characterised by an incandescent climate due to the expansion of youth skin groups throughout Europe. These saw many episodes of violence, especially arson and other attacks aimed at social centres, motivated mainly by the explicitly expressed hatred of new immigrants.[41] Despite the specificity of the Italian case, within the structure of the Mancino Law, it is possible to trace the classical argument of European and global liberalism, which is based on the fight against racism, and which translates into the common feeling according to which the opinions that openly incite violence and discrimination on racial, ethnic or religious grounds, should not enjoy the protection reserved for the freedom of expression of thought.

Nevertheless, if there is a general global consensus on the non-inclusion of such discourse and opinions that incite violence on such grounds, why should we tolerate those opinions that openly incite violence and discrimination on the grounds of sex and gender? Indeed, the historical arguments underlying the rules on the propagation and incitement to crime on the grounds of racial, ethnic and religious discrimination cannot represent an obstacle to the recognition of women as a protected group in the face of the propagation of ideas based on superiority or sexist hatred. The laws against racist hate speech have their origins in the post-war constitutionalism built on the ashes of World War II and the hate propaganda that was the basis of the world conflict. Contemporary constitutionalism based on the recognition of human rights and an inclusive concept of democracy must protect all those groups (and not just minorities in a quantitative sense) that have historically suffered specific discrimination and continue to live in conditions of profound vulnerability. This is the case for women, who still suffer much violence today and are a historically discriminated group, a situation that prevents them from democratic participation under the same conditions as men.

Therefore, if the "obstacles" that prevent women from being granted protection that is similar to that received by racial and religious minorities due to historical reasons can be easily overcome,[42] it remains to be defined which regulatory model would be the most appropriate.

4. Four models regulating hate speech

What are the values protected by anti-racist hate speech laws from the comparative perspective? Could we extend to sexist-type hate speech the definitions elaborated with reference to racist-type hate speech? The comparative panorama of racist hate speech offers us four different regulatory models that could also be extended to sexist hate speech:[43] the "freedom model," the "defence model"; the "no discrimination model" and the "multiculturalism model."

The first one is the "freedom model" in which the debate on "freedom of expression vs. hate speech" is characterised by the application of the "clear and present danger" principle, according to which freedom of expression is only limited to those expressions, under the specific circumstances of the case at hand, which are capable of having a clear and imminent danger on the protected values, i.e. the social order and the proper functioning of the democratic system. According to this model, hate speech would be unlikely to lead to any current and specific danger.

This model was born and developed in the jurisprudence of the Supreme Court of the United States of America and protects the democratic system by ensuring a "solid and open, without inhibitions" debate on issues of public relevance (on the basis of the application of the principles established in *New York Times v. Sullivan*).[44]

The "freedom model" has been adopted in other constitutional systems—such as in Argentina[45] and Israel[46]—where the "clear and present danger" principle is considered as the criterion to limit freedom of expression. In this model, the defence of social peace and the correct functioning of the democratic system are the fundamental values to be protected and where a prohibition on limiting freedom of expression based solely on the content of that expression has been established.

On the contrary, those expressive manifestations that, despite being offensive and scandalous and even though directed against a specific person in a degrading way with respect to race, ethnic origin, nationality or religion, would nonetheless be constitutionally admissible. In fact, in these cases, the immediacy of the causal link between hate speech and a particularly violent act (such as, in the most extreme cases, genocide or mass extermination) and taken for granted in many European laws, at least in terms of the probability of the worst possible hypothesis (such as limiting freedom of expression to avoid subordinating vulnerable groups or creating a climate of discrimination and violence or to protect the reputation of the members of a specific group) is excluded.

In the second model, the "defence model" (among which Germany, France, Italy and Austria, among others stand out),[47] the role of the protagonist is played by human dignity, which allows the limiting of all those expressions which, as a result of the content of the message they transmit constitutes a direct attack against it and, consequently, against the constitutional order. The protection of human dignity and the democratic system is carried out through a rather strict, almost militant approach, which is based on state ideology, whereby strict penal sanctions are applied. Configuring a system in such a "militant" way means the exclusion of certain expressions due to their "content" and of the "potential" danger they pose rather than the "real" danger.

In the "defence model," the state is responsible for combating those forms of expression considered abhorrent, balancing the different rights and freedoms recognised in the constitutional system, and in this weighing dynamic, human dignity plays a predominant role.[48] According to this scheme, the State must commit itself to repressing "anti-system" movements by adopting sanctions against those who practice intolerance, discriminate and incite hatred against those who are different. The protection of democracy in the "defence model" is based on the "paradox of tolerance" in an unfavourable sense for the intolerant since it legitimises preventive and repressive norms against them.[49]

The "non-discrimination model" (prevalent in international law and among Latin American countries) is the third model, and it is characterised by the exclusion from the area of protection of freedom of expression of all expressive "suitable" behaviours, which may have the ability, due to both its content and the circumstances, to generate a discriminatory context. Therefore, it is not considered necessary that the expressive conduct motivated by hatred linked to the belonging of the affected person to a specific racial, national, religious, ethnic or other groups consists of incitement to hatred or violence and, therefore, has the ability to generate an act of hatred or violence. What is guaranteed is protection against a discriminatory context, which therefore implies a differentiated and unjustified treatment.

Finally, in the "multiculturalism model," the protected value is constituted by harmony and peaceful coexistence between the different groups. Consequently, all those expressive behaviours which have the ability to endanger this "good" are punished. The multiculturalism model has been developed in Canada, where it has generated one of the most comprehensive, instructive and attractive systems at the normative and jurisprudential levels in the fight against the propagation of hate,[50] exerting its attractive force worldwide.[51] In this model, freedom of expression can be limited only in the case of "the most intentionally extreme forms of expression"[52] and only when values such as dignity and equality are put at risk, especially where it concerns minorities.[53]

Which of these models would be the most appropriate to discipline the problem of sexist hate speech?

5. Toward a proposal to regulate sexist hate speech? Final remarks

The tolerance to sexist hate speech that has been prevalent until now reflects a deeply patriarchal and misogynistic society, in which women are still considered in a hierarchical social plane where they are of less value than men. The problem of sexist hate speech has worsened with the strengthening and massification of the media and, with the digital age, has reached new profiles and problems, so much so that we can say that sexist hate speech represents one of the principal evils that afflict the twenty-first century. Why? Sexist hate speech makes women invisible as unworthy beings; it dehumanises them by denying their identity and existence as human beings.[54]

The dissemination of sexist hate speech, regardless of whether this leads to a violent act and only if this was more or less close to the performance of the act itself, would justify the sanctioning intervention of the law and the consequent exclusion of said phrases from the public arena, due to not only the potential violation that they can have on women's rights—including dignity, honour or equality—but also the tension that they can cause in society as a whole.[55]

Nevertheless, in this nebulous and sometimes slippery matter, one of the strong points is represented by the fact that we know that hate speech—and sexist hate speech is not an exception—is not something accidental. It is not an accident on the road.[56] Hate is being aware of what its object is; it is built *ad hoc*, through a slow and constant process, through practices and beliefs coldly calculated and transmitted over generations.[57]

The Internet has changed the rules of the game. If traditionally freedom of expression was "materially conditioned" since its exercise was linked to the availability of certain types of media,[58] the Internet forces us to reconsider public space.

In the digital world, hating is very easy.

Therefore, in this "liquid" context, I believe that the model that seems most appropriate to address sexist hate speech in the twenty-first century is that of multiculturalism, in which dialogue and tolerance are essential elements.

The "multiculturalism model," more than the others, pushes towards the rejection of hatred through criminal sanctions (necessary only as *extrema ratio*) and emphasises a culture of tolerance and respect through education. Although specific manifestations of hatred must be punished, the models that only foresee this sanction would not be adequate. To inflict punishment by imposing a sanction such as a fine or deprivation of one's personal liberty does not always lead to a transformation of the hate message and a solution to the main problem. The exclusive use of criminal law is only the expression of a seizure of power and an exercise of power by the "countries of fear."[59]

On the contrary, the "multiculturalism model" favours a more articulated response to hate speech: the state must intervene by restricting the freedom of expression of the person spreading hate only when it translates into an imminent threat of public disorder or a danger to life or another fundamental right. However, the law cannot solve everything. It is the responsibility of society to condemn these behaviours and try to confront the different forms of discrimination, including small and implacable exclusion strategies that are manifested in specific gestures and habits, in social practices and in convictions. The choice, therefore, must be in the sense of preferring the path of education to specific values since hatred and prejudice are children of ignorance and lack of knowledge.[60]

If the Holocaust and Auschwitz were built with words and not (only) with bricks, that is also true for the silent and invisible genocide that is killing women because they are women, which is built upon sexist discourse. And we must stop it.

As Alon Harel wrote, "treating the victims of racist speech more favourably than victims of sexist, homophobic, or other forms of abhorrent speech is itself a form of discrimination."[61]

Notes

* The author thanks Prof. Oscar Pérez de la Fuente for organizing the International Webinar "Free speech, democracy, and minorities" (20 July 2021), in which a preliminary version of this paper was presented. A special thank you also goes to Prof. Alexander Tsesis for his invaluable comments. Finally, the author would like to thank Dr. Chris Callan for the linguistic revision of the text.
1 "Feminicide" has been defined as "the killing of women by men *because* they are women" (Radford and Russell, 1992, xiv).
2 See UNODC (2018).
3 See in this regard: Article 4 of the International Convention on the Elimination of All Forms of Racial Discrimination (1965), according to which the propagation of theories based on the superiority of a race or a group of people of a certain colour or ethnic origin is prohibited; and Article 20 of the International Covenant on Civil and Political Rights (1966), according to which pro-war propaganda and advocacy of national, racial or religious hatred that constitutes incitement to discrimination, hostility or violence are prohibited.
4 See Article 13.5 of the American Convention on Human Rights (1969). Article 7 of the Universal Declaration of Human Rights (1948) refers only to incitement to discrimination. Article 1 of the Framework Decision on the fight against certain forms and manifestations of racism and xenophobia through criminal law (approved by the Council of the European Union) [Framework Decision 2008/913/JAI] manifests the objective to achieve the harmonization of the crime of incitement to hatred and violence in the EU countries and, in pursuing this aim, prohibits public incitement to violence or hatred even through the dissemination or distribution of writings, images or other materials directed against a group of people or a member of such a group, defined in relation to race, colour, religion, ancestry or national or ethnic origin, as well as denial of crimes of genocide, crimes against humanity and crimes of war.

5 Article 3 of the Convention for the Prevention and Punishment of the Crime of Genocide (1948).
6 Article IV of the International Convention on the Suppression and Punishment of the Crime of Apartheid (1973).
7 See Recommendation No. R (97) 20 of the Committee of Ministers of the Council of Europe. The case law issued by international bodies has subsequently broadened the spectrum of what is legally relevant, including "generating or reinforcing anti-Semitic sentiments," such as through the defence of Nazism. In this sense, see the ruling of the United Nations Human Rights Committee in the case *Faurisson v. France* [Communication No. 550/1993 (CCPR/C/58/D/550/1993), of 16 December 1996] and that of the Committee established within the scope of the ICERD (hereinafter ICERD Committee) in the case *The Jewish Community of Oslo et al. vs Norway* [Communication No. 30/2003 (ICERD/C/67/D/30/2003) of August 22, 2005], in which it was found that the statements defending Nazism are an incitement at least to racial discrimination, if not directly to violence. In this sense, see Kübler (1998, 335–376) and Castellaneta (2009, 157–172), according to which hate speech should be considered a crime against humanity insofar as it constitutes a form of persecution.
8 British law, for example, regulates incitement to racial and religious hatred (respectively, in Section 18 of the Public Order Act of 1986 and with the Racial and Religious Hatred Act of 2006), while the Russian Penal Code prohibits incitement to ethnic, racial and religious hatred through the use of the mass media (Article 282.1) and in Hungary public, incitement against an ethnic group, racial, religious or other groups of the population is prohibited (Article 269 of the former Penal Code and currently Article 232). Article 266b of the Danish Penal Code, on the other hand, prohibits incitement to hatred or violence as a result of a distinction between social classes, races, religions, denominations or regions (Article 312 of the Penal Code).
9 See Sternberg, 2009, 45–58 and, in particular, the "theory of the triangular structure of hatred."
10 Cf. *ex plurimis* on Canadian jurisprudence *R. v. Keegstra*, [1990] 3 S.C.R. 697, and the decision of the Italian Court of Cassation, Penal Section, Sez. V (*Paoletich* case), n. 44295/05, of 17 November 2005, commented on by Martinelli (2006, 2596 ff.).
11 Scholarship on this point is immense. *Ex plurimis* cfr. Cortese, 2006; Coliver, 1992, 363. The "crits" (Critical Legal Studies) focus mostly on the consequences that can potentially occur for the victim.
12 For a distinction between which types of speech are legally relevant to this point, see Nockleby (2000, 1277–1279). See also Hare and Weinstein, 2009.
13 On this point, see Parekh, 2012, 37–56, according to which hate speech is identified as being aimed at stigmatizing a specific individual or group by virtue of arbitrary or legally irrelevant characteristics, but perceived as undesirable and generally not removable, regardless of the carrying out of violent acts or other external consequences.
14 See Pizzorusso (2003, 667 ff., 1993), which underlines that hate speeches are not those that express conflicts not motivated by tendentially permanent characteristics, such as belonging to a group that generally constitutes a "minority," both from a merely quantitative point of view and as historically discriminated or politically weak groups. See also Matas (2000, 2 ff.).
15 See Frenda et al. (2019, 4744).
16 See Varela (2012, 36).
17 See Frenda et al. (2019, 4744).
18 This absence is explained in the Explanatory Memorandum of this Recommendation according to which "[i]t was considered necessary to avoid losing the focus of the text by covering all forms of intolerance (e.g. intolerance on grounds of sex, sexual orientation, age, handicap, etc.)" (para. 22).
19 Annex 1 to the Recommendation CM/Rec(2019)1 of the Committee of Ministers to member States on preventing and combating sexism define sexism.

Sexist hate speech against women 149

20 See the *Loi tendant à lutter contre le sexisme dans l'espace public et modifiant la loi du 10 mai 2007 tendant à lutter contre la discrimination entre les femmes et les hommes afin de pénaliser l'acte de discrimination*, adopted on 22 May 2014 and Article 444 of the Belgian Criminal Code.
21 See Sections 318(4) (as modified in 2014) and 319 of the Criminal Code of Canada.
22 See Articles 24, 32, and 33 of the *Loi du 29 juillet 1881 sur la liberté de la presse*, Article 621–1 of the French Penal Code, added by the *Loi n. 2018–703 du 3 août 2018 renforçant la lutte contre les violences sexuelles et sexistes*.
23 Article 170 of the Lithuanian Criminal Code.
24 Article 137d of the Penal Code of the Netherlands.
25 Article 510 of the Spanish Penal Code.
26 Bill n. S-2005 (better known as the Zan Bill). See *infra*.
27 Discrimination Act 1991, Sections 66(1)(c) and 67(1)(d)(iii)
28 Anti-Discrimination Act 1977, Sections 38R-38T.
29 Anti-Discrimination Act 1991, Sections 124A(1), and 131A(1).
30 Anti-Discrimination Act 1998, Sections 16(ea)-(eb).
31 Promotion of Equality and Prevention of Unfair Discrimination Act 2000, Sections 1(1) and 10(1).
32 Article 1 of the Law on Equal Opportunities for Women and Men.
33 See Section 26 of the Equality Act 2010.
34 See Section 23 of the Employment Equality Act, 1998.
35 See Article 3 of the Gender Equality Act, 1995.
36 *Estatuto de la Libertad de Opinión e Información y del Ejercicio del Periodismo*, Article 31.
37 See Article 24 of the *Loi du 29 juillet 1881 sur la liberté de la presse* (amended by Article 71 (V) of the *Loi n. 2019–222 du 23 mars 2019*).
38 OLG Köln, 09.06.2020—III-1RVs 77/20.
39 Law n. 205 of 1993, converting Decree-Law n. 122 of 1993.
40 Thus, the XII transitory and final provision of the Constitution of the Italian Republic, in the first paragraph, establishes that "The reorganization, in any form, of the dissolved Fascist party is prohibited"; in implementation of the aforementioned provision, the Law of 20 June 1952, n. 645, on the subject of "Implementation rules of the XII transitory and final provision (first paragraph) of the Constitution", in Article 1, specifies that there is a reorganization of the dissolved fascist party when an association, a movement or in any case a group of not less than five people pursues the anti-democratic aims of the fascist party: exalting, threatening or using violence as a method of political struggle, or advocating the suppression of the freedoms guaranteed by the Constitution, or denigrating democracy, its institutions and the values of the Resistance, or carrying out racist propaganda, or turning its activity to the exaltation of exponents, principles, facts and methods of the aforementioned party, or carrying out external manifestations of a fascist character. See also the Preamble and Article 4 of the International Convention on the Elimination of All Forms of Racial Discrimination, opened for signature in New York on 7 March 1966, was implemented by Italian law with Law no. 654.
41 See Tanzarella 92020, 119).
42 See Brown (2016).
43 I elaborated upon this categorization in a previous work: Spigno, 2018.
44 *New York Times Co. v. Sullivan* [376 U.S. 254 (1964)].
45 Argentina has adopted the criterion of clear and imminent danger, as well as the prohibition of restrictions on freedom of expression based solely on its content. In fact, Argentine jurisprudence has emphasized the need that, to limit freedom of expression, expressive conduct must be "suitable" to carry out prohibited racist propaganda, to instigate hatred and persecution of a particular group. Therefore, the emphasis is placed on the real harmful scope of the action that is considered discriminatory, with reference to each specific case (the evaluation of the damage to the protected legal

asset, the specific circumstances, the context in which the action is carried out, etc.). In this sense, see the decision of the *Cámara Criminal y Correccional Federal*, Sala II, *Bonavota, Liliana Graciela/inf. artículo 3ro., 2do. párrafo, Ley 23.592*, causa n. 13.682, of 19 February 1998, according to which «*Este Tribunal ha sostenido que "es exigencia para la configuración del delito imputado que la acción reprochada tenga capacidad como para alentar o incitar a la persecución o al odio contra una persona o grupo de personas a causa de su raza, religión, nacionalidad o ideas políticas." Esta capacidad a la que se hace mención debe ser merituada en cada caso concreto, debiéndose prestar particular atención a las circunstancias de modo y lugar en que la conducta es desplegada, a fin de poder asegurar que con ella se ha creado el peligro de que se produzcan las consecuencias que la ley intenta prevenir.*»

46 Please see Spigno (2018, 129 ff.). The Israeli Supreme Court, on the other hand, has considered the criterion of clear and imminent danger in terms of "probability": it is the so-called "near certainty test," which allows restrictions on freedom of expression to protect national security and public peace, when there is "almost certainty" that such assets are threatened by serious danger. This criterion would be a guarantee of democracy and freedom, since it reduces the risk of an arbitrary limitation of those expressions that only have a "mere tendency" to endanger public peace (see the judgement of the Supreme Court of Israel, *Kol Ha'am v. Minister of Interior* [HCJ 73/53, n. 73/53]). In the application of this criterion, freedom of expression in Israel also includes the right to express dangerous, irritating and deviant thoughts of the majority and hatred (see in this regard the judgement of the Supreme Court *Kahana v. The Broadcasting Authority*, [41 (3) P.D. 255 (HC 1987)]).

47 See Spigno (2018, 137 ff.).

48 See Rosenfeld (2003, 1523–1568), Eberle (1997, 97–901) and Whitman (2000, 1279–1398).

49 As can be read from the words of Karl Popper "if we are not willing to defend a tolerant society against the attack of the intolerant then the tolerant will be destroyed and tolerance towards them. . . . [For this] we must proclaim, in the name of tolerance, the right not to tolerate the intolerant"; cfr. Popper (2004, 346). See also Bobbio (1990): according to which "I firmly believe in my truth, but I have the duty to obey an absolute moral principle: respect for other people." According to Bobbio, respect for the other does not necessarily imply respect for what this man thinks or says: it rather means recognizing the right to be treated on a par with others, regardless of what he thinks or says. Respect for the other therefore serves as a condition and fundamental limit of tolerance: what violates respect for others is not tolerable. Tolerance loses value when it is exercised in comparison with tolerance, or when what is denied by the very conditions of tolerance is tolerated. See also Groppi (2005).

50 This model is based on a rich set of jurisdictional precedents and legislative acts, which include both criminal instruments and civil anti-discrimination remedies. On the configurability of a true "Canadian model," please see Spigno (2013, 283–295).

51 See Scaffardi (2006, 163–183).

52 *Regina v. Keegstra* (1990) 3 SCR 697, 787.

53 See Sileoni (2008, 449 ff.).

54 See Taguieff (1999, 12 ff.).

55 See Parekh (2012, 37–56), for whom hate speech is identified as having the objective of stigmatizing a specific person or group, by virtue of arbitrary or otherwise legally irrelevant characteristics, perceived as unwanted and generally unwelcome, regardless of the actual production of violent acts or other external consequences.

56 See Glucksmann (2005, 45).

57 See Emcke (2017, 43).

58 See Ansuátegui Roig (2017, 29–48).

59 See Todorov (2016, 14).

60 See Faloppa (2016, 69–123), according to which, there are numerous remedies to combat racism, all of which relate to education and culture.

61 Harel (1991–1992, 1906).

References

Ansuátegui Roig, F. J. 2017. "Libertà di espressione, discorsi d'odio, soggetti vulnerabili: Paradigmi e nuove frontiere." *Ars interpretandi, Rivista di ermeneutica giuridica* 1: 29–48.
Bobbio, N. 1990. *L'età dei diritti*. Torino: Einaudi.
Brown, A. 2016. "The 'Who?' Question in the Hate Speech Debate: Part 1: Consistency, Practical, and Formal Approaches." *Canadian Journal of Law & Jurisprudence* 29, no. 2: 275–320.
Castellaneta, M. 2009. "L'hate speech: da limite alla libertà di espressione a crimine contro l'umanità." In G. Venturini and S. Bariatti (eds.). *Diritti individuali e giustizia internazionale. Liber Fausto Pocar*. Milano: Giuffrè: 157–172.
Coliver, S. (ed.). 1992. *Striking a Balance: Hate Speech, Freedom of Expression and Non-Discrimination*. Article 19, International Centre against Censorship. London: Human Rights Centre.
Cortese, A. 2006. *Opposing Hate Speech*. Westport, CT and London: Praeger Publishers.
Eberle, E. J. 1997. "Public Discourse in Contemporary Germany." *Case Western Reserve Law Review* 47, no. 3: 797–901.
Emcke, C. 2017. *Contra el odio*. Barcelona: Taurus.
Faloppa, F. 2016. "Per un linguaggio non razzista." In M. Aime (ed.). *Contro il razzismo: Quattro ragionamenti*. Torino: Einaudi: 69–123.
Frenda, S. et al. 2019. "Online Hate Speech Against Women: Automatic Identification of Misogyny and Sexism on Twitter." *Journal of Intelligent & Fuzzy Systems* 36, no. 5: 4743–4752.
Glucksmann, A. 2005. *Le discours de la haine*. Vanves: Hachette.
Groppi, T. 2005. "Il Paradosso Della Democracia." *L'Unità*, January 28.
Hare, I. and Weinstein, J. (eds.). 2009. *Extreme Speech and Democracy*. Oxford: Oxford University Press.
Harel, A. 1991–1992. "Bigotry, Pornography, and the First Amendment: A Theory of Unprotected Speech." *Southern California Law Review* 65, no. 4: 1887 ff.
Kübler, F. 1998. "How Much Freedom for Racist Speech? Transnational Aspects of a Conflict of Human Rights." *Hofstra Law Review* 27, no. 2: 335–376.
Martinelli, D. 2006. "Nota a sentenza." *Giur. It.* III: 2596 ff.
Matas, D. 2000. *Bloody Words: Hate and Free Speech*. Winnipeg: Bain & Cox, Publishers.
Nockleby, J. T. 2000. "Hate Speech." In L. W. Levy and K. L. Karst (eds.). *Encyclopedia of the American Constitution*. Vol. 3. Detroit: Macmillan Reference USA: 1277–1279.
Parekh, B. 2012. "Is There a Case for Banning Hate Speech?" In M. Herz and P. Molnar (eds.). *The Content and Context of Hate Speech: Rethinking Regulation and Responses*. New York: Cambridge University Press: 37–56.
Pizzorusso, A. 1993. *Minoranze e maggioranze*. Torino: Einaudi.
Pizzorusso, A. 2003. "Limiti alla libertà di manifestazione del pensiero derivanti da incompatibilità del pensiero espresso con principi costituzionali." In *Diritti, nuove tecnologie, trasformazioni sociali, scritti in memoria di Paolo Barile*. Padua: Cedam: 651–670.
Popper, K. R. 2004. *La società aperta e i suoi nemici*. Vol. I. Roma: Armando Editore [*The Open Society and Its Enemies*. London: Routledge, 1945].
Radford, J. and Russell, D. E. H. (eds.). 1992. *Femicide: The Politics of Woman Killing*. New York: Twayne Publishers.
Rosenfeld, M. 2003. "Hate Speech in Constitutional Jurisprudence: A Comparative Analysis." *Cardozo Law Review* 24, no. 4: 1523–1568.

Scaffardi, L. 2006. "Istigazione all'odio e società multietnica: il Canada e l'hate speech." In G. Rolla (ed.). *Eguali, ma diversi. Identità e autonomia secondo la giurisprudenza della Corte Suprema del Canada*. Milano: Giuffrè: 163–183.

Sileoni, S. 2008. "Libertà di espressione e tutela dei minori e delle minoranze nella giurisprudenza della Corte Suprema." In G. Rolla (ed.). *L'ordinamento costituzionale canadese*. Milano: Giuffrè: 449 ff.

Spigno, I. 2013. "Libertà di espressione ed hate propaganda; verso un modello canadese?" In E. Ceccherini (ed.). *A trent'anni dalla Patriation canadese. Riflessioni della dottrina italiana*. Genova: Genova University Press: 283–295.

Spigno, I. 2018. *Discorsi d'odio. Modelli costituzionali a confronto*. Milano: Giuffré.

Sternberg, R. J. (ed.). 2005. *The Psychology of Hate*. Washington DC: American Psychological Association [trad. it. *Psicologia dell'odio. Conoscerlo per superarlo*. Gardolo, TN: Erikson, 2007].

Taguieff, P.-A. 1999. *Il razzismo. Pregiudizi, teorie, comportamenti*. Milano: Raffaello Cortina Editore.

Tanzarella, P. 2020. *Discriminare parlando. Il pluralismo democratico messo alla prova dai discorsi d'odio razziale*. Torino: Giappichelli.

Todorov, T. 2016. *La paura dei barbari: Oltre lo scontro delle civiltà*. Milano: Garzanti.

UNODC. 2018. *Global Study on Homicide: Gender-Related Killing of Women and Girls*. Vienna. www.unodc.org/documents/data-and-analysis/GSH2018/GSH18_Gender-related_killing_of_women_and_girls.pdf.

Varela, N. 2012. "La nueva misoginia." *Revista europea de Derechos Fundamentals* 19: 25–48.

Whitman, J. Q. 2000. "Enforcing Civility and Respect: Three Societies." *Yale Law Journal* 109: 1279–1398.

9 Artificial intelligence and hate speech

Migle Laukyte

1. Introduction

The International Covenant on Civil and Political Rights—along with many other international treaties—established that the restrictions to freedom of speech have to be legal and necessary to ensure respect of the rights or reputations of others and the protection of national security, public order or public health or morals (Article 19) and also that to advocate "national, racial or religious hatred that constitutes incitement to discrimination, hostility or violence shall be prohibited by law" (Article 20).

Hate speech—understood as "both a calculated affront to the dignity of vulnerable members of society and a calculated assault on the public good of inclusiveness"[1] (Waldron, 2012, 5–6)—is a limit that free speech cannot cross according to the legislation of the majority of democratic societies.[2] This is why the European Commission plans to include hate speech and hate crimes in the list of EU crimes as established in Article 83(1) of the Treaty on the Functioning of the European Union, together with such crimes as terrorism, trafficking in humans, corruption, money laundering, computer crime and other crimes.

Hate speech has enormously benefited from Internet-based technologies. Therefore, today when we refer to hate speech, more often than not, we refer to online hate speech. This kind of speech is much more difficult to fight because of anonymity, instantaneousness, ease of access and size of audience (Brown, 2017; Perez de la Fuente, 2019), besides other reasons. However, new technological advancements have emerged, and these advancements show that the problem of online hate speech is taking new forms. That is where this contribution comes into play: It addresses the link between online hate speech and a special group of new and disruptive technologies, known under the term of artificial intelligence (AI).[3]

In particular, this contribution adopts a three-dimensional perspective: first of all, I focus on AI as a tool to fight online hate speech, second, I look at AI as a way to generate hate speech, and, third, I explore the future scenario in which AI—together with other technologies—could offer the grounds for creating a new social group that could add to the list of social groups-targets of hate speech (such as immigrants, ethnic and other minorities).

DOI: 10.4324/9781003274476-12

The contents of this contribution could also be seen through the lens of the urgency of addressing it: indeed, right now, we focus on how we could use AI-based tools to fight the spread of hate speech online and prevent specific social groups from being attacked by haters. The development of such tools faces a few challenges related to the particularities of human language and the context in which certain expressions could completely change their meanings and turn into hatred. The initiatives and examples of how AI is helping us to fight hate speech are the focus of Part I.

Part II is dedicated to the next question that we probably will have to address in the near future. It is related to the use of AI to generate—or otherwise contribute to—hate speech. In this case, I refer to deepfakes and how they could be used to facilitate and foster hate speech online. The fact that deepfakes are a growing threat in the near future is also reflected in the EU Commission's proposal on harmonised rules on AI,[4] where for the first time the EU legislator is putting on the table the idea that deepfakes could become an issue that needs regulation and proposes to apply certain transparency requirements to them.

In Part 3, I completely change the standpoint and address a hypothetical scenario, based on the speculation about the evolution of hate speech. In particular, this part focuses on the idea that AI will also provide the haters with new social groups to attack. This group is represented by people who will use all the technological advancements to improve and enhance their physical and mental abilities and subscribe to the ideals of transhumanism. We already debate transhumanism as a possibility for humanity to overcome its own limitations with all the pros and contras,[5] but we still need to have a closer look at transhumanism through the lens of hate speech.

The chapter ends with concluding remarks about the present and future of hate speech and the different roles AI is already (and could potentially) play in it.

Finally and before I start, I also wanted to draw the reader's attention to the fact that I will not talk about freedom of speech in this chapter: I do not address how freedom of speech could be affected by AI that identifies the hate speech expressions in tweets or in other online environments, nor I address how the prohibition of deepfakes would affect people's freedom to say what they want and in the way they choose to do so. I do not do that not because I cannot see the relevance of it—of course, I can—but because I chose to focus on hate speech itself, and looking at freedom of speech would take away the protagonist role that hate speech has in this work. Focusing on hate speech and the harm it causes made me realise that more often than not, freedom of speech is given more importance than freedom from hatred, discrimination and intolerance (not to say physical violence) and maybe even rightly so: however, I just assume that freedom of speech is guaranteed and has much more safeguards in place than freedom from hatred and therefore focus on hate speech only.

2. Fighting hate speech with AI

It is not the goal of this chapter to list all the initiatives that have been launched to fight hate speech online on national and EU levels.[6] The focus of this section is to look at a few examples that would illustrate how AI has been—and is currently—used to fight hate speech. For example, in 2017 municipal elections, Finish researchers have used a hate speech detection system, based on supervised machine learning, to automatically monitor the social media of candidates to identify hate speech (Laaksonen et al., 2020). Their findings show that the main problem in making machines identify this kind of speech is the need to simplify it, i.e. to reduce it to the elementary essentials such "a complex socio-linguistic issue" as hate speech is (ibid., 2). The problem with this reduction is that we are dealing with hate speech that we, humans, ourselves still have difficulty to understand: "the concept of 'hate speech' is so slippery that it can be applied to almost any speech and any situation, . . . there are no discernible limits" (Coleman, 2016, 83). Obviously then, when a complex issue is reduced to the essence understandable to machines, many of its aspects—that form the different layers of complexity—are lost. This is particularly obvious in the case of hate speech when there are so many ways to express one's violent attitudes, discriminatory positions and harassing approaches towards other people.[7]

Indeed, the promise of AI— i.e. the promise to substitute humans in detecting and eliminating online hate speech—has clashed with the complexity of this speech and (for the moment) insufficient technological readiness to deal with this complexity: in fact, the types of language that are being used in hate speech include—but are not limited to—insults, prejudice and stereotyping, gossip, dividing language (us against them), trivialisation of violence and its justification as necessary, dehumanising metaphors, euphemisms, hyperboles and so on and so forth. In addition, what matters is not just the speech in itself but also who is speaking (the social, political and economic influence of the speaker) and the context of the speech.

The Al-re-co project is a good example of the Spanish public sector's attempt to fight hate speech online, in particular on Twitter and Facebook.[8] From a technical perspective, the goal is to build an algorithm that would be able—thanks to the indicators, elaborated on the basis of the words, expressions, phrases and other linguistic means that are being used to spread racist, xenophobic, Islamophobic and anti-Semitic hate speech—to identify hate speech on these social networks. The methodology of the training algorithm is based on supervised machine learning techniques, that is to say, the human supervision and support remain fundamental: it is a human operator who eliminates irrelevant information from the tweets and labels the tweets on the basis of the severity of hatred that a tweet involves[9] and then feeds these tweets to the algorithm. Then, the algorithm elaborates the data, while the human operator continuously feeds it with new data and supervises the results of the algorithmic performance.

However, the parties that are best-equipped resource- and technology-wise are private actors, represented by technological companies, such as Facebook, Twitter and Google. Facebook has published promising data as to the precision of its algorithms to spot hate speech in different languages (Schroepfer, 2021). This success, according to Facebook, has been achieved thanks to the improvements in semantic understanding of language, which permits to spot more sophisticated meanings, and also to the holistic approach towards understanding of content, that takes into account not only textual language as such but also comments, images and other elements. Differently from similar public initiatives, Facebook and other companies are investing in unsupervised learning and therefore advance the research in systems that would not need (that much?) human supervision and control.

The question is whether this lack of human supervision is desirable. On the one hand, human intervention does not guarantee that the algorithm will be errorless and, furthermore, could even produce a contrary effect: rather than decreasing, it could increase bias. As a matter of fact, this is what happened with Google's algorithm: people in charge of labelling tweets in terms of their toxicity were more prone to consider as toxic those tweets that were written in African American Vernacular English. This means that—at least, for some time—Google's algorithm associated African American speech with hate speech (for more about it, see Robitzski, 2019).

However, on the other hand, we might not be willing to completely erase humans from supervising the tools that make decisions on what can and cannot be said online. Moreover, recent research showed that, even if left without human supervision and bias, AI could all alone develop its bias: the experiment that involved a computational multi-agent system highlighted the trend that the agents preferred to interact with those agents that were similar to them, rather than with those that were different because they have learned that giving to the agent that is similar increases the probability of reciprocation (Robitzski, 2018). What does this research suggest? It suggests that (a certain level of) unfair discrimination is inherent in social and (social research based) computational interactions and that it is not feasible to completely eliminate it.

In addition, another conclusion is that we cannot avoid using AI, in particular online, because there is no other way to meaningfully fight the spread of hate speech in social networks and other digital environments. However, human supervision and control of algorithms are also very important. Therefore, hate speech cannot be seen as a purely technical problem—consisting in making machines understand and identify hate speech online—but as a multi-layered problem where both AI and humans have different roles to play and success will very much depend on each party's—human and AI—ability to do their tasks as best as they can.

3. Using AI for hate speech: the case of deepfakes

When we speak about the deepfakes, we have in mind the European Commission's definition in the AIA: here the deepfake is described in Article 52 (3) as "an AI system that generates or manipulates image, audio or video content that appreciably resembles existing persons, objects, places or other entities or events and would falsely appear to a person to be authentic or truthful" (European Commission, 2021) and requires its users to disclose that the content has been artificially generated and manipulated.[10]

This definition does not cover those deepfakes that are of low quality and clearly identifiable as fakes ("shallow fakes") nor applies to selectively edited videos, where certain expressions are taken out of context and put together into patchwork-like hate speech. In comparison, the U.S. definition of deepfake stays more neutral as to the involvement of AI: deepfake

> means any video recording, motion-picture film, sound recording, electronic image, or photograph, or any technological representation of speech or conduct substantially derivative thereof—(A) which appears to authentically depict any speech or conduct of a person who did not in fact engage in such speech or conduct; and (B) the production of which was substantially dependent upon technical means, rather than the ability of another person to physically or verbally impersonate such person.
> (Deep Fake Accountability Act, 2018)

Deepfakes can be used for a variety of purposes that range from completely innocuous, such as entertainment, to criminal, such as pornography. In reference to the latter, deepfakes give rise to the following two problems, identified by Franks and Waldman (2019): first of all, deepfakes subvert our capacity to distinguish the truth from falsity, and, second, they harm a person's dignity that can be neither challenged nor corrected. What deepfake pornography has in common with deepfake hate speech is that, in both cases, we are talking about false representation of reality and truth, and also about the use of apparently real images against a directly involved person (in the case of pornography), and against specific groups of people (in the case of hate speech). Indeed, Franks and Waldman affirm that:

> It is not hard to imagine deep-fake videos of racial minorities committing crimes or LGBT individuals abusing children, ... The danger is particularly acute where distrust of certain individuals or communities already exists: A deep-fake video can leverage our confirmation biases to edge its way into the national discourse.
> (ibid., 896).

From this perspective then, AI is a means to carry out even more sophisticated hate speech attacks by providing such speech with audiovisual contents that are almost impossible for humans to identify as fake. Besides, and in addition to this, what really changes with AI is that AI permits haters to use the social groups they feel hatred for against these social groups themselves: thanks to deepfakes, these people not only continue to be victims of hate speech but also become instruments to inflict more harm unto them. Furthermore, differently from deepfake pornography, which is banned as pornography from social networks, deepfake hate speech has much more space for manoeuvre and freedom to be accessed and shared online.

In the near future, when (or if?) the deepfakes will become more commonly used and sophisticated, and the technology to generate them will become more accessible, we might need to expand the use of AI to identify not only human-produced hate speech but also the hate speech generated by AI: work is already in progress as private and public stakeholders have already started to tackle this problem. For instance, Facebook has launched its deepfake detection challenge,[11] whereas academic researchers also offer methodologies to identify such false content: for instance, forensic techniques can be used to establish individual's speaking patterns that are usually violated by deepfakes (Agarwall et al., 2019). These are all ways that might be enormously helpful to identify high-quality deepfakes that the human eye is unable to distinguish from authentic audiovisual content.

In more general terms, we see that hate speech is just another means to increase our dependency and reliance on AI: both to fight hate speech and to generate it, we use AI because human means for both purposes (fight and generate) are insufficient and inadequate. As with many other spheres, we discover that our leaning on AI is growing exponentially and whether it is a progress or decline remains an open question.

After these two sections that address AI as a tool to fight hate speech (Part I) and as a tool to further develop hate speech (Part II), Part III is dedicated to AI as a reason for hatred and characteristic of special social groups that, as of today, do not exist but in the future might add to the list of those social groups that are more often than not objects of hatred.

4. Hate speech directed against AI-empowered transhumans

Part III of this chapter addresses the idea that in the future, AI (and other emerging and disrupting) technologies will contribute to creating a new social group which will represent a new target for (online and offline) haters. I am referring to those people who will use all the technologies to improve and enhance their physical and intellectual abilities, i.e. people whom we call transhumanists. These people have freely chosen to introduce mechanical, bionic or other kinds of non-organic parts in their physical bodies and/or have chosen to use other kinds of enhancement (drugs, hormones, neuro-interfaces, etc.) that make them function in a way that goes beyond the "normal" functioning of a human body or brain.[12]

In terms of AI, transhumanism sees it as a way to potential human beings through tools (today, these tools are smartphones[13]), but in the future, also by connecting the human brain to different objects and the Internet itself.[14]

It would be naïve to think that, in the future, we will not witness the emergence of new social groups-targets of hate speech: indeed, we already debate—at least on the academic level—the proposal to include animals as victims of speciesist hate speech (Milburn and Cochrane, 2021). Therefore, it should be even less difficult to imagine the transhumans as a social group that are subject to such attacks.

In the case of transhumans, we would be talking about a social group that has deliberately chosen to become different. Indeed, perhaps the AI and other disruptive and evolving technologies will bring into being new social groups whose difference is choice-based, and not innate or circumstantial as it is in the case of ethnic minorities or immigrants, respectively. The question is whether this choice-based character would influence the contents of hate speech and how: it would not be a mistake to speculate that the accessibility of these enhancements to the wider public will play a very important role in this. Related to this is the fact that (in the majority of cases, and at least at the beginning) transhumans will be people who belong to those classes of society that have certain levels of financial stability. But does high income save from hatred?

Research shows that, besides the question of income, it is a question of political influence: only those groups that have the biggest political influence, such as sexual or ethnic minorities, are protected from hate speech, whereas other groups (i.e. people with weight issues or vitiligo) would seldom get the same attention (Coleman, 2016). It seems then that there is a hierarchy of public attention among the discriminated and insulted social groups, which—if confirmed—opens debate over the reasons and justifications for the existence of such hierarchy. Could AI be functional not only in fighting or supporting AI but also in revealing to us our own bias and contradictions?

There is a further dimension to this link between transhumanism and hate speech: if science offers us a way to overcome our limitations—in this particular case, all those feelings that hate speech represents, starting with intolerance, hatred and refusal and ending up with violence—are we not morally obliged to use it or, at least, offer it to those haters who no longer want to feel these negative impulses to attack and denigrate other people? Indeed, Persson and Savulescu argue that:

> the mere realization that racism is false is not enough to wash away all xenophobic reactions in our nature. Racial differences signify lack of kinship, and mark off strangers from neighbours. People encode the race of each individual they encounter, and do so via computational processes that appear to be both automatic and mandatory. Encoding by race is a by-product of cognitive machinery that evolved to detect coalitional alliances. . . . If genetic and biomedical means of enhancement could counter such natural tendencies, they could have a crucial role to play in improving our moral character, that could complement traditional social and educational means of moral enhancement.
> (Persson and Savulescu, 2008, 168)

In addition, we already have therapies and drugs to treat many human features that are not acceptable, such as aggression and violent behaviour: the doubt is whether the means we already have—these therapies and pills—could not be improved with the help of technological advancements that the transhumanists believe so strongly in.

In the meantime, almost 10 years have already passed since what has been called the first cybernetic hate crime, when a person with Eyetap (an augmented reality headset) was assaulted by McDonalds staff who did not want him to use a video camera inside the restaurant and therefore tried to rip the Eyetap from his head, without taking into account that the Eyetap is not possible to remove from a person's skull without using specific instruments (Popper, 2012). The advancements in AI, neurosciences, bioengineering and robotics promise a new wave of enhancements, and it is still to be seen how these enhancements will be taken in by society as a whole, and how these advancements will affect hate speech: will we have more hate speech spreading through the Internet, would the current targets of hate speech—immigrants, Muslims, other minorities—feel the shift of haters towards new targets—transhumans—and therefore feel that they are hated less or will nothing change and we simply will be adding new targets of hatred?

5. Conclusions

Hate speech is like a cloud in Percy Bysshe Shelley's poem, which changes but cannot die.[15] How it will change, we still have to see: what we can see already is that new technologies—in our case, AI—have been used by both those who fight hate speech and those who see in AI new functionalities to express one's hatred and find supporters for it. In both cases, there are always people behind the AI, because hate speech continues to be an exclusively human kind of speech and is directed towards other human beings only.

Without a doubt, the speech that qualifies to be considered as hate speech, and therefore unacceptable and punishable by the legal system, is the one that is incompatible with the inclusive society and which sees some people as different and, therefore, threatening. The fact that we bring AI into play—either as a means to fight hate speech or as a means to make hate speech more effective—shows that there is no doom for hate speech, but on the contrary, hate speech is very much alive and flourishing.

We are still wondering how hate speech will affect—if at all!—the transhumanists who will use a variety of technologies to enhance and improve what nature (or God) has given them. From a purely academic perspective, transhumanism could offer us new insights about hate speech by helping us to understand how this kind of speech emerges, what triggers it and what makes it slow down, how it evolves and what kind of factors affect its evolution.

There are more questions related to transhumanism and hate speech: for instance, I have briefly addressed the idea of treating the human ability to feel hatred towards others with the help of human enhancement techniques (with medications, genetic engineering or other means), but I was also wondering whether we should all be submitted to such treatment: maybe we should approve ways to improve the human character and—in particular with reference to hate speech—we should be open to any means to make our minds hate less, become impenetrable to hate attacks and deaf to incitements of hatred towards others? If our human feebleness could be fixed, should we do it? These are all questions for the future, and while thinking about the future, we have to focus on the most urgent questions of today: these questions regard the use of AI in fighting hate speech. We have seen the tremendous difficulties that the researchers have to face so as

Artificial intelligence and hate speech 161

to understand first themselves, and then, in turn, make the algorithms understand what is not acceptable and what is in the online environment.

In addition, we also have to be aware that it is not just we, humans, who program, develop and supervise algorithms, but it is also algorithms who influence us, humans. In fact, we have been already warned that there are "two ways in which algorithmic power works by producing truths—both as outcomes or outputs of systems and as part of the discursive reinforcement of particular norms, approaches and modes of reasoning" (Beer, 2017, 11). It should be our purpose as a democratic society to look at these truths critically and never permit an algorithm to decide and dictate to us what the truth really is. So much less it should be permitted to do that in the case of hate speech.

Notes

1 Waldron defines dignity as a "person's basic entitlement to be regarded as a member of society in good standing, as someone whose membership of a minority group does not disqualify him or her from ordinary social interaction" (2012, 105) and the public good of inclusiveness as "an open and welcoming atmosphere in which all have the opportunity to live their lives, raise their families and practice their trades or vocations" (ibid., 16).
2 The U.S. position with respect to the EU position on hate speech is very different. For more about it, see, for instance, Kahn (2013), Waldron (2012), Schauer (2005) and many others.
3 For purposes of this chapter, AI is understood in the wide sense adopted by the EU Commission (2018), according to which "Artificial intelligence (AI) refers to systems that display intelligent behaviour by analysing their environment and taking actions—with some degree of autonomy—to achieve specific goals. AI-based systems can be purely software-based, acting in the virtual world (e.g. voice assistants, image analysis software, search engines, speech and face recognition systems) or AI can be embedded in hardware devices (e.g. advanced robots, autonomous cars, drones or Internet of Things applications)."
4 The full name is "Proposal for a Regulation of the European Parliament and of the Council laying down harmonized rules on Artificial Intelligence (Artificial Intelligence Act) and amending certain Union legislative acts." I will refer to it as AIA.
5 For more about this, see, among many, Llano Alonso (2018). Bartra calls transhumanism a postmodern shamanism (Bartra, 2019, 80ss.).
6 Just to cite a few, "Cyberespect: Guia Práctica de intervención en linea para ciberactivistas" (2017), www.sosracisme.org/wp-content/uploads/2018/01/11-12-5-11.admin_.CIBERESPECT_Guia_practica.pdf; or the work carried out by the Media Diversity Institute (www.media-diversity.org), Code of conduct on countering illegal hate speech online issued by the EU Commission (https://ec.europa. eu/commission/presscorner/detail/en/qanda_20_1135) and other initiatives.
7 Further particularity of hate speech is that it can be directed towards anybody, for example, it can be groups of people (ethnic minorities), but also against wider parts of society (women or elderly). Probably, the common denominator is that the hate speech is directed against someone who is perceived by the speaker as different, usually inferior, and this speech is severe enough to be considered illegal. This chapter adopts a wider concept of hate speech that covers any sort of speech that contributes to create a discriminatory, contrary to human rights and hate-based environment.
8 For more about this project co-financed by the EU, see https://alrecoresponse.eu/en/home/ (accessed 22 June 2021).

162 *Migle Laukyte*

9 Hate speech is classified into extreme hatred, hatred-offence, neutral discourse and upstander.
10 In addition, the Commission also specifies that those systems that were used by law enforcement to detect deepfakes are considered to be high-risk AI systems.
11 For more about it, see https://ai.facebook.com/blog/deepfake-detection-challenge-launches-with-new-data-set-and-kaggle-site/
12 I deliberately distinguish between people who chose to enhance themselves (transhumans) and those who had to do that because of disability, trauma or other similar reasons. For more about conceptual problems related to human enhancement, see Bess (2010).
13 Bartra calls the smartphone a "little electronic exobrain that connects our central nervous system to a social and cultural universe" and also argues that it expands the powers of the human ego (2019, 67; *my translation*).
14 Indeed, the researchers of the Brainternet project have already connected the human brain to the Internet (for more about this, see Caughill, 2017).
15 The poem is called "The Cloud" by Percy Bysshe Shelley and is available online at www.bartleby.com/41/517.html (accessed 2 May 2021).

References

Agarwall, S. et al. 2019. "Protecting World Leaders Against Deep Fakes." https://openaccess.thecvf.com/content_CVPRW_2019/papers/Media%20Forensics/Agarwal_Protecting_World_Leaders_Against_Deep_Fakes_CVPRW_2019_paper.pdf (accessed June 2, 2021).
Bartra, R. 2019. *Chamanes y Robots*. Barcelona: Anagrama Argumentos.
Beer, D. 2017. "The Social Power of Algorith." *Information, Communication & Society* 20, no. 1: 1–13.
Bess, M. 2010. "Enhanced Humans Versus 'Normal People': Elusive Definitions." *Journal of Medicine and Philosophy* 35: 641–655.
Brown, A. 2017. "What Is Special About Online (as Compared to Offline) Hate Speech?" *Ethnicities* 18, no. 3: 297–326.
Caughill, P. 2017. "Researchers Have Linked a Human Brain to the Internet for the First Time Ever." *The Futurism*. https://futurism.com/researchers-have-linked-a-human-brain-to-the-internet-for-the-first-time-ever (accessed June 22, 2021).
Coleman, P. 2016. *Censored: How European "Hate Speech" Laws Are Threatening Freedom of Speech*. Vienna: Kairos Publications.
Deep Fake Accountability Act. 2018. H.R. 3230, 116 Congress, 1st session, "A Bill to Combat the Spread of Disinformation through Restricions on Deep-fake Video Alteration Technology." https://www.congress.gov/bill/116th-congress/house-bill/3230/text.
European Commission. 2018. "Communication From the Commission to the EU Parliament, The EU Council, the Council, the EU Economic and Social Committee and the Committee of the Regions, Artificial Intelligence for Europe COM/2018/237 Final." https://eur-lex.europa.eu/legal-content/EN/TXT/?uri=COM%3A2018%3A237%3AFIN (accessed June 2, 2021).
European Commission. 2021. "Proposal for a Regulation of the EU Parliament and of the Council Laying Down Harmonized Rules on Artificial Intelligence (Artificial Intelligence Act) and Amending Certain Union Legislative Acts." https://eur-lex.europa.eu/legal-content/EN/TXT/HTML/?uri=CELEX:52021PC0206&from=EN (accessed May 22, 2021).

Franks, M. A. and Waldman, A. E. 2019. "Sex, Lies, and Videotape: Deep Fakes and Free Speech Delusions." *Maryland Law Review* 78, no. 4: 891–898.

International Covenant on Civil and Political Rights. 1966. www.ohchr.org/en/professionalinterest/pages/ccpr.aspx (accessed May 27, 2021).

Kahn, R. A. 2013. "Why Europeans Ban Hate Speech? A Debate Between Karl Loewenstein and Robert Post." *Hofstra Law Review* 41, no. 3: 545–585.

Laaksonen, S.-M. et al. 2020. "The Datafication of Hate: Expectations and Challenges in Automated Hate Speech Monitoring." *Frontiers in Big Data* 3. www.frontiersin.org/articles/10.3389/fdata.2020.00003/full (accessed May 31, 2021).

Llano Alonso, F. H. 2018. *Homo Excelsior: Los Límites Ético-Jurídicos del Transhumanismo*. Valencia: Tirant lo Blanch.

Milburn, J. and Cochrane, A. 2021. "Should We Protect Animals From Hate Speech?" *Oxford Journal of Legal Studies*. https://academic. oup.com/ojls/advance-article/doi/10.1093/ojls/gqab013/6289858? login=true (accessed June 29, 2021).

Perez de la Fuente, O. 2019. "How Can Internet Change Human Rights on Online Hate Speech Regulations?" In A. Sungurov et al. (eds.). *Current Issues on Human Rights*. Madrid: Dykinson: 93–103.

Persson, I. and Savulescu, J. 2008. "The Perils of Cognitive Enhancement and the Urgent Imperative to Enhance the Moral Character of Humanity." *Journal of Applied Philosophy* 25, no. 3: 162–177.

Popper, B. 2012. "New Evidence Emerges in Alleged Assault on Cyborg at Paris McDonald's." *The Verge*. www.theverge.com/2012/7/19/3169889/steve-mann-cyborg-assault-mcdonalds-eyetap-paris (accessed June 20, 2021).

Proposal for a Regulation of the European Parliament and of the Council laying down harmonized rules on Artificial Intelligence (Artificial Intelligence Act) and amending certain Union legislative acts 2021. https://eur-lex.europa.eu/legal-content/EN/TXT/?qid=1623335154975&uri=CELEX%3A52021PC0206 (accessed May 2, 2021).

Robitzski, D. 2018. "Left Unchecked, Artificial Intelligence Can Become Prejudiced All on Its Own." *Futurism*. https://futurism.com/artificial-intelligence-prejudiced (accessed June 23, 2021).

Robitzski, D. 2019. "Google's Hate Speech-Detecting AI Is Biased Against Black People." *The Byte*. https://futurism.com/the-byte/google-hate-speech-ai-biased (accessed June 22, 2021).

Schauer, F. 2005. "The Exceptional First Amendment." *KSG Working Paper* RWP05–021. https://ssrn.com/abstract=668543 (accessed June 12, 2021).

Schroepfer, M. 2021. "Update on Our Progress on AI and Hate Speech Detection." https://about.fb.com/news/2021/02/update-on-our-progress-on-ai-and-hate-speech-detection/ (accessed June 23, 2021).

Waldron, J. 2012. *The Harm in Hate Speech*. Cambridge, MA and London: Harvard University Press.

Part IV
Free speech and minorities

10 Disentangling "cancel culture"

David S. Han

1. Introduction

The debate over "cancel culture" has become a flashpoint within the present culture wars. Yet both the term itself (which is typically used in a pejorative sense) and its application to different contexts are nebulous. In the broadest sense, "cancelling" is simply socially shaming and withdrawing support from individuals or companies in response to past transgressions. Framed in this manner, cancel culture is nothing new, as group shaming of unpopular speech and actions has been around for time immemorial. But it also refers to a type of shaming and ostracism with characteristics unique to the social media age—one rooted in a technological context where records of one's past sins are easily accessible and retained indefinitely, where social reprobation can be disseminated broadly and rapidly and where the intensity of outrage (and resulting sanctions) can be greatly magnified through the mechanisms of social media.

This chapter seeks to disentangle multiple strands of the cancel culture debate as it relates to broad questions regarding free speech. It first seeks to define "cancel culture" and describe its characteristics within the present social and technological context. It then delineates the theoretical concerns on both sides of the debate, highlighting both the capacity of severe social shaming to chill speech and the use of the "cancel culture" term as a rhetorical cudgel for those seeking to minimise healthy social criticism. Finally, it discusses how we might best resolve this debate, which encompasses conflicting social and cultural norms regarding free speech that, in the social media age, will likely shape the nature of public discourse to a far greater extent than formal constitutional doctrine.

2. Defining "cancel culture"

Within the past few years in the United States, examples of people being "cancelled" abound. People have been cancelled for past bad conduct,[1] for making offensive or repugnant statements,[2] or for expressing socially unpopular views.[3] The conduct or statements in question may have occurred yesterday or years ago. The offender may be a public figure who suffers a fall from grace, or it might be a private person whose socially repugnant views or actions have been exposed to the public at large. And the consequences of cancellation can vary, ranging from fleeting social condemnation[4] to long-term ostracism and loss of employment.[5]

Despite the abundance of discussion and commentary on both sides of the "cancel culture" debate in recent years, however, the precise definition of "cancel" in this context is nebulous. We might take as a starting point the definition from the Merriam-Webster dictionary: "to withdraw one's support for someone, such as a celebrity, or something, such as a company, publicly and especially on social media."[6] The dictionary in turn defines "cancel culture" as "the practice or tendency of engaging in mass canceling . . . as a way of expressing disapproval and exerting social pressure."[7]

If we define cancel culture in these broad terms, it is certainly not a new phenomenon. It simply describes the sort of social shaming of unpopular speech and actions that have been around for time immemorial.[8] Everyone, of course, disapproves of particular viewpoints and actions. And few will seriously argue that social shaming and ostracism can *never* be justified in any context. Take, for example, a person who has unrepentantly committed atrocities against innocent children, or a person who stridently advocates for genocide. Few would argue that severe social condemnation and shaming of such people would be unjustified, even if such condemnation might lead to loss of employment or social ostracism. Rather, such a response would be viewed as merely the natural expression of people's right to criticise and socially sanction speech and actions with which they disagree, along with their right to choose those with whom they will associate.

In a narrower sense, however, the modern understanding of "cancel culture" might refer to a particular *type* of social shaming—one with features unique to the present age of the Internet and social media. Although cancellation in the modern sense is, at its root, no different from social shaming in pre-digital society, a number of technological and cultural factors have significantly broadened both the potential reach and severity of these sorts of social sanctions.

First, the advent of the Internet has allowed for a person's past sins to live on indefinitely. In the pre-Internet era, one's past actions and statements were largely subject to the vagaries of human memory and the limitations of physical documentation. Today, however, we live in an era of digital "receipts." As the common adage goes, "the internet never forgets"; decade-old tweets and compromising photos remain perfectly encased in digital amber, and with the advent of Internet archiving and screenshotting, incriminating digital content can often remain preserved long after the poster has deleted it. As one commentator observed, "All you need to do is have a particularly bad day, and the consequences could endure as long as Google" (Douthat, 2020).

Second, social media allows for any person to rapidly and broadly disseminate social condemnation throughout the world. In the pre-digital age, social reprobation might extend only to the limits of one's immediate community; thus, one might find a fresh start by, say, moving to a distant community. Furthermore, the speed at which word could spread would often be limited—by, for example, the physical limitations of person-to-person, word-of-mouth communication. Rapid and expansive communication of one's message to the general public was often realistically available only to a privileged few—those with sufficient wealth or fame to leverage mass media outlets.

In the Internet era, however, anyone with an Internet connection can disseminate social condemnation instantaneously and without geographic boundaries (Bromwich, 2020). This dissemination is no longer tethered to direct, person-to-person interaction, or to discrete personal or professional networks. Rather, social rebuke may be immediately disseminated to billions across the world—to friends, acquaintances and strangers alike. As one commentator has observed, "[U]nder the rule of the internet there's no leaving the village: Everywhere is the same place, and so is every time" (Douthat, 2020).

Third, social media platforms have broadly been designed in a manner that encourages and magnifies outrage, condemnation and vitriolic commentary. Because the business models of social media platforms rely heavily on ad revenue, platforms seek to maximise active user "engagement"—such as likes, retweets and comments (Morrison, 2015)—as this generates higher advertising rates.[9] And unsurprisingly, user engagement is strongly driven by negative emotions such as anger or condemnation, which incentivises platforms to draw users' attention to incendiary comments that generate backlash.[10]

Fourth, these factors lead not only to an increased likelihood of cancellation but also to increased sanctions on those who have been cancelled. Immediate and widespread dissemination of social condemnation makes it easier for social outrage to reach a tipping point at which offenders suffer severe consequences. And it places greater pressure on institutions affiliated with the offender—such as employers—who are more likely both to become aware of the offense in question and to face direct public pressure to sanction the offender. Thus, severe sanctions such as loss of employment and broad social ostracism might be more common. Furthermore, the advent of social media has made it much easier to impose social sanctions such as deplatforming[11] and doxxing[12] while greatly magnifying the severity of these sanctions far beyond what was possible in the pre-Internet era.

Finally, the impersonality of communication over the Internet—through tweets or Facebook status updates rather than direct, person-to-person communication—creates social distance between the shamer and the shamed. In the pre-digital era, personal knowledge and empathy might play a larger role in social shaming, as condemnation would tend to spread through networks of people with some sort of connection to the offender, which might serve to moderate the degree of social sanction imposed on offenders. In the social media era, however, shamers with no person-to-person contact with or personal connection to the offender can more readily create psychological distance between themselves and offenders, potentially leading to more incendiary condemnation and more frequent calls for severe sanctions.

Thus, on the one hand, cancel culture is nothing new. It is, at its essence, the same sort of mass shaming and social ostracism that has existed for time immemorial. Thus, as I will discuss in the following, the basic theoretical dimensions of the present cancel culture debate are no different than what they might have been in the pre-digital age. On the other hand, however, this long-standing issue has taken on a new resonance given the unique social and technological context of today, driven by the advent of the Internet and the ubiquity of social media. Thus, although the broad dimensions of the debate remain constant, the rapid and significant changes of the digital age might lead us to question whether some recalibration of free speech values is in order.

3. The theoretical dimensions of the cancel culture debate

In this section, I will delve into the theoretical arguments on both sides of the cancel culture debate. At the outset, however, it is worth emphasising a couple of things. First, the term "cancel culture" itself provides little in the way of meaningful illumination. As noted earlier, few will seriously argue that social shaming can *never* be justified in any context; as one commentator put it, "There is no human society where you can say or do anything you like and expect to keep your reputation and your job" (Douthat, 2020). In other words, "All cultures cancel; the question is for what, how widely and through what means" (Ibid.). The term itself therefore carries little analytical substance; rather, in the present debate, it is often used as little more than an epithet—a shorthand term that merely reflects the speaker's preexisting disapproval rather than any meaningful analytical standard.[13] Thus, in this chapter, I use the terms "cancel" and "cancel culture" not in any specialised manner, but merely as descriptive shorthand for social shaming of a person's speech or actions.

Second, my focus in this chapter is on the free speech implications of the cancel culture debate—more specifically, the extent to which it affects the marketplace of ideas. The degree to which a particular instance of cancellation implicates speech values in this manner, however, varies based on the circumstances. Cancellation for the expression of a viewpoint, for example, would most strongly and directly implicate such values, as it imposes social sanctions on the speaker simply for contributing to the marketplace of ideas. On the other hand, cancellation for criminal conduct occurring in the distant past might not implicate these values in as direct or significant a manner; rather, it might primarily raise different issues, such as the extent to which a person should continue to suffer negative consequences for bad deeds committed long ago. Thus, in the remainder of this chapter, I focus primarily on situations where cancellation occurs based on social disapproval of a particular viewpoint.

3.1. Critiques of cancel culture

The primary critique of cancel culture is its capacity to stifle a robust and diverse marketplace of ideas.[14] When speech is met with formal or informal social sanctions—such as social ostracism, deplatforming or doxxing—these sanctions may chill those with unpopular opinions from speaking or (in the case of deplatforming) prevent them from speaking directly. This creates the danger of groupthink and conformity within public opinion—a situation where people are afraid to articulate views outside of the socially acceptable norm lest they suffer the consequences of cancellation.

Taken to an extreme, this risks the creation of a public monoculture—a state of affairs that undermines all of the traditional rationales underlying the freedom of speech. The lack of a diverse and robust public discourse would stymie the pursuit of truth (Mill, 1859, 87), as socially accepted "truths" would remain unchallenged. It would hamstring the operation of democratic self-governance (Meiklejohn, 1948, 22–27), as citizens would be unable to consider all views and ideas—whether wise or unwise—in governing themselves. And it would undermine individual autonomy (Fried, 1992, 233), both with respect to speakers' rights to self-expression and with respect to listeners' rights to hear out all ideas and viewpoints in advancing their own self-actualisation.

Another potentially problematic aspect of present-day cancel culture is its arbitrariness. As commentator Ligaya Mishan has observed, cancellation has a quasi-judicial aspect to it, as offenders are effectively tried and sanctioned in the court of public opinion (2020). But there are of course no structures, rules or procedures guiding cancellation—no central tribunal, no standards of review and no preset sanctions (Ibid.). Some offenders may therefore be punished severely for relatively minor sins, while similar or worse offenders may never be affected. Particularly in the case of private figures, being selected for cancellation may often rest more on dumb luck and external circumstances rather than careful consideration and measured proportionality—for example, the happenstance of a bystander filming the incident, or unlucky timing within a slow news cycle ripe for a tale of outrage, or the arbitrary decision of a powerful influencer to draw attention to an incident. As Mishan has framed it, while many who are cancelled may be deserving of condemnation, they also often assume the role of the proverbial scapegoat—an example brought into the spotlight to bear public punishment and shaming as a stand-in for broad social ills (Ibid.).

This arbitrariness can extend to how those who are cancelled may be affected. Some might suffer severe repercussions like job loss or the inability to secure employment. Others might merely undergo a brief span of public disapproval without consequence, for reasons that have little to do with the gravity of the underlying offense (e.g. a fresher scandal or a breaking news story that causes the public to lose interest). This raises the risk that cancellation—which, as discussed later, has recently been used as a means to highlight and redress long-standing social inequities—can itself increase inequality. Perhaps the wealthy, privileged and famous are better equipped to weather the storm of cancellation with little long-term repercussions (Mishan, 2020), while it is the private figures of lesser means and influence that suffer far greater harm, regardless of the nature of their offenses.[15]

3.2. Cancellation as healthy counterspeech and accountability

Although critics decry cancel culture as contrary to free speech values, these same values are strongly reflected in the act of cancellation itself. Social shaming and criticism of a person's actions are, of course, nothing more than the normal exercise of the shamers' free speech rights. Just as people have the right to say what they please, people also have the right to criticise the speech of others through counterspeech. Freedom to speak does not include the right to be insulated against popular disapproval; this would of course be completely antithetical to fundamental free speech principles. Those who express socially unpopular viewpoints must therefore do so with the knowledge that others are free, in turn, to express their disdain and disapproval.

Furthermore, this disapproval might come in the form of social sanctions such as ostracism or loss of employment, and this is also consistent with free speech values. Just as we are free to criticise speech with which we disagree, we are also free to choose the people with whom we will associate. And these decisions will often rest on whether we approve or disapprove of a person's actions or opinions. In the abstract, few would disagree that an informal social group, or a community organisation, or an employer is entitled to choose not to associate with someone who expresses views deemed to be reprehensible.

An extreme backlash against cancellation therefore risks just as much damage to free speech values as cancellation run amok. This is clearly evident within the context of the present cancel culture debate. Many of the recent spates of cancellations have been rooted in social movements like #MeToo and Black Lives Matter—movements driven by the observation that important social issues have escaped notice for too long, and recognition and correction of these social ills are sorely needed. In this context, identifying and shaming offenders represents a form of long-overdue accountability.[16] To the extent that victims of sexual abuse or racism have long been forced to bear their sufferings in silence, public shaming of offenders gives voice to those who have lacked it, while imposing social sanctions on perpetrators who may have otherwise escaped any repercussions for their actions.

From this perspective, cancellation is the opposite of silencing. It is healthy criticism of existing social structures—specifically, entrenched social hierarchies that have long evaded scrutiny.[17] As such, accusations of "cancel culture" run amok might be wielded merely as a cudgel by those seeking to silence these viewpoints—an effort to entrench existing power structures against social criticism and reform. The anti-cancel culture movement can therefore be similarly criticised as seeking to silence important viewpoints in the marketplace of ideas—those that challenge existing social norms and structures.[18]

To be sure, some degree of arbitrariness with respect to cancellation might be inevitable and unfortunate. But symbolic social punishment of a selected few offenders—even if they are chosen somewhat arbitrarily—serves the ultimate goal of highlighting and redressing social injustices that have long been ignored.[19] And to the extent that cancellation creates a chilling effect on certain viewpoints, perhaps that is simply the natural result if those views are socially repugnant—an indication that the marketplace of ideas is working correctly to weed out false and harmful viewpoints, rather than an indication that it is broken.

3.3. *The rhetoric of speech versus the rhetoric of power*

The basic dimensions of the cancel culture debate can thus be summarised as follows. On the one hand, criticisms of cancel culture may be warranted, as severe social shaming can chill speech and effectively remove "unacceptable" viewpoints from public discourse. But on the other hand, what one side calls "cancel culture" might actually be healthy social critique and commentary—a corrective to a historically imbalanced public discourse built upon long-standing social and cultural hierarchies (Mishan, 2020).

The cancel culture debate thus parallels the long-standing debate within free speech theory regarding the operation of the marketplace of ideas. Each side of the cancel culture debate effectively adopts a different rhetorical mode.[20] Those critical of cancel culture tend to adopt what we might call the rhetoric of speech: we cannot chill expression because we need to let all ideas do battle within the open and neutral marketplace of ideas.[21] By contrast, those who support cancellation tend to adopt the rhetoric of power. This reflects the idea that the marketplace of ideas is not neutral: it is infected by a fundamental imbalance of power (Ingber, 1984, 17), such that appeals to high-minded free speech principles can act merely as cover for those who benefit from that imbalance.

The rhetoric of speech reflects the traditional understanding of the marketplace of ideas: an even playing field upon which conflicting ideas do battle and upon which the truth will ultimately prevail. Under this understanding, free speech principles are advanced by a laissez-faire approach to public discourse, whether in the context of government regulation or informal "regulation" through social shaming. The rhetoric of power, on the other hand, assumes a marketplace of ideas skewed in favour of socially powerful groups. Under this understanding, some degree of purposeful intervention into the marketplace of ideas—whether through government regulation or through the imposition of informal social sanctions—is necessary to level the playing field such that ideas disfavoured by dominant social groups are given real opportunities for public airing.

4. Working towards resolution of the debate

How might we work towards a healthy resolution of the present cancel culture debate? As a foundational matter, we need to recognise that the issue is not a simple, binary question of whether "cancellation" is a good or bad thing. Rather, the question is how we should calibrate public discourse to achieve the best balance between the free speech values on both sides of the debate. Heavy-handed cancellation can create chilling effects that stymie healthy public discourse; at the same time, public shaming is, at its core, counterspeech, so to decry all forms of cancellation is to decry any sort of healthy external critique. Extreme positions on either side therefore risk the creation or perpetuation of a public monoculture, either by instilling fear in those who wish to express unpopular views or by concretising norms regarding public discourse that, in practice, work to insulate preferred perspectives from critique.

Reaching a sensible balance regarding this issue therefore requires a measured and holistic perspective—a perspective that is unfortunately too often lacking within the present political climate. "Cancel culture" has become a buzzword for a debate that, in recent years, has taken on a highly politicised, "us versus them" orientation. Because the modern-day debate has arisen, to a significant extent, around the #MeToo and Black Lives Matter movements, support for cancellation has become associated with political progressives, while critiques of cancellation have become associated with political conservatives. Thus, given the highly polarised dynamic that has come to dominate American politics, much of the cancel culture debate has taken on a knee-jerk quality, stripped of the hard questions and nuance underlying it.

In the end, however, the cancel culture debate is ultimately about nuance and proportionality. It is not about whether cancellation is good or bad; it is about when, and to what extent, social shaming and sanctioning in response to certain actions or viewpoints are justified and desirable. And unlike traditional debates regarding the freedom of speech in the United States—which tend to revolve around the First Amendment's limitations on state action—this is not a question of legal doctrine, solvable by analytical means. Rather, it is ultimately an issue that can only be resolved through a broad cultural conversation about shared free speech values. What should freedom of speech look like in the age of the Internet and social media? How should we balance speakers' freedom to express their opinions against listeners' freedom to critique, condemn, and take action against those speakers? These are questions that have no singular and easy answers.

Any healthy resolution of the cancel culture debate must therefore emerge through a nuanced and measured cultural conversation regarding the sort of free speech culture and public discourse we wish to have. Thus, dialogue regarding cancel culture should reflect a posture and rhetoric of balancing and calibration, rather than absolutism and sloganeering. We cannot paint all social shaming and condemnation with the same brush by classifying it categorically either as cancel culture destroying the fabric of free speech or as necessary accountability for entrenched social injustices. Not all cancellations are the same, and reaching a healthy balance requires identifying circumstances under which social shaming ultimately undermines free speech values and those under which it advances those values.

We might consider, as an initial matter, the underlying basis for social shaming. Specifically, we might consider the extent to which a person is cancelled due to their association with a socially unpopular viewpoint, whether because they expressed such a viewpoint directly or because they undertook actions associated with that viewpoint. For example, a person who is cancelled because she embezzled money many years ago is not being cancelled because of her views. To be sure, one might reasonably debate the degree to which cancellation is justified in this particular instance, which might depend on factors such as the severity of the conduct, how long ago it occurred, the circumstances in question, the person's subsequent actions and so forth.

But this sort of cancellation does not carry the same sort of speech implications as, say, cancellation due to the expression of an unpopular viewpoint, which exacts a far higher cost with respect to free speech values. The chilling effects created by such cancellation extend not to conduct clearly recognised as socially harmful (like embezzlement), but rather to the articulation of socially unacceptable viewpoints. This sort of public shaming would not only chill the offender in question and other potential offenders from articulating similar viewpoints in the future, but it may also chill *all* speakers—across all parts of the political spectrum—from articulating views that they suspect may fall outside of prevailing social norms.

We might also consider the types and degrees of social sanctions imposed upon offenders. The most basic sanction imposed is social criticism—for example, social media posts condemning a person's stated views. As discussed earlier, this sort of criticism, by itself, is merely counterspeech that is an integral aspect of any well-functioning marketplace of ideas. Thus, to the extent offenders suffer harm as a result of such condemnation—social embarrassment, loss of friends and so forth—this is merely the marketplace of ideas operating as it should. Freedom of speech does not mean freedom from social condemnation of one's views, even if such condemnation might lead to some chilling effects.

Social condemnation, however, can develop into more significant institutional sanctions.[22] The most significant of these would be loss of employment through social pressure, but other sanctions might include deplatforming by social media companies or expulsion from community organisations. Examples of these sorts of institutional sanctions abound in recent cases of cancellation: public and private offenders alike have suffered the loss of employment and business opportunities, and—in the most notable case of deplatforming—Donald Trump was banned from Twitter following the attack on the United States Capitol on 6 January 2021 (Denham, 2021).

At this point, the costs of expressing one's views expand beyond social shaming into tangible harm: the loss of one's livelihood, formal ostracism from social groups or the direct silencing of one's voice. And here, the balancing judgement becomes more difficult. It is one thing to expect that speakers bear the social critique that accompanies the expression of their views; even if such critique is widespread and harsh, it is merely counterspeech at work within the marketplace of ideas. But it is another thing to expect speakers to bear the loss of their livelihoods, their ability to express their views to the public at large, or their community affiliations as a result of the expression of their views. These sorts of severe sanctions greatly magnify the chilling effect on all speakers, as few would be willing to bear these consequences for the sake of expressing their views.

On the other side of the ledger, however, employers, community organisations and private companies all have their own associational interests. An employer is broadly free to choose those with whom it will associate based on that person's publicly stated viewpoints. Thus, for example, an employer is entitled to fire an at-will employee with whom it no longer desires to associate because of the employee's publicly stated views, just as an employee could leave the employer under similar circumstances. This might be due to the employer's own disapproval of the employee's viewpoints, or it might be as a result of public pressure on the employer to take action against the employee. Either way, just as speakers have a right to say whatever they choose, individuals, companies and social media platforms have a right to choose those with whom they will associate.

In thinking through when these sorts of sanctions may be justified, we would also take into account the nature of the statement or viewpoint in question. Within public discourse, the degree of disapprobation naturally depends on the severity of the statement in question: one would expect minimal criticism of an employer firing an employee due to public statements supporting genocide, as opposed to firing the employee due to public statements opposing current tax policy. As one commentator has observed, "Today, almost all critics of cancel culture have some line they draw, some figure—usually a racist or anti-Semite—that they would cancel, too" (Douthat, 2020). And although this sort of distinct treatment of speech based on its perceived degree of reprehensibility would be flatly contrary to free speech principles from the perspective of government regulation, it is natural within broader public discourse. Certain viewpoints may be deemed so beyond the pale as to be deserving of severe social shaming and sanctioning, while others may be deemed to be sufficiently within the realm of sensible discourse such that such shaming is unwarranted (even if we disagree with them).

To be sure, much of the underlying debate regarding cancel culture is rooted in fundamental disagreements regarding these sorts of value judgements. Viewpoints that might be deemed sufficiently reprehensible to merit severe social sanctions to some may be deemed to be well within the realm of reasonable debate to others. Even if both conservatives and progressives agree that social sanctions are sometimes warranted for the expression of certain viewpoints, they will likely disagree significantly as to when particular viewpoints cross this line. But at the very least, public discourse surrounding the cancel culture debate should emphasise these sorts of relative severity judgements in order to maintain a broad sense of proportionality with respect to instituting social sanctions on offenders.

Furthermore, in evaluating the appropriateness of particular institutional sanctions, we might also take into account the nature of the relationship between the offender and the institution in question. The offender might have a close association with the institution in question, such that others may reasonably construe the person's views as reflecting (or at least not inconsistent with) the institution's views. This might be true, for example, of an employee of a small, family-owned restaurant or of a member of a community organisation. By contrast, few would likely construe the views of any one of Twitter's 300 million users as reflecting the views of Twitter itself, as Twitter seeks to act as a neutral third-party host of others' speech. The stronger this connection between the offender and the institution in question, the stronger the institution's associational interest in cutting ties with the offender, whether by terminating her employment or excluding her from membership.

To be sure, these broad guidelines in delineating the appropriate limits of cancellation provide little in the way of concrete guidance. But again, the cancel culture debate takes place outside of the realm of government regulation and constitutional doctrine. It is a wide-open, free-wheeling debate about our own cultural values—a debate with few doctrinal boundaries. It is ultimately up to us, as a civil society, to collectively deliberate as to what sort of public discourse we ought to have and to construct and preserve this discourse through the establishment of appropriate social norms. So perhaps our focus ought not to be on simply determining, as a theoretical matter, when cancellation is or is not justified. It is also imperative that we try to establish—through norms of civility, proportionality and reasoned public debate—the conditions within which this important cultural conversation can occur.

5. Conclusion

The present cancel culture debate is merely one aspect of a broad shift within the United States' free speech culture. Traditionally, debates regarding free speech in the United States have revolved around the strictures of the First Amendment—that is, the extent of the government's power to regulate speech. And this focus made sense in the pre-digital era, where many of the primary means of mass dissemination of information—such as protests, leafletting or organised rallies—took place within public forums under direct government control.

Most vital public discourse today, however, takes place on private forums—most notably, social media sites such as Twitter, Facebook, Instagram and Reddit. In these forums, fear of government censorship has given way to fear of private censorship.[23] And in this realm, legal and theoretical boundaries are of diminished importance (Balkin, 2018, 1154). Rather, the nature and parameters of our public discourse are dictated by the free speech culture that we collectively choose to adopt—one that is derived not from doctrinal analysis, but rather through broad social debate regarding free speech norms. It is therefore ultimately up to us—the participants in the marketplace of ideas—to collectively think through and delineate the rules of the game. Given the massive shift towards private speech platforms and the advent of "cheap speech" over the Internet (Volokh, 1995, 1806–1807), the contours and boundaries of public discourse lie largely in our own hands.

Thus, the best we might hope for with respect to the cancel culture debate may simply be a healthier national conversation regarding the issue—one that recognises proportionality, nuance and balance in evaluating the issue rather than political side-taking. Indeed, as history has shown us, political valences with respect to particular issues can shift rapidly.[24] Today's cancellers may become tomorrow's cancelled and vice versa.[25] Given that it is largely the public itself—rather than the government—that will be charting the future course of our public discourse, it is essential that we undertake this project seriously, through a continuous cultural conversation that recognises and seeks to balance the free speech values on both sides of the equation. Whether this sort of healthy social conversation is realistically possible within the highly polarised political climate of today is unclear—but that is what we should strive for.

Notes

1 Harvey Weinstein, Bill Cosby and Kevin Spacey, for example, were all cancelled due to allegations of sexual assault (Romano, 2021).
2 For example, tech CEO Michael Lofthouse was cancelled after his racist tirade towards an Asian-American family was captured on video and disseminated via social media (Elfrink, 2020).

3 Gina Carano, for example, was cancelled following a series of offensive and controversial statements over social media (Victor, 2021).
4 J.K. Rowling, for example, was "publicly excoriated . . . for expressing her views on gender identity and biological sex, but people continue to buy her books" (Mishan, 2020).
5 For example, Amy Cooper, who made false accusations to the police regarding a Black bird-watcher that transformed her into "an international symbol of the routine racism that Black people face in their daily lives," was "fired from her high-level finance job" (Nir, 2020).
6 *Merriam-Webster Dictionary*, s.v. "cancel." www.merriam-webster.com/dictionary/cancel#h1 (accessed 22 September 2022).
7 *Merriam-Webster Dictionary*, s.v. "cancel culture." www.merriam-webster.com/dictionary/cancel%20culture (accessed 22 September 2022).
8 Ligaya Mishan has observed, "Cancel culture doesn't exist because it has *always* existed, in rumors, whispers and smear campaigns" (2020). As many have noted, the current debate over "cancellation" may be viewed as merely a continuation of the debates surrounding "political correctness" in the 1990s (Romano, 2021).
9 As Mishan observed, "Every obsessive search on Google for proof of wrongdoing, every angry post on Twitter and Facebook to call the guilty to account, is a silent ka-ching in the great repositories of these corporations, which woo advertisers by pointing to the intensity of user engagement" (2020).
10 As Max Fisher and Amanda Taub observed, "Studies find that negative, primal emotions—fear, anger—draw the most engagement. So posts that provoke those emotions rise naturally. Tribalism—a universal human tendency—also draws heavy engagement" (2018).
11 In this context, to deplatform is "to remove and ban (a registered user) from a mass communication medium (such as a social networking or blogging website)." *Merriam-Webster Dictionary*, s.v. "deplatform," accessed 22 September 2022. www.merriam-webster.com/dictionary/deplatform.
12 To dox is "to publicly identify or publish private information about (someone) especially as a form of punishment or revenge." *Merriam-Webster Dictionary*, s.v. "dox," accessed 22 September 2022. www.merriam-webster.com/dictionary/dox.
13 As Mishan has observed, "To say 'cancel culture' . . . is already to express a point of view, implicitly negative" (2020).
14 This critique lay at the core of the much-discussed "Letter on Justice and Open Debate," an open letter published in *Harper's Magazine* that was signed by notable writers, journalists and academics across the political spectrum (Ackerman et al., 2020). The letter argued that the present culture has "steadily narrow[ed] the boundaries of what can be said without the threat of reprisal," thus leading to "greater risk aversion among writers, artists, and journalists who fear for their livelihoods if they depart from the consensus, or even lack sufficient zeal in agreement" (Ibid.).
15 As Ross Douthat observed, "[c]elebrities are the easiest people to target, but the hardest people to actually cancel" (2020). Similarly, Sarah Manavis observed that "[t]he majority of those 'cancelled,' like JK Rowling, Dave Chappelle, or Aziz Ansari, go on to experience continuing commercial success," and "[i]n some cases, backlash becomes part of their brand – a fresh, new pivot that benefits their growing bottom line" (2020).
16 "'Cancel culture' could . . . be defined as a collective desire for those in positions of power to be held responsible for their perceived wrongdoings. Most of the time, this is when it is believed the actions or opinions in question oppress the marginalised, or put the safety of others at risk" (Manavis, 2020).

17 "[T]he origins of cancel culture are rooted in giving marginalized members of society the ability to seek accountability and change, especially from people who hold a disproportionate amount of wealth, power, and privilege" (Romano, 2020).
18 This view is reflected in an open letter criticizing the *Harper's* letter as "reflect[ing] a stubbornness to let go of the elitism that still pervades the media industry, an unwillingness to dismantle systems that keep people like [the *Harper's* signatories] in and the rest of us out" (Binkowski et al., 2020).
19 As Douthat observed, "The goal [of cancellation] isn't to punish everyone, or even very many someones; it's to shame or scare just enough people to make the rest conform" (2020).
20 As Ryan Lizza observed, "One person's online mob is another person's vehicle to hold someone accountable" (Lizza, 2020). As one commentator quoted by Lizza argued, "What we're seeing described as cancel culture isn't so much a new kind of behavior but a new set of actors in our political discourse who get to say what isn't ok—young people, African Americans, transgender people. . . . Everyone thinks there are lines. The question is where are those lines and who gets to draw them" (Ibid.).
21 Abrams v. United States, 250 U.S. 616, 630 (1919) (Holmes, J., dissenting).
22 Douthat has defined cancellation to require these sorts of serious sanctions that extend beyond mere public criticism, stating, "You are not being canceled if you are merely being heckled or insulted, . . . no matter how vivid and threatening the heckling becomes. You are decidedly at risk of cancellation, however, if your critics are calling for you to be de-platformed or fired or put out of business" (Douthat, 2020).
23 As Jack Balkin has observed, "digital speech flows through an elaborate privately-owned infrastructure of communication," such that "our practical ability to speak is subject to the decisions of private infrastructure owners, who govern the digital spaces in which people communicate with each other" (2018, 1153).
24 Today, for example, it is currently the political right fighting for the broad expansion of First Amendment protections while the political left seeks to restrain this expansion—the polar opposite of the political landscape 60 years ago.
25 As Douthat observed, "[t]he right and the left both cancel; it's just that today's right is too weak to do it effectively" (2020).

References

Ackerman, E. et al. 2020. "A Letter on Justice and Open Debate." *Harper's Magazine*, July 7. https://harpers.org/a-letter-on-justice-and-open-debate.

Balkin, J. M. 2018. "Free Speech in the Algorithmic Society: Big Data, Private Governance, and New School Speech Regulation." *U.C. Davis Law Review* 51: 1149–1210.

Binkowski, B. et al. 2020. "A More Specific Letter on Justice and Open Debate." *The Objective*, July 10. https://objectivejournalism.org/2020/07/a-more-specific-letter-on-justice-and-open-debate.

Bromwich, J. E. 2020. "Why 'Cancel Culture' Is a Distraction." *New York Times*, October 27. www.nytimes.com/2020/08/14/podcasts/daily-newsletter-cancel-culture-beirut-protest.html.

Denham, H. 2021. "These Are the Platforms That Have Banned Trump and His Allies." *Washington Post*, January 14. www.washingtonpost.com/technology/2021/01/11/trump-banned-social-media.

Douthat, R. 2020. "10 Theses About "Cancel Culture." *New York Times*, July 14. www.nytimes.com/2020/07/14/opinion/cancel-culture-.html.

Elfrink, T. 2020. "Tech CEO Apologies for Racist Tirade Against Asian American Family Caught on Video." *Washington Post*, July 8. www.washingtonpost.com/nation/2020/07/08/lofthouse-racist-video-tech-ceo.

Fisher, M. and Taub, A. 2018. "How Everyday Social Media Users Become Real-World Extremists." *New York Times*, April 25. www.nytimes.com/2018/04/25/world/asia/facebook-extremism.html.

Fried, C. 1992. "The New First Amendment Jurisprudence: A Threat to Liberty." *University of Chicago Law Review* 59: 225–253.

Ingber, Stanley. 1984. "The Marketplace of Ideas: A Legitimizing Myth." *Duke Law Journal* 1984: 1–91.

Lizza, R. 2020. "Americans Tune in to 'Cancel Culture'—and Don't Like What They See." *Politico*, July 22. www.politico.com/news/2020/07/22/americans-cancel-culture-377412.

Manavis, S. 2020. "'Cancel Culture' Does Not Exist." *New Statesman*, July 16. www.newstatesman.com/science-tech/2020/07/cancel-culture-does-not-exist.

Meiklejohn, A. 1948. *Free Speech and Its Relation to Self-Government*. New York: Harper Brothers Publishers.

Mill, J. S. 1859/2003. *On Liberty*. New Haven: Yale University Press.

Mishan, L. 2020. "The Long and Tortured History of Cancel Culture." *New York Times*, December 3. www.nytimes.com/2020/12/03/t-magazine/cancel-culture-history.html.

Morrison, K. 2015. "Cutting Through the Social Media Jargon: What Are Reach, Impressions and Engagement?" *Adweek*, September 17. www.adweek.com/digital/cutting-through-the-social-media-jargon-what-are-reach-impressions-and-engagement.

Nir, S. M. 2020. "How 2 Lives Collided in Central Park, Rattling the Nation." *New York Times*, June 14. www.nytimes.com/2020/06/14/nyregion/central-park-amy-cooper-christian-racism.html.

Romano, A. 2021. "The Second Wave of 'Cancel Culture'." *Vox*, May 5. www.vox.com/22384308/cancel-culture-free-speech-accountability-debate.

Victor, D. 2021. "Gina Carano Is Off 'Mandalorian' Amid Backlash Over Instagram Post." *New York Times*, February 11. www.nytimes.com/2021/02/11/arts/television/gina-carano-lucasfilm.html.

Volokh, E. 1995. "Cheap Speech and What It Will Do." *Yale Law Journal* 104: 1805–1850.

11 Government speech and minority rights

The American view

William D. Araiza[*]

1. Introduction

What should a democratic government's responsibilities be when it speaks in ways that attack or disparage minorities? Beyond physical atrocities against ethnic, religious and political minorities, the twentieth century also witnessed brutal verbal attacks by government speakers against minority groups, often as a precursor to those physical assaults. The relationship between speech attacks and physical attacks persists even when the violence occurs at less horrific levels. For example, many observers found a connection between President Trump's ethnically-tinged attacks on the Chinese government during the COVID-19 pandemic and increased hate crimes against Asian Americans.

American law differs from the law of many of its advanced democratic siblings in its refusal to recognise such group hate speech as an unprotected category of speech. Nevertheless, American law implicitly recognises a difference depending on whether such speech is made by private parties or the government itself. At first glance, that last statement is an odd one. Over the last two decades, the U.S. Supreme Court has slowly developed a doctrine, called the "government speech" doctrine, that seemingly allows the government to speak as it wishes, just as private speakers can. The government speech doctrine states that, when the government (state or federal) is deemed to be speaking, the normal limits the First Amendment imposes on the government do not apply. The logic of such a doctrine is straightforward: the government, it is argued, must have the latitude to speak to promote its goals, unencumbered by basic rules of American free speech law. In particular, when the government speaks, the so-called "content neutrality rule"—the rule that presumptively prevents the government from distinguishing favoured from disfavoured speech based on its content—does not apply.

Simple examples reveal the necessary truth of this proposition. Surely, the government can engage in content discrimination by choosing the topics about which it wishes to speak. Indeed, it can go farther and choose the viewpoints it wishes to express about those topics. Thus, a government that wishes to speak about

DOI: 10.4324/9781003274476-15

smoking and voting can do so; moreover, if it sends anti-smoking, pro-voting messages, it should not thereby be required to give equal time to pro-smoking and anti-voting messages. Both practical social goals (e.g. combatting smoking) and maintenance of a healthy political system (e.g. encouraging voting) should be within the government's power to promote without having to impair its own message by being required to send the opposing one.

Yet this straightforward idea uncritically applied proves too much. The government's appropriate latitude to send certain messages should not allow it *carte blanche* to send any messages it wishes. Some justices' opinions in some government speech cases attempt to find a structural limitation on the government's ability to speak by insisting that government be transparent about its status as the source of the speech in question (*Johanns v. Livestock Marketing Association*, 2005 [Souter, J.]). The idea is that such transparency will ensure democratic control of the message the government sends.

But this limitation on the government's latitude to speak accomplishes too little. If we are concerned about government speech that harms minorities, then relying on the democratic process to prevent such harmful speech is exactly the wrong response. For at least nearly a century, the intuitions of American justices have rebelled at the idea that counter-majoritarian interests such as minority rights can be safely guarded by the majoritarian political process (*United States v. Carolene Products Co.*, 1938; Gey, 2010, 1293).

Thus, other limits on government speech must be found when that speech relates, not to shifting economic and social arrangements which can be safely consigned to the political process, but rather to the counter-majoritarian interests of minority groups. This essay considers this challenge as it threads its way through a variety of American constitutional law doctrines. To provide a context for its analysis, it offers five plausible examples of government speech or expression that arguably denigrates or subordinates minorities:

- A government statement, issued in the form of a proclamation from the governor's office, asserting that the state is a Christian society;
- A government decision to include the confederate battle flag as a part of the state's official flag or seal;
- A government statement, issued via guidance from a state department of education, mandating that public school sex education classes teach that same-sex sexual conduct is immoral;
- A law prohibiting gender-affirming surgery (i.e. surgery that conforms persons' physical characteristics to their gender self-identification);
- A government anti-obesity program that urges citizens to summon what it calls "the willpower and self-control" to limit the consumption of fatty foods.

The rest of this chapter considers limits on government speech that denigrates minorities, using these examples and several variants thereon as contexts for its analysis.

2. First Amendment rights for government?

Begin with the most foundational question: does the government have a First Amendment right to speak? On reflection, the answer seems to be "no." The traditional justifications for protecting the right to speak either do not apply to the government or raise thorny conceptual or practical questions.

One basic justification for free speech is that it enables speakers to define themselves by using the uniquely human attribute of speech to present themselves to the world (Baker, 1992; Emerson, 1963). Because government lacks a personality that would be actualised by speech, this justification for free speech simply does not apply to it. To be sure, other non-human associations—for example, businesses, unions, universities and civic groups—enjoy free speech rights. However, at least some such associations exist solely or largely in order to allow their human members to express themselves by associating for expressive purposes (*Federal Election Commission v. Massachusetts Citizens for Life*, 1986). At least in modern liberal democracies, the government should not be thought of as an association of like-minded persons coming together to express themselves. A modern republican government—a *res publica*, a "public matter"—belongs to all its citizens. The inevitable pluralism of views and outlooks and the government's obligation to respect such differing views render the self-actualisation idea a bad fit with a government speaker.

Even more serious questions attend the prospect of granting free speech rights to the government under the theory that free speech enables self-government (Bhagwat, 2017, 1450–1451). Democratic government is, of course, the product of democratic deliberation. To say that government itself can participate in the process of that deliberation raises difficult questions, not just of logical circularity but, more fundamentally, about whether the currently ascendant political faction should be allowed to wield public power to advocate for its continued political authority. In short, the self-government rationale arguably refutes itself.

But what about the third, and in some ways, the most powerful justification for free speech: the idea that that speech contributes to "a marketplace of ideas" in which truth is generally thought to ultimately prevail and is at least entitled to compete (*Abrams v. United States*, 1919 [Holmes, J.])? This theory, unlike the self-government idea, appears to give the freest possible rein to speech, since, presumably, every speech act contributes to the marketplace. At first glance, the marketplace theory perhaps provides a justification for government speech.

One response to this question is easy. As scholars have noted, according to the government a right or authority to speak creates a tension with the First Amendment because government speech often takes the form of action that limits other persons' rights to speak (e.g. Blocher 2011, 698). For example, when in 2009 the Court held that a city was engaging in its own speech when it accepted one religious monument for placement in a park but declined to accept another monument offered by a different religious group, that "government speech" had the effect of restricting the speech of the group whose offer was declined (*Pleasant Grove*

City v. Summum, 2009). Similarly, when the Court held that a state was speaking when it allowed some privately-designed images on state automobile license plates and rejected other designs, that "government speech" effectively restricted the rights of those who wished to display the rejected designs (*Walker v. Sons of Confederate Veterans*, 2015).

The lesson is simple: when the government is held to be speaking, that characterisation often comes at the cost of private parties' speech rights. In other words, it often comes at the expense of the marketplace. Indeed, given that characterising the speech in question as governmental allows the government to engage in content and viewpoint discrimination, the government speech characterisation allows the government not only to restrict the marketplace but also to distort it in favour of views the government favours.

But leave aside such situations, and consider government speech that has no direct impact on private speech. Scholars have worried that the government's uniquely powerful voice threatens to drown out or displace private speech, thus distorting the marketplace of ideas even absent direct restriction of private speech (e.g. Blocher, 2011, 698). To be sure, the extent to which this displacement occurs may be open to debate. Nevertheless, even that suggestion cuts against any confident assertion of the marketplace metaphor as a reason to accord First Amendment rights to the government.

These objections to the idea of government as a First Amendment rights holder help us begin to construct an argument about government speech and minority rights. A basic tenet of First Amendment doctrine is that speakers are generally free to choose the topics about which they wish to speak and the viewpoints they wish to express about those topics. Thus, accordingly, First Amendment rights to the government would raise difficult questions about the legal restrictions that would limit the government if it wished to engage in speech disparaging minorities. For example, just as private parties in the United States are free to express the view that racial minorities are inferior, religious minorities damned or sexual minorities immoral, so too could government express such views, if in doing so they were held to be exercising First Amendment rights.

Of course, such private liberty to engage in such speech may not exist in other advanced democratic nations that restrict abusive or disparaging speech as, for example, the German Basic Law does by limiting free speech in pursuit of ensuring "the inviolability of personal dignity" (Grundgesetz [GG] art. 5 § 2 (F.R.G.)). By contrast, American free speech law allows private persons to speak in ways that would likely be forbidden by many other democracies. To deny similar latitude to the government while still characterising it as holding First Amendment rights would thus distort First Amendment law in ways that could ultimately threaten the foundational freedom of speech commitment the nation has made with regard to private speakers. Therefore, accordingly, First Amendment rights to the government would either open the door to presumptive government latitude to express such disparaging views, subject only to the doubtful protections of the democratic process, or require modifications to First Amendment doctrine that could ultimately undermine basic speech freedoms as Americans have come to understand them.

For these reasons and others, many scholars have concluded that the government should not be thought of as having a First Amendment right to speak (e.g. Bezanson and Buss, 2001; Gey, 2010). And yet, the government constantly speaks—and should be allowed to do so. The task then becomes finding an approach that recognises the government's authority to speak while also limiting the ability of democratic majorities (or even smaller factions who manage to obtain control over a particular government entity or program) to wield that authority to engage in speech denigrating minorities. Denying the government the same First Amendment rights that private parties enjoy is a good first step.

3. Limits on government's authority to speak: preliminary issues

Rejecting First Amendment *rights* for government shifts the terrain to government *authority* to speak. The government clearly has this authority. Speech is an inevitable part of legitimate government action. To conduct its business effectively, the government must publicise its initiatives and urge public support and compliance. Anti-smoking programs inevitably include public messages urging people to stop smoking. Pro-vaccination programs include similar outreach urging people to get vaccinated.

Governments at all levels have the authority to engage in such speech. The Constitution's Necessary and Proper Clause (U.S. Constitution Art. I § 8) provides Congress ample power to take actions appropriate to put into effect the regulatory powers the rest of the Constitution gives it. At the state and local levels, the concept of police power is easily broad enough to allow similar speech. But such broad authority is not limitless. In particular, the government's authority to speak does not constitute authority to transgress other constitutional boundaries (*Pleasant Grove City v. Summum*, 2009, 468). Those boundaries include those imposed by the Equal Protection Clause, the fundamental constitutional guarantee of equality. The question then becomes, when can government speech disparaging minorities be said to discriminate in a way that violates that clause?

Thinking about the government speech question as one that implicates the government's legitimate authority may help delineate the allowable scope of—and the limitations on—government speech that harms minorities. However, before considering the appropriate scope of that authority, it is helpful to consider several preliminary issues.

3.1. Is the government communicating a message?

The most basic question is whether the government is communicating a meaningful message at all. Of course, as illustrated by the examples provided at the end of the Introduction, some cases are clear. A government proclamation about the state's Christian identity obviously sends a message. But other cases are more ambiguous. Consider a government ban on gender-affirming surgery.

Those ambiguous cases hearken back to the classic 1896 case *Plessy v. Ferguson*, where the Court, over only one dissenting vote, upheld state-mandated racial segregation on railroads and thus, by implication, across every realm of public activity. One of the key points of Justice Henry Billings Brown's majority opinion was his statement that any subordinating or disparaging message Blacks received from the racial segregation law was a message they themselves chose to put on it:

> We consider the underlying fallacy of the plaintiff's argument to consist in the assumption that the enforced separation of the two races stamps the colored race with a badge of inferiority. If this be so, it is not by reason of anything found in the act, but solely because the colored race chooses to put that construction upon it.
>
> (*Plessy v. Ferguson*, 1896, 551)

While the *Plessy* Court did not phrase it in these terms, its analysis of whether the train law communicated a message of inferiority can be understood as an early application of the state action concept—that is, the rule that any constitutional violation requires unconstitutional action by the state itself (e.g. Strasser, 2000, 48). One way to understand Justice Brown's statement was as simply denying that the state was sending any particular message by enacting the segregation law.

Today, we are far more willing than the *Plessy* Court was to acknowledge the role that government regulation can play in sending disparaging messages. One need only look at *Brown v. Board of Education*'s classic statement recognising that segregation communicates to minority students a message of inferiority to realise that *Plessy*'s wilful blindness to the message the train segregation law sent is no longer the law (*Brown v. Board of Education*, 1954, 494; Strasser, 2000, 49–50). Later Supreme Court justices have made the point even more explicitly. For example, in 1995, Justice John Paul Stevens chastised the Court for striking down a race-based contracting preference. He argued that the majority, by applying the same level of scrutiny to such preference laws that it applied to exclusionary laws such as the ones in *Plessy* and *Brown*, had "disregard[ed] the difference between a 'No Trespassing' sign and a welcome mat" (*Adarand Constructors, Inc. v. Peña*, 1995, 245 [Stevens, J.]). Regardless of whether his critique was well-taken, his use of those metaphors—a sign and a welcome mat—reveals the potential for regulatory laws to send messages.

3.2. Is a message sufficient for a finding of unconstitutionality?

But recognising that the government can send messages through regulation is not the same as concluding that such messages by themselves may violate the Constitution. Consider a 1971 case, *Palmer v. Thompson*. In *Palmer*, the City of Jackson, Mississippi had been ordered to desegregate its public swimming pools. Rather than complying, it chose instead to close its pools or transfer them to private ownership. The question for the Court was whether that conduct violated the Equal Protection Clause.

A bare five-justice majority of the Court held that it did not. Justice Hugo Black's majority opinion rejected the argument that any city's purpose to prevent integration violated equal protection without a differential material effect on the Black plaintiffs. Because both Blacks and whites suffered from the pools' closures and transfers, that differential material impact was lacking. In other words, a mere intent to discriminate, divorced from any material impact on the minority group, may be insufficient to make out an equal protection violation.

Palmer dealt with the impact of government conduct—the decision to close government facilities rather than integrate them—rather than the impact of government speech. Nevertheless, it suggests that, under current American law, speech that might be seen as sending a disparaging message, just like conduct that might be seen as sending such a message, could still be inadequate for the purpose of demonstrating an equal protection violation. But before considering this possible obstacle, and ways litigants might be able to surmount it, this essay considers two complicating factors with regard to equal protection-based limits on government speech.

3.3. Government speech and its relation to private conduct

The first complicating factor deals with government endorsement of private conduct. To illustrate this issue, consider a variant of one of the examples of government speech offered at the end of the Introduction. Consider a government statement that, rather than directing public schools to teach the immorality of same-sex sexual activity, instead merely endorses private schools' right to teach that idea. Hypothesise a situation in which the government takes no position on the appropriateness of such teaching. Instead, it simply endorses the right of private persons and associations to act on their beliefs.

This situation is parallel to one the Court confronted in a 1967 case, *Reitman v. Mulkey*. *Reitman* involved the decision by the people of California, via a referendum, to repeal a fair housing law the legislature had enacted and to enshrine in the state constitution the right of landowners to dispose of their property as they wished. The question *Reitman* presented was whether that referendum result violated equal protection by officially endorsing private discriminatory conduct.

A bare five-justice majority held that it did. Writing for that majority, Justice Byron White emphasised that the referendum did more than simply repeal the statute that had prohibited such discrimination. Rather, it had enshrined in the state constitution the right to discriminate. The dissent disagreed and warned that the majority's result would impede non-discrimination legislation, since, after the Court's decision, such legislation, once enacted, would become presumptively unrepealable.

Reitman poses a difficult question about whether the Court's analysis does indeed make anti-discrimination legislation effectively unrepealable. But for our purposes, the more interesting question is simply whether a government statement endorsing private views effectively imputes those views to the state. Of course, *Reitman* itself involved more than a mere government statement; rather, it involved government *regulation* authorising private discrimination. But if the question on the table is the constitutionality of government *messaging*, then the attribution question *Reitman* confronted still applies: does government speech endorsing private discrimination violate equal protection just as government speech directly espousing discrimination might?

3.4. Endorsing constitutionally protected conduct

We can take the question posed at the end of the last sub-section and problematise it as an additional step. What in the analysis, if anything, changes if the conduct the state endorses enjoys significant constitutional protection? This step distinguishes *Reitman*. Even though the Constitution protects property interests, those rights remain subject to substantial regulation. But the rights to speak and to hold religious views enjoy significant constitutional protection. So too does a religious entity's right to act on those views in the course of employing a ministerial employee (a category that extends far beyond the traditional conception of "minister") (*Our Lady of Guadalupe School v. Morrissey-Berru*, 2020; Barrick, 2020).

Does the analysis change if the government endorses viewpoints or conduct that enjoy significant constitutional protection? Is the government thereby freer to endorse such views, despite any harm they may cause minorities? Christians have the right to believe that the United States is, or should be, a Christian country. Sexual traditionalists have a right to believe that same-sex conduct or gender fluidity is immoral. Churches have the right to discriminate when they select their ministers. Can the government, as in *Reitman*, endorse those views or that conduct, or does such endorsement unconstitutionally disparage the groups harmed by such private views or conduct?

4. Equal protection-based limits on the government's authority to speak

Part III's discussion of preliminary issues allows us now to consider the limits of the government's authority to speak when its speech disparages minorities. That question is posed as one of the government's authorities, rather than its right, in recognition of Part I's demonstration that government should not be thought of as enjoying First Amendment rights. Nevertheless, as the introduction to Part II made clear, the government's legitimate regulatory powers include the power to speak—for example, to urge people to stop smoking as part of a campaign to regulate tobacco, or to urge people to get vaccinated, as part of an overall plan of health regulation. The question then becomes what types of government speech constitute legitimate adjuncts to such regulatory conduct and what types constitute illegitimate disparagement of minority groups?

4.1. Obstacles to an equal protection approach

Framing the question in this way does not necessarily make it easier. It may be that much government speech denigrating minorities is not reasonably related to legitimate government regulatory activities. But, as discussed later, some ordinary regulatory activities could include government speech that might be thought of as denigrating. For example, a program of tobacco regulation and control could include government speech a smoker might interpret as demeaning (Dorf, 2011). Perhaps more seriously, limitations on the ability of sexually-active gay men to donate blood, expressed via official governmental communications, could be interpreted as stigmatising them (Diaz, 2013). Challenges to such government speech will encounter the defence that government has the authority to regulate tobacco and the blood supply and that such regulatory authority carries with it the power to engage in speech, even if that speech has a collateral effect of demeaning a minority group.

Different obstacles attend instances of more explicit government speech. For example, consider a state government's decision to display the confederate battle flag, either as its own unique banner or as part of a state flag design. In two cases, lower federal courts concluded that Black plaintiffs alleging that such decisions violated equal protection could not show that the government's display of the flag caused them a distinct harm (*NAACP v. Hunt*, 1990; *Coleman v. Miller*, 1997). The courts in those cases did not take issue with the plaintiff's argument that the state's display of the confederate design impacted him, and Black persons generally. However, they concluded that some white persons were equally offended by the state's conduct. On that basis, the court concluded that the state's conduct did not inflict a particular discriminatory burden based on race.

One can detect in *Hunt* and *Coleman* the ghost of *Palmer v. Thompson*, the Mississippi swimming pool case discussed earlier. As with the display of the flag in *Hunt* and *Coleman*, the Court in *Palmer* held that the city's closure of its swimming pools inflicted harm on all citizens, and thus did not impose a discriminatory burden on racial minorities. While the analysis may seem paradoxical, not to mention troubling, the offense that persons of different races might have taken at a state's decision to display the confederate flag design proved fatal to any claim directly based on equal protection analysis. This restrictive approach to equal protection has potentially broad ramifications for government speech disparaging minorities. If flying a confederate flag design does not impose a disparate burden on Black Americans, then presumably neither would other racially disparaging speech—nor, for that matter, disparaging speech targeting any other minority that nevertheless also offended a broad segment of society.

4.2. Limits on the government's authority to speak: equal protection, animus, and government's legitimate power

But we can identify another path to attack disparaging government speech. It should be possible to challenge such speech by conjoining the government powers argument offered earlier with equal protection reasoning. The analysis here requires considering a style of equal protection reasoning that has hovered around the edges of Supreme Court jurisprudence for 50 years, but which has become more prevalent in its recent jurisprudence.

In 1973, in *Department of Agriculture v. Moreno*, the Court famously stated that "a bare . . . desire to harm a politically unpopular group cannot constitute a legitimate governmental interest" (p. 534). *Moreno* struck down a federal statute that restricted the availability of food assistance to unrelated groups of persons living and sharing household expenses in one dwelling unit. While the named plaintiff, Jacinta Moreno, was an elderly woman who lived and shared resources with an unrelated family in order to save money, the sparse legislative history of the law suggested that Congress was motivated by a desire to deny food assistance to the "hippies" and "hippy communes" who comprised a distinct social group when the statute was enacted. According to the Court, Congress's "bare . . . desire to harm" that group was an illegitimate government interest that could not suffice to uphold the law against an equal protection challenge. Indeed, as I have discussed in other writing, the illegitimacy of that interest also appeared to have led the Court to accord closer scrutiny to the other, presumptively legitimate, interests the government cited in defence of the law (Araiza, 2017, 32–34).

Moreno has come to be understood as the genesis of a strand of equal protection law that condemns certain laws because they are motivated by "animus." The progress of the animus idea has been uneven, and it remains under-theorised. However, in a series of gay rights and religious freedom cases, the Court has relied on that idea to strike laws down (Araiza, 2021). Without delving too deeply into the details, those decisions have rested on conclusions either that the legislature was affirmatively motivated by "simple dislike" (Araiza, 2017, 2) of the burdened group, or that animus was the only possible explanation for a law that could not be otherwise justified. In other words, courts have found animus based on either direct evidence or by implication.

The animus idea can advance the constitutional argument for prohibiting government speech disparaging minorities. As an equality argument, it implicates the core reason such speech is problematic—i.e. because it intentionally subordinates persons based on their minority status, or, in *Moreno*'s words, because such speech rests on "a bare . . . desire to harm" a vulnerable group. But as an argument that relies on the lack of a legitimate reason for the government speech, it may avoid the difficulties that attend more conventional equal protection arguments, such as the disparate impact requirement that doomed the confederate state flag lawsuits in *Hunt* and *Coleman*. Instead, by focusing on the lack of any legitimate government purpose attending such speech, the animus approach emphasises the lack of government *authority* to engage in the challenged government speech. As such, it rests on the distinction between the government's authority to speak in support of its legitimate regulatory objectives and its lack of authority to speak simply because it wishes to disparage or suppress a recognisable minority.

4.3. The categories of government's disparaging speech

A reader might respond to the aforementioned argument by observing that the government often has legitimate interests in expressing certain viewpoints, not

Government speech and minority rights 191

as a matter of First Amendment right but, rather, as a matter of performing legitimate government functions. That response requires teasing out four situations, differentiated by two variables: the nature of the government's expression and the presence or absence of a legitimate government interest. The resulting landscape is reflected in this grid:

	Pure Expression	Expression Related to Substantive Regulation
No legitimate government interests	1	3
Legitimate government interests	2	4

The placement of a situation or case along the vertical, or y-axis, is determined by whether the government action is supported by a legitimate government interest. The placement of a situation or case along the horizontal, or x-axis, is determined by whether the government action reflects purely expressive government interests or interests related to substantive government regulation.[1] This subsection considers each of the resulting four situations, as identified by the box numbers provided earlier.

1. Box 1: pure government expression lacking a legitimate government interest

Despite the general legitimacy of a state's interest in expressing public values, the Court has made clear that government lacks a legitimate interest in expressing certain ideas. In *Lawrence v. Texas*, Justice O'Connor cited the canonical animus cases to conclude that moral disapproval of lesbian, gay and bisexual persons is not a legitimate government interest sufficient to justify a law even under the rational basis standard of constitutional review, traditionally the most deferential level of such review (2003, 582 [O'Connor, J.]). Exactly a decade later, a Court majority again relied on those cases to find a constitutional violation in the federal government's communication of a message that same-sex marriages sanctioned under state law were nevertheless "second-tier" marriages "unworthy of federal recognition" (*United States v. Windsor*, 2013, 772).

For its part, the First Amendment's Establishment Clause has been read to prohibit, if nothing else, government favouritism toward one religion over another (*Larson v. Valente*, 1982), while some justices have gone farther to argue that it prohibits government endorsement of any particular religion or even religion over irreligion (*County of Allegheny v. ACLU*, 1989). Thus, the Introduction's example of a state's proclamation of its Christianity identity would likely run afoul of the principle that any government speech must further a legitimate government interest. More generally, the animus and religious establishment cases make clear that the expression of certain values, such as simple moral disapproval or disfavouring of a group, does not constitute a legitimate government interest.

2. Box 2: pure government expression that reflects a legitimate government interest

The cases located in Box 2 reflect situations in which the government is conceded to possess a legitimate interest in expressing particular public values. The confederate flag controversy is a prime example of this situation. Except in unusual circumstances, the act of flying a flag is purely expressive. As the prior sub-section demonstrated, some cases of government expression reflect nothing but constitutionally illegitimate discriminatory animus or, in the case of religion, favouritism that is prohibited by a freestanding constitutional provision. But as suggested by *Wooley*, some expressive interests are perfectly legitimate.

The confederate flag controversy presents a situation where illegitimate and legitimate messages might both exist. As is well-known, many persons find the confederate flag to express hateful, disparaging ideas of racial oppression and, indeed, the slavery for which the confederate states went to war. Others perceive a much more benign message: tradition, reverence for fallen ancestors or local autonomy.[2] The question then becomes, whose perceptions count, either in discerning an overall message or in deciding whose perceptions outweigh others', in a case where it is simply impossible to distil one predominant message.

In considering this question, Michael Dorf offers a variety of options, from crediting any denigration claim made by an identifiable social group and requiring careful judicial scrutiny of the challenged expression, to limiting such scrutiny to situations where the complaining party constitutes a class—known in American law as a "suspect class"—that merits heightened judicial protection. He also posits the opposite presumption, in which any reasonable benign reading of the expression insulates it from a challenge (Dorf, 2011).

There is no neutral answer to this question. Rather, the answer will inevitably depend on the relative weights one allots to the community's desire to express (presumptively democratically-adopted) views and to minority groups' sensitivities. It may be that any such balancing also requires considering the depth of feeling each side has about their perceptions and the extent to which the democratic majority has accounted for minorities' perceptions in other expressive contexts.

3. Box 3: regulation-based expression lacking a legitimate government interest

Consider now expression that is tied to, or collateral to, substantive government regulation. As with the pure expression discussed in the previous two sub-sections, government expression tied to regulation can be further differentiated based on whether that expression features or lacks a legitimate government interest. This sub-section considers regulation-related expression that lacks such an interest.

Such expression seems to present an easy case, since its lack of a legitimate government interest renders the government action vulnerable to being struck down as simply irrational—or, if the court chooses, as being grounded in animus. *Moreno* itself would present such a situation if the food assistance cut-off could have been understood as reflecting government expression. But consider an example that perhaps has a stronger expressive element: a government law prohibiting gender-affirming surgery. Presumably, if the law reflected "simple dislike" of transgender persons (Araiza, 2017, 2), then animus would present a straightforward vehicle for striking it down.

To be sure, any animus-grounded strike-down of such a law would require the court to reject any proffered justifications for the regulation. In cases involving expression tied to regulation, rather than pure government expression, this requirement could present an obstacle, given courts' traditional deference to government regulatory decisions. For example, an animus-based challenge to a prohibition on gender-affirming surgery would encounter the government's undoubted power to regulate unsafe or inappropriate medical practices. On the other hand, some regulatory action may strike courts as inherently suspect, given its underlying context. For example, the culturally-contested nature of transgender identity may well lead a court to immediately suspect that a ban on gender-affirming surgery is, like the food assistance cut-off in *Moreno*, motivated by "a bare . . . desire to harm" transgender persons or by "moral disapproval" of them (*Lawrence v. Texas*, 2003, 582 [O'Connor, J.]). Of course, a court might well find it easier to conclude that such a motivation justifies striking down the law without even considering any expression that attends the substantive government action. In that case, it is not the expression itself that triggers the court's decision.

4. Box 4: regulation-based expression that features legitimate government interests

A particularly difficult question arises when minority disparagement indisputably occurs but is defended as an adjunct to an appropriate regulatory policy government might adopt. Consider an anti-obesity campaign. As Professor Dorf explains, such a campaign might well have as a collateral effect the denigration of obese people (Dorf, 2011). For example, government advertisements might urge persons to summon the willpower necessary to exercise and resist eating fatty foods. Such advertisements might be perceived, both generally and by obese persons, as implicit attacks on the latter's presumed lack of self-control. Smokers might take similar offense at anti-smoking campaigns. Similarly, regulation of the blood supply for safety might lead the government to exclude men who actively engage in same-sex sexual conduct. When such restrictions are publicised, gay and bisexual men may feel similarly demeaned (Diaz, 2013).

Animus analysis does not provide an easy pathway to striking down such expression, given the government's ability to justify the challenged speech as vindicating legitimate regulatory interests. Thus, one might recognise that, say, anti-obesity and anti-smoking programs are primarily legitimate regulatory programs aimed at changing *conduct* and that collateral imputations of a particular *status'* inferiority are simply the unfortunate consequences of such regulation. As Steven Gey noted in a different context, "there are important distinctions between broad, general government programs that also happen to involve speech and narrowly focused programs that involve nothing but speech" (Gey, 2010, 1293). This might suggest that the government's legitimate authority to engage in expression related to a regulatory program is broader than when it engages in pure expression. Another possibility, not inconsistent with that suggestion, is to subject regulation-related expression to meaningful scrutiny only when it impacts a historically-marginalised group or what was earlier identified as a "suspect class." This approach would not only acknowledge the government's legitimate regulatory prerogatives but would also recognise that government often fails to adequately account for the interests of such marginalised groups, even if that failure is inadvertent rather than intentional (Karst, 1977).

5. Conclusion

The intricacy of much of the analysis this essay has presented traces, in large part, to American constitutional law's general lack of explicit limits on denigrating speech. Indeed, if such explicit limits existed, then accepting that the government itself had First Amendment rights would not present an obstacle to limiting denigrating government speech, since such speech would presumably be subject to those same general limits.

But because American law lacks those explicit speech limits in general, the search for such limits on government speech requires that we look beyond the First Amendment. The animus principle provides some of those limits. By focusing on the lack of a legitimate government interest supporting some types of denigrating government speech, that principle, when applied to a governmental powers approach to the question, potentially skirts problems that attend more conventional equal protection attacks on such speech.

However, the animus principle is less useful when the government can readily point to legitimate interests underlying its denigrating speech. Those situations raise difficult questions of balancing the government's legitimate interests, whether in engaging in pure speech (as with flying the confederate flag) or speech that attends a legitimate regulatory program (as with anti-obesity speech that is made as part of a government health program). Finding the correct balance in such situations poses a difficult challenge, one that requires us to choose how much to value the feelings of threat and exclusion disparaged groups experience from such speech and the appropriate latitude government should enjoy when it makes regulatory and expressive decisions through the normal democratic process.

Notes

* Thanks to Thu Nguyen and Jillian Horowitz for excellent research assistance.
1 To be sure, a particular government action may be supported by both expressive and substantive interests. For example, in *Wooley v. Maynard* (1977), the Supreme Court struck down a state's requirement that passenger automobiles display state-issued license plates that expressed an ideological message. The Court in that case recognized two state interests: first, a regulatory interest in identifying passenger autos and distinguishing them from other vehicles licensed by that state and, second, an expressive interest in "promot[ing] appreciation of history, individualism, and state pride" (p. 716). Even though the Court found those interests insufficient to justify the law's requirement that

the motorist express the state's message, for our purposes, the important point is that the Court recognized the legitimacy of both the state's regulatory and expressive interests.
2 To be sure, even such benign references can also be understood more darkly. Tradition might carry very different connotations for Blacks and whites in a southern community, reverence for fallen ancestors might mean something very different in a German World War II military cemetery than in another country's and local control may be inextricably bound up in the morality of the underlying issue (here, slavery) that was the subject of the local-versus-national control struggle.

References

Adarand Constructors, Inc., v. Peña [1995] 515 U.S. 200.
Araiza, W. 2017. *Animus: A Brief Introduction to Bias in the Law*. New York: New York University Press.
Araiza, W. 2021. "Regents: Resurrecting Animus/Renewing Discriminatory Intent." *Seton Hall Law Review* 51: 983–1033.
Baker, C. E. 1992. *Human Liberty and Freedom of Speech*. New York: Oxford University Press.
Barrick, R. 2020. "The Ministerial Exception: Seeking Clarity and Precision Amid Inconsistent Application of the *Hosanna-Tabor* Framework." *Emory Law Journal* 70: 465–519.
Bezanson, R. and Buss, W. 2001. "The Many Faces of Government Speech." *Iowa Law Review* 86: 1377–1511.
Bhagwat, A. 2017. "In Defense of Content Regulation." *Iowa Law Review* 102: 1427–1475.
Blocher, J. 2011. "Viewpoint Neutrality and Government Speech." *Boston College Law Review* 52: 695–767.
Brown v. Board of Education [1954] 347 U.S. 483.
Coleman v. Miller [1997] 117 F.3d 527.
County of Allegheny v. ACLU [1989] 492 U.S. 573.
Department of Agriculture v. Moreno [1973] 413 U.S. 528.
Diaz, V. 2013. "A Time for Change: Why the MSM Lifetime Deferral Policy Should Be Amended." *University of Maryland Law Journal of Race, Religion, Gender, and Class* 13: 134–155.
Dorf, M. 2011. "Same-Sex Marriage, Second-Class Citizenship, and Law's Social Meanings." *Virginia Law Review* 97: 1267–1346.
Emerson, T. 1963. "Toward a General Theory of the First Amendment." *Yale Law Journal* 72: 877–956.
Federal Election Commission v. Massachusetts Citizens for Life [1986] 479 U.S. 238.
Gey, S. 2010. "Why Should the First Amendment Protect Government Speech When the Government Has Nothing to Say?" *Iowa Law Review* 95: 1259–1314.
Johanns v. Livestock Marketing Association [2005] 544 U.S. 550.
Karst, K. 1977. "The Supreme Court's 1976 Term: Foreword: Equal Citizenship Under the Fourteenth Amendment." *Harvard Law Review* 91: 1–68.
Larson v. Valente [1982] 456 U.S. 228.
Lawrence v. Texas [2003] 539 U.S. 558.
NAACP v. Hunt [1990] 891 F.2d 1555.
Our Lady of Guadalupe School v. Morrissey-Berru [2020] 140 S.Ct. 2049.
Palmer v. Thompson [1971] 403 U.S. 217.
Pleasant Grove City v. Summum [2009] 555 U.S. 460.

Plessy v. Ferguson [1896] 163 U.S. 537.
Reitman v. Mulkey [1967] 387 U.S. 369.
Strasser, M. 2000. "Plessy, Brown, and HBCUs: On the Imposition of Stigma and the Court's Mechanical Equal Protection Jurisprudence." *Washburn Law Journal* 40: 48–69.
United States v. Carolene Products Co. [1938] 304 U.S. 144.
United States v. Windsor [2013] 570 U.S. 744.
Walker v. Sons of Confederate Veterans [2015] 576 U.S. 200.

12 SLAPP

Between the right to a fair trial and the chilling effect in favour of free speech

Jędrzej Skrzypczak

1. Introduction

In the beginning, it is worth decoding the abbreviation used in the title of this chapter, namely SLAPP. It means Strategic Lawsuits Against Public Participation. This is considered a form of legal harassment. Generally, it consists in undertaking deliberate legal actions, that is, bringing lawsuits, private indictments (or notifying law enforcement agencies) by law firms representing influential persons, organisations or state institutions to exhaust financially and mentally, with a view to suppress critical voices and opinions, to the detriment of public participation, and to avoid public scrutiny of persons acting to protect the public interest (Bárd et al., 2020).

On the other hand, in democratic systems, no one can be prevented from seeking legal aid in independent courts. Therefore, it is crucial in this area to properly and precisely define this unambiguously negative phenomenon to find appropriate legal instruments that can counteract such occurrences and, at the same time, will not close the legal path to court for the parties concerned.

The critical element of this phenomenon is the disproportion between the parties to court proceedings. On the one hand, it is about entities with enormous financial, political, organisational and social capabilities, that is, most often representing a certain majority (national, ethnic, political, religious or resources-related), and on the other hand, persons who do not have such capabilities. Hence, it should be emphasised that representatives of various minorities sometimes fall victim to this type of legal action. According to the report The Coalition Against SLAPPs in Europe (CASE, 2022) and Amsterdam Law Clinics—discrimination cases referring to those SLAPP instances that were initiated against individuals that represented or shared the views/beliefs of a marginalised group constitute only less than 3% in Europe. Although it can be assumed that other types of cases of this type do, in fact, concern certain minorities of opinion (Ibid.). In addition, currently, this type of legal action is most often a consequence of previous statements and publications posted in public debate on Internet forums or social media.

DOI: 10.4324/9781003274476-16

2. SLAPP definition

The term SLAPP was first proposed by George W. Pring and Penelope Canan in the late eighties of the twentieth century (Pring, 1989; Pring and Canan, 1988, 506–526; Pring and Canan, 1992, 937–940; Segal, 2006, 643–646). The authors defined this abbreviation as any type of legal action such as lawsuits, indictments prepared by influential entities (e.g. a corporation, public official, high profile businessman) against journalists, human rights defenders, academics and civil society organisations, who expressed a critical position on a significant issue of political or social importance. One of the main characteristics of this type of action is the disproportion of resources between the plaintiff's substantial private or public institutions and the defendants (journalists, whistleblowers, etc.). As an example, the European Court of Human Rights in the case of Steel and Morris v. the United Kingdom (*Steel and Morris v. the United Kingdom*, 2005) reasoned

> that since there was a vast inequality between Steel and Morris and McDonald's, denying legal aid to the Applicants deprived them of their ability to present the case effectively, and therefore violated Article 6. In addition, the court noted that there was strong public interest in the opinions of non-mainstream groups regarding the environment and health.

As emphasised in public debate,

> the aim of a SLAPP suit is not to genuinely assert a right. SLAPP suits are often based on meritless, frivolous, or exaggerated claims. They are deliberately initiated with the intent to intimidate and drain their targets' financial and psychological resources, rather than genuinely exercise, or vindicate a right or obtain redress for a certain wrong.
> (Public Participation Project, 2022)

The actions discussed here are based on resource depletion and the strategy of affecting the morale of the defendant. Often such lawsuits have little chance of success, but the point is to stay in a court dispute as long as possible. Plaintiffs usually know from the outset that their allegations are unfounded or exaggerated. But they also know that being a defendant and facing an investigation and potential trial is both costly and time-consuming.

Consequently, harassing lawsuits can have a strong "chilling" effect, preventing a journalist or activist from re-exercising their right to criticise. As the European Court on Human Rights stressed in the case Dink v. Turkey (*Dink v. Turkey*, 2010)

> States were required to create a favourable environment for participation in public debate by all the persons concerned, enabling them to express their opinions and ideas without fear. In a case like the present one, the State must not just refrain from any interference with the individual's freedom of expression, but was also under a "positive obligation" to protect his or her right

to freedom of expression against attack, including by private individuals. In view of its findings concerning the authorities' failure to protect Fırat Dink against the attack by members of an extreme nationalist group and concerning the guilty verdict handed down in the absence of a "pressing social need", the Court concluded that Turkey's "positive obligations" with regard to Fırat Dink's freedom of expression had not been complied with. There had therefore been a violation of Article 10 (Ibid.).

And even when the court dismisses the claim, the length of the trials and the threat of damages or penalties frequently lead to such an effect. These goals are attempted by making outrageous claims for compensation or allegations designed to slander, harass and overwhelm activists and/or civil society organisations. This is a deliberate action that is expected to lead to the effect mentioned here. The effectiveness of such strategies depends on various factors, including the amount of the costs of the trial, legal representation, provisions on infringement of personal rights and defamation and the existence of safeguards, e.g. anti-SLAPP law or awarding costs against abuse of law (Johnston, 2002/2003, 263–264).

As far as we can judge, the problem of this type of legal action is significant and challenging, unfortunately, not only in the United States but also in other parts of the world. The European Union recently drew attention to this issue (Council of Europe, 2021). It is worth reviewing the definition of the SLAPP concept in official EU documents.

According to the definition proposed in the European Union document The European democracy action plan,

> SLAPPs are groundless or exaggerated lawsuits initiated by state organs, business corporations or powerful individuals against weaker parties who express criticism or communicate messages that are uncomfortable to the litigants, on a matter of public interest. Their purpose is to censor, intimidate and silence critics by burdening them with the cost of a legal defence until they abandon their criticism or opposition.
>
> (European Union, 2020)

The meaning of an extensive and more precise definition is presented in the draft directive of the European Parliament and of the Council on protecting persons who engage in public participation from manifestly unfounded or abusive court proceedings (Strategic lawsuits against public participation—Monitoring Media Pluralism, 2022, 1–3) of April 2022 (European Union, 2022). Pursuant to Article 3 item 3 of this document: "'abusive court proceedings against public participation' mean court proceedings brought in relation to public participation that are fully or partially unfounded and have as their primary purpose to prevent, restrict or penalise public participation" (EU Legislation in Progress, 2022, 6). As seen from the above, the basic premises of SLAPP include, first, cases relating to public debate; second, such legal actions aimed at preventing or limiting public debate or punishing for public debate and third, total or partial groundlessness of such prima facie legal actions. Such nature of the initiated legal actions may be indicated by the exemplary instances described in the quoted Article 3 item 3 of the draft directive, that is,

> Indications of such a purpose can be: (a) the disproportionate, excessive or unreasonable nature of the claim or part thereof; (b) the existence of multiple proceedings initiated by the claimant or associated parties in relation to similar matters; (c) intimidation, harassment or threats on the part of the claimant or his or her representative (European Union, 2022).

At the same time—as explained in Article 3 item 1 of this document—"public participation" should be understood as

> any statement or activity by a natural or legal person expressed or carried out in the exercise of the right to freedom of expression and information on a matter of public interest, and preparatory, supporting or assisting action directly linked thereto. This includes complaints, petitions, administrative or judicial claims, and participation in public hearings (Ibid.).

In turn, "matter of public interest" means any matter which affects to such an extent that the public may legitimately take an interest in it, in areas such as: (a) public health, safety, the environment, climate, or enjoyment of fundamental rights; (b) activities of a person or entity in the public eye or public interest; (c) matters under public consideration or review by a legislative, executive, or judicial body, or any other public official proceedings; (d) allegations of corruption, fraud or criminality and (e) activities aimed to fight disinformation (Ibid.).

3. SLAPP in practice

According to a recent European Commission analysis, SLAPP suits are "increasingly conducted across the EU Member States, in an environment that is getting increasingly hostile towards journalists, human rights defenders, and various NGOs". (Bárd et al., 2020). In Europe, for every European journalist or activist who is threatened with violence, there are 100 more persons silenced by law firms (Ibid.). Many examples of this type of legal action can be found in European countries (Kraski, 2017, 923; Mhainín, 2020b, 63–65; Perrone, 2020, 66–68; Musscat, 2019, 44–46; World Rainforest Movement, 2010) such as Spain[1] (Greenpeace, 2020), France[2] (Ibid.), Bulgaria, Romania, Portugal, Slovenia (Ibid.), Croatia (Vale, 2019; Philips, 2020), Germany (Verza, 2020), Italy[3] (Greenpeace, 2020) and the United Kingdom (Mhainín, 2020b).

According to the report Shutting out Criticism: how SLAPPs threaten European Democracy, the pretext for bringing SLAPP lawsuits was alleged cases such as defamation (by far the most frequently occurring issue), insult, privacy, denigration, GDPR, harassment, honour, disclosure of secret information, trespass and breach cease-and-desist (Greenpeace, 2020). Moreover, the legal procedures used in this type of trial may be of the criminal, civil or administrative type.

4. SLAPP in Poland

According to the Polish Journalism Society report, there were recently 172 cases in Poland (between 2015 and 2021) that can be classified as harassing journalists and the media (Iwanowa, 2021). These are instances of both civil claims for damages and cases for rectification, but also criminal proceedings (including Article 212 of the Criminal Code)-criminal libel, or other issues, e.g. detention or attempts to waive journalistic secrecy, as well as proceedings initiated by journalists in the field of law, work in response to dismissal or discrimination on political grounds (18 cases) (Ibid.). According to these studies, the most common entities that legally harass the media and journalists are public institutions, e.g. ministries—31, politicians—26, the Public Prosecutor's Office—15, persons associated with a politician—15, judges—15, state-owned companies—10, TVP (Polish public TV)—8, prosecutors—3 and the ruling party—3. The most often attacked media are "Gazeta Wyborcza" (63 cases), Ringier Axel Springer Poland (Ringier Axel Springer Polska is the leading publisher in Poland), acting on traditional (such well-known brands as "Fakt," "Newsweek," "Forbes" and "Przegląd Sportowy") and the Internet media market (Onet.pl.—one of the most popular Polish Internet portals)—41, OKO.press (OKO.PRESS is an independent Internet portal conducting journalistic investigations)—8, "Polityka"—weekly news magazine—9 and TVN (a private TV channel)—4 cases.

In turn, according to the report Shutting out Criticism: How SLAPPs Threaten European Democracy, there are a total of 119 such cases in Poland, which, per 1,000 inhabitants, places the country in seventh place (index 0.31). According to the criterion of the number of cases per 1,000 inhabitants, the first three countries are Malta (index 8), Slovenia 1.95 and Bosnia and Herzegovina (1.22). This negative ranking is followed by Croatia (0.82), Luxembourg (0.63) and Ireland (0.52) (CASE, 2022; Global Freedom of Expression, 2018).

5. ANTISLAPP law

Recently, there have been many examples of adopting anti-SLAPP law regulations, generally aimed at more reliable safeguards for the defendants in this type of trial. Anti-SLAPP laws were more developed in the United States, Canada and Australia (Borg-Barthet et al., 2021), while in Europe, SLAPP regulations are rather unknown. According to some researchers, this situation results from different considerations of the right to freedom of expression in the constitutional systems of some countries. While freedom of speech is protected as an almost absolute right by the U.S. First Amendment, the necessary balance between this fundamental right and other interests—such as reputational rights—is ensured in the European national and regional system, e.g. in Article 10.2 of the European Convention on Human Rights (Borg-Barthet et al., 2021).

Generally, the idea of such anti-slapp regulation provides that the court looks at these lawsuits at a very preliminary stage and decides whether it is a question of public affairs or a voice in the public debate or not. If not, the court dismisses the case (Segal, 2006, 640–641).

6. ANTISLAPP regulation in the United States

It is worth noting that there is no federal anti-SLAPP law in the United States. However, there are some such provisions in particular states. According to The Public Participation Project, SLAPP protection standards vary from state to state. They can be divided into five categories of legal guarantee degree against SLAPP: A = Excellent (California, Colorado, District Columbia, Hawaii, Kentucky, Nevada, New York, Oklahoma, Oregon, Washington), B = Good (Connecticut, Georgia, Indiana, Kansas, Louisiana, Missouri, Rhode Island, Tennessee, Texas, Vermont), C = Adequate (Arkansas, Florida, Massachusetts), D = Weak (Delaware, Maine, Maryland, Nebraska, New Mexico, Pennsylvania, Utah), F = no anti-SLAPP law (Alaska, Dakota, Idaho, Iowa, Michigan, Minnesota, Mississippi Montana, New Hampshire, New Jersey, North Carolina, North Dakota, Ohio, South Carolina, Virginia, Wisconsin, Wyoming) (Public Participation Project, State Anti-SLAPP Laws, 2022).

The first such anti-LAPP Statute was adopted in California in 1992 (California Anti-Slapp Law, Cal. Civ. Proc. Code § 425.16, 1992). As it is recalled in the doctrine,

> the Act gave defendants the possibility to file a special motion for a strike when the reason resulted from the act of the defendant to exercise the constitutional right of the defendant to file a petition or the right to freedom of expression in relation to a public matter.
>
> (Segal, 2006, 646–647)

However, the case of Washington is very interesting (*Maytown Sand & Gravel, LLC v. Thurston City*, 2018). This state adopted the first version of anti-SLAPP regulation in 2010 and passed the Uniform Public Expression Protection Act in May 2021. This is a kind of model anti-SLAPP provision, which

> applies to claims based on an individual's exercise of the rights of expression, freedom of the press, assembly, petition, and association on matters of public interest. Thus, it essentially enables defendants to bring applications for a summary judgment at a much earlier stage in the proceedings rather than after a long and costly discovery period.
>
> (Vining and Matthews, 2020)

As these authors point out, "In 2017, Virginia amended its anti-SLAPP law to include actions in "matters of public interest that would be protected under the First Amendment" and to allow selected defendants to recover attorney fees and costs. However, unlike most anti-SLAPP provisions, Virginia law still does not provide for any special procedures allowing a defendant to take advantage of these safeguards early in the proceedings. In June 2019, Colorado became the state to adopt anti-SLAPP law. The Act allows the defendant to make a special request to dismiss claims arising from exercising the right to petition or freedom of speech in connection with a public matter. Tennessee much improved its anti-SLAPP law in 2019 to protect the public from lawsuits "brought in response to [their] exercise of the right to freedom of expression, the right to petition, or the right of association". The law allows defendants to file a motion to dismiss SLAPP's lawsuit before commencing a costly discovery process, appeal an anti-SLAPP denial immediately and recover attorney's fees if a court rules in their favour. In November 2020, New York significantly expanded its anti-SLAPP law, which previously only covered cases brought by plaintiffs seeking public permits, zoning changes or other authority from a government body. The 2020 amendment extended the anti-SLAPP law to include matters relating to "any communication in the open place or in the public forum concerning a matter of public interest" or "any other lawful conduct aimed at exercising the right to freedom of expression in relation to the public interest". Not all changes in recent years have strengthened anti-SLAPP safeguards. In 2019, Texas amended its anti-SLAPP law to limit the types of claims that can receive protection. While the previous version of the Texas law allowed defendants to seek the dismissal of actions broadly "related" to an individual's exercise of the right to freedom of expression, petition or association, the new statute requires the claim to be more "based on" or "in response to" the exercise of one of these rights. Lawmakers also dropped anti-SLAPP safeguards for statements about trade secrets or non-competition agreements, potentially allowing employers to intimidate whistleblowers with employee trials" (Vining and Matthews, 2020).

7. ANTISLAPP in Europe

It is believed that anti-SLAPP regulations can also be based on international and regional principles that protect freedom of expression, such as Article 19 of the International Covenant on Civil and Political Rights (United Nations, 1966) and Article 10 of the European Convention on Human Rights (Council of Europe, 1950). In the case of Article 10 of the European Convention of Human Rights, the guidelines of the European Court of Human Rights may also be helpful, which in the case of Handyside v. Great Britain (*Handyside v. Great Britain*, 1976) stated that a democratic society should also tolerate those ideas which "offend, shock or disturb the state or any sector of the population". Another key case was Steel Morris v. The United Kingdom (*Steel and Morris v. the United Kingdom*, 2005), in which the European Court of Human Rights found

> a violation of Article 10 of the Convention: the applicants, namely two members of London Greenpeace, were asked to reimburse EUR40,000 for damaging McDonald's reputation through a brochure entitled "What's wrong with McDonald's?" According to the Court, the violation resulted from the state's inability to provide legal aid to activists—who were persons with very low incomes towards one of the wealthiest companies in the world—and from the size of the ruling given to them.
>
> (Verza, 2020)

Currently, no EU Member State has introduced targeted legislation that specifically protects against SLAPP lawsuits. EU-wide rules providing strong and consistent protection against SLAPP lawsuits would be essential to ending this abuse in the EU Member States and serve as a benchmark for countries in the rest of Europe and beyond. It would contribute to a safer environment for public oversight authorities and public participation in the EU (Article 19, 2020). As Sofia Verza underscores, since February 2018, a group of European MEPs called on the European Commission to prepare an EU anti-SLAPP directive that

> would give investigative journalists and media groups the power to request to rapidly dismiss 'vexatious lawsuits' and would create a fund for the financial support of media group resisting such lawsuits. Moreover, MEPs also proposed the creation of a new EU register that would "name and shame" firms practicing SLAPPs. One of the reasons that induces the EU MEPs to promote such a regulation is the case of Daphne Caruana Galizia, a Maltese investigative journalist that was murdered in a car bomb . . . October (2019). . . .
> (Verza, 2020)

In November 2020, the coalition of non-governmental organisations from across Europe (ARTICLE 19, Association of European Journalists and many others)[4] appealed to policymakers to protect public watchdogs such as journalists, rights defenders, activists and whistleblowers from Strategic Lawsuits Against Public Participation (CASE, 2022).

On 3 December 2020, the Commission announced the European Democracy Action Plan (European Union, 2020). which announced the implementation of a set of measures into the legal system aimed at, among other things, supporting free and independent media, including this initiative and the recommendation on the safety of journalists (European Union, 2021). The action plan is complemented by other initiatives, including a strategy to strengthen the application of the Charter of Fundamental Rights EU, which sets out actions to empower civil society organisations and rights defenders (Roadmap EU, 2021).

As already mentioned, in April 2022, the European Parliament and the Council announced a draft directive on protecting persons involved in public participation from manifestly unfounded or abusive legal proceedings ("strategic lawsuits against public participation"). As one can optimistically assume, the adoption of this document will take place in a few to several months, and it will enter into force in the EU Member States within the next two years (European Union, 2022).

8. SLAPP v. the right to a fair trial

We must remember that according to Article 6 of the European Convention on Human Rights, everyone is entitled to a fair and public hearing within a reasonable time by an independent and impartial tribunal established by law (Council of Europe, 1950).

This conflict of rules of law (rights to a fair trial and freedom of expression) is possible. The best example of this challenge is the decisions of the U.S. courts in this matter. As we mentioned earlier, Washington passed the anti-SLAPP bill in 2010. Still, the state's supreme court rejected it five years later, stating that it had violated the state's constitutional right to a jury trial (*Davis v. Cox*, 2015; European Union, 2022).

A similar trend can also be observed in other U.S. states (Vining and Matthews, 2020). For example, in 2016, a local court of appeals in Minnesota ruled that the state's anti-SLAPP law was unconstitutional, stressing that the law violated the principle of the right to a jury trial (*Mobile Diagnostic Imaging v. Hooten*, 2016). In 2017, the Minnesota Supreme Court confirmed that the state's anti-SLAPP bill is unconstitutional (*Leiendecker v. Asian Women United of Minn*, 2017; Vining and Matthews, 2020).

As indicated in the doctrine (Vining and Matthews, 2020),

> defendants in the USA have to face one more challenge in SLAPP proceedings. As mentioned, the US Congress never passed federal anti-SLAPP law, and different courts in each state hold divergent positions as to whether or not state such provisions apply in federal court. Some federal appeals courts have allowed defendants to take advantage of these safeguards in federal court. But other such courts, especially in recent years, have disagreed. The Supreme Court has not yet dealt with the case (Ibid.).

As already mentioned, in April 2022, the European Commission proposed a draft directive of the European Parliament and of the Council on protecting persons who engage in public participation from manifestly unfounded or abusive court proceedings (European Union, 2022).

It should be noted that this document contains significant restrictions on its use, that is, only in the so-called cross-border implications. All cases will be considered as such when both parties are not domiciled in the same Member State as the court seized. In addition, a cross-border case will be considered in instances where, despite the failure to comply with the aforementioned condition, the ongoing public debate may be necessary for more than one EU Member State regarding events or discussions organised by the Union institutions (e.g. a public hearing on environmental pollution or laundering dirty money).[5]

Most importantly, the draft directive contains proposals for legal solutions to counteract juridical actions of the SLAPP type. There are several possible procedural guarantees here.[6] First, various kinds of procedural safeguards. It is about such legal solutions that the court hearing the case is entitled to oblige the claimant to provide security for procedural costs or procedural costs and damages if it deems such deposit to be appropriate due to the existence of elements indicating that the court proceedings constitute abuse.[7] Second, the directive proposes that a court may dismiss all or part of manifestly unfounded actions intended to stifle public debate very early. An application for such early dismissal of the claim should be examined in an accelerated procedure (European Union, 2022).

Moreover, it should be the claimant's responsibility to prove that the claim is not manifestly unfounded.[8] Third, the directive proposes the possibility of a number of additional measures of protection against such abusive court proceedings.[9] Thus, it is the plaintiff who instituted the acrimonious court proceedings to quell the public debate that should be ordered to pay all the costs of the proceedings, including the total fees of legal representation borne by the defendant. In addition, a respondent who has suffered damage as a result of SLAPP should be able to claim compensation for the damage. Finally, it is suggested that solutions be introduced to impose effective, proportionate and dissuasive penalties on the party that initiated this SLAPP procedure. In addition, it points to the possibility of refusing the recognition and enforcement of decisions of the SLAPP type given in a third country because such recognition and enforcement are clearly contrary to public policy (ordre public) (European Union, 2022; Gio and Nasreddin, 2022).

The draft directive proposes to introduce special jurisdiction over SLAPP cases. Namely, where abusive court proceedings were instituted before a court of a third State concerning a public debate against a natural or legal person domiciled in a Member State, such a person could claim compensation for damages and costs before the court having jurisdiction over their place of residence or seat, incurred in connection with proceedings before a court of a third country, regardless of the location of residence or seat of the claimant in proceedings in a third country (European Union, 2022).

Additionally, it is worth paying attention to one of the regulatory postulates raised during the discussion on anti-SLAPP solutions in Poland. This idea has originated because often, the reasons for this type of court proceedings are organs of public influence at various levels. Hence, the postulate that the personal rights of a legal person should not be related to that person's authority. In other words, the president of the city, its mayor or the commune head, that is, a set of legal measures, cannot use the public money of this entity to defend their own good name. If he wants to argue with the press, he should bring his own trial. Such a legal solution would ensure a balance between the parties to the proceedings (European Union, 2022; Gio and Nasreddin, 2022).

9. Conclusions

Strategic Lawsuits Against Public Participation are methods of silencing criticism far less brutal than an assassination, but their "chilling" effects could often be just as destructive.

Given the importance of the role of social oversight bodies such as investigative journalists, activists and whistleblowers for the rule of law and the fight against corruption, when their security is not ensured, they endanger not only freedom of expression but also, increasingly, the viability of democracy.

However, we should always look for a balance between two essential, constitutional (on the national levels) and conventional (on the international and European levels) rules, the right to a fair trial and freedom of expression (Mhainin, 2020a). The best solution is to look for symmetry between those principles that should be introduced, which would allow the rejection of SLAPP cases at the initial stage of the judicial process but also impose sanctions on SLAPP users for abusing the law and court proceedings and provide the victims of these attacks with tools of defence.

As was mentioned, one of the main characteristics of this type of action is the disproportion of resources between the plaintiff's vital private or public institutions and those of the defendants (journalists, whistleblowers, etc.). Those actions are based on resource depletion, and the strategy of affecting the morale of the defendant and being a defendant and facing an investigation and potential trial is both costly and time-consuming. As seen previously, the plaintiffs usually represent various types of majority (political, market, financial, religious, national), and the defendants belong to one or other minority. Therefore, it can be assumed that anti-slapp regulations are an accurate means of protecting various types of minorities. And this is necessary for a democratic system.

From a European point of view, it seems that the European Union should adopt laws protecting European citizens across the EU from SLAPP attacks. Despite all its shortcomings (limited only to cross-border cases), it seems that the aforementioned draft EU directive may be a model or even a template for national legislation. It proposes legal measures against SLAPP, which are balanced and adapted to the principles of a democratic state ruled by law, and, on the other hand, guarantees the right to a fair trial (Borg-Barthet et al., 2021).

Notes

1 Spanish meat processing company Coren is demanding €1 million in damages from an environmental activist for exposing its waste management practices.
2 French businessman Vincent Bolloré and his Bolloré Group companies were flooding journalists and non-governmental organisations (NGOs) with personal rights' lawsuits to stem the critical revelation of his African interests.
3 An example is the case of journalist Amalia De Simone, who has conducted several harrowing trials (mostly defamation criminal cases) in the past few years by businessmen as well as public officials after she reported on their allegedly illegal activities.
4 Access Info Europe, Amnesty International, ARTICLE 19, ANTICOR (France), Blueprint for Free Speech, Centre for Free Expression (CFE) (Canada), CEE Bankwatch Network, Chceme zdravu krajinu ("We want a healthy country," Slovakia), Citizens Network Watchdog Poland, Civil Liberties Union For Europe, Civil Rights Defenders (CRD), Civil Society Europe, Clean Air Action Group (Hungary), Committee to Protect Journalists, Common Weal, Corporate Europe Observatory, Defend Democracy, Earth League International, Environmental Paper Network (EPN), ePaństwo Foundation (Poland), Eurocadres—Council of European Professional and Managerial Staff, European Centre For Not-For-Profit Law (ECNL), European Centre for Press and Media Freedom (ECPMF), European Coalition for Corporate Justice (ECCJ), European Environmental Bureau (EEB), European Federation of Journalists (EFJ), European Trade Union Confederation (ETUC), FIDH (International Federation for Human Rights), Forest Initiatives and Communities (Ukraine), Forum Ökologie & Papier Four Paws International, Free Press Unlimited (FPU), Global Forum for Media Development (GFMD), Global Justice Ecology Project, GMWatch, Government Accountability Project, Greenpeace EU Unit, Human Rights House Foundation (HRHF), Human Rights Without Frontiers, IFEX, Index on Censorship, Institute for Sustainable Development

Foundation, International Media Support, International Partnership for Human Rights (IPHR), International Press Institute (IPI), Iraqi Journalists Right Defence Association, Journalismfund.eu, Justice and Environment, Justice Pesticides, Maison des Lanceurs d'Alerte (France), Mighty Earth, Milieudefensie—Friends of the Earth Netherlands, MultiWatch (Switzerland), Netherlands Helsinki Committee, Nuclear Consulting Group (NCG), OBC Transeuropa, OGM dangers, Oživení (Czech Republic), Pištaljka (Serbia), Polish Institute for Human Rights and Business, Protect, RECLAIM, Rettet den Regenwald (Rainforest Rescue), Reporters Without Borders (RSF), Sherpa, Sciences Citoyennes, Society for Threatened Peoples (STP) (Switzerland), SOLIDAR and SOLIDAR Foundation (European networks, based in Belgium), Speakout Speakup Ltd (United Kingdom), Stefan Batory Foundation (Poland), SumOfUs, The Daphne Caruana Galizia Foundation, The Good Lobby Italia, The International Rehabilitation Council for Torture Victims (IRCT), The New Federalist, The Signals Network, Transnational Institute, Transparency International—Bulgaria, Transparency International EU, Transparency International Italy, Umweltinstitut München, Vouliwatch, Whistleblower Netzwerk (WBN) (Germany), Whistleblowing International Network, Women Engage for a Common Future—WECF International, Xnet (Spain) and Young European Federalists (JEF Europe).

5 According to Article 4, 1 of European Union, 2022. For the purposes of this Directive, a matter is considered to have cross-border implications unless both parties are domiciled in the same Member State as the court seised. 2. Where both parties to the proceedings are domiciled in the same Member State as the court seised, the matter shall also be considered to have cross-border implications if: (a) the act of public participation concerning a matter of public interest against which court proceedings are initiated is relevant to more than one Member State or (b) the claimant or associated entities have initiated concurrent or previous court proceedings against the same or associated defendants in another Member State.

6 According to Article 5, Member States shall ensure that when court proceedings are brought against natural or legal persons on account of their engagement in public participation, those persons can apply for: (a) security in accordance with Article 8; (b) early dismissal of manifestly unfounded court proceedings in accordance with Chapter III and (c) remedies against abusive court proceedings in accordance with Chapter IV. Such applications shall include: (a) a description of the elements on which they are based and (b) a description of the supporting evidence. Member States may provide that measures on procedural safeguards in accordance with Chapters III and IV can be taken by the court or tribunal seised of the matter *ex officio*.

7 According to Article 8, Member States shall ensure that in court proceedings against public participation, the court or tribunal seised has the power to require the claimant to provide security for procedural costs, or for procedural costs and damages, if it considers such security appropriate in view of presence of elements indicating abusive court proceedings.

8 Under Article 9.1, Member States shall empower courts and tribunals to adopt an early decision to dismiss, in full or in part, court proceedings against public participation as manifestly unfounded. 2. Member States may establish time limits for the exercise of the right to file an application for early dismissal. The time limits shall be proportionate and not render such exercise impossible or excessively difficult. Article 10, Stay of the main proceedings. Member States shall ensure that if the defendant applies for early dismissal, the main proceedings are stayed until a final decision on that application is taken. According to Article 11 (Accelerated procedure), "Member States shall ensure that an application for early dismissal is treated in an accelerated procedure, taking into account the circumstances of the case and the right to an effective remedy and the right to a fair trial. Article 12 (Burden of proof), Member States shall ensure that where a defendant has applied for early dismissal, it shall be for the claimant to prove that the claim is not manifestly unfounded". Article 13 (Appeal), Member States shall ensure that a decision refusing or granting early dismissal pursuant to Article 9 is subject to an appeal.

9 See Chapter IV of European Union, 2022 Remedies against abusive court proceedings. Under Article 14 (Award of costs), Member States shall take the necessary measures to ensure that a claimant who has brought abusive court proceedings against public participation can be ordered to bear all the costs of the proceedings, including the full costs of legal representation incurred by the defendant, unless such costs are excessive. Article 15 Compensation of damages, Member States shall take the necessary measures to ensure that a natural or legal person who has suffered harm as a result of an abusive court proceedings against public participation is able to claim and to obtain full compensation for that harm. Article 16 Penalties, Member States shall provide that courts or tribunals seised of abusive court proceedings against public participation have the possibility to impose effective, proportionate and dissuasive penalties on the party who brought those proceedings.

According to Article 5, Member States shall ensure that when court proceedings are brought against natural or legal persons on account of their engagement in public participation, those persons can apply for: (a) security in accordance with Article 8; (b) early dismissal of manifestly unfounded court proceedings in accordance with Chapter III and (c) remedies against abusive court proceedings in accordance with Chapter IV. Such applications shall include: (a) a description of the elements on which they are based and (b) a description of the supporting evidence. Member States may provide that measures on procedural safeguards in accordance with Chapters III and IV can be taken by the court or tribunal seised of the matter *ex officio*.

References

Article 19. 2020. "Protecting Public Watchdogs Across the EU.2020: A Proposal for EU Anti-SLAPP Law." www.article19.org/wp-content/uploads/2020/12/Anti_SLAPP_Model_Directive-2-1.pdf.

Bárd, P., Bayer, J., Luk, N. C. and Vosyliute, L. 2020. "SLAPP in the EU Context." https://ec.europa.eu/info/sites/default/files/ad-hoc-literature-review-analysis-key-elements-slapp_en.pdf.

Borg-Barthet, J., Lobina, B. and Zabrocka, M. 2021. "The Use of SLAPPs to Silence Journalists, NGOs and Civil Society, European Union, Policy Department for Citizens' Rights and Constitutional Affairs Directorate-General for Internal Policies, PE 694.782- June 2021." www.europarl.europa.eu/RegData/etudes/STUD/2021/694782/IPOL_STU(2021)694782_EN.pdf.

California Anti-SLAPP Law. 1992. "Cal. Civ. Proc. Code § 425.16." www.casp.net/california-anti-slapp-first-amendment-law-resources/statutes/.

CASE. 2022. "Coalition Against SLAPPs in Europe, Shutting out Criticism, 2022, How SLAPPs Threaten European Democracy." https://datastudio.google.com/u/0/reporting/2222427e-5b20-4678-bb44-90565410d86b/page/p_o5rvo18gqc.

Council of Europe. 1950. "Convention for the Protection of Human Rights and Fundamental Freedoms." www.echr.coe.int/Documents/Convention_ENG.pdf.

Council of Europe. 2021. "Annual Report by the partner organisations to the Council of Europe Platform to Promote the Protection of Journalism and Safety of Journalists." https://rm.coe.int/final-version-annual-%20report-2021-en-wanted-real-action-for-media-freed/1680a2440e.

Davis v. Cox, 351 P. 3d 862, 864. 2015. https://caselaw.findlaw.com/wa-supreme-court/1702446.html.

Dink v. Turkey. 2010. App. No 2668/07, 6102/08, 30079/08, 7072/09, and 7124/09. https://webcache.googleusercontent.com/search?q=cache:ierUGL2uHg8J:https://hudoc.echr.coe.int/app/conversion/pdf/%3Flibrary%3DECHR%26id%3D003-3262169-3640194%26filename%3D003-3262169-3640194.pdf&cd=1&hl=pl&ct=clnk&gl=pl&client=safari.

EU Legislation in Progress. 2022, Strategic lawsuits against public participation (SLAPPs), https://www.europarl.europa.eu/RegData/etudes/BRIE/2022/733668/EPRS_BRI(2022)733668_EN.pdf.

European Union. 2020. Communication from the Commission to the European Parliament, the Council, the European Economic, and Social Committee and the Committee of the Regions on the European Democracy Action Plan, 2020. COM/2020/790 Final. https://eur-lex.europa.eu/legal-content/EN/ALL/?uri=COM:2020:790:FIN.

European Union. 2021. Commission Recommendation on Ensuring the Protection, Safety, and Empowerment of Journalists and Media Professionals in the European Union, 2021. C (2021) 6650 Final. https://eur-lex.europa.eu/legal-content/EN/TXT/?uri=PI_COM:C(2021)6650.

European Union. 2022. Proposal for a Directive of the European Parliament and of the Council on Protecting Persons Who Engage in Public Participation from Manifestly Unfounded or Abusive Court Proceedings. ("Strategic Lawsuits Against Public Participation") COM(2022) 177 Final. https://ec.europa.eu/info/law/better-regulation/have-your-say/initiatives/13192-Działania-UE-przeciwdziałajace-naduzywaniu-drogi-sadowej-SLAPP-wobec-dziennikarzy-i-obroncow-praw_pl.

Gio, R. B. and Nasreddin, D. 2022. SLAPPS Threaten European Democracy. A Report by Case, A Report by The Coalition Against SLAPPs in Europe (CASE). https://static1.squarespace.com/static/5f2901e7c623033e2122f326/t/6231bde2b87111480858c6aa/1647427074081/CASE+Report+on+SLAPPs+in+Europe.pdf.

Global Freedom of Expression. 2018. "SLAPPs' 5 W's: A Background of the Strategic Lawsuits Against Public Participation." July 12. https://globalfreedomofexpression.columbia.edu/publications/slapps-5-ws-background-%20strategic-lawsuits-public-participation/.

Greenpeace. 2020. "Sued Into Silence, How the Rich and Powerful Use Legal Tactics to Shut Critics Up." www.greenpeace.org/static/planet4-eu-unit-stateless/2020/07/20200722-SLAPPs-Sued-into-Silence.pdf.

Handyside v. Great Britain. 1976. App. No 5493/72, E.C.H.R. https://globalfreedomofexpression.columbia.edu/cases/handyside-v-uk/.

Iwanowa, E. 2021. "Towarzystwo Dziennikarskie, Raport. Monitoring represji wobec wolnych mediów2015–2021." http://towarzystwodziennikarskie.pl/2021/05/21/monitoring-represji-wobec-wolnych-mediow-2015-2021/.

Johnston, M. E. 2002/2003. "A Better SLAPP Trap: Washington State's Enhanced Statutory Protection for Targets of Strategic Lawsuits Against Public Participation." *Gonzaga Law Review* 38, no. 2: 263–264. http://blogs.gonzaga.edu/gulawreview/files/2011/02/Johnston.pdf.

Kraski, R. 2017. "Combating Fake News in Social Media: U.S. and German Legal Approaches." *St John's Law Review* 4, no. 91: 923–955.

Leiendecker v. Asian Women United of Minn. 2017. State of Minnesota in Supreme Court N.W.2d 623. https://casetext.com/case/leiendecker-v-asian-women-united-of-minn-6.

Maytown Sand & Gravel, LLC v. Thurston City, 2018, 423 P. 3d 223. 2018. https://casetext.com/case/maytown-sand-gravel-llc-v-thurston-cnty-2.

Mhainin, J. N. 2020a. "A Gathering Storm: The Laws Being Used to Silence the Media." *Index on Censorship 2020*. https://euagenda.eu/upload/publications/a-gathering-storm.pdf.pdf.

Mhainín, J. N. 2020b. "Fighting the Laws That Are Silencing Journalists: Vexatious Legal Threats Are Part of the European Media Landscape. We Need to Take Action Against Them, Says a New Index Report." *Index on Censorship* 49, no. 3: 63–65.

Mobile Diagnostic Imaging v. Hooten. 2016. 889 N.W.2d 27, (Minn. Ct. App. 2016). https://casetext.com/case/mobile-diagnostic-imaging-inc-v-hooten-2.

Monitoring Media Pluralism. 2022. "Monitoring Media Pluralism in the Digital Era. Application of the Media Pluralism Monitor in the European Union, Albania, Montenegro, the Republic of North Macedonia, Serbia and Turkey in the year 2021, Centre for Media Pluralism and Media Freedom." https://cadmus.eui.eu/bitstream/handle/1814/74712/MPM2022-EN-N.pdf?sequence=1&isAllowed=y

Musscat, C. 2019. "If You Can Keep Your Head When All About You are Losing Theirs...": It's Lonely and Dangerous Running an Independent News Website in Malta, but Some Lawyers Are Still Willing to Stand Up to Help." *Index on Censorship* 48, no. 2: 44–46.

Perrone, A. 2020. "A Slap in the Face: Meet the Italian Journalist Who Has Had to Fight Over 126 Lawsuits All Aimed at Silencing Her." *Index on Censorship* 49, no. 1: 66–68. https://journals.sagepub.com/doi/10.1177/0306422020917084.

Philips, G. 2020. "How the Free Press Worldwide is Under Threat." *The Guardian*, May 28. www.theguardian.com/media/2020/may/28/how-the-free-press-worldwide-is-under-threat.

Pring, G. W. 1989. "SLAPPs: Strategic Lawsuits Against Public Participation." *Pace Environmental Law Review* 7, no. 1. https://digitalcommons.pace.edu/cgi/viewcontent.cgi?article=1535&context=pelr.

Pring, G. W. and Canan, P. 1988. "Strategic Lawsuits Against Public Participation." *Social Problems* 35, no. 5: 506–526.

Pring, G. W. and Canan, P. 1992. "Strategic Lawsuits Against Public Participation (SLAPPS): An Introduction for Bench, Bar, and Bystanders." *Bridgeport Law Review Quinnipiac Collage* 12, no. 4: 937–940.

Public Participation Project. 2022. "State Anti-SLAPP Laws." https://anti-slapp.org/your-states-free-speech-protectio.

Roadmap EU. 2021. "EU Package Against Abusive Litigation (SLAPP), Targeting Journalists and Rights Defenders. https://eur-lex.europa.eu/legal-content/EN/TXT/HTML/?uri=PI_COM:Ares(2021)6011536

Segal, J. 2006. "Anti-SLAPP Law Make Benefit for Glorious Entertainment Industry of America: Borat, Reality Bites, and the Construction of an Anti-SLAPP Fence around the First Amendment." *Cardozo Arts & Entertainment* 26.

Steel and Morris v. the United Kingdom. 2005. App. No 68416/01), E.C.H.R. https://globalfreedomofexpression.columbia.edu/cases/steel-v-united-kingdom/.

United Nations. 1966. "International Covenant on Civil and Political Rights Adopted and Opened for Signature, Ratification and Accession by General Assembly Resolution 2200A (XXI) of December 16, Entry Into Force March 23, 1976." www.ohchr.org/en/instruments-mechanisms/instruments/international-covenant-civil-and-political-rights.

Vale, G. 2019. "Croatia: Over a Thousand Ongoing Trials Against Journalists or Media." *European Centre for Press and Media Freedom*. www.rcmediafreedom.eu/Tools/Legal-Resources/Media-freedom-in-Croatia-the-problem-is-not-the-laws-but-their-application.

Verza, S. 2020. "SLAPP: The Background of Strategic Lawsuits Against Public Participation." *European Centre for Press and Media Freedom*. www.ecpmf.eu/slapp-the-background-of-strategic-lawsuits-against-public-participation/.

Vining, A. and Matthews, S. 2020. "Overview of Anti-SLAPP Laws." www.rcfp.org/introduction-anti-slapp-guide/.

World Rainforest Movement. 2010. "French Economic Group Bolloré Attempts to Intimidate Journalists Who Expose Abusive Practices on Its Plantations in Cameroon." *WRM Bulletin* 155, June 29. www.wrm.org.uy/other-information/french-economic-group-bollore-attempts-to-intimidate-journalists-who-expose-abusive-practices-on-it.

13 The freedom of speech and the protection of religious feelings

The case of Dorota Rabczewska—comparative analysis

Tomasz Litwin

1. Introductory remarks

Dorota Rabczewska is a Polish singer and celebrity whose behaviour is sometimes controversial. In 2009, she made an interview for an online edition of a newspaper and presented her opinion on the Bible: "it is difficult to believe in something that was written by somebody who was drunk with wine and smoked some kind of grass." This statement motivated two persons to accuse her of offending their religious feelings. In 2012, Warsaw-Mokotów Local Court on the basis of Article 196 of the Polish Penal Code (PC) found her guilty of offending religious feelings by insulting the object of worship concerning the authors of the Bible. She received a fine of 5,000 PLN (approximately €1,165). This verdict was sustained by the District Court in Warsaw where Rabczewska appealed. Then she complained to the Polish Constitutional Tribunal, questioning the constitutionality of PC Article 196. The Constitutional Tribunal, however, decided that the rule was constitutional.

There are different legal approaches towards the punishment of such types of crimes in other democratic states. In the United States, blasphemy is not penalised, whereas in Austria, Finland, Germany, Italy, Lithuania and Switzerland, it is penalised (Gorman, 2013) and the judgements of the European Court of Human Rights (ECHR) on this matter are diverse. These different legal approaches towards this issue requires an analysis of the arguments supporting and contradicting the punishment of verbal or graphic blasphemy. Blasphemy associated with a physical action could include a criminal act (e.g. material damage), hence it is not considered in this article.

The main research hypothesis of the article is that in the modern democratic state a verbal or graphic creation strongly criticising, mocking or insulting a particular religion or religion regarded as a social phenomenon, including different religious practices (further also: blasphemy or blasphemy crime), should not be penalised because of the general characteristics of a democratic state.

The article is written from the constitutional-legal research perspective based on the assumption that in a democratic state, the constitution is the most important law. Therefore, there is a common catalogue of constitutional principles that are present

DOI: 10.4324/9781003274476-17

in the legal systems of democratic states, such as a democratic state ruled by law, freedom of speech or equality before the law, which are understood in a similar fashion in different countries. In this article, different methods for interpreting legal rules are used: language-logical, systematic, teleological, doctrinal and, mostly, judicial. The main sources are the judgements, legal acts and scientific literature.

1.1. The detailed analysis of Rabczewska's case

Dorota Rabczewska in 2012 was convicted by the Warsaw-Mokotów Local Court of being guilty of the crime from Article 196 of the PC. The penalty was a fine (Constitutional Tribunal of Poland, 2015, para. 1.1.).

According to Article 196 of PC:

> Anyone found guilty of offending religious feelings [of other persons—TL] through public calumny of an object or place of worship is liable to a fine, restriction of liberty or a maximum two-year prison sentence.
> (Venice Commission, 2010, 202)

The analysis of this rule based on its substance and literature (Wróbel, 2017; Kozłowska-Kalisz, 2021; Zgoliński, 2020; Kłączyńska, 2014; Hypś, 2021; Banaś-Grabek, 2020) leads to such assumptions:

- Offensive behaviour should concern religious issues.
- The court undertaking the verdict should regard the average sensitiveness of the believer of a particular religion.
- Some authors present the opinion that it requires only one person to report the crime and others that it requires at least two persons.
- The term "calumny" should be understood in this context as a behaviour or action that are mocking or offending only with the purpose to humiliate other persons.
- The "calumny" should be made "publicly" which means that many persons have an access to observe such action. In the literature, however, a view could be found that the described crime is committed only when the victim has a direct access to observe it.
- The "object or place of worship" should be understood broadly, not only as a physical object of cult but also as theological dogma or principle.
- Penalty for committing the described crime could be alternatively: fine of amount established on the basis of the rules from Article 33 PC: from 100 PLN (approximately: 22 EURO) even up to 1,080,000 PLN (approximately: 240,000 EURO), restriction of liberty from one month up to two years (unpaid work for social purposes from 20 up to 40 hours monthly) and/or (if the convicted person is employed) deduction from 10% up to 25% from monthly salary for social purposes; the court could also, apart from the mentioned penalties, sentence the convicted person to pay additional cash benefit even up to 60,000 PLN (approximately: 13,333,33 EURO) or to prison (maximum two years).

After the verdict of the Local Court, Rabczewska appealed to the District Court in Warsaw which sustained the previous verdict (Constitutional Tribunal of Poland, 2015, para. 1.1.). In 2012, Rabczewska submitted a constitutional complaint to the Constitutional Tribunal of Poland.

The Constitutional Tribunal did not consider the merits of the objection that Article 196 is not in accordance with Article 25 para. 2 and Article 32 para. 1 of the Constitution (principle of the neutrality of the state authorities concerning the worldview of individuals and principle of equality before the law). As the Tribunal observed, both rules invoked in the complaint are not guaranteeing any rights or freedoms of the individual, as their addressee are public authorities. Therefore, the Tribunal noticed that complaint should concern the violation of the individual's rights and freedoms and quashed the proceedings concerning this objection (Constitutional Tribunal of Poland, 2015, para. 2.4.).

The Constitutional Tribunal also did not support the objection that Article 196 of PC was not precise enough according to the constitutional standards (nonconformity with Article 42 para. 1 linked with Article 2 of the Constitution). The Tribunal shared with the complainant the view that penal legal rules should be constructed so precisely that an individual could know which actions are legally neutral and which put them at the risk of penalty. However, the Tribunal judged that precise meaning of such terms as "religious feelings," "offence," "offence of religious feelings," "calumny," "calumny of an object of worship" and "object of worship" were established by the doctrine of penal law. The term "religious feelings" means such human emotions that concern multiple aspects of a particular religion to which the particular person is an adherent. The right to protect religious feelings is not only a freedom from offensive actions concerning those feelings but also a freedom to manifest to be the adherent of religion. According to the Tribunal, "offence of religious feelings" in the context of Article 196 of PC should be understood as the emotional reaction of an individual caused by "calumny of the object of worship"—humiliating, contemptuous, insulting or derisive action towards the object of worship. Therefore, the source of "offence of religious feelings" could be every action that is a calumny of the object of worship. The term "calumny" means such sort of statement whose purpose is to humiliate or violate the dignity of individual. The analysis of a particular statement is a calumny should focus on the way of expressing it. The "calumny of the object of worship" not only concerns inanimate material religious objects, but it also should be understood as contempt of or offence against what these objects are symbolising, e.g. deity. Calumny could be done in many forms, similarly to the offence of religious feelings. Therefore the terms "calumny of the object of worship" and "object of worship" have a precise legal meaning, especially concerning the religions that are widespread among the society (Constitutional Tribunal of Poland, 2015, para. 4).

The Tribunal also rejected the argumentation of the complaint concerning non-conformity of Article 196 of PC with Article 53 para. 1 linked with Article 54 para. 1 of the Constitution. The Tribunal agreed that Article 196 protects only religious feelings but did not find this to be a privilege of believers, but only a precise description of the object of protection. The Tribunal found it justified because religious feelings are a special category of feelings that only believers share and no equivalent exists in case of non-believers. Hence, non-believers cannot be offended by "calumny of an object or place of worship." Article 196 cannot also be regarded as a privilege of believers because the crime described there can be committed by a believer of a particular religion or by another person—religiously indifferent or non-believer (Constitutional Tribunal of Poland, 2015, para. 5).

The Tribunal did not also find non-conformity of Article 196 of PC with Article 54 linked with Article 31 para. 3 of the Constitution. It presented the opinion that freedom of expression (Article 54) allows the criticism of religion. However, the criticism should be made in an appropriate form. The essence of the freedom of expression cannot be regarded as the right to present statements that have the form of "calumny" concerning religious issues and their main aim is to humiliate and hurt the feelings of others. According to the Tribunal, penalisation of offending religious feelings is justified by the protection of constitutionally guaranteed freedom of religion and human dignity. Regarding the judgements of the ECHR, on the basis of a few selected verdicts, the Tribunal emphasised the view of the ECHR that in general national authorities have the best competences to evaluate the significance of religion in a particular society. The statements concerning religion with the only aim to offend and spread hatred are not protected by the freedom of expression. This freedom is connected with the obligation to omit statements that would have unnecessarily offensive character. In such circumstances, the state authorities have the right to penalise such type of statement to protect freedom of religion and spirit of tolerance. As Rabczewska was sentenced to a fine, the Tribunal only evaluated this penalty and found it appropriate (Constitutional Tribunal of Poland, 2015, para. 6).

2. An overview of the judicial cases concerning blasphemy considered in different states and in the ECHR

Blasphemy in the context of the protection of religious feelings has been the subject of legal judgements in many democratic states other than Poland. This overview will focus on the most important established case law from the United States, Lithuania and Austria, as well as on the judgements of ECHR.

The judgement of U.S. Supreme Court in the case of Burstyn v. Wilson from 1952 is particularly important. It concerned the prohibition on the distribution of the film "Miracle" in New York State. This decision was made under the provisions of New York's Education Law that forbid distribution when a film was officially regarded as "sacrilegious." The Supreme Court stated that the First Amendment concerns films as well as books and newspapers. As the Court noted:

> However, from the standpoint of freedom of speech and the press, it is enough to point out that the state has no legitimate interest in protecting any or all religions from views distasteful to them which is sufficient to justify prior restraints upon the expression of those views. It is not the business of

government in our nation to suppress real or imagined attacks upon a particular religious doctrine, whether they appear in publications, speeches, or motion pictures.

(*Burstyn, Inc. v. Wilson*, 1952, 505)

The Court also stated that the legal protection of one religion concerning the cases of "sacrilegious" acts would be against the principle of "separate church and state with freedom of worship for all" as it could also be regarded as favouring one religion over the others, which would violate the First Amendment (*Burstyn, Inc. v. Wilson*, 1952, 504–505).

In Lithuania, several judgements and decisions in 2013–2014 concerned the case of Sekmadienis Ltd. company and advertisements of jeans that were a part of its advertising campaign. The advertisements presented a young, tattooed man with long hair wearing jeans and a young woman wearing a white dress and they were accompanied by the captions: "Jesus, what trousers!"; "Dear Mary, what a dress!" and "Jesus [and] Mary, what are you wearing!" The company was fined the equivalent of EUR 580. According to the reasons for judgement, the advertisements were an offence against public morals, as they were offending the religious feelings of religious people (*Sekmadienis Ltd. v. Lithuania*, 2018, para. 5–30).

In Austria, the case of E.S. (2011–2014), who suggested that Muhammad was a paedophile because he married a 6-year-old girl, is particularly illustrative. E.S. was sentenced a fine of EUR 480. The court justified the judgement by stating that although "harsh criticism of churches or religious societies and religious traditions and practices is lawful, the permissible limits are exceeded when criticism descends into insults or mockery of a religious belief or person of worship" (*E.S. v. Austria*, 2018, para. 12–23).

The ECHR does not seem to establish sentencing guidelines. The Court supported the judgements of a domestic court in the case of E.S. vs Austria. It justified its judgement by stating that freedom of expression allows criticism of religion and religious communities but not abusive attacks. The ECHR also emphasised the importance of the protection of public order by safeguarding religious peace (*E.S. v. Austria*, 2018, para. 42–58).

Another case concerned the film "Visions of Ecstasy," presenting St Teresa of Avila and her visions of Jesus Christ. The film was regarded by the British court as soft pornography, with elements of blasphemy, in that it depicted St Teresa having sex with the crucified Christ. The film was prohibited from being distributed. The ECHR regarded this measure as being in accordance with freedom of speech because it was justified on the grounds of protecting the religious feelings of Christians (*Wingrove v. the United Kingdom*, 1996, para. 57–64).

In a similar case, the court blocked the distribution of the film "Das Liebeskonzil" (The Council of Love). The film portrays God as a senile old man, the adult Jesus Christ as "a low grade mentally defective" and the Virgin Mary as "unprincipled wanton" erotically interested in contacts with the Devil. They all appear to cooperate with the Devil to punish mankind and concoct a sexually transmitted disease so that men and women will infect one another without realising it. The

ECHR supported the decision of the national courts, arguing that it was justified on the grounds of protecting religious feelings, religious peace and public order, as well as the principle of tolerance, and on the basis of "social need," which was assumed from the declarations of the majority of Tyroleans (87%) as being Catholics (the film was planned to be shown in Tyrol) (*Otto-Preminger-Institut v. Austria*, 1994, para. 21–22, 52–57).

However, in the case of Sekmadienis Ltd. v. Lithuania, ECHR considered freedom of speech as more important than the protection of religious feelings. The Court did not find the advertisements that were the subject of the case to be offensive. Moreover, the Court stated that religious people in a democratic pluralistic society should be prepared for criticism and the "propagation by others of doctrines hostile to their faith" (*Sekmadienis Ltd. v. Lithuania*, 2018, para. 75–83).

In another case, the ECHR approved the hostile criticism of Archbishop Ján Sokal, a prominent representative of the Slovakian Catholic Church, as an element of freedom of expression. In that case, the Court accepted the criticism of Slovakian Catholics for not leaving the Catholic Church because of Sokal's leadership (*Klein v. Slovakia*, 2006, para. 50–54).

The last case worth considering is that of Paul Giniewski. Although Giniewski was sentenced on the basis of the law concerning public defamation of a group of persons on the basis of their membership of a religious community, in his article, he only criticised the encyclical of John Paul II, *Veritatis Splendor*, and did not make any references to Catholics. This situation could be regarded as being similar to the blasphemy cases described earlier, as the Pope's encyclical is a form of religious writing which contains binding explanations and interpretations of religious issues. Giniewski criticised the approach of John Paul II who seemed to regard the New Testament as being more important than the Old Testament and stated that such an approach was the source of anti-semitism which led to fascism and Holocaust. According to the judgement of the ECHR, Giniewski's comments could be defended on the basis of freedom of expression. The Court stated that Giniewski's article was not hostile towards believers or Catholicism. The ECHR viewed it as a contribution to the historical analysis of the causes of the Holocaust, which is very important for democratic states, and did not present any radical views. Similar considerations on Catholic dogmas as the source of antisemitism and fascism, are present in the writings and speeches of the Catholic Church's representatives (*Giniewski v. France*, 2006, para. 45–55).

The verdict of the ECHR is difficult to be predicted, as shown in the case of I.A. In this case, the Court approved the verdicts of domestic (Turkish) courts that imposed a fine on I.A. for publishing the novel "Forbidden Phrases," which was regarded as blasphemous. The novel could be described as the presentation of the author's views on philosophical and theological issues in a literary style. The Court rendered its judgement on the fragment of the book, assessing it as "offensive attacks on matters regarded as sacred by Muslims" that cannot be protected by the principle of freedom of speech (*I.A. v. Turkey*, 2005, para. 21–31).

The judgement was undertaken by four votes to three, with three judges jointly presenting a separate opinion. They emphasised that the book probably had a negligible impact on Turkish society, as only 2,000 copies were printed. Moreover, although Turkish society is religious and the author's approach concerning all religions could be regarded as atheistic, this did not justify the imposition of a penalty on the publisher of the book. Although the cited fragment could be regarded as offensive to Muslims, it still did not justify the penalty, as it was only a small part of the book. The judges also expressed the opinion that there is no obligation to read this book, hence the public authorities had no grounds to start legal proceedings. Although the penalty was mild, it could potentially have a "chilling effect" on other persons and lead to the publishing only of works that were "politically (religiously) correct." This could be very dangerous for the essence of freedom of speech and also for democracy (*Joint Dissenting Opinion İ.A. v. Turkey*, 2005, para. 1–9).

3. The weaknesses of arguments supporting the penalisation of blasphemy

Although the main arguments supporting the penalisation of blasphemy presented in the described judgements seem to be respectable, they do have weaknesses when placed in the context of a modern democratic state.

It is obvious that adherents of a particular religion have the same rights as other citizens including the right to protect their dignity. The assumption that blasphemy violates their dignity (Constitutional Tribunal of Poland, 2015, para. 6.3.2) requires answering questions: how can it be violated, and is it possible to violate the human dignity of a social group like believers of a particular religion. Human dignity can be violated in many ways: through humiliation, instrumentalisation, degradation, debasement, torture, rape, slavery or poverty (Pollman, 2011, 245). Moreover, such a violation could inflict a collective, such as believers of a religion. An example would be extraordinary airport security controls against people who look like Muslims. However, Christian Neuhäuser regards the famous Muhammad caricatures as a form of mocking but not humiliation (2011, 22–24); therefore, according to the aforementioned criteria, this case should not be regarded as a violation of human dignity. It seems that although some statements or drawings can be regarded as mocking or insulting for the believers of a particular religion, it is not enough to consider such cases to be a violation of dignity. As Neuhäuser states, "the defilement of a group symbol must be connected to a real threat in order to constitute a symbolic group humiliation and not merely a form of mocking" (2011, 24). When we analyse the cases presented earlier, they concern the statements on some elements of religious doctrine or symbols, which have only form of mockery. They do not directly concern the believers; it seems, therefore, that they cannot be treated as a threat to the rights and freedoms of individuals. Moreover, if a statement or drawing has the form of a general satire and is not addressed directly towards a particular person, it cannot be regarded as a violation of the dignity of the individual. Such an act can be differently perceived by believers: some of them could feel offended, but others, even while not accepting the form, could find some of its substance to be truthful, or at least indicate a problem with the way believers are engaged in a democratic society.

There is also no clear evidence that such a form of blasphemy limits the freedom of religion (*Otto-Preminger-Institut v. Austria*, 1994, para. 46–47). It is only a hypothetical possibility that harsh criticism could lead to restriction of the freedom of religion because, in response to the criticism, the majority of citizens in the society would oppose the supporters of a particular religion.

Moreover, the possibility that such a form of blasphemy might incite a breakdown in public order (*E.S. v. Austria*, 2018, para. 43–50) seems only hypothetical. In a democratic state, public debate is sometimes very intense because of different views, but one of the main tasks of the state is to ensure free public debate and not to allow violence to become the method of practicing politics. A democratic state should ensure public order without restricting freedom of expression.

In a democratic political system, the number of believers should not have influence upon the right to criticise a particular religion. The opposite conclusion leads to the assumption that criticism could be made only against a religion whose adherents constitute a minority in the society. The democratic system in the Western world has a liberal, not a majoritarian character: although the political majority is entitled to govern the state, the protection of minority rights and freedoms is still a binding principle.

The problem with the argument concerning public morals as justifying the blasphemy law is how the term "public morals" should be understood in a democratic state. Its citizens differ in their worldviews, including the role of religion in their life. Hence, the assumption that a particular act of blasphemy is insulting for the majority of citizens seems to be wrong.

Of course, from a historical perspective, a particular religion could play a very important role in the history of a particular state. However, one of the main characteristics of the modern democratic state is its neutrality towards the worldviews of its citizens. Therefore, a conception that public morals justify the state restricting freedom of speech because a particular religion should be regarded as an important factor in the construction of its identity is also wrong.

The term "public morals" should be understood differently. An action could be restricted on the grounds of public morals if it limits the rights and freedoms of others or is deleterious to society. The lack of acceptance of a particular action or behaviour as the only reason to restrict it cannot be justified on the basis of public morals (Nowlin, 2002, 278–285). Such an approach towards public morals was shared by the ECHR in the case of Jeffrey Dudgeon in 1981. It concerned a Northern Ireland law that prohibited male homosexual contacts with adult men, even if they were done privately and with mutual consent. Dudgeon regarded these rules as contravening the European Convention of Human Rights. In the procedure before the ECHR, the rules were defended on the grounds of public morals. However, the Court did not support this argumentation, as it did not find depenalisation of the homosexual acts causing "risk of harm to vulnerable sections of society." The Court also emphasised that this law had "detrimental effects" on the life of homosexual persons. Therefore, the ECHR regarded this law as unjustified even if the homosexual acts "shock, offend or disturb" a part of the society (*Dudgeon v. United Kingdom*, 1981, para. 46–62).

The blasphemy can be regarded as being discordant with the principle of tolerance, showing disrespect towards the worldview of believers of a particular religion. Still, it seems that this argument is too weak to limit freedom of speech, a fundamental value for a democratic state. In the judgement of the ECHR, where the argument concerning tolerance was expressed, the ECHR also emphasised the role of freedom of expression, even if used in a way that "shocks, offends or disturbs the State or any sector of the population," as a fundamental value for a democratic society, among such values like "pluralism and broad-mindedness." Such argumentation would support the right to criticise a religion, even if the criticism is harsh and unfair, as remaining in accordance with the values of a democratic society (*Otto-Preminger-Institut v. Austria*, 1994, para. 49).

A similar line of arguments could be adopted to support decriminalisation of blasphemy. Even though such acts "shock, offend or disturb" members of society, there is no justification for penalising them. The penalisation of such acts requires proving "the risk of harm to vulnerable sections of society." There is no proof that acts of blasphemy in all the presented cases undermined the broadly regarded social position of the adherents of a particular religion.

These arguments could also be used against the assumption that blasphemy laws are protecting the believers of a particular religion from hate speech. However, it is essential to consider what hate speech is, as there is no definition of this term in acts of international law. According to one of the UN documents, hate speech concerns a particular person or group of persons, who may share the same religion (Guterres, 2019, 2); it does not, however, seem to concern deities, religious figures and symbols or religious cults. The only possibility that a statement or drawing could be regarded as hate speech is when it somehow directly refers to a person or group of persons who are adherents of a particular religion. The prohibition of hate speech cannot be regarded as the prohibition of the criticism of religious groups, even if it is harsh or unfair. The key to distinguish hate speech from permissible criticism is the sort of language that is used. Statements that could be regarded as hate speech are characterised by offensive language, the purpose of which is to humiliate, degrade or discriminate a particular person or group of persons. The analysis of the presented cases leads to the conclusion that those acts that were the subjects of the judgements concerned the principles of religion and not its believers. Therefore, they should not be regarded as hate speech cases (Lemmens, 2018, 91). Only four cases seem to require a more detailed investigation in an effort to elucidate whether they could be associated with hate speech: E.S. versus Austria, I.A. versus Turkey, Klein versus Slovakia and Giniewski versus France.

Language-logical analysis of the fragment of the E.S. judgement leads to the conclusion that there are statements concerning Muhammad as a historical figure and Muslims as a social group. In my opinion, a harsh or even unfair criticism of Muhammad is not a hate speech towards Muslims. Of greater interest are statements regarding male Muslims. E.S. stated that "the highest commandment for a male Muslim is to imitate Muhammad, to live his life." In the context of this statement, according to the rules of Islam, a male Muslim should "be a warlord, have many women and like to do it with children." Still, this statement does not mean the same as "all male Muslims behave like warlords, want to have many women and are paedophiles" because it concerns the rules of Islam and not the behaviour of male Muslims. The Austrian court also seemed to come to a similar conclusion that E.S. "was not suggesting that all Muslims were paedophiles, but was criticising the unreflecting imitation of a role model" (*E.S. v. Austria*, 2018, para. 13–14).

In another statement on Muslims, E.S. stated that they "get into conflict with democracy and our value system" (*E.S. v. Austria*, 2018, para. 13). This could be regarded as unfair criticism but not hate speech.

The subject of the I.A. case was the evaluation of the novel "The forbidden phrases" and its most controversial fragments. One of the fragments criticises the deity and has no relation to its believers. The following text concerns only the believers of religion in general and the author regards them rather as victims (of a deity?) (*İ.A. v. Turkey*, 2005, para. 8). Therefore, the language used in the fragment devoted to believers cannot be classified as hate speech. The second fragment criticises Muhammad as an example of a good Muslim. The most controversial phrase of that fragment states that Muhammad did not forbid necrophilia and zoophilia. Nevertheless, such a statement cannot be regarded as a suggestion for the acceptance of such behaviours by Muslims (*İ.A. v. Turkey*, 2005, para. 13).

In the case of Klein versus Slovakia, the subject of the evaluation was an article of Martin Klein in response to the statement of Archbishop Ján Sokol who publicly demanded a prohibition on the promotion of the film "The People vs. Larry Flynt" through a poster showing the main character with the flag of the United States around his hips, depicted as crucified on a woman's pubic area dressed in strings, and also a prohibition on the distribution of the film. Although the author was accused of offending the religious feelings of a group of believers, this case does not really concern blasphemy, as Klein's article does not criticise the principles of the Christian faith. The article is a harsh criticism of Sokol for his public statement which did not concern religious issues. The author accused the archbishop of a "lack of honour" only because in the past Sokol cooperated with the communist authorities. The author calls Sokol an "ogre" and also assesses his behaviour as "scurrilous," but from the context of the article, it is clear that he does not want to humiliate Sokol; he uses these expressions to strengthen his objection to Sokol's statement. It should be mentioned that this statement, demanding the prohibition of film distribution, should be considered in the context of the history of Slovakia, which belonged to the communist bloc where preventive censorship was an element of the political-legal system. Klein also criticises Catholics, regarding them as conformists who accepted Sokol's leadership, despite his past and present views (*Klein v. Slovakia*, 2006, para. 12). This form of criticism cannot be regarded as hate speech.

The last case that should be mentioned concerned Giniewski's article where he wrote:

> Many Christians have acknowledged that scriptural anti-Judaism and the doctrine of the "fulfilment" [accomplishment] of the Old Covenant (Testament) in the New led to antiSemitism and prepared the ground in which the idea and implementation [accomplishment] of Auschwitz took seed.
> (*Giniewski v. France*, 2006, para. 14)

It is obvious that antisemitism in Europe was present before the birth of fascism and could be regarded as one of its sources. Furthermore, the New Testament could be assessed as negatively presenting the Jewish community. Still, when we analyse the cited most controversial fragment of Giniewski's article, he is not claiming that the Catholic religion is a direct source of fascism or that Catholics are fascists, therefore his statements cannot be regarded as hate speech.[1]

4. Analysis of the legal arguments against penalisation of blasphemy

The main argument against the criminalisation of blasphemy in a democratic state is based on its general characteristics. The term "democratic state" could be regarded as the antithesis of the "theocratic state" (*Joint Dissenting Opinion İ.A. v. Turkey*, 2005, para. 5; Lemmens, 2018, 102–103). In a democratic state, the legal system respects that society is pluralistic and its members can have different views on religious issues. No view, including one based on religion, should be privileged by law. A democratic state should be neutral insofar as the worldview, including the religious views, of the individual is concerned (Nisnevich, 2012, 35–36). Moreover, one of the fundamental principles in a democratic state is continual public debate, sometimes very intense and divergent, concerning different subjects. Such a debate, fully open for willing participants and presented views, is a way of replacing violence as a method of conducting politics. Freedom of speech becomes one of the fundamental principles of public debate, so criticism of religion, even radical, should be included within it.

Moreover, religious movements often want to influence political life, e.g. they postulate the introduction of regulations that would concern not only believers but all members of society. Therefore, this type of religious movement becomes *de facto* a kind of political movement. In a democratic state, political movements and doctrines are subject to constant criticism, which is sometimes harsh, because freedom of speech is one of the state's fundamental principles, so it should also concern those aspects of religions and the actions of its believers (Lemmens, 2018, 108). Political satire—often mean, mischievous and exaggerated—can also concern religious movements, especially if they want to influence the whole of society's daily life. Satire of this kind could be regarded as blasphemy; however, it focuses public attention on important issues that concern the functioning of a particular community in a democratic state.

The ECHR emphasised the importance of freedom of expression (speech) for a democratic society:

> Freedom of expression constitutes one of the essential foundations of such a society, one of the basic conditions for its progress and for the development of every man. Subject to paragraph 2 of Article 10 (art. 10–2), it is applicable not only to "information" or "ideas" that are favourably received or regarded as inoffensive or as a matter of indifference, but also to those that offend, shock or disturb the State or any sector of the population.
> (*Handyside v. United Kingdom*, 1976, para. 49)

Therefore, freedom of expression should also be exercised in the cases of statements, texts, drawings and so on containing harsh and unfair criticism of religion, even if they are regarded by believers as blasphemy.

One of the principles of a democratic state is also equality of the individual before the law and a prohibition on discrimination. Most religions, however, are based on the conviction that believing in a particular deity and following the rules established by that religion is the only accepted way of having a worthy life. Those who do not follow such a way of life are sinners whose life has less value than that of believers and who for their sins will be punished in the afterlife or even during present life (Nisnevich, 2012, 33, 36–37). It remains an open question how believers treat "sinners." In the Western world, a tolerant approach seems to predominate, but hostility can also sometimes be observed. This simplified analysis of religion as a sort of social phenomenon leads to the conclusion that the introduction of strict religious values or principles to the legal system would lead to discrimination against non-believers. Therefore, the criminalisation of blasphemy is a way of supporting religion. There is often no equivalent of blasphemy criminalisation when it comes to offending the feelings of atheists.

In a democratic state, criminal law should be very precise and every person should generally know whether a particular action will have legal consequences (Bingham, 2008, 124–125; *Sunday Times v. United Kingdom*, 1979, para. 49). The problem with blasphemy when regarded as a crime is that it is very difficult, especially for a non-believer of a particular religion, to find the boundary which separates allowed criticism from the blasphemy. The criminalisation of blasphemy leads to the nonsensical assumption that every citizen should know what is sacred for the believer of a particular religion even if he/she is a non-believer. Moreover, the perception of a statement, text or drawing as blasphemy depends on the individual sensitivity of the believer. As previously mentioned, there may well be significant differences of opinion among the adherents of a particular religion. Finally, possible punishment depends more on the individual, i.e. the personal characteristics of the judge evaluating the case than on the substance of the law (Lemmens, 2018, 103).

5. Final remarks

Verbal or graphic blasphemy can be committed in many ways: a drawing, a caricature, a film, a book, an article in a newspaper or an interview. Unlike in the United States, it is still penalised in some democratic European states and the person who commits such an act can be fined or given a custodial sentence.

Furthermore, contrary to the verdict of the U.S. Supreme Court (Burstyn v. Wilson), there are no sentencing guidelines for the ECHR, which often accepts the penalisation of blasphemy. The justification for the penalisation of blasphemy is based on the protection of human dignity, protection of freedom of religion, protection of public order and religious peace. However, it seems that these arguments have many weaknesses, and there are more persuasive arguments against the penalisation of blasphemy acts. These arguments include the general characteristics of a democratic state: neutrality concerning the individual's worldview, freedom of expression and equality before the law.

Therefore, democratic states should repeal the rules that penalise such acts. Although some of them might offend the believers of a particular religion, penalisation is not an appropriate way for a modern democratic state to handle such an issue. The most important task for the state to limit the number of blasphemy cases is the promotion of tolerance, based on respect for persons of different worldviews, and the education of youngsters, emphasising values deemed to be important for a democratic society, like pluralism, tolerance and broadmindedness.

Note

1 To similar conclusion, that Klein and Giniewski cases are not hate speech cases, came Oscar Pérez de la Fuente (2019, 58–60) using different methods of text analysis.

References

Literature

Banaś-Grabek, M. 2020. "Uwagi do art. 196 [Comments on art. 196]." In M. Banaś Grabek et al. (eds.). *Kodeks karny część szczególna art. 148–251. Komentarz [Penal Code Detail Part art. 148–251. Commentary]*. Warsaw: C.H. Beck. LEGALIS online.

Bingham, T. 2008. "Rule of Law." *The Irish Judicial Studies Institute Journal* 8, no. 1: 121–144.

Hypś, S. 2021. "Uwagi do art. 196 [Comments on art. 196]." In A. Grześkowiak and K. Wiak (eds.). *Kodeks karny. Komentarz [Penal Code. Commentary]*. Warsaw: C.H. BECK. Legalis Online.

Kłączyńska, N. 2014. "Uwagi do art. 196 [Comments on art. 196]." In J. Giezek (ed.). *Kodeks karny. Część szczególna. Komentarz [Penal Code Detail Part. Commentary]*. Warsaw: Lex a Wolters Kluwer Business, LEX Online.

Kozłowska-Kalisz, P. 2021. "Uwagi do art. 196 [Comments on art. 196]." In M. Mozgawa (ed.). *Kodeks karny: Komentarz aktualizowany [Penal Code. Updated Commentary]*. London: LEX Online.

Lemmens, K. 2018. "'Irreligious' Cartoons and Freedom of Expression: A Critical Reassessment." *Human Rights Law Review* 18, no. 1: 89–109.

Neuhäuser, C. 2011. "Humiliation: The Collective Dimension." In P. Kaufmann et al. (eds.). *Humiliation, Degradation, Dehumanization. Human Dignity Violated*. Dordrecht and New York: Springer: 21–36.

Nisnevich, Y. 2012. "Political and Legal Concept of Modern Democratic State." *American Journal of Sociological Research* 2, no. 3: 32–37.

Nowlin, C. 2002. "The Protection of Morals under the European Convention for the Protection of Human Rights and Fundamental Freedoms." *Human Rights Quarterly* 24, no. 1: 264–286.

Pérez de la Fuente, O. 2019. "On Religious Defamation or Religious Hatred in Some Case of the ECHR." In V. A. Shamakhov (ed.). *Modern Challenges to the European Integration: International Policy and Legal Aspects*. Saint Petersburg: RANEPA: 52–63.

Pollman, A. 2011. "Embodied Self-Respect and the Fragility of Human Dignity: A Human Rights Approach." In P. Kaufmann et al. (eds.). *Humiliation, Degradation, Dehumanization. Human Dignity Violated*. Dordrecht and New York: Springer: 243–261.

Venice Commission. 2010. *Blasphemy, Insult and Hatred: Finding Answers in a Democratic Society*, no. 47. Science and Technique of Democracy. Strasbourg: Council of Europe Publishing.

Wróbel, W. 2017. "Uwagi do art. 196 [Comments on art. 196]." In W. Wróbel and A. Zoll (eds.). *Kodeks karny. Część szczególna. Tom II. Część I. Komentarz do art. 117–211a [Penal Code Detail Part art. 117–211a. Commentary]*. Warsaw: Wolters Kluwer. LEX Online.

Zgoliński, I. 2020. "Uwagi do art. 196 [Comments on art. 196]." In V. Konarska-Wrzosek (ed.). *Kodeks karny. Komentarz [Penal Code. Commentary]*. Warsaw: Wolters Kluwer. LEX Online.

Judicial cases

The Constitutional Tribunal of Poland [2015] OTK ZU 9A/2015, item 142.
Dudgeon v. United Kingdom [1981] 4 EHRR 149.
E.S. v. Austria [2018] ECHR 891.
Giniewski v. France [2006] ECHR 82.
İ.A. v. Turkey [2005] ECHR 590.
Joseph Burstyn, Inc. v. Wilson [1952] 343 U.S.
Handyside v. United Kingdom [1976] 1 EHRR 737.
Klein v. Slovakia [2006] ECHR 909.
Otto-Preminger-Institut v. Austria [1994] ECHR 26.
Sekmadienis Ltd. v. Lithuania [2018] ECHR 112.
Sunday Times v. United Kingdom [1979] 2 EHRR 245.
Wingrove v. the United Kingdom [1996] ECHR 60.

Other materials

Gorman, S. 2013. "Blasphemy Is a Crime Not Only in Pakistan, but Europe too." www.france24.com/en/20181031-blasphemy-middle-east-asia-bibi-europe-law-religion-ireland (accessed July 18, 2021).

Guterres, A. 2019. "United Nations Strategy and Plan of Action on Hate Speech." www.un.org/en/genocideprevention/documents/UN%20Strategy%20and%20Plan%20of%20Action%20on%20Hate%20Speech%2018%20June%20SYNOPSIS.pdf (accessed July 18, 2021).

Part V
Conclusion

14 Conclusion

Alexander Tsesis and Jędrzej Skrzypczak

It would seem that the era of the Internet and social media, that is, a decentralised global network and the possibility of free dissemination of information and opinions by each user, would provide a genuinely unhindered, cross-border circulation of information and opinions. Many expected it to be an enormous opportunity for freedom of speech for all, including all kinds of minorities, which would thus gain a say in the public debate. As it turns out, such a vision has not come true. On the contrary, the actual dissemination of public discussion, for example, on social media, activated many persons but very often to promote hate speech aimed at various types of minorities, who have become the "favourite" target of such attacks. This is also one of the hypotheses in this book. Reading the following chapters of this collective work, a gloomy picture of the digital world emerges from the point of view of freedom of speech and minority rights. The second hypothesis of our book concerns the law and media policy, which in the digital age and the global Internet network could, on the one hand, give the right way to enjoy the benefits of freedom of speech and, on the other, provide legal instruments for the protection of minorities. It should be remembered that the Internet as a global network seems to be non-territorial. Still, the most prominent players among Big Tech or GAFA platforms are companies of American law, so "immersed" in the idea of freedom of speech on the one hand but also of profit maximisation on the other. In addition, other entities derived from a different tradition of respecting freedom of speech, such as TikTok, are trying to play an increasingly important role in the fight for the rule of the souls and minds of digital users. In addition, boot devices and artificial intelligence play a specific role in this digital world, although behind them are, after all, particular interests and offensive strategies. Hence, the question arises as to what regulation method to adopt in this area.

Laws have been enacted by individual countries or as regional provisions, for example, within the European Union—or if it can be metaphorically stated that the invention of the Internet is like the discovery of a new, virtual continent—and therefore it is necessary to create a world super-government in this area. But there is always a temptation among the rulers, sometimes under the pretext of providing real or imaginary threats, to introduce significant restrictions on freedom of speech or even censorship. The best example is the regulation of the functioning of social media in undemocratic countries. For instance, after the military aggression against Ukraine began on 24 February 2022, the Russian parliament urgently adopted a regulation extending the prohibition of any criticism of the Russian armed forces and the prohibition of disparaging any actions of the Russian authorities abroad. As a result, using the term "war in Ukraine" on social media instead of Putin's "special military operation" may be punishable by up to 15 years in prison. Hence, it is imperative to evaluate all the positions and views claiming that in the global era of the Internet should be self-regulating. We live in an era when communications are often governed by non-territorial norms. One of the most contested issues concerns the extent to which government privacy regulations should govern an electronic medium of communication that is largely nonterritorial. Many scholars and policy makers regard such laws to be overreach into a area that should be self-regulated by social media platform.

As Alexander Tsesis argues in Chapter 1, entitled *Democratic values and the regulation of hate speech*, the spread of denigrating ideas has historically been essential for groups to amass followers willing to commit various injustices. Among the many examples of hate speech turning into violent conduct are the Rwanda genocide, Jewish Holocaust, black slavery and aboriginal removal. On these and many other occasions around the world, rhetoric can influence mass violence. Supremacist groups whip up collective harm by steadily appealing to easily identifiable prejudices and adopting them to win support for violent or discriminatory conduct.

His chapter studies various international and national regulations of speech. The focus is on Universal Declaration of Human Rights, the International Covenant on Civil and Political Rights and the European Convention on Human Rights. They hold in common the erection of limits that balance speech against countervailing harms against groups and individuals. These international approaches differ from the libertarian one that is typically determinative and formalistic in the United States. In addition to contrasting those approaches to free expression, Tsesis discusses European national laws—such as those from Germany, Belgium, Great Britain and Spain—that recognise the central importance of free speech to democratic society but also balance it with other constitutional values, including dignity and public safety.

In the next chapter, Jędrzej Skrzypczak quotes, unfortunately still valid, the words of William Shakespeare who stated that "conversation should be pleasant without scurrility, witty without affectation, free without indecency, learned without conceitedness, novel without falsehood." Freedom of speech can lead to intercultural or cross-cultural conflict. Since the Internet plays a vital role in connecting people around the world, communication on the Internet can increase intercultural or cross-cultural conflict where there are differing levels of free speech protection.

Skrzypczak argues that access to the Internet could be considered a human right in the twenty-first century. Nevertheless, he argues that such freedom should not be protected by law; rather, he advocates that private entities develop mechanisms and structures conducive to evaluating inappropriate content and for governments to initiate dialogue with stakeholders, states and tech companies to develop the necessary skills and expertise required to combat hate speech online while avoiding censorship of minority communities.

In his chapter, "Free speech and Internet," Perez de la Fuente applies Robert Dahl's classic typology of political systems to analyse how Russia and China monitor, regulate and restrict access and interaction on the Internet. He focuses his analytical lens on Dahl's classifications of political systems as democracies, hegemonies and polyarchies.

China, as de la Fuente explains, is generally a hegemony because it restricts speech on the Internet and thereby impacts political participation and inclusiveness. While there are some forums for debate, government heavy-handedly monitors these communications. Political dissidents are repressed and incarcerated; moreover, by its very structure, a one-party state is hegemonic. Turning his attention to Russia, Perez de la Fuente notes the paradox of the country's having adopted constitutional protections for free speech and ratifying the European Convention on Human Rights including its safeguard for free expression and the country's suppression of dissidents under the overblown and aggressive pursuit of "extremism." Laws that are vaguely drafted to fight extremism are manipulated by the government to quash critics of Vladimir Putin's regime. Anti-government rhetoric appearing online often falls prey to government censorship. The government also blacklists websites under pretexts of anti-extremist policies whose purpose is to prevent opposition voices from spreading ideas. Moreover, the government blocks websites and tracks its citizens' data. Russia, Perez de la Fuente concludes, should be classified as a hybrid regime, more nearly a hegemony than a polyarchy. Russia demonstrates its overt disrespect for free expression, alternative views and associational liberties.

In turn, Helen Norton's essay, *Manipulation and the First Amendment*, describes the harms of manipulative speech and practices. She distinguishes ordinary commercial speech from data disseminated covertly to impose hidden, coercive and deceptive digital content on persons. She also posits a framework for explaining when, how and why government's interests are sufficiently strong to justify regulations of online manipulation without violating the First Amendment of the U.S. Constitution.

The government may sometimes protect comparatively vulnerable audiences in a manner that is consistent with First Amendment jurisprudence. Differences in power and information can matter to First Amendment law, permitting the government to intervene where harm can be caused to vulnerable listeners. Norton asserts that the First Amendment allows regulators to intervene where malicious speakers endeavour to manipulate listeners, just as the government can intervene in cases of discrimination and fraud. Ultimately, Norton proposes that the court should expand the parameters of the commercial speech doctrine by adding "manipulative" speech to the list of speech that does not fall under First Amendment protection. Norton also touches upon online political manipulation but recognises that strict judicial review in the latter sphere would render any meaningful regulation in this area unlikely.

Filimon Peonidis, in the chapter *Fake news published during the pre-election period and free speech theory*, focuses on "fake news," articulating a proposal for constitutional regulation of political fake news published in the period prior to elections. He instead argues that no protection should be given to fake news because it poses a legally cognisable harm. This is especially the case when fake news undermines democratic integrity in electoral processes or otherwise encourages attitudes that harm healthy democracy. He argues that political content that is published during an election contest could constitute a legally cognisable harm when it is likely to undermine electoral integrity, referenda and campaigns. Damages from fake news at these times sensitive to the democracy are impairment of free and fair participation, instigation to violence and epistemic self-righteousness or bigotry.

Peonidis acknowledges there are legal "hurdles" that governments must overcome before fake news could be regulated. He stresses that empirical research should be conducted to verify or disprove his assumptions about the impact of political fake news on voters' choices. Throughout the chapter, Peonidis stresses that his argument is preliminary meant to generate reflection, discussion and deliberation rather than immediate legislative implementation.

In his chapter, *Misinformation and hate speech: when bad becomes even worse*, Gustavo Ferreira Santos argues that policies for combatting Internet misinformation and hate speech are essential because they radicalise groups and create distrust rather than promote dialogue. Without public policies preventing nefarious campaigns, democracy is threatened and can be undermined by basic conditions necessary for its functioning and for co-existence.

Santos contrasts the United States and German approaches to free speech. He criticises the former for only allowing the regulation of hate speech when confronted with an imminent danger of illegality. The American system, he believes, empowers harassers at the expense of targeted individuals. German jurisprudence, on the other hand, allows law enforcement to crack down on hate speech as it appears on social media or other parts of the world wide web. As in Germany, many human rights treaties that embrace free speech nevertheless emphasise that hate speech does not enjoy any protected status.

The Internet in particular, Santos points out, amplifies misinformation and hate speech resulting in individual and social harms. Bots and social network algorithms help to proliferate data transmission faster and further than ever before. Santos also turns to French and German legislation to emphasise how democratic societies can protect free speech while curbing this harm. French law prohibits parties from engaging in disinformation about campaigns and the electoral process. German legislation enjoins social media networks to report about performance, create fines on noncompliant parties, require the "appointment of responsible persons in Germany and impose a duty to disclose details about the offenders to those affected by criminal offenses." Santos concludes that misinformation and hate speech be countered with French and German legislation serving as starting points for policy developments.

The chapter by Irene Spigno, *Sexist hate speech against women: towards a regulatory model*, asserts that sexist hate speech should be subject to unique regulations and proposes regulatory models. Spigno draws attention to cases in countries such as Germany where she argues sexist hate speech was acquitted because the penal code protected "minorities" but not, specifically, women.

Spigno offers four models of regulating hate speech. First, under the freedom model, which is the rule in the United States, freedom of expression is limited only to speech which poses a clear and present danger to protected values. Second, under the defence model, exercised by states such as Germany and France, expressions that directly attack personal dignities are restricted by penal sanctions that apply to hateful speech. In these and other European countries, governments are responsible for combating hate speech. Judicial analysis is done by balancing democratic values. Third is the no-discrimination model, characterised by exclusion from free speech safeguards of content likely to generate discrimination, even when it is not motivated by hatred against protected groups. circumstances. Finally, under the multiculturalism model, punishment is incurred from expressive behaviours that endanger the ability of different groups to coexist.

Spigno asserts that the multiculturalism model best allows governments to combat sexist hate speech, particularly when it is spread online. She insists that this model adopts criminal sanctions to preserve cultural tolerance. Additionally, it teaches the importance of social responsibility, thereby addressing the ignorance that often leads to hatred. Although specific manifestations of hatred must be punished, Spigno emphasises that social tolerance can only be achieved by conjoining sanctions and education.

In the next chapter of this book, *Artificial intelligence and hate speech*, Migle Laukyte probes into the link between online hate speech and artificial intelligence. She relies on a three-part mode. She focuses on AI as a tool to combat Internet hate speech, AI as a means of promoting hate speech and a future possibility of AI as a generator of social groups who might then be social-group targets of hate speakers. The targets of hate speech might be immigrants, ethnic groups and other minorities.

Laukyte delves into how AI is currently being used to detect, identify and remove hate speech from websites by means of supervised machine learning. She draws attention to Spanish public sector efforts to rely on message chains to identify hate speech on social media and then to refine software algorithms to spot hate speech in different languages and dialects. Yet, she warns that technologies can also be abused despite their autonomous efficiencies, AI can generate its own biases. Thus, human supervision and control of algorithms that would prevent them from being sources of misinformation and hatred remain essential to democratic societies in the age of the Internet.

In his chapter *Government speech and minority rights: the American view*, William D. Araiza concentrates his attention on how the U.S. doctrine of government speech affects minority rights. First Amendment doctrine does not require the government to remain content- nor viewpoint-neutral in its messaging. Araiza points out that the troubling implication of the government speech doctrine is that it provides no explicit restrictions against the denigrations of minority groups.

Araiza explains that the authority of government to speak might nevertheless be challenged when political majorities or even powerful factions deploy government statements to denigrate minorities. His chapter presents hypotheticals to assess some of the legal challenges that would confront litigants seeking injunctions or damages for harms resulting from discriminatory government speech.

Araiza argues that because the First Amendment is inapplicable to government entities, the Equal Protection Clause is better suited to efforts meant to prevent governments that disparage minorities. He argues that doctrines and theories of speech in modern liberal democracies should neither promote a single viewpoint nor chill the marketplace of ideas by punishing dissent. Government speech might, for instance, be limited when it is used to make statements motivated by public officials motivated by animus to disparage or suppress minority groups. Araiza's animus approach to government speech looks beyond the First Amendment. His animus approach provides a means of demonstrating that government expression illegitimately denigrates targeted groups. He suggests that democratic societies balance the interests of disparaged groups against governmental requirements to express legitimate policies essential to the operation of a democratic society.

David S. Han, in the chapter entitled *Disentangling "cancel culture,"* endeavours to provide a definition for "cancel culture" in the technological context. Particularly, Han explains that the modern "cancel culture" can be described as a type of social shaming that relies on unearthing past, socially undesirable statements and disseminating them broadly to facilitate social condemnation.

Han explains how cancel culture can harm free speech, both because it can be exploited to chill speech and to shame those who articulate unpopular ideas. On the flip side, cancellation can require accountability for discriminatory social constructs—including sexism and racism. In this way, Han points out, cancellation can be a means of empowering voices that heretofore have been silenced from fully engaging in the marketplace of ideas. Public discourse, Han writes, can best be balanced by balancing both sides of the debate. Nuance and proportionality are needed to identify the extent to which social shaming or sanctioning is justifiable and desirable. Law is unlikely to be the solution; rather, Han advocates for cultural discourse. Social condemnation is not something that can readily be regulated by law; rather, Han explains that societal norms "will likely shape the nature of public discourse and to a far greater extent than formal constitutional doctrine." One form of social condemnation might be deplatforming by social media companies of persons who exploit digital venues to attack specific groups or democratic institutions. Another means of engaging in proportionality might be for employers to terminate employees who engage in extremist speech such as apologetics for genocide.

In the next chapter, *The freedom of speech and the protection of religious feelings—the case of Dorota Rabczewska—comparative analysis* by Tomasz Litwin, it is indicated that

> verbal or graphic blasphemy can be committed in many ways: a drawing, a caricature, a film, a book, an article in a newspaper or an interview. Unlike in the United States, it is still penalised in some democratic European states and the person who commits such an act can be fined or given a custodial

sentence. Furthermore, contrary to the verdict of the US Supreme Court (*Burstyn v. Wilson*), there are no sentencing guidelines for the European Court of Human Rights, which often accepts the penalisation of blasphemy. The justification for the penalisation of blasphemy is based on the protection of human dignity, protection of freedom of religion, protection of public order and religious peace. However, it seems that these arguments have many weaknesses, and there are more persuasive arguments against the penalisation of blasphemy acts. These arguments include the general characteristics of a democratic state: neutrality concerning the individual's worldview, freedom of expression and equality before the law. Therefore, democratic states should repeal the rules that penalise such acts. Although some of them might offend the believers of a particular religion, penalisation is not an appropriate way for a modern democratic state to handle such an issue. The most important task for the state to limit the number of blasphemy cases is the promotion of tolerance, based on respect for persons of different worldviews, and the education of youngsters, emphasising values deemed to be important for a democratic society, like pluralism, tolerance and broadmindedness.

As Jędrzej Skrzypczak proves in the last chapter entitled "SLAPP—between the right to a fair trial and the chilling effect in favour of free speech"—"such type of legal actions are methods of silencing criticism far less barbaric than a car bomb or a headshot, but their 'chilling' effects are often just as destructive."

The authors of the subsequent chapters attempted to answer the question raised in the introduction, that is, how should a reasonable internet policy be shaped to protect minorities and what should be avoided in this sphere? Sometimes they proposed it by directly formulating specific postulates, while others did it by describing negative examples and trends and how not to act.

It should be emphasised that representatives of various minority groups are victims of this type of legal action. Undoubtedly, every constitutional democracy should be based on a triad of values: democracy, rules and human rights. There is also no doubt that there is no democracy without the protection of minority rights. One can even risk the thesis that the protection of minority rights defines the quality of democracy in a given country. Unfortunately, in many places around the world, including Europe, democracy is retreating or is at least seriously threatened. This regrettably means a danger to various minorities, including in the Internet space and social media platforms. What is no less important and dangerous, these threats not only occur in the virtual sphere but also result in real violence aimed at representatives of minorities. Paradoxically, it is social media that has become a space for inflaming resentment against specific groups, antagonising and polarising them. It was supposed to be so beautiful. And yet without a minority, the world, societies and democracies would not be so pluralistically diverse.

There is no doubt today, that human rights, especially human dignity, are inalienable and inviolable and must, therefore be guaranteed not only in traditional, offline fora "settings but also in the online world." On the other hand, the online world is in some ways more lawless than the wild west without much regulatory order to protect human rights, political information and government transparency. In addition to hard law—especially by constitutional norms and statutes-soft law—especially through agreements, principles and declarations-should play a role in the evolution of domestic and international policies. For all that, it cannot mean the absence of any rules in this online world, and therefore complete anarchy, i.e. a world where the exclusive right and the will of the strong reigns to the detriment of privacy, reputation, representation, clarity, information and democracy.

The effects of social media on stability have in many places become acute. For example, false political advertisements in countries from Sri Lanka to Indonesia, Libya, India, Myanmar and Mexico have been used to subvert democratic processes by saturating the marketplace of ideas with false propaganda that instigates violence. Efforts to deal with the international implications of online media will continue to pose colossal complications today and will continue to do so in the future. The challenge in the years ahead will be to articulate a theory of the private and public realm that will sustain democratic values while simultaneously preventing the manipulation of the Internet for nefarious purposes. Any such effort must avoid the autocratic evils of censorship and preserve and evolve this malleable media that has in the last three decades become intrinsic to communication and association.

Notes on contributors

William D. Araiza is Stanley A. August Professor of Law at Brooklyn Law School, United States. His teaching and scholarly interests focus on administrative and constitutional law and he has written widely, including on First Amendment Law and Constitutional Law. He is a member of the American Law Institute, has served as Chair of the Administrative Law Section of the Association of American Law Schools and on the LexisNexis Law School Publishing Advisory Board and holds several leadership positions in the Southeastern Association of Law Schools.

Gustavo Ferreira Santos is Professor of Constitutional Law at the Catholic University of Pernambuco, Brazil, where he was Coordinator of the law course and the graduate law school (Master's and Ph.D. programs). His research focuses on the relationship between constitutionalism and democracy, and for some years, he has been studying and supervising theses on fundamental rights in communication, such as freedom of expression, and, more recently, these rights on the Internet.

David S. Han is Professor of Law and the Associate Dean for Faculty and Research at Pepperdine University Caruso School of Law, United States, where he teaches in the areas of First Amendment law, tort law and criminal procedure. His scholarship focuses on First Amendment law and tort law.

Migle Laukyte is Tenure-Track Professor in Cyberlaw and Cyber-Rights at the Law Faculty of the Pompeu Fabra University, Spain. Her work is mainly dedicated to legal and ethical questions related to Artificial Intelligence, such as legal personhood of AI, consumer protection and robotics, governance of AI and human rights and AI. She is Co-founder of the academic unit on Human Rights, Diversity and New Technologies at UC3M, Spain. She is a member of the European Group on Ethics in Science and New Technologies, and a member of the EBP Expert Group on Blockchain Ethics, as part of the European Blockchain Service Infrastructure.

Tomasz Litwin is Assistant Professor at the Jesuit University Ignatianum in Krakow, Poland. His interests are focused on constitutional law, parliamentary systems and human rights. He has published widely, particularly on the Polish political system.

Helen Norton is University Distinguished Professor and Rothgerber Chair in Constitutional Law at the University of Colorado School of Law, United States. Her scholarly and teaching interests include constitutional law (especially free speech and equality) and civil rights law. She served as Leader of President-elect Obama's transition team charged with reviewing the Equal Employment Opportunity Commission. She has been honoured with the Excellence in Teaching Award on multiple occasions and was appointed a University of Colorado Presidential Teaching Scholar in 2014.

Filimon Peonidis is Professor of Moral and Political Philosophy at the Aristotle University of Thessaloniki, Greece. He has had visiting and teaching appointments at various universities in London, Toronto, Vancouver, Melbourne, Antwerp, Hamburg and Berlin. He has written on moral theory, liberalism, freedom of expression, normative democratic theory and the history of democratic traditions.

Oscar Pérez de la Fuente is Associate Professor of Philosophy of Law and Political Philosophy in the Department of International and Ecclesiastical Law and Philosophy of Law and in the "Gregorio Peces-Barba" Human Rights Institute at Carlos III University of Madrid, Spain. He has written on cultural pluralism, free speech and legal interpretation. He is Coordinator of the "Cultural pluralism and rights of minorities" workshop and Chair of the Research Committee 26 on Human Rights of the International Political Science Association.

Jędrzej Skrzypczak is Head of the Department of Media Systems and Press Law in the Faculty of Political Science and Journalism at Adam Mickiewicz University in Poznan, Poland. In 2016 and 2022, he was nominated as an official candidate for the National Broadcasting Board by the coalition of opposition parties. He is Chair-elect of the Research Committee 26 on Human Rights of the International Political Science Association and Vice President of the Polish Press Law Association.

Irene Spigno is General Director of the Inter-American Academy of Human Rights of the Autonomous University of Coahuila, Mexico, and Director of the Center for Comparative Constitutional Studies of the Inter-American Academy of Human Rights. Her research interests include freedom of expression—and in particular hate speech—political freedoms, constitutional justice and multiculturalism from a comparative perspective. She participates in many research projects on human rights, political participation and democracy and comparative constitutional law.

Alexander Tsesis is Raymond & Mary Simon Chair in Constitutional Law and Professor of Law at the Loyola University in Chicago, United States, and Visiting Professor at George Washington University Law School, United States. He has written on cyber speech, constitutional interpretation, civil rights law and human rights. His scholarship focuses on a breadth of subjects, including constitutional law, civil rights, constitutional reconstruction, interpretive methodology, free speech theory and legal history.

Index

access 3–12; and artificial intelligence 157–159; European perspective 51–56, 59–60; and human rights 69–78, 83–86; and misinformation 129–132; and the protection of religious feelings 230–231
accountability 171–172
America *see* United States
American Indian removal 21
analogue era 45, 47–52, 60
animus 189–194, 234
ANTISLAPP 201; Europe 203–204; United States 202–203
anti-semitism 20
Arendt, Hannah 129
Argentina 144, 149n45
artificial intelligence 153–161
Australia 9, 26, 123, 142, 201
Austria 27, 216–217, 219–221
authoritarianism 4–5, 103, 131; authoritarian deliberation 72–75, 87–88
authority to speak, government 188–194; *see also* government speech

ban on opposition 85–86
Beausoleil, Lauren E. 128
Belgium 26–27
Berlin, Isaiah 4
blasphemy: judicial cases concerning 215–218; legal arguments against penalisation of 222–223; weaknesses of arguments supporting the penalisation of 218–222; *see also* protection of religious feelings
Bosnia and Herzegovina 201
Brazil 24, 131, 133
Brown, Henry Billings 186
Bulgaria 200

Calo, Ryan 94, 96–98, 100
Canada 24, 139, 145–146, 201
cancel culture: defining 167–170; theoretical dimensions of the debate 170–173; working towards resolution of the debate 173–177
censorship 4–5, 75–79, 82–85
central propaganda spaces 75
Chile 142
chilling effect 172–175, 198–199, 206, 218, 234–235
China 71, 83, 85–89; approach to free speech and the Internet 72–79
civic spaces 75
Cohen, Julie 94, 97–98, 102–104
commercial settings and spaces 75, 94–95, 99–104
conduct, private 187–188
constitutionality 34–35, 59–60, 230–236; and fake news 111–116; and government speech 185–194; and misinformation 124–128; and the protection of religious feelings 212–215; and sexist hate speech against women 144–145
contestation, public 12, 70, 72–75, 80–85, 87
counterspeech 171–173, 175
Croatia 200–201
cyberattacks 77
Cyprus 24

deepfakes 156–158
Deibert, Richard 131
deliberation *see* authoritarian deliberation
deliberative spaces 74–75
democracy: American free speech law and hate incitement 33–35; and artificial

240 Index

intelligence 153–161; and fake news 108–119; international consensus and nuance 23–33; and manipulation 93–106; and misinformation 123–135; pressing and substantial concern 19–23; and sexist hate speech against women 137–147
Denmark 28–29
devices, control of 78
digital era 11, 44; freedom of speech in 45–46; majority and minority in 47–52
dignity *see* protection of the dignity
disconnection, localised 78
disparaging speech 184, 189, 190–194
domain-name controls 78
Douthat, Ross 168–170, 176

effects, manipulative 101–104
elections 56–57, 73–75, 85–88, 111–118, 131–132
electronic controls 75–79
emergent civic spaces 75
equal protection 185–194, 234
Europe 44–45, 60–61; access of minorities to the media and the protection of the dignity 52–55; ANTISLAPP in 203–204; freedom of speech in the digital era 45–46; and Internet media 55–60; majority and minority in the analogue and digital era 47–52; *see also specific countries*
European Commission on Human Rights (ECHR) 24, 30–33, 54, 79–82, 212, 215–220, 223–224
extremism 28–29, 80–87, 123, 129, 231, 234

fair trial, right to 197, 206–207; ANTISLAPP in Europe 203–204; ANTISLAPP law 201; ANTISLAPP in United States 202–203; SLAPP definition 198–200; SLAPP in Poland 201; SLAPP in practice 200; SLAPP v. the right to a fair trial 204–206
fake news 108, 118–119; and lies 109–110; a regulatory proposal 111–119
fake plurality 85–86
false speech 113, 120n7
features, manipulative 92, 102–104, 106
Finland 29
First Amendment 93–95, 105–106; and the government's interventions to protect listeners from manipulation 99–105; government speech 183–185; and the harms of manipulation 95–98
forum, Internet as 3–7
France 6, 9, 59, 132–135, 217, 220–222
freedom, Internet 4–7, 83–84
free speech 11–14, 44–46, 60–61, 197, 206–207, 212–215; access of minorities to the media and the protection of the dignity 52–55; American free speech law 33–35; ANTISLAPP in Europe 203–204; ANTISLAPP law 201; ANTISLAPP in United States 202–203; and cancel culture 167–177; China's approach to 72–79, 87–88; and democratic values 19–35; and government speech 181–194; and human rights 69–88; and the Internet 3–7, 55–60; judicial cases concerning blasphemy 215–218; and majority and minority 8–11, 47–52; and the penalisation of blasphemy 218–225; and polyarchies and hegemonies 69–72; Russia's approach to 79–88; SLAPP definition 198–200; SLAPP in Poland 201; SLAPP in practice 200; SLAPP v. the right to a fair trial 204–206
free speech theory 108, 118–119; and lies 109–110; and regulation 111–119

Gelfert, Axel 12, 109–110
genocide 22–23, 34, 139, 145–147, 168, 176, 234
Germany 9, 24–27, 59, 126–128, 132–135, 142, 232–233; anti-semitism 20
government interventions 99–105, 133
government-regulated commercial spaces 75
government speech 181–182; and First Amendment rights 183–185; and limits on government's authority to speak 185–194
Graber, Mark 106
Great Britain 27–28, 56–57, 198–200, 203, 223
Guterres, António Manuel de Oliveira 56, 220

Harel, Alon 147
harms 93–99, 105–106, 230–234
Hartzog, Woody 105
hate incitement 33–35
hate speech 123–127, 134–135, 137–139; American free speech law and hate incitement 33–35; and artificial

intelligence 153–161; combating 132–134; and fake news 108–119; international consensus and nuance 23–33; and the Internet 129–130; and manipulation 93–106; and misinformation 123–135; pressing and substantial concern 19–23; and public policies 127–129; regulation of 142–147; sexist speech considered as 139–141, 146–147; and social media 130–131
hegemonies 69–72
human rights 6–7; China's approach to 72–79, 87–88; and polyarchies and hegemonies 69–72; Russia's approach to 79–88
Hungary 31–32

inclusiveness 70–72; China 75–79; Russia 85–86, 88
India 24, 32, 130–131, 133, 236
Ingber, Stanley 173
international deliberative spaces 75
Internet, the 44–45, 55–61; access of minorities to the media and the protection of the dignity 52–55; amplification of misinformation and hate speech 129–130; China's approach to 72–79, 87–88; combatting misinformation and hate speech 132–134; and democratic values 19–35; and freedom of speech 11–14, 45–46; and human rights 69–88; Internet freedom 4–7, 83–84; and majority and minority 8–11, 47–52; as a new forum 3–7; and polyarchies and hegemonies 69–72; Russia's approach to 79–88
interpretation 24–25, 71, 73, 81, 87
Ireland 142, 201, 219
Israel 31, 144

judicial cases concerning blasphemy 215–218; see also protection of religious feelings

Kant, Immanuel 110
Kerr, Ian 102, 105

law see SLAPP; ANTISLAPP; First Amendment; regulation
legal cultures: and democratic values 19–35; and human rights 69–88; and minorities 44–61
legitimate power of government 189–190
Leisegang, Daneil 25

Lewis, Bernard 22
liberalisation 70, 87; China 72–75; Russia 80–85
Libya 32, 236
lies 108–110, 112–114, 116–118, 130–131
listeners 93–98; protection from manipulation 99–105
Lithuania 54, 142, 212, 215–217
Luxembourg 26, 201

majority 8–10, 86–88; in the analogue and digital era 47–52
Malta 201
manipulation 93–95, 105–106; government's interventions to protect listeners from 99–105; harms of 95–98
manipulative speech 94, 99–103, 106, 231
Mauritanian slavery 21–22
media, the: access of minorities to 52–55; new challenges for minorities 55–60; see also social media
Mexico 32, 236
minorities 8–11, 44–45, 60–61; access to the media and the protection of the dignity 52–55; and cancel culture 167–177; and free speech 11–14, 45–46; and government speech 181–194; and the Internet 3–7, 55–60; majority and minority in the analogue and digital era 47–52; and the protection of religious feelings 212–224; and SLAPP 197–207
minority rights 181–182; and First Amendment rights 183–185; and limits on government's authority to speak 185–194
Michan, Ligaya 171, 173
misinformation 123–127, 134–135; and artificial intelligence 153–161; combating 132–134; and fake news 108–119; and the Internet 129–130; and manipulation 93–106; and misinformation 123–135; and public policies 127–129; and sexist hate speech against women 137–147; and social media 130–131
Myanmar 32, 236

Native Americans 21
Neuhäuser, Christian 218
networks, control of 78
news see fake news
New Zealand 123
Norton, Helen 12, 99, 110, 116, 118, 231

Norway 30–31
nuance 174, 234

opposition, ban on 85–86

Pakistan 33, 78
participation 70, 72, 74; China 75–79; Russia 83, 85–86, 88
Peonidis, Filimon 12, 110, 231–232
Pérez de la Fuente, Oscar 7–11, 71, 153, 231
plurality, fake 85–86
Poland 30, 46, 59–61, 212–215, 218; SLAPP in 201, 206
policies *see* public policies
political settings 95, 97, 100, 102–106
polyarchies 69–72
Portugal 200
Post, Robert C. 115–116
power: government's legitimate power 189–190; rhetoric of speech versus rhetoric of 172–173
Pring, George W. 198
private conduct 187–188
propaganda spaces 75
protection of religious feelings 212–215; judicial cases concerning blasphemy 215–218; and the penalisation of blasphemy 218–225
protection of the dignity 51–55
public contestation 12, 70, 72–75, 80–85, 87
public policies 123–129, 206, 232

Rabczewska, Dorota 212–215
regulation 137–139; American free speech law and hate incitement 33–35; China's approach to 72–79, 87–88; and fake news 111–112; of hate speech 142–147; international consensus and nuance 23–33; of manipulative speech 100–101, 102–103; and polyarchies and hegemonies 69–72; Russia's approach to 79–88; and sexist speech 139–141, 146–147; *see also* ANTISLAPP
religion *see* protection of religious feelings
restriction, localised 78
rhetoric 19, 22–23, 26, 167, 172–174, 230–231
rights *see* fair trial, right to; First Amendment; human rights; minority rights

Romania 54–55, 200
Russia 32–33, 79–88, 230–231
Rwandan genocide 22–23

sexist hate speech against women 137–139; considered as hate speech 139–141; and regulation of hate speech 142–147
Shakespeare, William 60, 230
Skrzypczak, Jędrzej 11, 13, 46
SLAPP 197, 206–207; ANTISLAPP in Europe 203–204; ANTISLAPP law 201; ANTISLAPP in United States 202–203; definition 198–200; in Poland 201; in practice 200; and the right to a fair trial 204–206
slavery: American 20–21; Mauritanian 21–22
Slovakia 217, 220–221
Slovenia 200–201
social media 229–236; and cancel culture 167–170, 174–177; and democratic values 24–25, 29–32; European perspective 44–46, 51–57, 59–61; and misinformation 128–133
South Africa 9, 142
Spain 26, 155, 233
speech: rhetoric of power vs rhetoric of 172–173; *see also* disparaging speech; free speech; government speech; hate speech; manipulative speech; sexist hate speech against women
Spigno, Irene 12, 232–233
Sri Lanka 32, 235
Strossen, Nadine 34
Sunstein, Cass 96, 98, 117
surveillance 32, 72, 75–79, 97, 131
Sweden 29–30, 56–57
Switzerland 24, 142, 212

tailoring: through targeting 103–104; through tools 104–105
transhumans, AI-empowered 158–160
trial *see* fair trial, right to
Tsesis, Alexander 7, 11, 13, 24, 35
Turkey 26, 55, 198–199, 217–218, 220–222

unconstitutionality 59, 113, 186–188, 205
United Kingdom *see* Great Britain

United States 181–182; American Indian removal 21; ANTISLAPP in 202–203; First Amendment rights 183–185; free speech law and hate incitement 33–35; limits on government's authority to speak 185–194; slavery 20–21

values, democratic: American free speech law and hate incitement 33–35; international consensus and nuance 23–33; pressing and substantial concern 19–23; *see also* democracy

Vietnam 33

Waldron, Jeremy 126–128, 153
Winthrop, John 21
women *see* sexist hate speech against women
Wu, Felix 100

Zeldin, Wendy 25

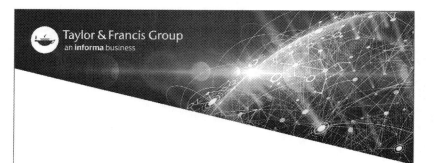

Printed in the United States
by Baker & Taylor Publisher Services